Introduction to Business Taxation
'Finance Act 2005'

AF678652

CIMA
PUBLISHING

Introduction to Business Taxation 'Finance Act 2005'

Chris Jones, BA CTA (Fellow) ATT

ELSEVIER

AMSTERDAM • BOSTON • HEIDELBERG • LONDON • NEW YORK • OXFORD
PARIS • SAN DIEGO • SAN FRANCISCO • SINGAPORE • SYDNEY • TOKYO

Elsevier Butterworth-Heinemann
Linacre House, Jordan Hill, Oxford OX2 8DP
30 Corporate Drive, Burlington, MA 01803

First published 2006

Copyright © 2006, Lexis Nexis UK. All rights reserved

No part of this publication may be reproduced in any material form (including photocopying or storing in any medium by electronic means and whether or not transiently or incidentally to some other use of this publication) without the written permission of the copyright holder except in accordance with the provisions of the Copyright, Designs and Patents Act 1988 or under the terms of a licence issued by the Copyright Licensing Agency Ltd, 90 Tottenham Court Road, London, England W1T 4LP. Applications for the copyright holder's written permission to reproduce any part of this publication should be addressed to the publisher

Permissions may be sought directly from Elsevier's Science and Technology Rights Department in Oxford, UK: phone: (+44) (0) 1865 843830; fax: (+44) (0) 1865 853333; e-mail: permissions@elsevier.co.uk. You may also complete your request on-line via the Elsevier homepage (www.elsevier.com), by selecting 'Customer Support' and then 'Obtaining Permissions'

British Library Cataloguing in Publication Data

Library of Congress Cataloguing in Publication Data
A catalogue record for this book is available from the Library of Congress

ISBN 0 7506 6938 1

For information on all Elsevier Butterworth-Heinemann publications visit our website at http://books.elsevier.com

Typeset by Integra Software Services Pvt. Ltd, Pondicherry, India
www.integra-india.com
Printed and bound in Great Britian

Working together to grow
libraries in developing countries

www.elsevier.com | www.bookaid.org | www.sabre.org

ELSEVIER BOOK AID International Sabre Foundation

CONTENTS

PREFACE

This book provides all the material you need for the CIMA Professional Development Certificate in Business Taxation. Within each chapter you will find some examples for you to try, to test you on the important rules covered in the chapter.

At the end of each chapter, there is a short summary which contains a "pocket digest" of the rules covered within the chapter. These individual summaries form a comprehensive overview of the syllabus.

As this manual has been written specifically to cover all areas of the syllabus we are confident you will find this an invaluable tool leading to success in the examination.

CIMA
Tax Tables

Income Tax rates	**2005-06**	**2004-05**
	%	%
Starting rate	10	10
Basic rate	22	22
Higher rate	40	40
	£	£
Starting rate band	1 - 2,090	1 - 2,020
Basic rate band	2,091 - 32,400	2,021 - 31,400

Income Tax reliefs	**2005-06**	**2004-05**
	£	£
Personal allowance	4,895	4,745

Income Tax – Pension contributions

Stakeholder / Personal pension premiums

Age	%
Up to 35	17.5
36–45	20
46–50	25
51–55	30
56–60	35
61 or over	40

Age is taken at the start of the fiscal year

Pension Plan earnings cap	2005-06: £105,600	2004-05: £102,000
Stakeholder pension limit	2005-06: £3,600	2004-05: £3,600

Company cars and fuel

Company cars

Cash equivalent (2004/05) 15% of list price for cars emitting 140g/km (2005/06), 145g/km (2004/05)
Increased by 1% per 5g/km over the 140g/km/145g/km limit
Capped at 35% of list price
3% supplement on diesel cars not meeting the Euro IV emission standards
(subject to 35% cap) or registered after 1 January 2006

Van scale charge

£500 (reduced to £350 if more than four years old at the end of the fiscal year). There is no taxable benefit where an employee takes a van home but is not allowed any other private use.

Fuel scale benefits

For **2005-06** (& 2004-05) the benefit is £14,400 multiplied by the percentage used in calculating the car benefit (ie based on carbon dioxide emission rating)

HMRC Authorised Mileage Rates

	2005-06 and 2004-05	
Vehicles	**First 10,000 business miles**	**Additional business miles**
Car or van *	40p	25p
Motorcycles	24p	
Bicycles	20p	
Passenger payments	5p	

* For NIC purposes, a rate of 40p applies irrespective of mileage.

Value Added Tax

Standard rate		$17\frac{1}{2}\%$
Annual registration limit	From 1 April 2004	£58,000
	From 1 April 2005	£60,000
De-registration limit	From 1 April 2004	£56,000
	From 1 April 2005	£58,000

Annual accounting / cash accounting	**Post 31.3.04**
	£
Turnover threshold to join scheme	660,000
Turnover threshold to leave scheme	825,000

Capital allowances

Principal writing down allowance rates	
Plant and machinery, patent rights and know-how	25%
Industrial buildings and Agricultural buildings	4%
Long life assets	6%

First year allowances available	
Small-sized businesses	40% (1) (2)
Medium-sized businesses	40%

(1) 50% rate applies from 1 April 2004 to 31 March 2005 for companies.
(2) 50% rate applies from 6 April 2004 to 5 April 2005 for unincorporated businesses.

Small sized businesses

100% on computers and related equipment acquired between 1 April 2000 and 31 March 2004

First year allowances available to all businesses

100% on Energy Saving Plant acquired from 1 April 2001 (extended definition from 17 April 2002) and on designated water efficient plant from 1 April 2003

100% on cars registered between 16 April 2002 and 31 March 2008 if the car either emits not more than 120g/km of CO_2 or it is electronically propelled.

100% on the renovation or conversion of vacant business premises, in any of the disadvantaged areas of the UK designated as Enterprise Areas, for the purpose of bringing those premises back into business use. (The Business Premises Renovation Allowance).

Small and medium sized company limits

	Small	Medium
(i) Turnover	£5.6m (£2.8m)	£22.8m (£11.2m)
(ii) Balance sheet assets	£2.8m (£1.4m)	£11.4m (£5.6m)
(iii) Employees	50	250

Note. The figures in brackets apply to accounting periods ending prior to 30 January 2004.

Corporation Tax

Financial year	**2004 and 2005**
Full rate	30%
Small companies' rate	19%
Starting rate	0%
Profit limit for lower rate	£10,000
Profit limit for lower rate marginal relief	£50,000
Profit limit for small companies' rate	£300,000
Profit limit for small companies' marginal relief	£1,500,000
Marginal relief fraction for profits between £10,000 and £50,000	19/400
Marginal relief fraction for profits between £300,000 and £1,500,000	11/400

There is a minimum corporation tax charge of 19% on PCTCT distributed to non corporate shareholders.

Research and Development expenditure and transfer pricing limits: small and medium sized company limits

	Small	Medium
Employees	50	250
Turnover	€10m	€50m
Balance sheet assets	€10m	€43m

National Insurance contributions

	2005-06		2004-05	
Class 1 contributions	**Annual**	**Weekly**	**Annual**	**Weekly**
Lower earnings limit	£4,264	£82	£4,108	£79
Earnings threshold	£4,895	£94	£4,745	£91
Upper earnings limit	£32,760	£630	£31,720	£610

Employee's contributions in 2005-06 (2004-05)

Not contracted out:	11% (11%) on earnings between £94 (£91) and £630 (£610) 1% (1%) above £630 (£610) per week
Contracted out:	9.4% (9.4%) on earnings between £94 (£91) and £630 (£610) 1% (1%) on earnings above £630 (£610) per week 1.6% rebate on earnings between £82 (£79) and £94 (£91)

Employer's contributions in 2005-06 (2004-05)

Not contracted out:	12.8% (12.8%) on earnings in excess of £94 (£91)

Contracted out: Salary related: 9.3% (9.3%) on earnings between £94 (£91) and £630 (£610)
12.8% (12.8%) on earnings in excess of £630 (£610)
3.5% (3.5%) rebate on earnings between £82 (£79) and £94 (£91)

Contracted out: Money purchase: 11.8% (11.8%) on earnings between £94 (£91) and £630 (£610)
12.8% (12.8%) on earnings in excess of £630 (£610)
1% rebate on earnings between £82 (£79) and £94 (£91)

	2005-06	**2004-05**
Class 1A contributions	12.8%	12.8%
Class 1B contributions	12.8%	12.8%
Class 2 contributions		
Normal rate	£2.10 pw	£2.05 pw
Small earnings exception	£4,345 pa	£4,215 pa
Class 3 contributions	£7.35 pw	£7.15 pw
Class 4 contributions		
Annual lower earnings limit	£4,895	£4,745
Annual upper earnings limit	£32,760	£31,720
Percentage rate between limits	8%	8%
Percentage rate above upper limit	1%	1%

Capital Gains
Retail Prices Index

Where Retail Price Indices are required, it should be assumed that they are as follows.

	Jan	Feb	Mar	Apr	May	Jun	Jul	Aug	Sep	Oct	Nov	Dec
1982	-	-	79.44	81.04	81.62	81.85	81.88	81.90	81.85	82.26	82.66	82.51
1983	82.61	82.97	83.12	84.28	84.64	84.84	85.30	85.68	86.06	86.36	86.67	86.89
1984	86.84	87.20	87.48	88.64	88.97	89.20	89.10	89.94	90.11	90.67	90.95	90.87
1985	91.20	91.94	92.80	94.78	95.21	95.41	95.23	95.49	95.44	95.59	95.92	96.05
1986	96.25	96.60	96.73	97.67	97.85	97.79	97.52	97.82	98.30	98.45	99.29	99.62
1987	100.0	100.4	100.6	101.8	101.9	101.9	101.8	102.1	102.4	102.9	103.4	103.3
1988	103.3	103.7	104.1	105.8	106.2	106.6	106.7	107.9	108.4	109.5	110.0	110.3
1989	111.0	111.8	112.3	114.3	115.0	115.4	115.5	115.8	116.6	117.5	118.5	118.8
1990	119.5	120.2	121.4	125.1	126.2	126.7	126.8	128.1	129.3	130.3	130.0	129.9
1991	130.2	130.9	131.4	133.1	133.5	134.1	133.8	134.1	134.6	135.1	135.6	135.7
1992	135.6	136.3	136.7	138.8	139.3	139.3	138.8	138.9	139.4	139.9	139.7	139.2
1993	137.9	138.8	139.3	140.6	141.1	141.0	140.7	141.3	141.9	141.8	141.6	141.9
1994	141.3	142.1	142.5	144.2	144.7	144.7	144.0	144.7	145.0	145.2	145.3	146.0
1995	146.0	146.9	147.5	149.0	149.6	149.8	149.1	149.9	150.6	149.8	149.8	150.7
1996	150.2	150.9	151.5	152.6	152.9	153.0	152.4	153.1	153.8	153.8	153.9	154.4
1997	154.4	155.0	155.4	156.3	156.9	157.5	157.5	158.5	159.3	159.5	159.6	160.0
1998	159.5	160.3	160.8	162.6	163.5	163.4	163.0	163.7	164.4	164.5	164.4	164.4
1999	163.4	163.7	164.1	165.2	165.6	165.6	165.1	165.5	166.2	166.5	166.7	167.3
2000	166.6	167.5	168.4	170.1	170.7	171.1	170.5	170.5	171.7	171.6	172.1	172.2
2001	171.1	172.0	172.2	173.1	174.2	174.4	173.3	174.0	174.6	174.3	173.6	173.4
2002	173.3	173.8	174.5	175.7	176.2	176.2	175.9	176.4	177.6	177.9	178.2	178.5
2003	178.4	179.3	179.9	181.2	181.5	181.3	181.3	181.6	182.5	182.6	182.7	183.5
2004	183.1	183.8	184.6	185.7	186.5	186.8	186.8	187.4	188.1	188.6	189.0	189.9
2005*	188.9	189.6	189.8	190.0	190.2	190.4	190.6	190.8	191.0	191.2	191.4	191.6
2006*	191.8	192.0	192.2	192.4	192.6	192.8	193.0	193.2	193.4	193.6	193.8	194.0

* = assumed

A: Introduction to the UK Tax System

In this chapter you will cover the following areas in overview:
- the various taxes levied in the UK;
- the period for which income tax is charged;
- the categorisation of sources of income;
- the sources of income that are exempt from income tax.

A1.1 Taxes in the UK

The UK government raises in the region of 230 to 250 billion pounds in taxation each year.

Income tax is the single largest earner for the government making up **30%** of total revenue. Income tax is charged on salaries from employment, on rental income from properties let out, on interest from banks and building societies, on dividends from companies and on the profits of the self employed.

The second largest earner for the government is value added tax (**VAT**). This makes up about **23%** of the total government revenue and is charged by businesses to customers on supplies of goods or services in the UK.

National Insurance contributions (**NIC**) make up **21%** of total government income. National Insurance contributions are generally paid by both employers and employees on earnings from employment, although NIC is also levied on self employed persons on the profits of their trade.

Income tax, VAT and NIC are the three most important taxes as far as raising money is concerned, making up about 75% or so of total government revenue.

A large part of the remainder (**16%**), is made up of **duties**, being taxes on alcohol, petrol and tobacco, as well as certain levies on goods coming into the UK.

Corporation tax makes up about **8%** of total government revenue, being the tax paid by UK companies on their taxable profits.

The remaining slice consists of the **"capital taxes"** being capital gains tax (CGT), inheritance tax (IHT), stamp duty (SD) and stamp duty land tax (SDLT). Capital gains tax is the tax levied when individuals sell assets and make a profit.

A1.2 The tax year

Individuals pay income tax by reference to the "tax year". The UK tax year runs from **6 April to the following 5 April**. For example, the tax year that begins on 6 April 2005 and ends on 5 April 2006 is known as the tax year 2005/06.

The tax rates and tax allowances for the 2005/06 tax year, were set in the March 2005 Budget.

There are two stages in calculating an individual's tax liability. First we compute the individual's taxable income from all sources in the relevant tax year. Having arrived at **taxable income** we then apply the 2005/06 **tax rates and allowances** to that income, to arrive at the **tax liability** for the year. This tax will be collected by the HM Revenue & Customs ("the Revenue") under the "self-assessment" system. This will be dealt with in a later chapter.

A1.3 Sources of income

The tax legislation categorises various sources of income. Each type of income has its own special rules. This is why we need to decide what type of income an individual has received.

When we looked at income received by individuals in the past, the **types of income** were sorted into **Schedules** and sometimes further divided into **Cases.** This was called the **Schedular system.** It still operates for **companies** and so we will be looking at it in detail when we study companies. You may well find references to the old system in past questions. So we will mention the main points of the old system as we explain the current way of sorting out the types of income.

The first type of income that we will think about is **trading income**. This covers profits from a trade. So, for instance, a **self employed** person in business as a taxi driver, or a market trader, or a builder or plumber, would be taxed on his **trading income.** This used to be called **Schedule D Case I income**.

Trading income also covers profits from a profession or vocation. For instance, a **self employed** professional such as a solicitor or barrister would also **have trading income**. This used to be called **Schedule D Case II** income. Trading income is a very important type of income and we will deal with it in a separate module.

The second type of income we need to consider is **property income**. This is income from **land and buildings**, such as **rental** income. We need to keep property income from **UK** land and buildings separate from property income from **non-UK** land and buildings. Income from UK land and buildings used to be taxed under Schedule **A**. Income from non-UK land and buildings used to be taxed under Schedule **D** Case **V**.

Next, there is a very important type of income called income from **earnings and pensions. Earnings** covers **salaries, bonuses** and **non-cash benefits**. We will look at these in detail in later sessions. This type of income used to be taxed under Schedule **E**.

There are various types of **savings and investment** income. A very common one is interest arising from **UK banks** and **building societies**. We call this **interest income**. This type of income used to be taxed under Schedule **D** Case **III**.

Another type of investment income is **dividends received from companies**. These used to be taxed under Schedule **F**. As we will see later, **dividend income** needs to be kept separate from other types of investment income because it has different rates of tax applied to it.

These are the two **main types** of savings and investment income, but there **are some others** which we will explain more about later in this course.

An individual may have income from **outside the UK**. We have already seen that he may have **property income** from **non-UK land and buildings**. He may also have **investment income** from outside the UK such as **non-UK bank interest** or **non-UK dividends**. All income arising outside the UK is now called **foreign income**. Foreign investment income used to be taxed under Schedule **D** Case **V**.

It is important to note here that income can still be **taxable** in the UK, even if it arises from a source **outside** the UK. As a general principle, individuals who **live** in the UK and who were **born** in the UK will pay UK income tax on their **worldwide** income wherever it comes from. So, a **UK resident** will generally pay income tax on foreign income.

Finally, there is income which is chargeable to income tax which does not fall within any of the categories that we have just looked at. This is called **miscellaneous income**. It is the Revenue's way of covering itself and making sure that taxable income doesn't fall through the net. Miscellaneous income used to be taxed under Schedule **D** Case **VI**. We will consider miscellaneous income in more detail later in the course.

A1.4 Exempt income

There are a few sources of income which are specifically exempt from income tax. Income from **National Savings Certificates** is exempt from tax, as are any winnings on **Premium Bonds**. Any income from **betting, gaming** or **lotteries** is exempt from income tax. s. 692 ITTOIA 2005

Most **social security benefits** are also exempt from income tax. The notable exceptions to this are the state pension and any job-seekers allowances. These are taxable income. s.660 ITEPA 2003

Any **statutory redundancy pay** received on the termination of an employment is also exempt from income tax. s. 309 ITEPA 200

Scholarship awards are exempt, as is any income from **ISAs** (individual savings accounts). SI 1998/18

Q	Now test your understanding by attempting the example which follows.

Example 1

Which of the following sources of income are exempt from income tax:

		Taxable	Exempt
a)	Interest on National Savings Account		
b)	Dividend from a foreign company		
c)	Child's wages from a newspaper round		
d)	Income from National Savings Certificate		
e)	Housing benefit		
f)	State retirement pension		

Answer 1

	Taxable	Exempt
Interest on National Savings Account	✓	
Dividend from a foreign company	✓	
Child's wages from a newspaper round (note)	✓	
Income from National Savings Certificates		✓
Housing benefit		✓
State retirement pension	✓	

Note:
Wages are taxable as employment income. The fact they are paid to a child is irrelevant. However, in most instances, the child's income will be covered by Personal Allowances so no tax will be due.

SUMMARY - INTRODUCTION TO THE UK TAX SYSTEM

The main taxes in the UK are income tax, VAT, NIC, corporation tax, capital gains tax and inheritance tax.

Income tax is paid for a tax year which runs from 6 April to 5 April.

Income is categorised into the following sources:

Trading income
Property income - UK
- non-UK
Employment income
Savings and investment income - interest income
- dividend income
Foreign income
Miscellaneous income

Some income is exempt from income tax such as:

Income from National Savings Certificates
Premium bonds winnings
Income from Betting and Lotteries
Most social security benefits
Statutory redundancy pay
Income from ISAs

B: Computation of Taxable Trading Profit

B1: TRADING INCOME AND THE BADGES OF TRADE

In this chapter we will look at trading income including:
- the schedule for taxing trading income;
- the definition of a trade;
- the "badges of trade" arising from case law;
- land transactions;
- the anti-avoidance provisions;
- whether receipts are taxable or not.

Statutory references are to ITTOIA 2005 unless stated otherwise.

B1.1 Trading Income

The category "trading income" encompasses both **income from a trade,** for example plumbing or building and **income from a profession or vocation.** A profession would include accountancy or law. A vocation includes acting, ballet dancing, theatrical performing, sport etc.

Previously, under the old schedular system income from a trade was taxed under Schedule D Case I, whereas income from a profession or vocation was taxed under Schedule D Case II. There were no notable differences between the way profits were taxed under DI or DII.

B1.2 The definition of trading

Income tax is charged on "the profits of a trade, profession or vocation". s. 5

A trade is defined as **"every manufacture, adventure or concern in the nature of trade".**

A "trade" is defined in the legislation as a "trade", which is a circular definition and does not take us a great deal further. Therefore, the interpretation of what is meant by the term "trade" has been left largely to the Courts. The Courts have developed a number of tests to determine whether somebody is trading. These tests are known as the **"badges of trade"**.

B1.3 The Badges of Trade

Profit seeking motive

When a person enters into a transaction, we need to identify whether there is a **profit seeking motive**. It is not the **existence** of a profit that is important, it is the **motive to earn one**. However HM Revenue and Customs (the Revenue) will really be interested in this issue if a profit has **actually** been earned, because then they have something to tax.

A taxpayer may argue that they are trading in order to utilise a loss to reduce their tax bill. The taxpayer must demonstrate the **motive** rather than the existence of profit to establish that a trade is being carried on.

Frequency and number of similar transactions

If we do something once, never to be repeated again, it is unlikely that we would be treated as carrying on a trade. However if we **keep doing it**, it is more likely that we are trading. For instance, assume I sold my car which I had owned for four years. I then bought myself another car and sold that one two years later. It is unlikely the Revenue would consider that I am **trading** in cars. If, however, I bought and sold cars every month, it is more likely that they will seek to tax the profits as trading income.

The most notable case in this area is *Pickford v Quirke* where a taxpayer purchased a mill with the object of using it for trading purposes. However it turned out that the mill was in a much worse state than they had imagined and the best thing the taxpayer could do was to strip all the items out of it and sell them piecemeal. He made a considerable profit doing this, so he did it again and again and again. As a result of the **repeated number of transactions**, it was held that the profits were taxable as trading income.

Modification of the asset in order to make it more saleable

If we buy something, do nothing to it then sell it, it is unlikely we are trading. However, if we bought a car, put a new engine in it, resprayed the body and made it more attractive to buy, it is possible we would be considered to be trading.

Nature of the asset

We cannot pin a trading label onto a single one-off transaction simply because we cannot justify that the particular asset was purchased for any other purpose than to resell it. The most notable case in this area is *Rutledge v CIR*.

In this case, a taxpayer purchased 1 million rolls of toilet paper in one single transaction. He then sold them on at a profit in another single transaction. This was held to be trading (an "adventure" in the nature of trade) as there was no other justifiable reason to purchase such a large quantity of toilet paper - he could not argue that this was simply overstocking!

Connection with an existing trade

Taking an example of a car, let us say that as a tax accountant I sell a car. It is unlikely that I would be trading in cars because there is no link between selling cars and being a tax accountant. If however I was a car mechanic who occasionally sold a car, the Revenue are much more likely to successfully tax the profits on the sale of cars along with my existing trade as there is a **direct link** between repairing cars and selling cars. Other badges of trade would also need to apply, but such a link is something that the Revenue will look very closely at.

Financing arrangements

If an asset is purchased on a short term loan which the taxpayer is unable to fund without selling the asset again, then the Revenue can successfully argue that the asset was purchased specifically with a view to selling it.

This was cited in the case of *Wisdom v Chamberlain* where the comedian Norman Wisdom bought a mound of silver bullion on a short term loan. He could not service the interest payments from his existing money, but as soon as he sold the bullion and repaid the loan he found he had made a substantial profit. This profit was taxed as trading income.

Length of ownership

If you have owned something for a long time, it is much easier to justify that you bought it for its enjoyment or for your own private consumption. A profit on sale would not therefore be treated as a trading profit. If however you have only owned it for a **short period** it is much more likely that the Revenue could successfully argue that it was purchased with the aim of selling it at a profit.

The existence of a sales organisation

In the case of *The Cape Brandy Syndicate,* a syndicate of chartered accountants distilled brandy. They distilled far more than they could actually drink themselves and sold the surplus. The Revenue sought to tax them as trading income. They argued that they were simply selling what they could not physically drink themselves. However as they had set up a special phone line and information desk and published brochures and adverts advertising their brandy, the Revenue successfully argued that they had commenced a trade.

Reason for the acquisition/sale

Finally, we will look at **how the asset was acquired** - ie, whether purchased or otherwise acquired by gift or inheritance - and what is the **reason for the sale** of the asset? By way of an example, consider Maud who inherits a wardrobe full of fur coats from her late mother. She does not want to wear them, so she puts an advert in the local paper to sell them. The Revenue spot this advert and seek to tax Maud for any profits earned. As Maud **inherited** the coats it is highly unlikely that a trading label can be pinned to these transactions. However if Maud had **purchased** a wardrobe full of fur coats, advertised them and then sold them at a profit, it is much more likely that she would be held to be trading. Simply realising an inheritance for cash is not the commencement of a trade.

In some circumstances, the existence of one single badge is enough to show trading (as in the case of *Rutledge v CIR).* However **in other cases we need to look at a combination** of the badges of trade. The trigger to get the Revenue interested in the transaction in the first place is the existence of a **profit**.

B1.4 Land transactions

The Revenue often look closely at the purchase and sale of land and buildings, simply due to the size of the profits involved. It is in the area of land transactions that the most cases involving the badges of trade have been taken to the Courts.

One of the important questions to ask is whether the taxpayer is "**investing in land" or "dealing in land"** - "dealing" is trading. This question which was posed in the case of *Marson v Morton.* Here a taxpayer purchased some land with the intention of holding on to it as an **investment** for at least two years. In order to increase the value of the land, the taxpayer applied for planning permission. Looking at the badges of trade, this will be regarded by the Revenue as a **modification to an asset to make it more saleable**.

It was held in this case that because the **original intention was the purchase of an investment**, no trade was being carried on. It is not what the taxpayer **says** which determines intentions, it is what the **surrounding evidence supports**. Documented intentions made the difference.

Another question that we must ask is, is whether our taxpayer is a **resident in the property**, or a **developer who is refurbishing a property for onward sale**. In the case of *Kirkby v Hughes,* a builder purchased a run-down house. He carried out a lot of repair and refurbishment work and sold the house at a healthy profit. He then purchased a strip of land and built a house on it, again selling it at a substantial profit. He then purchased a barn and converted it into a house.

The Courts believed that he was trading because they could apply **enough of the badges of trade** to him. There clearly was a profit seeking motive, he had modified the assets he purchased, there was a connection with an existing trade, and the length of ownership in each case was fairly short. The profits on the first house were held to be taxable as trading income along with all of the other properties he had bought and sold.

Looking specifically at **one** of the badges of trade we should also identify a **reason for the purchase and a reason for the sale**. In the case of *Taylor v Good,* a husband purchased a property to be used as a family home. However on seeing the house, his wife refused to live in it. As a result he had no option but to sell the house. Despite it being a one-off transaction, the Revenue felt that the badges of trade applied because the asset was only owned for a very short period of time. However, there was clearly **another reason for the acquisition and subsequent sale** - there was a genuine **intention** by the taxpayer to live in the house rather than simply to make a quick profit. Therefore the transaction was held **not** to be a trading transaction.

B1.5 Frequency of transactions

Michael buys unprofitable restaurants, turns the businesses around and sells them at a profit. He has done this 12 times. The idea came to him when he sold his first restaurant which he had run as the owner and manager for 10 years.

The question we are asking is whether he is chargeable to tax on trading income, first in respect of the restaurants in general, which he had run for a short period, but also in respect of the first restaurant which he had run for a long period.

We must look closely at the badges of trade. Clearly there is a profit seeking motive which is readily identifiable. The frequency of transactions which Michael is undertaking points towards a trade. Modifications to the asset purchased (taking an unprofitable restaurant and turning it around), the length of ownership (he owns them for a relatively short period of time) and the reason for the sale (to make money), lead us to draw the conclusion that these transactions will clearly be trading transactions.

The next question is - **do the future transactions taint the first one?** Unfortunately the answer to this question is **yes.** In the case of *Leach v Pogson,* an individual had owned a driving school for a long period of time before he sold it at a profit. He then purchased, turned around and sold numerous other driving schools in the future. It was held by the Courts that not only were profits from sales of the **later** driving schools charged to tax as trading income, but the **original disposal, although originally treated as a capital transaction, will be turned into a trading transaction because of later events**.

B1.6 Share Dealing

Muriel thinks she has an infallible system to predict share price movements. Over a two year period she entered into over 100 transactions buying and selling shares. She made a profit on some but overall she made a loss, so her system was not as infallible as she thought! Will she manage to obtain loss relief against her general income?

In order to set a loss against other income, the **loss must be a trading loss** - we will come to losses later in this course. The question is whether Muriel is **dealing or investing.** In the case of *Salt v Chamberlain* it was held that **all share transactions are capital** in their nature unless they are undertaken by a properly registered share dealer. Therefore if a private individual (not a share dealer) buys and sells shares many many times, he can never have the badges of trade pinned on to those transactions. Such profits will be taxable as **capital gains** and subject to CGT with all the advantages of indexation and taper relief.

B1.7 Taxable and Non-Taxable Receipts

If receipts are **wholly unexpected and unsolicited,** they are **not taxable**. This is highlighted in the case of *Simpson v John Reynolds & Co.*, in which a taxpayer received a voluntary payment from an ex-customer when they were asked to cease to act as their insurance broker. Because the payment was not invoiced, not expected and was purely an unsolicited gift, it was not held to be part of the taxable trading income.

In *Murray v Goodhews,* an ex-gratia payment given to a pub landlord as a result of the cancellation of his pub tenancy was held not to be taxable. The reason for this was that the receipt of the compensation had nothing to do with him buying and selling alcoholic drinks and running a pub - it was as a result of the termination of the pub tenancy.

However, if amounts are **expected** then they will be **taxable**. In the case of *Creed v H & M Levinson Limited,* a taxpayer was offered an ex-gratia amount from an ex-customer and successfully sued for more. As the receipt was clearly solicited and expected, it was taxable. In the case of *McGowan v Brown & Cousins*, an estate agent who received compensation for not being appointed as letting agent, was taxed on the income as it related specifically to the trade and was solicited and expected.

SUMMARY - TRADING INCOME AND THE BADGES OF TRADE

Trading income encompasses both income from a trade and income from a profession or vocation.

The statutory definition of a trade includes the word "trade", so tests known as the "badges of trade" have developed from case law. These include:

- profit seeking motive
- frequency and number of similar transactions
- modifications to sell an asset
- nature of the asset
- connection with an existing trade
- financing arrangements
- length of ownership
- existence of a sales organisation
- how the asset was acquired and the reason for sale.

Land transactions have featured in many cases and the questions to ask also include:

- is the taxpayer investing or dealing?
- is the taxpayer resident in the property or a developer?

If a series of transactions are treated as trading this will taint the first time such a transaction was carried out so it can no longer be regarded as a capital transaction.

If a taxpayer has deliberately taken steps to turn a trading transaction into a capital one, the profits may be taxed as miscellaneous income.

Wholly unexpected and unsolicited amounts are not taxable, however if amounts are expected then they will be taxable.

B2: ADJUSTMENT OF PROFIT

In this chapter you will cover the rules that apply for adjusting accounting profits to obtain the taxable trading profits. In particular you will cover:

- depreciation;
- capital expenditure;
- the wholly and exclusively rule;
- entertaining;
- gifts;
- luxury car rental payments.

Statutory references are to ITTOIA 2005 unless stated otherwise.

B2.1 Introduction

Assume a trader prepares a set of accounts and those accounts show a profit. However, in computing this profit the trader could have deducted expenditure which the Revenue may not like. Consequently we are required to make a number of adjustments in arriving at the trader's taxable profit.

We **start** with the **profit per accounts.** We then **add certain disallowed expenditure,** and **deduct items which are not taxed as trading income**.

This gives us the "tax adjusted profit", which is acceptable to the Revenue.

Profit per accounts	X
Add: Disallowed expenditure	X
Deduct: Items not taxed as trade profits	(X)
Tax adjusted profit	X

It is this profit which is taxable as trading income.

B2.2 Depreciation

Depreciation is **not allowed** for tax purposes. This is because there are so many rates and methods of depreciation the Revenue feel that traders will be encouraged to choose depreciation rates which maximise tax relief.

Instead businesses are able to claim capital allowances (CAs). CAs are normally given at a rate of 25% on a reducing balance basis on assets that qualify as plant and machinery. CAs are covered in a later chapter.

B2.3 Items not taxed as Trading Income

Traders might include all of their income in their accounts, but it is only trading income which is taxed as trade profits. Therefore all **other sources of income are deducted** in arriving at the profit figure. This other income will then be brought back in the main income tax computation and taxed accordingly. Typical examples of non-trading income are: s.4

- **rental income**;
- **interest income**;
- **dividends received**;
- **any sundry miscellaneous income**.

Illustration 1

A trader has the following results;

Profit & Loss Account;	£'000
Turnover	850
Cost of sales	(400)
Gross Profit	450
Rental income	50
Interest receivable	20
Gross profit	520
Office expenses	(80)
Premises expenses	(100)
Depreciation	(60)
Profit before tax	**280**

Tax Computation;		£'000
Profit per accounts		280
Add:	Depreciation	60
Deduct:	Rental income	(50)
	Interest	(20)
Trading Income		270

It is this Trading Income which is brought into the trader's income tax computation as earned income.

B2.4 Disallowed expenditure

There are three main categories in this area.

- **Capital expenditure** - this is any expenditure which gives an "enduring benefit" to the business. There is a large amount of case law in this area which we will cover shortly. s. 33

- **Expenditure** which has **not been incurred "wholly and exclusively"** for the purposes of the trade. Again there is a large amount of case law in this area. s. 34

- **Specific disallowables** given by tax statute and case law.

We shall examine each of these in turn.

B2.5 Capital expenditure

The purchase of **capital equipment** should be **included on a trader's balance sheet,** as the balance sheet shows all the fixed assets of the business. These would include:

- motor cars;
- premises;
- other equipment (photocopiers, computers etc).

These items are **eligible for capital allowances or industrial buildings allowances** (IBAs) and these rules will be covered in later chapters.

If the trader has included any **capital additions** in the Profit and Loss Account, they should be **disallowed** and **added back** in arriving at the Trading Income. Where capital additions qualify as plant or machinery, capital allowances will be given instead.

We also **disallow profits or losses on the sale of assets**. Losses on sales of assets are a disallowed expense and should therefore be **added back.** Profits on sales of assets are not taxable as Trading Income and should therefore be **deducted** in arriving at trading profits.

The trader may have also incurred **legal fees on the acquisition** of capital assets. These are disallowed as they **relate to a capital item**. However, legal fees incurred on the **renewal of a short lease are specifically allowed**. A short lease in this context is a lease of less than 50 years.

B2.6 Wholly and exclusively

Expenses are only deductible if they are incurred **"wholly and exclusively"** for the purposes of the trade. s. 34

Private expenditure

When preparing accounts, traders often include items which relate in whole or in part to their own private affairs (ie not to the business). For example a trader may decide to deduct a **"salary"** which he pays to himself out of the profits of the business. This "salary" is not taxable on him as employment income since his profits are charged to tax as a self-employed individual (he is not an employee).

Consequently we **add back** any salary or wages drawn from the business by the proprietor in arriving at the tax adjusted profit. **Salaries paid to employees are allowable** as there is a corresponding charge to income tax on the employment income.

Mortgage interest relating to the traders private residence is clearly a private expense and is not incurred "wholly and exclusively for the purposes of the trade". It should therefore be **added back**. However, interest paid on a loan to buy **business premises** (shop, office etc) will be allowed as a deduction.

Motor expenses are a good example of a private expenditure. Assume a trader drives a car, and he agrees with the Revenue that the car **is used 70% of the time for business purposes.** However, he deducts **all** of the costs of running the car in his profit and loss account (eg, all fuel, repairs, insurance, road tax etc). If 70% of the costs are incurred for business purposes, **30% of the costs must be disallowed** as they relate to private expenditure which has not been incurred wholly and exclusively for the purposes of the trade. **30% of the motor expenses should be added back** to the profit.

Provided the taxpayer proposes a percentage which reasonably reflects the private element of the expense, the Revenue will usually accept it.

The private use adjustment can apply to **any expenditure**. For example, if a taxpayer uses, say, 20% of his house as an office for the purposes of the trade, he will be able to deduct 20% of the mortgage interest in arriving at his taxable profit. If he has deducted the full amount in his accounts, we would need to add back 80%.

Travel expenses

There has been a large number of cases going before the Courts with regard to the "wholly and exclusively" test for travel expenses.

In the case of *Newsom v Robertson,* a self employed barrister claimed the costs of **travel from his home in Surrey to his Chambers** in Central London. The barrister argued that he worked in both locations - from time to time he needed to prepare cases and read through client files at home. However, he was not listed in the telephone directory as a barrister at his home address, and he did not want his clients visiting him at his home. He could have carried out his paperwork in Chambers, it was just that he **chose** to work from home. As a result, the Courts were **not satisfied** that the travel expenses had been incurred **wholly and exclusively** for the purposes of his profession and therefore **disallowed** the costs.

In *Horton v Young,* a bricklayer worked at a number of different sites. He negotiated his contracts and kept his records at his home. In order to lay bricks he obviously had to **travel to the site** at which the bricks needed laying. Therefore the Courts were satisfied that any travel costs were incurred wholly and exclusively for the purposes of the trade. The builder's **fixed place of business was his home, therefore travel costs to the site were allowed.**

In *Sargeant v Barnes,* a dentist travelled from his home every morning to his surgery. Costs of travelling from **home to work are not allowed** as a deductible expense for self-employed individuals as they are **not incurred for the purposes of the trade**. However, the dentist would stop off at the lab on his way to work to pick up bits and pieces of equipment he required to insert into his patients' mouths. He then drove on to the surgery.

The dentist argued that the costs of travel between the **lab and the surgery** were allowed, effectively saying that his work started on reaching the lab. However the Courts were not satisfied that the costs were deductible as the dentist would have passed the lab in any event as it was on his normal route into to work. Therefore as he **did not incur any extra travel costs,** the expenses were not deductible.

Clothing

In *Mallalieu v Drummond,* a barrister claimed that the costs of her dark Courtroom dress were allowable as an expense against her professional income because she was required to wear them in Court and would not otherwise wear such clothing in her everyday life. However the Courts were **not satisfied** that this was the case, as they argued that she would be **wearing clothing in Court in any event** in order to provide her with **warmth and normal decency**. The clothing costs were therefore **disallowed** as they satisfied a private purpose.

Therefore, an accountant who only normally wears his suit when he is acting as an accountant, would **not** be able to claim the costs of that suit as a trading expense because he would have to wear something when meeting clients.

However, the Revenue do accept that **protective clothing** (hard hats, overalls, chefs aprons etc) is an expense incurred wholly and exclusively for the purposes of the trade and **will allow such items**. The same applies for actors' costumes.

Children's wages

In *Dollar & Dollar v Lyon,* the precedent was set that wages paid to the children of the trader are only deductible provided they can satisfy the "wholly and exclusively" test. We therefore need to demonstrate that if we did not employ our own children, we would need to employ somebody else's children to perform those jobs (for instance, working in the shop on a Saturday or doing a paper round). The wages paid should be at a **reasonable market rate**, nowadays bearing in mind the National Minimum Wage. If in the Revenue's view the children's' wages put through the accounts are simply their pocket money (as in the *Dollar & Dollar* case), the costs would not be deductible.

Accountancy fees

In *Smiths Potato Estates Limited v Bolland,* the **costs of a tax appeal**, even though it was successful, were **not allowed** as they were not incurred wholly and exclusively for the purposes of the trade. The company had incurred the costs **in its capacity as a taxpayer,** not in its capacity as a trader. Therefore the costs did not relate specifically to its **trade**.

Following on from this case, the Revenue will not accept a deduction for the cost in preparing an individual's personal tax return even though the return will include details of the Trading Income. This is because the cost is being incurred in the individual's capacity as a **taxpayer**, not in his capacity as a trader.

So how do we treat accountancy fees levied for dealing with a **tax enquiry?** The Revenue has issued a Statement of Practice stating that if the enquiry relates **specifically to the trading income** and as a result of the enquiry **no additional profits are brought within the charge to tax**, any costs incurred in dealing with that enquiry **will be allowed** for tax purposes. SP 16/91

Finance lease assets

The rule on finance lease assets derives from the case of *Gallagher v Jones.* SP 3/91
Prior to this case, many taxpayers claimed actual rentals payable under finance leases rather than the commercial charges which had been put through the accounts. However in the case of finance leased assets, a deduction is given for **the depreciation element together with the interest charge**. This is the **only exception to the rule that depreciation is not allowed** for **tax purposes**. This rule is referred to in the Revenue's Statement of Practice 3/91.

B2.7 Specific disallowables

Costs incurred by a trader in **entertaining anyone except the trader's own staff** are specifically **disallowed** by tax legislation. S.45

Gifts of items are also generally **disallowed** unless;
(i) the assets gifted **cost under £50**; and
(ii) the gift must bear the **business name, logo** or a **clear advertisement;** and
(iii) the gift should **not** include **food, drink** or **tobacco.**

The Revenue are reluctant to give full relief for the leasing costs of luxury cars. A **luxury car** in this context is a car costing **more than £12,000**. In this instance, we only allow rental payments given by the formula below: s. 48

$$\textbf{Allow:} \quad \frac{£12{,}000 + P}{2P} \times \textbf{Rental payment}$$

where P = retail price of the car when new

This formula can be found at s.48(2) ITTOIA 2005.

The luxury car restriction does not apply to the leasing of cars which:

(i) are electrically propelled; or

(ii) have carbon dioxide emissions less than or equal to 120g/km.

This exemption applies to expenditure incurred on or after 17 April 2002 on the hiring of a car which is first registered on or after that date.

Q	Now test your understanding by attempting the examples which follow.

Example 1

A Mercedes SLK is leased for £6,000 p.a. The car cost £25,000

Calculate the amount of the expense that would be allowable and the amount that would be disallowed.

Example 2

State whether the following expenses incurred by a sole trader are allowable or disallowable for tax purposes:

		Allowable	*Disallowable*
a)	Loss on sale of a computer		
b)	Amortisation of goodwill		
c)	Employee steals the petty cash		
d)	Entertaining the local vet		
e)	Legal fees incurred on purchase of a new building		
f)	Interest on late paid VAT		
g)	Depreciation on a finance leased asset		
h)	Purchase of a new washing machine		

Answer 1

Allow: $\frac{£12{,}000 + £25{,}000}{2 \times £25{,}000} \times £6{,}000 =$ **£4,440**

Disallow: £(6,000 - 4,440) = **£1,560**

i.e. £1,560 would be added back in the adjustment to profits calculation.

Answer 2

		Allow	*Disallow*
a) Loss on sale of computer	(Capital)		X
b) Amortisation of goodwill	(Type of depreciation)		X
c) Employee theft of cash	(Business risk - wholly and exclusively)	✓	
d) Entertaining the local vet	(Not staff)		X
e) Legal fees on new building	(Capital)		X
f) Interest on late paid VAT	(Fine)		X
g) Depreciation on finance leased asset	(Gallagher v Jones SP3/91)	✓	
h) Purchase of a new washing machine	(Capital item)		X

SUMMARY - ADJUSTMENT OF PROFIT

Adjustments must be made to the profit per accounts to arrive at a tax adjusted figure.

Items not taxed as trading income must be deducted in arriving at the tax adjusted profit and include:

- rental income
- interest income
- dividend income
- sundry income
- profits on sales of fixed assets

Disallowed expenditure must be added back and includes:

- depreciation (except on finance leased assets)
- capital expenditure
- losses on sales of fixed assets
- legal fees on acquisition of assets (except renewal of lease < 50 yrs)
- expenses not incurred wholly and exclusively for the trade
- private expenditure
- travel expenses from home to work
- normal clothing (but not protective clothing which is allowable)
- children's wages if really pocket money
- costs of a tax appeal
- entertaining (unless staff)
- gifts (unless < £50, bearing the business name and not food, drink nor tobacco)
- a proportion of luxury car rentals (not "green" cars)

$$\frac{£12{,}000 + P}{2P} \times \text{Rental payment (P = retail price of new car)}$$

A measure of relief for capital expenditure is available for traders instead of depreciation. Certain items will be eligible for capital allowances or industrial buildings allowances (covered later).

B3: *CAPITAL* v REVENUE

In this chapter we shall look more closely at the rules for distinguishing whether expenditure is capital in nature (and therefore disallowable) or revenue in nature and hence would not lead to any adjustment to profits. You will learn about:

- the general principles;
- initial repairs;
- repairs v replacements;
- staff costs;
- training costs;
- one-off costs

Statutory references are to ITTOIA 2005 unless stated otherwise.

B3.1 General Principles

Section 33 ITTOIA 2005 disallows **any sum employed as capital** in the business. This would include items such as **loan repayments**. If for instance, a taxpayer borrows money to purchase a business premises, any repayments he makes back to the bank relating to the capital of the loan will not be tax deductible. However any interest element will be allowable. s. 33

The **cost of capital acquisitions** is also disallowed. A capital acquisition for these purposes is any expense which gives an **enduring benefit** to the business.

The cost of **improvements** to business premises is disallowed. The replacement of a part of the premises with the nearest modern equivalent, reflecting technological improvements, is allowable. However, if an item is substantially upgraded, the whole expenditure may be capital.

Specifically the Revenue now accepts that replacing single glazed windows by double glazed equivalents counts as a repair. The Revenue's previous view was that such expenditure would 'normally' be an improvement and therefore disallowed.

B3.2 Initial repairs

If a trader purchases an asset and then spends money on it, is this expense capital? In *Law Shipping Company v IRC,* a company purchased a ship which needed some immediate repair work as it did not possess a certificate of sea-worthiness. They spent the money and claimed the repairs as a revenue expense in the profit and loss account. However, the Courts held that the repairs were part and parcel of the **acquisition costs** of the asset as they **enabled the ship to be used for the very first time**. As a result, these "repairs" were **held to be capital** - i.e. linked to the capital acquisition of the ship.

Could we argue that the costs are revenue? In the case of *Odeon Associated Theatres Limited v Jones,* a number of cinemas were purchased just after the war in a very run down state. However, Odeon kept them open to the public and continued to show films. Over a period of time they gradually repaired and renovated the cinemas and brought them up to a much smarter state. As much of repair work related to dilapidations arising prior to Odeon's purchase, the Revenue argued under the *Law Shipping* precedent that the repairs expenses were part and parcel of the acquisition cost - ie, they were capital. However, as the **repairs took place to useable assets**, the Court held that the **costs were revenue in nature and therefore allowable**. The most important factor with regard to repairs on newly acquired assets, is whether the asset was **purchased in a useable state** and was **actually used** in that state.

B3.3 Repair v Replacement

A **repair** to an item is normally allowed as a **revenue expense** whereas **replacing** an entire item is normally considered a **capital** acquisition. There are two contrasting cases here. In *Bullcroft Main Collieries v O'Grady,* a business owned a factory. On the same site there was a freestanding chimney. The chimney was in a poor state of repair and the most economic thing to do was to knock it down completely and rebuild it. This was held to be a **replacement of an entire asset** and **capital** in nature - i.e. a capital acquisition of a brand new chimney.

However, in *Samuel Jones & Co (Devondale Ltd) v CIR,* a company owned a factory which had a chimney actually attached to it. The chimney was demolished and replaced with another one. The taxpayer successfully argued that this was a **repair to a subsidiary part of the factory** and not the replacement of an entire asset. The costs were **revenue** in nature and therefore allowable.

Therefore as far as repairs are concerned, if a trader actually repairing a **part** of an asset, that is a genuine repair and the costs will be allowed. However, if a trader is replacing an asset in its **entirety**, that is a capital item.

B3.4 Staff costs

Staff costs are generally a **revenue expense unless they relate to a capital project.** For example, if a firm of builders employs its own staff to construct a new head office, we would capitalise those particular staff costs on the balance sheet as they are part of the acquisition costs of the new head office (the new office being a capital asset employed in the business).

Another example would be a firm of accountants employing staff who have developed a new internal accounting software package to be used long-term in the business. The staff costs here are likely to be linked to a capital transaction and they should be disallowed. Capital allowances should instead be claimed on the software development costs. We will deal with capital allowances in a later session.

In *IRC v The New Zealand Forest Institute Limited*, the company purchased a number of research undertakings from the New Zealand Government. When the undertakings were purchased, the company took over all of the employees' contracts of employment. Some of the staff were entitled to accrued holiday pay, which was duly paid by the company who claimed it as a revenue expense. However, the Privy Council held that this was **capital**, relying on the decision of *Law Shipping*. The holiday pay formed part of the **acquisition costs of the undertakings**, and were contractual obligations. The company had purchased an asset (the new research undertakings) and were immediately required to spend money on it. That is a capital transaction.

James Snook & Co Limited v Blasdale involved a company owned by a number of directors. The directors were also shareholders. The buyer was purchasing the shares in the company in return for a cash payment to the shareholders.

The acquisition of shares is normally treated as a capital transaction and the purchaser would therefore not be able to obtain tax relief in arriving at their taxable profits. However, two of the board directors (who were also shareholders) were to be made redundant as well as selling their shares.

The purchaser negotiated with these two members that the cash they receive would be treated as **compensation for loss of office**. This way the purchaser could treat the payment as part of **staff costs** (ie, as an allowable revenue expense). However, the Courts did not agree. The transaction was treated as capital as there was a **direct link between the cash and the sale of shares.** The Revenue will try to link a payment to a capital transaction wherever possible. In this situation, it would have been better for the purchaser to buy the shares (at a discounted price), keep the board members on for, say, 6 months, then make them redundant. The redundancy payment in this instance payment would most likely be treated as a revenue expense.

B3.5 Training costs

The acquisition of new expertise is treated as capital. For example, assume an individual wants to trade as an accountant. The costs incurred by that individual to acquire the relevant expertise and pass the accountancy exams will not be treated as an expense in arriving at his taxable profit but will simply be a **cost incurred to enable him to trade** in the first place.

In a similar situation, the costs incurred by an individual putting themselves through training to become a driving instructor would also be **treated as capital** as these are costs to put that person in the **position to trade**, and are not incurred **as part of actually trading**.

Ongoing, update or development training, once qualified, will be **allowed** as a revenue expense because there is a direct link between the expense being incurred and the income being received as an accountant or driving instructor.

Staff training costs are always allowable as a trading expense whether this is for the staff to acquire new expertise or simply keep up to date. In addition, such training is a tax free benefit for those members of staff because the Government is keen to encourage employers to train and improve their employees.

B3.6 One-off costs

A one-off payment may either be capital or revenue, depending on the nature of it. A one-off payment will be capital if it results in the **purchase of either a tangible or an intangible asset**. An example of an intangible asset would be something like a licence agreement or a patent royalty. This was given in the case of *Morgan Crucible Company Limited v IRC.*

If the payment **affects the value of a capital asset** it will also be treated as capital as decided the case of *Tucker v Granada Motorway Services Limited.* Here a payment to reduce future rentals on a lease was held to be capital in nature because it **increased the value of the lease** on the balance sheet.

A one-off payment will be revenue (and allowable) if it is **made to reduce future revenue obligations** and does not result in either the acquisition or the increase in value of a capital asset. This was given in the case of *Hancock v The General Reversionary and Investment Co Limited.*

Q	Now test your understanding by attempting the example which follows.

Example 1

You are required to state which of the following are revenue or capital items for tax purposes.

	Capital	*Revenue*
a) Replacement of a photocopier		
b) New rollers on a photocopier		
c) Repairs to a second hand photocopier to enable it to be used.		
d) Redecoration of a new office building in line with the business's "corporate image".		
e) Redundancy payments made to staff as a result of the takeover of the company		
f) Redundancy payments made to a director / shareholder as a result of a takeover.		
g) CPE training for a self-employed accountant.		
h) A one-off payment to reduce rental payments on a leased building.		
i) Purchase of an annuity to enable a business to make pension payments to retired staff.		

Answer 1

	Capital	*Revenue*
a) Replacement of a photocopier	✓	
b) New rollers on a photocopier		✓
c) Repairs to a second hand photocopier to enable it to be used.	✓	
d) Redecoration of a new office building in line with the business's "corporate image".		✓ (see Note)
e) Redundancy payments made to staff as a result of the takeover of the company		✓
f) Redundancy payments made to a director / shareholder as a result of a takeover.	✓	
g) CPE training for a self-employed accountant.		✓
h) A one-off payment to reduce rental payments on a leased building.	✓	
i) Purchase of an annuity to enable a business to make pension payments to retired staff.	✓	

Note:

We will assume that the trader purchased a useable office block, and therefore it is likely we could treat this as a revenue expense given the *Odeon* decision. However we might end up with a battle from the Revenue if they could argue that the asset was actually unusable - i.e. because the walls were not decorated in the corporate identity.

SUMMARY - CAPITAL v REVENUE

If expenditure is capital in nature it must be disallowed for tax purposes. Capital acquisitions giving an enduring benefit to the trade and improvements to business premises must be disallowed. Loan repayments must also be added back although interest is allowable.

Initial repairs to an asset to enable it to be used are disallowed. However initial repairs to a useable asset are allowable.

Repairs to a subsidiary part of an asset are allowable but replacement of an entire asset is capital expenditure. Replacing single glazed windows with double glazed equivalents counts as a repair.

Staff costs are allowable unless they relate to a capital project.

If on takeover of a company a cash payment is made to shareholders being made redundant this will be linked to the sale of the shares and will be disallowed.

Training costs to enable an individual to trade will be disallowed although CPE and staff training costs are allowable.

A one-off payment to purchase an intangible asset is also disallowable, as are payments that affect the value of a capital asset.

B4: CAPITAL ALLOWANCES – DEFINITION

In this chapter you will cover the rules for determining whether plant and machinery qualify for capital allowances – the tax deduction available instead of depreciation. You will learn about:
- the statutory definition of non-qualifying expenditure;
- the exclusion for buildings;
- the exclusion for structures and land;
- the override to the exclusions;
- case law test of function v setting.

Statutory references in this chapter are to CAA 2001 unless otherwise stated.

B4.1 Introduction

Capital allowances are a **tax deductible allowance given when a trader incurs qualifying capital expenditure.** The trader would not get a revenue deduction for the expenditure because it has an **enduring benefit** for the trade and is therefore regarded as capital. It will however be a business cost and therefore the trader should be able to claim a deduction against taxable profits. This is done by means of a capital allowance. s. 2

The amount of the capital allowances available depend on the type of qualifying expenditure. All allowances are laid down in statute. The allowance could be as little as 4%, it could be as high as 100% - it **depends on the type of expenditure and the type of business incurring the expenditure**.

Capital expenditure falls into 3 broad categories:

a) expenditure on **plant and machinery** (by far the most common); and s. 1(2)(a)

b) expenditure on **industrial buildings** (very common); and. s.. 1(2)(b)

c) **other** expenditure (less common), such as on agricultural buildings..

In this chapter we will look at the **definition of plant and machinery.** In subsequent chapters we will look at how we calculate the various types of allowances.

You should note that capital expenditure will **include any irrecoverable VAT.** This is VAT which the trader is **unable to claim back** for various reasons - this will become clearer once you have studied the VAT part of your course.

B4.2 Definition of "Plant and Machinery"

s. 21-
s. 33

The definition of plant and machinery is found in the Capital Allowances Act of 2001 (CAA 2001). There is also a **significant body of case law** discussing what is and what is not plant.

CAA 2001 defines what is non-qualifying expenditure. Therefore if an item is not within the non-qualifying expenditure, by elimination it is likely to be regarded as plant.

The non-qualifying expenditure is broken down into **"buildings", and "structures and land".** The non qualifying expenditure included under buildings can be found within **S.21 CAA 2001**. There is a list called **List A** in this section. If a particular item is within List A, it is specifically excluded **and is therefore unlikely to qualify** as plant and machinery s. 21

Similarly within **S.22 CAA 2001**, there is a list **(List B)**, which identifies expenditure in connection with structures and land which should **not be regarded as plant or machinery.** So you can see that the legislation is very useful in determining whether something is plant or not. s. 22

There is also a very important **override** within the legislation. This can be found at **S.23** CAA 2001 within **List C**. Essentially if expenditure **is within List C it is likely to qualify** as plant and machinery. s. 23

It could therefore be that expenditure looks as though it falls within S.21 CAA 2001 (and would therefore not qualify for allowances), but if you can specifically find it within S.23, then **S.23 overrides the original exclusion**, and the expenditure will probably be treated as plant and will qualify for allowances

Even if an item in included within List C, it **must still satisfy the case law test of "function versus setting"**.

This very important test asks whether;

(i) the asset in question forms **part of the setting in which the trade is carried on?**; or

(ii) the asset in question is something which a trader actively uses in his trade, i.e. **does the asset perform a function in the business?**

If the asset **has a function,** it will be **plant** and capital allowances can be claimed. However, if expenditure has been incurred by the trader on **part of the setting** within which he runs his business, it will **not be plant** and no allowances can be claimed. This was established of *J Lyons & Co v Attorney General* and has been revisited many times by the Courts in deciding what is or is not "plant".

B4.3 Buildings - s. 21 CAA 2001 s. 21

Under the buildings exclusion within S.21 CAA 2001, the term "building" includes:

a) an asset which is **incorporated in the building**;

b) an asset which, although **not incorporated** in the building (because perhaps it is moveable), is **in the building** and is of a kind which **would normally be incorporated** in the building;

c) an asset that is **in or connected with the building and is in List A.**

You can see that if an item is incorporated in the building, or it is normally incorporated, but on this particular occasion it is moveable, it is likely to be excluded under (a) or (b).

List A provides further clarification as to items included within the term "building", specifically detailing the following:

1) Walls, floors, ceilings, doors, gates, shutters, windows, stairs.

2) Mains services and systems for water, electricity and gas.

3) Waste disposal systems.

4) Sewerage and drainage systems.

5) Shafts or other similar structures.

6) Fire safety systems.

No great surprises there, but List A does clarify that expenditure on these particular items (unless later overwritten by List C), would be **regarded as expenditure on "buildings" and therefore would not qualify as "plant".**

B4.4 Structures and Land - s.22 CAA 2001 s. 22

Under S.22, **plant and machinery does not include expenditure on the following**:

a) The provision of a structure or other asset **in List B**; or

b) Any works involving the **alteration of land.**

Land is not plant, but List B is worth a close look and contains the following:

1) Tunnel bridge, viaduct etc.

2) Pavement, road, car park.

3) Canal or basin.

4) Dam, reservoirs etc.

5) Docks, harbours, wharfs.

6) Dykes and sea walls.

Again no great surprises here. You would have to be fairly optimistic to argue that a tunnel, for example, was a piece of plant. However, to be safe do **check that your item is not within List C** as anything in List C **overrides List B.**

B4.5 Override - s. 23 CAA 2001 s. 23

S.23 tells us that that S.21 and S.22 **do not apply to the following**:

a) Thermal insulation of industrial buildings.

b) Fire safety.

c) Safety at designated sports grounds.

d) Safety at regulated stands at sports grounds.

e) Safety at other sports grounds.

f) Personal security.

g) Software and rights to software.

h) List C items.

Therefore expenditure on any of the items above will be treated as expenditure on "plant" and **will qualify** for capital allowances.

List C is a long list of very specific items. The majority of these items have been derived from case law. Indeed Lists A, B and C have largely been constructed as a summary of case decisions regarding whether assets constitute plant or not. Therefore, in this area, we no longer need to refer to much case law as case precedents have now been put on the statute books and incorporated into the Capital Allowances Act. The new legislation is very comprehensive and is a great help in determining whether a particular item is plant or not.

Taking a closer look at List C, which comprises some 33 items, it should be noted that whilst List C items **normally qualify as plant**, it does not **automatically** mean the asset is plant. The asset must **also fulfil the case law test of function v setting.**

In the majority of cases the "function" test will be passed. However you should be aware that just because an asset appears on List C, it does not automatically mean that capital allowances can be claimed. If a "List C" asset forms part of the "setting" in which a business is carried on, a capital allowances claim will be denied.

Illustration 1

Consider a dry dock. A dry dock is mentioned in S.22 List B, item 5 (ie a dock, harbour, etc). These are the items which are considered to be part of a structure or land, therefore you would think it would **not** be plant and would not qualify for capital allowances.

Now take a look at List C in S.23.

In List C, item 23, we have the provision of dry docks. In the case of *CIR v Barclay, Curle & Co Ltd*, a dry dock was held to perform a function in the business, ie, removing a ship from the river, holding it upright whilst it was being repaired and then returning it to the river when the repairs were complete. Consequently the dry dock fulfilled a function in the business rather than just being part of the setting in which the business was carried on.

Therefore the dry dock will qualify as plant, providing of course the functional test has been met, which it should do following the *Barclay Curle* case.

From this exercise we see an item that initially looked as though it was **excluded** from being plant because it was in List B. However, on an inspection of overrides in List C we find it specifically mentions the item concerned. Therefore we can assume that we are a long way to establishing that a dry dock is plant.

B4.6 Case Law

Various cases on the "function v setting" test demonstrate this very important principle.

In *Dixon v Fitch's Garage Ltd (1975),* it was held that a **garage canopy** over a petrol filling station did not actually help in the supplying of petrol. It was therefore held to be part of the setting, and therefore not plant. However, if the canopy was more than just a canopy (ie, it performed a greater role in the business such as attracting customers to the garage), then the Revenue may accept that the canopy fulfils a function and capital allowances could be claimed. In an Irish case (*O'Culachain v McMullan Brothers*) the taxpayer succeeded in such a claim as the canopy carried advertising in illuminated lettering.

In *Schofield v R & H Hall Ltd (1975),* dockside concrete **grain silos** were held to be plant as they fulfilled a function in the trade. They held the grain in a position from which it could be discharged to purchasers. This was a function, and the silos were therefore plant. This has now been specifically included in List C - Item 28 states the provision of silos provided for temporary storage or storage tanks are specifically included as plant.

In *Cooke v Beach Station Caravans Ltd (1974),* a caravan park with leisure facilities, claimed that the construction of their **swimming pool** fell within the "function" provisions, and was therefore plant. The Revenue argued it was setting. The Courts agreed that the pool performed a function, i.e. the caravan park used the swimming pool for carrying on its trade, and it was a major attraction to the caravan park. Again this case has now been included in the legislation at List C, item 16.

In *Jarrold v John Good & Sons Ltd,* **moveable partitions** in an office to sub-divide floor space were considered not to be part of the structure. The Revenue contended that they were part of the setting, i.e. part of the building in which the trade was carried on.

The Court of Appeal agreed with the taxpayer and decided that the partitions performed a function as they were moveable and were intended to be moved in the course of the business. The partitions were therefore plant. This is now included in List C at item number 13.

As you can see, a lot of case law is now incorporated into List C in S.23 CAA 2001. It is certainly worth looking this up if you have not already done so.

Q	Now test your understanding by attempting the example which follows.

Example 1

Which of the following types of expenditure do you feel qualifies as plant?

a) General lighting in a retail store
b) Display lighting in store windows
c) Decorative tapestries in a hotel
d) Ship used as a floating restaurant
e) Advertising hoardings
f) Suspended ceiling over a stairwell
g) Suspended ceiling over eating area

Answer 1

		Plant?
a)	General lighting in a retail store	X
b)	Display lighting in store windows	✓
c)	Decorative tapestries in a hotel	✓
d)	Ship used as a floating restaurant	X
e)	Advertising hoardings	✓
f)	Suspended ceiling over a stairwell	X
g)	Suspended ceiling over eating area	✓

a) General lighting in a retail store does not normally qualify for plant. It is just considered to be part of the setting. When acquiring a building, general lighting is an integral part. In List A item 2, mains services such as electricity systems are not regarded as plant.

b) Display lighting in store windows can be regarded as plant. The lighting is normally much more specialised and with that it fulfils a function, i.e. to attract customers into the shop. In List C item 2, electrical systems which meet the requirements of a particular activity are treated as plant.

In *Cole Brothers v Phillips*, capital allowances claims were made in respect of lighting in a retail shop (part of the John Lewis Group). General lighting was held not to be plant whilst more specialised lighting (eg, for window displays etc) was held to perform a function. This established the principle that the Revenue could review capital allowance claims on a "piecemeal basis" (ie, considering each piece of "plant" on its own merits).

c) Decorative tapestries in a hotel are regarded as plant. In List C item 14, decorative assets provided for the enjoyment of the public in a hotel, restaurant or similar trade will be treated as plant. This was established in the case of *CIR v Scottish & Newcastle Breweries Ltd* where tapestries and murals fitted to the walls of pubs and hotels created an "ambience and atmosphere" with which to attract customers. Therefore such expenditure had a function rather than being part of the setting.

d) A ship used as a floating restaurant was not regarded as having a function, it was actually the setting in which the trade was carried on. (*Benson v Yard Arm Club Limited (1979)*).

e) Advertising hoardings are specifically within List C, item number 15. Therefore it will be safe to assume that they qualify as plant.

f) A suspended ceiling over a stairwell is not regarded as plant. It does not fulfil a function, but instead is merely part of the setting. *Hampton v Fortes Autogrill Ltd (1980).*

g) A suspended ceiling over an eating area however, could be regarded as plant as it fulfils a function in the trade creating a general atmosphere. Exposed wiring over an eating area is not attractive for customers!

SUMMARY - CAPITAL ALLOWANCES - DEFINITION

Depreciation is not allowable for tax purposes. Instead a deduction in respect of some types of qualifying expenditure is available.

Capital allowances are given on plant and machinery. Different allowances are available for certain buildings such as industrial buildings and agricultural buildings. Note that no allowances are available for office buildings.

In the legislation the definition of non-qualifying expenditure includes buildings and structures and land. Two lists, List A and List B, tell us what is meant by these terms and hence what does not qualify for plant and machinery allowances.

There are some exceptions to the exclusions given in List C which must therefore always also be checked.

The final test which comes from case law and must always be satisfied is 'function v setting'.

To qualify for capital allowances the asset must fulfil a function in the trade rather than be simply part of the setting in which the trade is carried on.

B5: CAPITAL ALLOWANCES - COMPUTATION

In this chapter you will learn the rules for computing capital allowances on plant and machinery including:
- the basic layout;
- pooling of expenditure;
- the FYA pool;
- the general pool;
- cheap cars;
- long life assets;
- expensive cars;
- short life assets.

Statutory references in this chapter are to CAA 2001 unless otherwise stated.

B5.1 Basic computational layout

Capital allowances computations are prepared for accounting periods, eg for the year ended 31 December 2005. Capital allowances are a trading expense for a business and should be deducted in arriving at the trading income figure for the accounting period. s. 6

Year ended 31 December 2005:

	£
Adjusted profits before CAs	X
Less: capital allowances (CAs)	(X)
Trading Income	**X**

The trading income (i.e. after CAs) would then be taxed in 2005/06 under CYB.

To calculate the CAs we start with the **tax written down values brought forward** from the previous period. We then **add** in any **additions** in the period (the price paid for any plant or machinery) and **take off** any **disposals** (the sale proceeds). When deducting proceeds we restrict the deduction to the original costs of the asset (see later). This gives us the total amount on which we can claim allowances.

Allowances are calculated at **25%.** These are deducted leaving the written down value to carry forward to next year. s. 56

	£
Written down value (WDV) brought forward	X
Additions (purchase price)	X
Disposals (sale proceeds - restricted to cost)	(X)
	X
Allowances @ 25%	(X)
Written down value (WDV) carried forward	X

B5.2 Pooling of expenditure s. 53

Within the capital allowance computation there will be various "heads" of expenditure. These are:

- First year allowance pool
- General pool
- Long life assets
- Expensive cars
- Short life assets

B5.3 The first year allowances pool s. 39

The first year allowance (FYA) pool will include **expenditure on plant & machinery qualifying for first year allowances.** FYAs are normally available at s. 52
40% on qualifying purchases. This 40% rate has been in force since July 1998.
However, for some businesses a 50% rate applies (which we shall look at in the s. 46
next session). Qualifying purchases excludes cars - more on this later.

Additions qualifying for first year allowances are entered into this FYA pool. The FYA is deducted and the **balance is transferred to the general pool at the end of the period.** There will never be a balance carried forward or brought forward on the FYA pool.

Illustration 1

Assume a trader has a written down value brought forward on the general pool of £100,000. In the year assets qualifying for 40% FYAs are purchased for £50,000. The capital allowances computation will be:

	FYA Pool	*General Pool*	*Allowance*
	£	£	£
WDV b/f		100,000	
Additions	50,000		
FYA (40%)	(20,000)		20,000
WDA (25%)		(25,000)	25,000
Transfer to general pool	(30,000)	30,000	
WDV c/f		105,000	
Total allowances			45,000

B5.4 The general pool

The general pool **includes anything which is not specifically included elsewhere.** For example, plant and machinery would go into the general pool if it did not qualify for a first year allowance.

B5.5 Cheap cars s. 74

For accounting periods ending **before 1 April 2000, all cars** purchased which **cost £12,000 or less were pooled together in the "cheap car pool".**

The cheap car pool has now been **abolished.** Additions of "cheap" cars now go into the **general pool** and obtain writing down allowances (WDAs) at 25%. There are no FYAs on cars.

B5.6 Long life assets s. 91

Long life assets are assets with a predicted **useful life of at least 25 years.** We are looking at very distinctive expenditure here - eg, in power stations etc, where the expected useful life of assets used in the business is a long time.

Long life assets are kept in a **separate pool** - they do not qualify for FYAs and do not go into the general pool. Expenditure on long life assets will qualify for a **writing down allowance of only 6%.** This is substantially lower than the normal 25% because the life of the asset is longer than a normal asset - 25 years is longer than you would expect a normal piece of plant or machinery to last. s. 102

However, these **rules will not apply** (i.e. the asset will **not** be treated as a long life asset), **where expenditure in the year on such assets** does **not exceed £100,000** in total. These special "6%" rules will therefore most commonly apply to large companies. s. 99

If the special rules do not apply, the asset would qualify for FYAs and any residue would be transferred to the general pool at the end of the period.

This £100,000 limit is **adjusted for short accounting periods.** For example, if a trader draws accounts for a six month accounting period, the long life asset limit would be £50,000. The £100,000 limit is also adjusted for the **number of associated companies** - more on that when you cover associates within your Corporation Tax studies.

If an asset is acquired second-hand and had originally received a 25% writing down allowance, it will continue to obtain relief at 25%.

If an asset has been treated as a long life asset by a seller, the buyer (regardless of how much he buys the asset for) will also have to treat the asset as a long life asset - once a long life asset, always a long life asset.

B5.7 Expensive cars

An expensive car is any car costing **more than £12,000. Each expensive car** must be shown separately in its own capital allowances column. Expensive cars are **not pooled with any other assets.** s. 74

The annual **writing down allowance** is restricted to the **lower of**: s. 75

- **25%; or**
- **£3,000**

When the car is sold, a balancing allowance or charge will arise.

Illustration 2

A trader draws accounts to 31 December. At 1 January 2005, the written down value brought forward is £90,000 on the general pool and £20,000 on a BMW 735. In the year the trader bought an Audi A6 for £24,000 and sold the BMW for £12,000. The capital allowances computation will be:

Y/e 31.12.05

	Pool	*BMW 735*	*Audi A6*	*Allowances*
	£	£	£	£
WDV b/f	90,000	20,000		
Addition			24,000	
Disposal		(12,000)		
Balancing Allowance		8,000		8,000
WDA (25%)	(22,500)			22,500
WDA (restricted)			(3,000)	3,000
WDV c/f	67,500		21,000	33,500

A balancing adjustment is made every time a "non pooled" asset (such as an expensive car) is sold.

In this instance, as the car has been sold for **less than its "tax value"**, a balancing allowance arises. The balancing is allowance is treated in the same way as a normal capital allowance, i.e. it increases the total CAs due for the period.

If the car had been sold for **more than its "tax value"** (ie for more than £20,000 in this example), a balancing charge would have arisen. A balancing charge is effectively a "negative" allowance and will reduce the total CAs available for the period.

The written down values brought forward at 1 January 2006 are £67,500 and £21,000.

The capital allowances computation for the next period (y/e 31 December 2006) will be:

Y/e 31.12.06	*Pool*	*Audi A6*	*Allowances*
	£	£	£
WDV b/f	67,500	21,000	
WDA (25%)	(16,875)		16,875
WDA (restricted)		(3,000)	3,000
WDV c/f	50,625	18,000	19,875

B5.8 Short life assets s. 83 – s. 84

An election can be made to **depool** certain assets which have a predicted **useful life of no more than 4 years.** The effect of the election is that the assets s. 85

are dealt with separately, i.e. they are not put into the general pool but instead stand on their own in a separate column.

A **balancing allowance** will usually arise if the asset is sold within the 4 year period. s. 86

If the asset is still in use more than 4 years of the end of the year of acquisition (i.e. after 5 lots of WDAs have been claimed on it), the written down value is transferred to the general pool.

There is no downside to making a short life asset election (other than having to do the associated paperwork). We deal with the asset separately for 4 years. If it is sold within 4 years of the end of the period of acquisition and proceeds are less than the written down value brought forward, a balancing allowance will arise. If the asset is still owned after 5 write-downs, the balance in the short life asset column is transferred across to the general pool.

Illustration 3

A trader draws accounts for the year ended 31 October 2004. The written down value brought forward on the general pool was £30,000. A computer was bought for £12,000 in the period (no first year allowances were available on the computer).

A short life asset election has been made in respect of the computer. The capital allowances computation will be:

Y/e 31.10.04	*General pool*	*Computer*	*Allowances*
	£	£	£
WDV b/f	30,000		
Addition		12,000	
WDA (y/e 31.10.04)	(7,500)	(3,000)	10,500
	22,500	9,000	
WDA (y/e 31.10.05)	(5,625)	(2,250)	7,875
	16,875	6,750	
WDA (y/e 31.10.06)	(4,219)	(1,688)	5,907
	12,656	5,062	
WDA (y/e 31.10.07)	(3,164)	(1,266)	4,430
	9,492	3,796	
WDA (y/e 31.10.08)	(2,373)	(949)	3,322
	7,119	2,847	
Transfer to pool	2,847	(2,847)	
	9,966		
WDA (y/e 31.10.09)	(2,492)		2,492
	7,494		

If the computer had been sold at any time during the first four years for less than its written down value, a balancing allowance would have been available.

If however the original expenditure had been put into the general pool, the proceeds would simply be deducted from the general pool and no balancing allowance would be given.

The effect of "depooling" an asset into its own column is to give the trader the opportunity of **realising the balancing allowance sooner** than would otherwise be the case.

Q	Now test your understanding by attempting the examples which follow.

Example 1

Below is a proforma capital allowance computation for the year ended 30 June 2005. There is a written down value brought forward on the general pool and a BMW car. We are then given the normal headings - additions, disposals, first year allowances at 40%, writing down allowances at 25%, balancing allowance, transfer and written down value carried forward.

Assume that the BMW car is sold for £11,000 in the year, a Skoda car is bought for £8,000 and some equipment is purchased for £6,000.

Compute the allowances due and complete the computation.

	FYA Pool	*General Pool*	*BMW car*	*Allowances*
	£	£	£	£
WDV b/f		102,000	15,000	
Additions:				
Disposals:				
FYA	( )			
WDA		( )		
BA			( )	
Transfer to general pool	( )			
WDV c/f				
Total allowances				

Example 2

Ted owns an engineering business in Sheffield. In the year to 30 September 2005 the following information is given:

	£
WDV b/f	
General pool	60,000
Expensive car	10,000
Long life asset	104,000
Short life asset (acquired 1.7.00)	20,000
Additions:	
Plant and equipment (40% FYA due)	12,000
Renault Clio	9,000
Disposals – plant (original cost £2,000)	2,800

Calculate the total allowances due for the year.

Answer 1

	FYA Pool	*General Pool*	**BMW car**	*Allowances*
	£	£	£	
WDV b/f		102,000	15,000	
Additions:				
Car		8,000		
Equipment	6,000			
		110,000		
Disposals			(11,000)	
FYA	(2,400)			2,400
WDA		(27,500)		27,500
BA			(4,000)	4,000
Transfer to general pool	(3,600)	3,600		
WDV c/f		86,100		
Total allowances				**£33,900**

It is best to approach these proforma computations by **dealing with additions and disposals in the year first**.

The BMW was sold for £11,000. Disposals proceeds of £11,000 are therefore deducted in the BMW car column.

A Skoda was purchased for £8,000, so it will be entered into the general pool. Remember £8,000 is not enough for the Skoda to be regarded as an expensive car. Also **first year allowances are not available on cars - 25% WDAs are given on cars**.

Finally, equipment purchased for £6,000 goes into the FYA pool.

Now deal with the allowances. The BMW car has a **balancing adjustment** as it is in its own column - the written down value is £15,000, the disposal proceeds are £11,000, therefore we have a **balancing allowance** of £4,000. We take that across to the allowances column.

In the general pool there are qualifying costs of £110,000 on which WDAs are available at 25%. WDAs of £27,500 are deducted and these allowances are taken across to the allowances column. Finally, the expenditure in the FYA pool will qualify for 40% first year allowances of £2,400 (again the amount claimed is taken across and reflected in the allowances column). Total allowances for the period are £33,900. This is a trading expense for Trading Income purposes.

In order to complete the computation, £3,600 is **transferred from the FYA pool into the general pool.** The written down value carried forward on the general pool is £86,100.

Answer 2

	FYA Pool	*General Pool*	*Expensive Car*	*Long life assets*	*Short life assets*	*Allowances*
	£	£	£	£	£	£
WDV b/f		60,000	10,000	104,000	20,000	
Transfer		20,000			(20,000)	
Additions	12,000	9,000				
Disposal		(2,000)				
		87,000				
FYA (40%)	(4,800)					4,800
WDA (25%)		(21,750)	(2,500)			24,250
WDA (6%)				(6,240)		6,240
Transfer	(7,200)	7,200				
WDV c/f		72,450	7,500	97,760		**35,290**

The short life asset was acquired on 1 July 2000. This means that by the start of this year we would have **already taken 5 WDAs** to date, so we must **transfer that short life asset to the general pool**.

The Renault Clio bought for £9,000 goes into the general pool. Remember there are no first year allowances are given on cars.

We also have a disposal in the year. We **restrict the disposal proceeds to the actual cost of the asset**. So £2,000 is deducted in the general pool. This leaves us with £87,000 of expenditure in the general pool which will qualify for the 25% writing down allowance.

Next we will deal with the first year allowance of 40% on the equipment costing £12,000. £4,800 goes across into the allowances column.

We also have WDAs of 25%. These are £21,750 on the general pool and £2,500 on the expensive car. That means we put a further £24,250 in the allowances column.

The **long life asset** gets a 6% WDA. £6,240 goes into the allowances column.

We transfer the balance on the FYA pool into the general pool at the year end and show the carried forward values for completeness.

SUMMARY - CAPITAL ALLOWANCES - COMPUTATION

Capital allowances are given on the general pool of plant and machinery at 25% p.a. on a reducing balance basis.

The WDV b/f is increased by additions, decreased by disposals and the balance is written down at 25%.

Some additions will qualify for a higher allowance in the first year prior to being added into the general pool.

Cars costing less than £12,000 go into the general pool.

Expensive cars costing more than £12,000 are not pooled but have their own column. The 25% WDA is limited to £3,000 p.a.

Assets costing at least £100,000 in aggregate and with a predicted useful life of 25 years or more are pooled separately. Such long life assets are only written down at 6% p.a.

If asset is expected to be sold at a loss within 4 years, an election can be made to depool it to crystallise a balancing allowance on sale. If still in use 4 years after the end of the period of acquisition, a short life asset is transferred into the general pool.

B6: INDUSTRIAL BUILDINGS ALLOWANCES

In this chapter you will cover the rules for allowances on industrial buildings including:
- definition of an industrial building;
- qualifying trades;
- relevant interest;
- qualifying expenditure;
- the allowances;
- disposal of an industrial building;
- purchasing a used building;
- buildings in Enterprise Zones.

Statutory references in this chapter are to CAA 2001 unless otherwise stated.

B6.1 Introduction s. 271

The definition of an industrial building is important because only those buildings qualifying as "**industrial**" buildings will be entitled to industrial buildings allowances (IBAs).

IBAs are available if;

(i) the expenditure concerned is **incurred in the course of construction** of a **qualifying building;** and

(ii) the expenditure is **qualifying expenditure.** Not all costs incurred in the construction of a building are qualifying expenditure for IBA purposes.

B6.2 Qualifying building

A qualifying building is a **building used in a qualifying trade** or a **qualifying hotel**.

The specific criteria for a qualifying hotel can be found at S.279 CAA 2001. A qualifying hotel should have at least 10 letting bedrooms, be open for at least 4 months during the period April to October and provide a service of the making s. 279 of beds, cleaning of rooms and offering breakfast and dinner as a normal part of the hotel's business.

A **qualifying sports pavilion** is also a qualifying building. In this instance it does not matter what the trade or the business is. For example, a bank could have a s. 280 sports club with a sports pavilion which is made available for staff - that sports pavilion would qualify for industrial buildings allowances.

Finally, a qualifying building would also be a **building in an Enterprise Zone.** The s. 281 strict criteria are laid out at S.281 CAA 2001.

B6.3 Qualifying expenditure

The definition of "qualifying expenditure" is found at S.292 CAA 2001. Broadly this will include capital expenditure on the construction of a qualifying building. s. 292

It should be appreciated that allowances are given to the person with the **relevant interest** in the building. This is normally the **freeholder** - we will look at this later on in this chapter. s. 286

All the detailed rules are laid out logically in the legislation.

"Construction costs" do **not include the cost of acquiring the land** or any planning fees that may be incurred. Construction costs **will include preparing, cutting, tunnelling or levelling** the land and any **architects, quantity surveyors and engineers fees**, providing that the building is actually constructed. s. 273

B6.4 Qualifying Trade s. 274

In order for a building to be qualifying, it must be used in a "**qualifying trade**". The definition of a "qualifying trade" is extremely important and is and defined at s.274 CAA 2001.

A qualifying trade means a **trade of a kind described in Table A** or an **undertaking of a kind described in Table B,** if the undertaking is carried on by way of a trade. **Table A trades** are the more important of the two and are more common.

S.275 CAA 2001 includes an extension to normal qualifying trade buildings and states that a building is also in use for a qualifying trade if it is a **staff welfare building**. This could be a **canteen** or a **social club** of a manufacturing company. s. 275

Staff welfare buildings are different to sports pavilions because to qualify as a staff welfare building, **the building has to be used by a company with a qualifying trade.** Sports pavilions, as we saw earlier, did not need a qualifying trade attaching - **any trade** with a sports pavilion would qualify for IBAs on that sports pavilion.

B6.5 "Table A" trades

Table A qualifying trades are important and are laid out at S.274 CAA 2001.

Qualifying trades are strictly defined as:

a) **manufacturing** goods or materials;

b) **processing,** i.e. the subjection of goods or materials to some sort of process;

c) **storage** of goods or materials;

d) agricultural contracting, for example contract harvesting.

e) working farm plantations, fishing and mineral extraction.

The most common areas are **manufacturing, processing** and **storage**.

B6.6 Processing

The legislation states that processing is the "**subjection of goods or materials to a process**". This definition has been tested in various cases where traders felt they had buildings which were used for the subjection of goods or materials to a process.

The case of *Bourne v Norwich Crematorium Limited (1964)* concerned a crematorium. The trader felt that he was "subjecting goods to a process", therefore his crematorium should qualify as an industrial building. In this case it was held that human bodies are not goods and therefore no IBAs were available.

Kilmarnock & Equitable Co-operative Society Ltd v CIR (1966) involved a trader screening and packing coal. It was held that this **was** subjecting goods or materials to a process. Consequently the building in which this task was undertaken was an industrial building and IBAs were due.

Buckingham v Securitas Properties Ltd (1980) concerned wage packeting. This involved coins and notes being counted and put into pay packets. Although it was held that a process was being undertaken, notes and coins were not held to be goods, therefore this was not an industrial building.

Another case involved unpacking, relabelling and repacking. This could quite conceivably be a supermarket where labelled brands are received, unpacked and then put into boxes with the supermarket's own brand. In this particular case it was held that unpacking, relabelling and repacking was **not** a process - it was a mere preliminary to a sale.

B6.7 Storage

The other important area of qualifying trades is storage. Within S.274 CAA 2001, "storage" could be a **trade which consists of the storage** of goods or materials which are to be **used in the manufacture** of other goods or materials.

Storage could also mean the storage of goods or materials which are to be **subjected in the course of trade to a process.** In this latter case, goods or materials could be stored by one trader and **be subjected to a process by another trader.**

The most relevant case here is *Crusabridge Investments Ltd v Casings International Ltd (1979).* In this case, a building was used to store used tyres which were to be sent to manufacturers to be remoulded. "Remoulding of tyres" was considered to be an **industrial process**. Consequently, the **building storing the tyres was an industrial building**. It did not matter that the tyres were not to be subject to a process by the trader - they were to be subject to a process by **another** trader and that is sufficient for the building to qualify for IBAs.

The Revenue thought this was too generous a provision and have tried to clarify the limitations of this legislation. They saw this provision as potentially opening all kinds of doors for claims, for example IBA claims for the storage facilities of builders' merchants. Following the *Crusabridge* decision, these storage facilities would qualify for IBAs as the goods stored and sold by a builders merchant were to be used in a further process.

Consequently - according to a Revenue interpretation - storage should form a **significant, separate and identifiable part of the trade** and it should be **conducted as a purpose and end in itself,** not just a necessary and transitory incident of the business. In the *Crusabridge* case, the building would still qualify for IBAs as the collection and storage of tyres was deemed to be an **essential part of the business in itself**. However, following this interpretation, it is unlikely that storage facilities used by builders merchants and similar trades would qualify for IBAs.

Part C of the legislation says storage will also include the storing of **goods or materials which have been manufactured, or produced or subjected in the course of a trade to a process, but have yet to be delivered** to any purchaser. Note here that we must have a **purchaser.** Therefore if a trader is involved in a retail trade and has a warehouse storing goods prior to their being sold through **his own retail outlets**, that warehouse is **unlikely to qualify** as an industrial building as the goods are not being delivered to a purchaser.

Finally the **storage of goods or materials on their arrival in the UK from a place outside the UK** also qualifies.

B6.8 "Table B" trades s. 286

Going back to S.274 CAA 2001, a qualifying trade also means an **undertaking of a kind described in Table B** if the undertaking is carried on by way of a trade. The trades listed are electricity, water, hydraulic power, sewerage, transport, highway undertakings, tunnels, bridges, inland navigation and docks. They are not as common as manufacturing trades, and if you are studying for exams it is unlikely that you will be asked questions concerning these kinds of trades. It is much more likely you will be dealing with trades as laid down in Table A.

B6.9 Relevant Interest

IBAs will be available to the person who has the "relevant interest" in the particular property. Relevant interest is defined within S.286 CAA 2001.

The **relevant interest** is the interest in the building to which the person who incurred the expenditure on the construction of the building was entitled when they incurred the expenditure. Therefore if a person owns the freehold and spends money on the construction of a building, then the relevant interest is the freehold - that is the interest the person had when he spent the money.

If a trader (individual or company) owns the freehold of a factory, in all probability that freeholder will claim IBAs on that factory as he has the "relevant interest" in a building and carries on a qualifying trade.

If the trader were then to build an extension to the factory, this is treated as a separate "pot" of expenditure for IBA purposes, ie, as a separate asset within the IBA computations. The relevant interest in the **extension expenditure** is the interest that the person had when they spent the money. So in this example, the relevant interest is the **freehold** as that is the interest that the trader had when he incurred the expenditure.

Relevant interest becomes more complicated when we are dealing with lessors and lessees. Assume, for example, a trader has a freehold factory which cost £1m. The freeholder does not actually use the factory himself. He grants a **lease** to another trader and it is this trader (the"lessee") who uses the factory in his trade. Who has the relevant interest?

In this example, it will be the **freeholder**. The freeholder spent £1m on the factory and when he spent it he owned the freehold. The relevant interest therefore lies with the freeholder.

It is the **freeholder** who may be entitled to IBAs. These allowances will be set against the freeholder's **rental income from the letting of the factory** and would therefore be an allowable expense for Property Income purposes.

The availability of IBAs depends on what the **lessee** is using the building for. If the lessee uses the building for a qualifying trade, IBAs can be claimed by the freeholder (ie, the landlord). So although the **freeholder may be entitled to IBAs, his entitlement is based on the lessee's use of the building**. Accordingly, clauses are often inserted into rental agreements to ensure that lessees must use the building for a qualifying trade.

If the lessee built an extension and paid for the extension themselves, the **lessee would hold the relevant interest in the extension,** i.e. when they spent the money on the extension they owned the lease, so therefore the relevant interest for the extension is the lease. The lessee would be entitled to IBAs on the **extension expenditure**.

B6.10 Granting a long lease s. 290

There is one quirk to relevant interest and long leases. This is highlighted in S.290 CAA 2001. "Long leases" in this case are leases of **more than 50 years duration.**

Consider a freeholder who grants a 60 year lease on his factory to a lessee for a premium of £200,000. Currently the relevant interest is owned by the freeholder. However, the freeholder may not need the IBAs - for example the freeholder may be a non-taxpayer, such as a local authority (such organisations are not generally liable to tax). Therefore IBAs could go to waste.

When a long lease is granted, it is possible for the freeholder and lessee to **jointly elect to transfer the relevant interest from the freeholder to the lessee.** The lessee is deemed to have acquired an industrial building for the purchase price of £200,000 - the lease premium. Therefore the lessee will obtain IBAs on this £200,000 - he now owns the relevant interest by election and can claim IBAs to set against trading profits.

Example 1

Which of the following buildings may qualify as an industrial building?

	Yes ?	*No ?*
a) Building used for the mechanical processing of cheques.		
b) Plant hire depot used for repair and maintenance of plant between hirings.		
c) Warehouse storing bought-in goods for onward sale to the public.		
d) A sports pavilion owned by Bank Plc for employee use.		
e) A hotel with eight letting bedrooms		

B6.11 Industrial buildings allowances

In summary IBAs are available on:

- general industrial buildings;
- qualifying hotels ;
- buildings in enterprise zones; and
- sports pavilions.

Specifically **excluded** are:

- dwellings;
- retail shops;
- showrooms;
- non-qualifying hotels; and
- offices.

B6.12 Qualifying expenditure s. 292

Qualifying expenditure is based on the construction cost of the building. **Land** is always **excluded** but the **preparing, cutting, tunnelling** or **levelling** of the land, together with the **architects fees** are **included**. Legal fees do **not** qualify.

Qualifying expenditure also **includes the non-industrial parts** if together they amount to **less than 25%** of the total construction cost. The percentage was 10% for buildings constructed before March 1993. Therefore if a trader builds a factory which has some office space in it, we look at the total construction cost. If the costs of the offices are less than 25% of total cost, IBAs are given on the total construction cost, including the offices. s. 283

Example 2

Clarke Kent purchased some land on 1 October 2003 for £200,000. In the year to 30 June 2004 he spent the following:

	£
Levelling and cutting the land	35,000
Architects fees	15,000
Factory construction (including offices £160,000)	600,000

Calculate the qualifying expenditure for IBA purposes.

B6.13 The allowances

The allowances that can be claimed on industrial buildings are:

a) The initial allowance

Initial allowances used to be available in the period in which the expenditure is incurred. Currently, however, there is no initial allowance available.

b) The writing down allowance s. 309 - s.310

This is a **4% straight line allowance** - i.e. 4% on cost every year.

Writing down allowances are given if the **building is in industrial use on the last day of the accounting period.** What the building is used for throughout the accounting period is not relevant - it is the use on **that last day** which is important.

If a building is **in non-industrial use at the end of the accounting period, no IBA will be given.** Instead a **notional 4% writing down allowance** is deducted from the pool of qualifying expenditure. **The notional WDA** does not reduce taxable profits for that year - it merely reduces the balance of qualifying expenditure going forward.

Empty periods (ie, when the building is vacant and not being used for any purpose) take on the **same form as the immediate preceding use.** Therefore if on the last day of an accounting period the building was empty, we look back to the immediately preceding use and treat the "empty" period exactly the same as that preceding use. You may see this referred to as "temporary disuse". s. 285

The **WDA is time-apportioned** for short accounting periods. If the business has a 7 month AP, the WDA would be 7/12 x 4%. s. 310(2)

There is **no writing down allowance in the year of sale**. Balancing allowances / charges may apply instead as we shall see later.

Illustration 1

Clarke Kent incurred qualifying expenditure of £650,000 on a building in the year to 30 June 2004. The building was brought into use on 1 August 2004. It was used for industrial purposes until 30 September 2007. The property remained empty until 31 August 2008. The property was in non-industrial use from 1 September 2008 to 30 June 2009.

We will demonstrate how the IBA history is compiled. The IBA computation will be;

	Cost	Allowances
Y/e 30 June 2004	£	£
Addition	650,000	
Not in use on last day so no WDA yet		
Y/e 30 June 2005		
In industrial use on last day so WDA given		
WDA @ 4%	(26,000)	26,000
Y/e 30 June 2006		
In industrial use on last day so WDA given		
WDA @ 4%	(26,000)	26,000
Y/e 30 June 2007		
In industrial use on last day so WDA given		
WDA @ 4%	(26,000)	26,000
Y/e 30 June 2008		
Empty on last day - preceding use was industrial so WDA given		
WDA @ 4%	(26,000)	26,000
Y/e 30 June 2009		
Non-industrial use on last day so Notional WDA		
Notional WDA 4%	(26,000)	Nil
WDV at 1 July 2009	£520,000	
Allowances given		£ 104,000

Note that as the building was specifically being used for a non-industrial purpose on 30 June 2009, no IBAs are available for this period. Instead the residue of expenditure is reduced by a "notional" WDA of £26,000 but "nil" in entered into the claim column.

Non-industrial use is different from the building being "empty" which implies that no activities at all are being conducted in the building. If a building is empty at the end of the period, IBAs will be given as normal if the building was in industrial use in the preceding period (as is the case here).

B6.14 Disposal of an industrial building s. 314 - s. 324

The amount of sale proceeds is the key factor when dealing with the disposal of an industrial building. This is best shown by a flowchart.

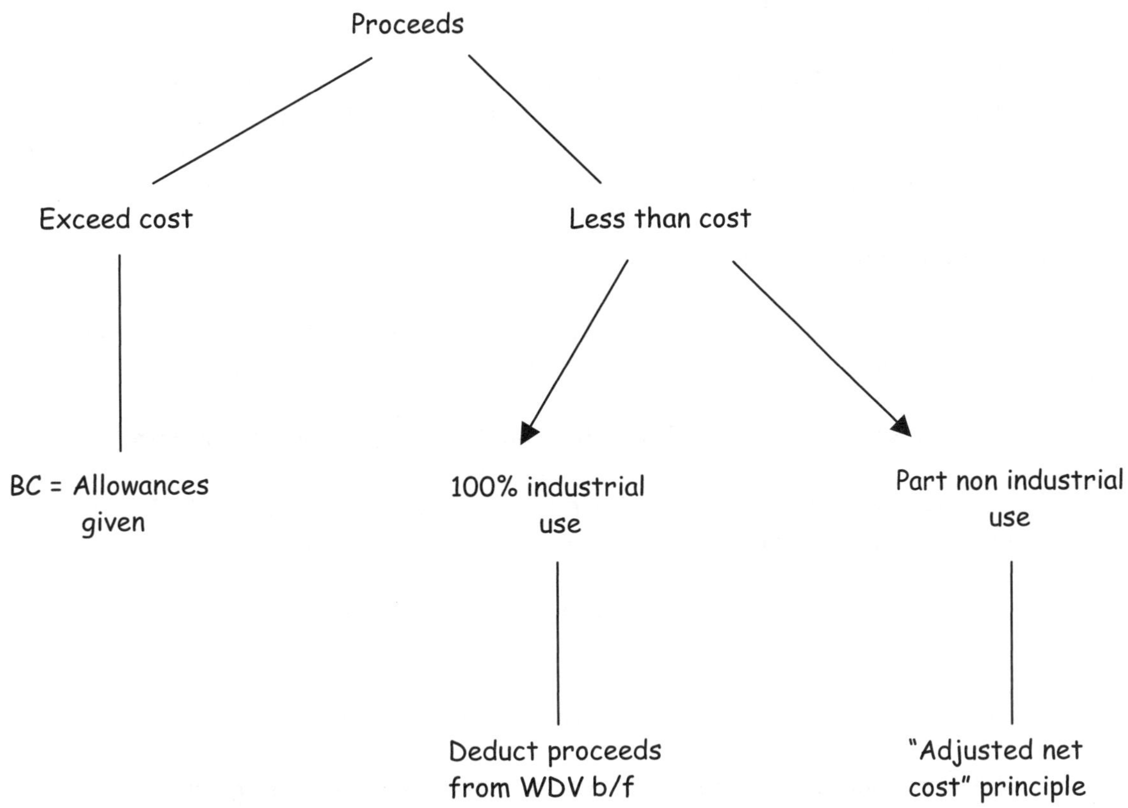

If proceeds exceed cost, there is a **profit**. Where a building is sold at a profit within its "25 year tax life", **the balancing charge on disposal will always be equal to the allowances previously given. There is no exception to this rule.** IBAs compensate a trader for the fall in value of an industrial building. Therefore if the building is sold at a profit, there is no fall in value. The Revenue will then reclaim the allowances given because there has been no cost to the business; they have made a profit. s. 318 s, 320

s. 314(4)

No balancing adjustment (allowance or charge) will arise if the building is sold outside its "tax life". The tax life of a building is **25 years**, starting from when it was first brought into use. For planning purposes, a balancing charge can be avoided by selling the building once the tax life has expired.

A profit on the sale of a building could give rise to a chargeable gain (regardless of whether the tax life has expired). A gain can be deferred under the "roll-over relief" provisions if a building is replaced with another.

Where the building is sold for less than cost, i.e. a loss has been made, there are two different treatments.

If the property had been used for 100% industrial purposes throughout its period of ownership, we simply **deduct the proceeds from the written down value brought forward**. This gives a **balancing allowance or balancing charge** in the same way as non-pooled plant & machinery (eg, an expensive car). Note that a balancing charge could still arise where a cash loss has been made on the sale of a building. s. 318

If, however, there was **part industrial and part non-industrial use**, we have to compute the "adjusted net cost". s. 319

Before we move on and look at the adjusted net cost rules, a quick reminder - as discussed in the previous chapter - that FA 2003 has introduced specific anti-avoidance legislation to deny businesses relief for balancing allowances arising where proceeds are low as a result of a tax avoidance scheme.

B6.15 Adjusted net cost (ANC) s. 323

The net cost is the loss on sale. If we bought a property for £900,000 and sold it for £750,000, we have a net cost of £150,000.

The **adjusted net cost** (ANC) is the **industrial proportion of this loss.**

For example, if the building was used for 50% of the time for industrial purposes and 50% for non-industrial purposes, the adjusted net cost is;

£150,000 x 50% = £75,000

That is the industrial proportion of the net cost (ie the loss the trader has made whilst the building was being used for industrial purposes).

We then **compare the adjusted net cost to the allowances given.**

	£
Adjusted net cost	ANC
Less: IBAs previously given	(IBAs)
BA / (BC)	BA / (BC)

The difference is a balancing charge or balancing allowance, depending on the level of allowances given. For example, if the allowances given were, say, £70,000, there would have a balancing allowance of £5,000 because adjusted net cost is £75,000.

	£
Adjusted net cost	75,000
less IBAs previously given	(70,000)
Balancing Allowance	£5,000

Effectively, the trader has made a loss of £75,000 whilst using the building for industrial purposes. The Revenue has given him £70,000 of IBAs to compensate him for the loss. The Revenue will give the "balance of allowances" of £5,000 in the year of sale.

If IBAs previously given were, say £85,000, a balancing charge would arise;

	£
Adjusted net cost	75,000
Less: IBAs previously given	(85,000)
Balancing Charge	£(10,000)

The trader made a loss of £75,000 whilst using the building for industrial purposes. The Revenue gave £85,000 of IBAs to compensate him for the loss. This is too much, so the Revenue will claw-back £10,000 in the year of sale.

Example 3

Continuing Clarke Kent above, calculate the balancing adjustment if the factory is sold for £800,000 on 1 December 2009.

Example 4

Assume that Clarke Kent sold the property on 1 December 2009 for £475,000. The property was in industrial use from 1 July 2009 to the date of sale.

Complete the steps for the calculation as follows:

(a) Calculate the net cost

(b) Calculate the number of months of industrial usage

(c) Calculate the number of months of Total usage

(d) Calculate the ANC = $\frac{\text{Industrial usage}}{\text{Total usage}}$ x net cost

(e) Calculate the balancing adjustment

(f) Establish whether it is a balancing allowance or a balancing charge

B6.16 The purchaser's position s. 311

The purchaser receives allowances based on the following formula:

$$\frac{\textbf{Residue after sale}}{\textbf{Remaining tax life (months)}} \times 12 = \textbf{Annual WDA}$$

The purchaser cannot claim 4% allowances. They must use the formula above to determine their annual writing down allowance. The purchaser is entitled to the WDA if the building is in industrial use on the last day of their accounting period.

By "**Residue after sale**" we mean the **written down value before sale, minus any balancing allowance at sale or plus any balancing charge at sale, ie**

	£
TWDV at start of AP of sale	X
Less BA or Plus BC	(X)
Residue after sale	X

Residue after sale **can never exceed the price paid by the new user.**

Remaining tax life is simply the **unexpired proportion of the tax life.** The tax life of an industrial building is 25 years (ie 300 months).

Remaining tax life = 300 months - months of use to date

Example 5

Continuing Clarke Kent above, calculate the allowances available to the purchaser in each of the two scenarios (ie examples 3 & 4).

Remember:

	(a)	(b)
Sale price	£800,000	£475,000
WDV at 30 June 2009	£520,000	£520,000
Balancing charge/(allowance)	£104,000	(£43,656)
Expired usage	64 months	64 months

B6.17 Buildings in Enterprise Zones s. 281

If a commercial building is constructed in a designated Enterprise Zone (EZ), initial allowances are available on the construction costs at **100%.** The initial allowance is intended to encourage investment in areas where regeneration is required. s.306

Note that 100% initial allowances are available for "**commercial**" buildings in EZs. "Commercial" in this context will include **shops and showrooms** etc as long as they are used for the purposes of a trade. **Offices** will always qualify for 100% initial allowances regardless of what they are used for (except if they are used as a dwelling house!). s. 281(b)

All or part of the initial allowance may be **disclaimed**. Thereafter, writing down allowances are given on the balance of expenditure at a rate of **25%** on a reducing balance basis. s.306(2)

Allowances are given either against trading income (if the person having the relevant interest is a trader) or against Property income (if the person having the relevant interest lets the building to a trader).

Allowances are only given if the construction expenditure is incurred within **10 years** of the zone being officially designated as an Enterprise Zone. s. 298-s. 299

Balancing allowances and charges will apply as for other industrial buildings if the building in the EZ is sold within **25 years**. If 100% initial allowances have been claimed, a sale within 25 years will inevitably lead to a **balancing charge**. s. 314

Answer 1

		Yes	No
a)	Building used for the mechanical processing of cheques.		✓
b)	Plant hire depot used for repair and maintenance of plant between hirings.		✓
c)	Warehouse storing bought-in goods for onward sale to the public.		✓
d)	A sports pavilion owned by Bank Plc for employee use.	✓	
e)	A hotel with eight letting bedrooms		✓

a) A building used for the mechanical processing of cheques is not an industrial building. In the case of *Girobank Plc v Clark (1998)* the processing of cheques was deemed to be a process, but pieces of paper carrying information were not deemed to be goods.

b) A plant hire depot used for repair and maintenance of plant between hiring is not an industrial building. In the case of *Vibroplant Ltd v Holland (1982),* the depot was not deemed to be a factory and the plant was not subject to a process.

c) A warehouse storing bought in goods for onward sale to the public is not an industrial building. In *Dale v Johnson Brothers (1951),* a retailer or wholesaler who stores goods for resale cannot claim IBAs because he himself is the purchaser.

d) A sports pavilion owned by a bank for the use of employees is an industrial building. S.280 CAA 2001 says that a building occupied by a person carrying on a trade and used as a sports pavilion for the welfare of employees is an industrial building - it does not matter that the bank is not carrying on a qualifying trade.

e) A hotel with 8 letting bedrooms is not an industrial building. In order to qualify as an industrial building the hotel must have at least 10 letting bedrooms (S.279 CAA 2001).

Answer 2

	£
Construction (see Note)	600,000
Levelling and cutting	35,000
Architects' fees	15,000
	650,000

Note
£650,000 x 25% = £162,500
Offices cost £160,000 so they qualify as below 25%

Answer 3

The building was sold at a profit so a **balancing charge** arises equal to the allowances given of **£104,000**.

Answer 4

a) Net cost: £(475,000 - 650,000) = **£175,000**

b) and (c)

	Total Use	*Industrial Use*	*Non-Industrial Use*
1.8.04→30.9.07	38	38	
1.10.07→ 31.8.08	11	11	
1.9.08→30.6.09	10		10
1.7.09→1.12.09	5	5	
	64	**54**	**10**

(d) ANC $= £175,000 \times \frac{54}{64}$ = **£147,656**

(e) Balancing adjustment = £147,656 - 104,000 = **£43,656**

(f) This is a **balancing allowance** as the business can claim allowances on £147,656 but has only claimed £104,000 so far.

Answer 5

	(a)	(b)
Residue before sale	520,000	520,000
BC/(BA)	104,000	(43,656)
Residue after sale	624,000	476,344
Limited to price paid		£475,000

(a) Allowances for purchaser = $\frac{624,000}{300 - 64} \times 12$

= **£31,729**

(b) Allowances for purchaser = $\frac{475,000}{300 - 64} \times 12$

= **£24,153**

SUMMARY - INDUSTRIAL BUILDINGS ALLOWANCES

Industrial buildings are buildings used in a qualifying trade. Qualifying hotels with 10 letting bedrooms, open for 4 months from April to October offering normal hotel services also qualify for allowances. Sports pavilions always qualify no matter what the trade is. Buildings in Enterprise Zones qualify for 100% allowances.

Qualifying trades include manufacturing, processing and storage. Processing means the subjection of goods to a process. Storage qualifies if it is of raw materials, finished goods or goods arriving from overseas. The storage of retail goods prior to sale does not qualify.

The allowances are given to the taxpayer with the relevant interest in building. This is usually the freeholder but could be the lessee in respect of enhancement expenditure. If a long lease is granted (over 50 years) a joint election can be made to transfer the relevant interest to the lessee.

The allowances are given on qualifying expenditure which is the construction cost. It excludes land but preparing/cutting the land and architects fees qualify. Any non-industrial parts such as offices, shops or showrooms will also qualify if they amount to less than 25% of the construction cost.

The allowance is 4% p.a. straight line on cost (tax life of 25 years) and is given provided the building is in industrial use on the last date of the accounting period. If the period is not 12 months in length, the 4% WDA is time apportioned.

If the building is in non-industrial use on the last day a notional allowance is given. Empty periods take on the same form as the immediate preceding use.

If the building is sold as a profit, there is a balancing charge in the year of sale. The balancing charge will equal IBAs previously given

If the building is sold at a loss, the 'adjusted net cost' (or industrial proportion of the loss) is compared to the allowances given and a BA or BC computed accordingly.

$$\text{Adjusted net cost} = \frac{\text{Industrial usage}}{\text{Total usage}} \times \text{net cost}$$

The purchaser of a used building does not get a 4% allowance, instead their allowances are:

$$\frac{\text{Residue after sale}}{\text{Remaining tax life}} \times 12 = \text{Annual WDA}$$

The residue after sale is the WDV of the building including the balancing adjustment at sale computed for the seller. It is restricted to price paid.

B7: INTANGIBLE FIXED ASSETS

This chapter outlines the tax treatment of IFAs looking at:
- trade v non trade IFAs;
- relief for losses on IFAs;
- rollover relief on disposal of an IFA;
- special rules for groups.

B7.1 Introduction

IFAs are recognised as income as they are **debited / credited in determining the company's profit or loss.** The rules are similar to the loan relationship rules. Para 1 Sch 29 FA 2002

B7.2 Intangible fixed assets

The term "Intangible Fixed Asset" has the same meaning as it has for accounting purposes. In particular it includes **intellectual property** which means any **patent**, registered **trademark**, design or **copyright** etc. It also **includes goodwill**, again as defined for accounting purposes.

B7.3 Trade and non-trade IFAs

Para 30-34 Sch 29 FA 2002

It is important to classify IFAs according to whether they relate to a trade, a property business, or are non-trade.

Trading debits and credits form part of **DI** as they are accrued to the profit and loss account.

Debits and credits relating to a property business are treated as part of the expense/income of that property business.

Non-trade debits and credits are pooled. If the non-trade credits exceed non-trade debits then there is a gain chargeable under **DVI.**

If non-trade debits exceed non-trade credits then there is a **non-trade loss on IFAs.** Certain reliefs are available for this loss.

B7.4 Relief for non-trade loss on IFAs

Para 35 Sch 29 FA 2002

A claim can be made to set the **whole or part** of the loss against the company's **total profits** for that period. There is **a two year time limit** for this claim.

A claim can be made to use the loss under the **group relief** provisions which we will look at later.

To the extent that the loss has not been used in a current year claim or surrendered as group relief it will be **carried forward** as a non-trade debit to the next accounting period.

B7.5 Impact on tax computations

Royalty payments are allowed under **DI or DVI on an accruals basis.**

Patent and copyright royalties are paid gross between UK companies. Remember that all figures that appear in the tax computation must be gross figures.

Royalty receipts are taxed on an **accruals basis under DI or DVI.**

Goodwill (which was previously part of the capital gains tax regime) will now only give rise to **income gains or losses.** Goodwill has **ceased to be a qualifying asset for capital gains tax rollover.** However, **a form of rollover relief is available.** The rules apply to goodwill **bought or created after 1 April 2002.**

For goodwill purchased and other IFA assets acquired or created after 1 April 2002 the company is allowed a **deduction for the amortisation or impairment charged** in the accounts. Alternatively they can claim a **straight line deduction of 4% on cost.** International Accounting Standard No 38 (IAS 38) does not allow a company to amortise goodwill. Goodwill will be stated in the balance sheet at fair value and subject to an impairment review. Para 10 & 1 Sch 29 FA 2002

When a company first adopts IAS 38 it may be required to increase the carrying value of goodwill. Schedule 29 ensures that the write up is a taxable credit, limited to the amount of relief already given. Any impairment from written up cost will be deductible. Para 116A - 11 116F Sch 29 FA 2002

B7.6 Rollover relief for IFAs

Para 37 Sch 29 FA 2C

If an IFA is sold then any gain arising will be an income gain.

Illustration 1

A Ltd purchased goodwill on 1 May 2004 for £250,000 and sold it for £300,000 on 31 December 2004. The company amortised the goodwill at 10% per annum. Its year end is 30 June.

The amortisation charged for the 8-month period for which the company owned the goodwill (1 May to 31 December 2004) will be:

£250,000 x 10% x 8/12 = £16,667

The written down value of the goodwill is:

	£
Cost	250,000
Less: amortisation to date	(16,667)
	233,333

The sale takes place in the accounting period ended 30 June 2005 and the income gain will be:

	£
Proceeds of sale	300,000
Less: WDV	(233,333)
Income gain	66,667

Where a company reinvests the proceeds of sale in other goodwill (or other IFA) it can claim rollover relief. The proceeds need to be reinvested in the period **12 months before to 36 months after** the sale of the old IFA. To get **full relief** the **whole of the proceeds need to be reinvested**. Paras 39-41 Sch 29 FA 2002

Illustration 2

Continuing the example of Company A Ltd. The company buys replacement goodwill for £400,000. All proceeds have been reinvested so rollover relief will be available in full.

The amount rolled over will be:

	£
Proceeds reinvested	300,000
Less: cost of old IFA	(250,000)
	50,000

Note that we do **not** take account of the amounts written off the cost in this calculation.

	£
Income gain	66,667
Amount rolled over	(50,000)
	16,667

Following the claim, the company will still show a credit in its P&L of £16,667 representing a reversal of the write-off.

The cost of the new goodwill going forward will be:

	£
Cost of new IFA	400,000
Less: income gain rolled over	(50,000)
	350,000

If only **part of the proceeds are reinvested,** the amount available for **rollover** is the **amount by which the amount reinvested exceeds the cost of the old asset.** Para 41(3) Sch 29 FA 2002

Illustration 3

If A Ltd above decides to reinvest only £270,000, as this is less than the proceeds received, relief will only be available for:

	£
Amount reinvested	270,000
Less: cost of old asset	(250,000)
	20,000

The gain for the year will be:

	£
Income gain	66,667
Amount rolled over	(20,000)
	46,667

The cost of the new asset going forward will be:

	£
Cost of new IFA	270,000
Less: income gain rolled over	(20,000)
	250,000

Special rules apply where the asset sold was created before 1 April 2002. IFAs that existed before this date stay within the capital gains tax regime however they **do not stay within the capital gains tax rollover relief rules.**

On disposal the asset will give rise to a capital gain from 1 April 2002. This gain can only be rolled over under the rules set down in the FA 2002.

This is achieved by making certain amendments to the rollover provisions that we looked at above. Para 130 Sch 29 FA 2002

The net proceeds received (i.e. proceeds less incidental cost of disposal) are compared to cost. Cost is defined as net proceeds less the chargeable gain as calculated for capital gains tax in other words we include indexation allowance where applicable.

Illustration 4

X Ltd sells goodwill it has held since December 1990 for £300,000 paying solicitors fees of £30,000 in relation to the sale. The goodwill originally cost £55,000. IA is 20%. X Ltd is considering the following investments in a new IFA:

a) £280,000
b) £220,000

The gain arising will be:

	£
Proceeds	300,000
Less: expenses	(30,000)
Net proceeds	270,000
Less: Cost	(55,000)
	215,000
IA £55,000 x 20%	(11,000)
Chargeable gain	£204,000

Under option a) there will be full reinvestment as the new asset costs £280,000 which is more than the net proceeds for the old asset of £270,000.

The gain that can be rolled over is £204,000 giving a base cost for the new asset of £280,000 - £204,000 = £76,000.

Under option b) there will be partial reinvestment. The new asset cost £220,000 which is less than the net proceeds received of £270,000.

The gain that can be rolled over will be £220,000 - £66,000 = £154,000. This gives the same result to that which would have arisen under the CGT rules whereby net proceeds not reinvested remain chargeable.

The base cost of the new asset will be £220,000 - 154,000 = £66,000.

B7.7 Groups

Paras 46-54
Sch 29 FA 2002

For IFA purposes, groups are essentially the same as those defined for **capital gains** purposes. We examine this definition and rules similar to those below in a later chapter.

Transfers of IFAs within a group are **tax neutral**, provided that the asset is a chargeable IFA before and after the transfer.

Rollover is allowed on a group wide basis provided that the company that buys the new asset is within the same group at the time of purchase. In addition the new asset must be bought from outside the group.

SUMMARY - INTANGIBLE FIXED ASSETS

From 1 April 2002 new rules were introduced for Intangible Fixed Assets (IFAs).

Debits and credits in relation to IFAs are taxed/relieved in line with the accounting treatment.

Amortisation of an IFA is allowed or the company can elect for a 4% straight line write off.

Royalties are brought in on an accruals basis for tax following the accounts.

Debits and credits relating to IFAs are DI or DVI depending on whether they relate to the trade.

Non-trade debits and credits go to a DVI pool. If there is a net deficit this can be set off in the current year against other income, group relieved or carried forward.

Disposals of IFAs such as goodwill give rise to an income gain or loss however, a form of rollover relief is available.

Transfers of IFAs in a CGT group are tax neutral. A degrouping charge can arise following the transfer of an IFA. This degrouping charge can be transferred to another company. Group wide rollover is possible for IFAs.

B8: RESEARCH AND DEVELOPMENT EXPENDITURE

This chapter will outline the relief available for expenditure on research and development, covering in particular:

- the 150% tax relief available to small and medium sized companies;
- the tax credits available to loss making small and medium sized companies;
- the 125% tax relief available to large companies.

B8.1 Introduction

This relief was originally introduced for **small and medium sized companies** by **Finance Act 2000**. Note that the relief is not available to traders - only to companies.

The relief has now been **extended and improved** by subsequent Finance Acts to include relief for **large companies** and for work **subcontracted to** small and medium companies

Useful guidance can be found in the legislation in the Miscellaneous Non Statutory Material, Number VI.

B8.2 Small and medium sized companies

A company incurring qualifying Research and Development (R&D) expenditure will be able to claim a **deduction equal to 150% of the costs** incurred in calculating its PCTCT. Para 13 Sch 20 FA 2000

The usual effect of this is that the **further 50%** of the R&D expenditure needs to be **deducted in arriving at the adjusted profits for tax purposes**.

Illustration 1

Small Limited spends £65,000 on qualifying R&D in its accounting period ended 31 December 2005.

In calculating PCTCT for the year to 31 December 2005 the total deduction for R&D will be:

£65,000 x 150% = **£97,500**

If the £65,000 has already been deducted in arriving at the accounting profit, this means that an additional deduction of

(£97,500 - 65,000) = **£32,500** i.e. 50% of £65,000

should be put through as an adjustment in arriving at the profits for tax purposes.

To qualify for the relief the company **must spend £10,000** on qualifying R&D. This limit was £25,000 before April 2003. Para 1 Sch 20 FA 2000

This figure is for a **12 month accounting period** and will be proportionally reduced where the accounting period is less than 12 months e.g. for a six month period the limit will be £5,000.

To **qualify as a small or medium sized enterprise (SME)** the company must have:

(i) fewer than 250 employees; and

(ii) either annual turnover of less than 50m Euros or an annual balance sheet total of less than 43m Euros.

These limits are in your Tax Tables.

B8.3 Qualifying R&D

Certain conditions have to be met in relation to the expenditure: Para 3 Sch 20 FA 2000

(i) it must be **revenue not capital** in nature;

(ii) it must be **related to a trade** carried on or to be carried on by the company;

(iii) it must be incurred on:
- (a) **staff costs**;
- (b) **software**;
- (c) **consumable or transformable materials**;
- (d) **subcontracted R & D costs**; or
- (e) **externally provided workers**.

(iv) Any **intellectual property** created as a result of the expenditure must **vest in the company**;

(v) It is **not incurred** in the carrying on of **activities** which are **contracted out** to the company by any person (although under FA 2002 these rules have been extended in certain circumstances - we will look at this later);

(vi) It is **not subsidised**, (although an SME is allowed a 25% enhanced deduction on 'subsidised' expenditure provided it would be available to a large company in the same circumstances).

B8.4 R&D Tax Credits

This relief allows companies with trading losses to **"surrender"** part of that loss to the government in return for a tax refund.

A company with a trading loss that has incurred qualifying R&D can surrender all or part of the loss as follows.

Firstly the **surrenderable amount** needs to be calculated. This is the **lower of:** Para 15 Sch 20 FA 2000

(i) the **unrelieved trading loss;** and

(ii) **150% of the qualifying R&D expenditure**.

For these purposes an unrelieved trading loss means the **trading loss** of the period **reduced by any actual and potential claims for relief for that loss in the current period** and any other actual loss relief claims made in respect of the loss.

No account is taken of **losses brought forward or carried back to** this accounting period.

Once this loss has been surrendered the amount of **credit given is the lower of:** Para 16 Sch 20 FA2000

(i) **16%** of the surrenderable loss for the period; and

(ii) the company's **PAYE and NIC bill** for the period.

Illustration 2

Medium Ltd has the following results:

Trading loss	£170,000
Qualifying R&D	£45,000
PAYE/NIC bill	£85,000

The surrenderable loss is the lower of:
(i) £170,000
(ii) £45,000x 150% = £67,500

i.e. £67,500

The tax credit given will be the lower of

(i) 16% x £67,500 = £10,800
(ii) £85,000

i.e. £10,800

This tax credit of £10,800 will either be used to reduce Medium Ltd 's tax bill if it has other sources of income or will be received as a tax free refund.

The trading loss of the company carried forward is now:

£170,000 - £67,500 = £102,500

For expenditure of £45,000 the company has received a refund of £10,800 which equates to 24% (10,800/45,000) or **150% x 16% = 24%.**

Illustration 3

Rafael Ltd, a small company, spends £125,000 on qualifying R&D. The company has a trading loss of £135,000 and has DIII income of £40,000. The company's PAYE/ NIC bill of £67,000.

The surrenderable loss is the lower of:
(i) £135,000 less the £40,000 potential CY loss claim i.e. £95,000
(ii) £125,000 x 150% = £187,500

i.e. £95,000

The tax credit given will be the lower of
(i) 16% x £95,000 = £15,200
(ii) £67,000

i.e. £15,200

B8.5 Large Companies

Sch 12 FA 2002

Large companies qualify for R&D relief for **accounting periods ending on or after 1 April 2002**.

Large companies are those that do not qualify as SMEs under the rules above.

The relief given to large companies is **a 125% deduction** in calculating PCTCT. The usual effect of this is that the **further 25%** of the R&D expenditure needs to be **deducted in arriving at the adjusted profits for tax purposes**.

Para 11 Sch 12 FA 2002

Illustration 4

Large Limited spends £245,000 on R&D during the accounting period ended 31 March 2006.

The deduction in calculating the PCTCT will be:

£245,000 x 125% = £306,250

If the £245,000 has already been deducted in arriving at the accounting profit, this means that an additional deduction of

(£306,250 - 245,000) = **£61,250** i.e.25% of £245,000

should be put through as an adjustment in arriving at the profits for tax purposes.

The definition of research and development is the same as that which is applied to small and medium sized enterprises.

To qualify for the relief the company has to spend a **minimum of £10,000** (£25,000 for APs beginning before 9 April 2003) during the accounting period. This limit is again pro rated for accounting periods of less than twelve months.

A large company **can claim for expenditure on work contracted to it** provided it is contracted by another large company or any person otherwise than in the course of a trade chargeable to Schedule D Cases I or II. Para 4 Sch 12 FA 2002

There is **no requirement for the intellectual property** created by the R&D **to vest** in the company.

Example 1

Lamp Ltd, a small company, spends £35,000 on R&D during the year to 31 March 2006. Profits before R&D deductions are £155,000.

You are required to calculate the PCTCT

Example 2

Net Ltd, a small company, spends £150,000 on R&D. During the year the company makes a trading loss of £70,000 and had a PAYE/NIC bill of £35,000.

You are required to calculate the amount of tax credit the company may claim.

Answer 1

	£
Profits	155,000
Less R&D 35,000 x 150%	(52,500)
PCTCT	**£102,500**

Answer 2

The surrenderable loss will be the lower of:

	£
Unrelieved loss	70,000
150% x 150,000	225,000
Therefore	70,000

The tax credit will be the lower of

16% x 70,000	11,200
The NIC/PAYE bill =	35,000

Therefore the tax credit will be **£11,200**

SUMMARY – RESEARCH AND DEVELOPMENT EXPENDITURE

R&D relief of 150% is available to SMEs.

The relief relates to revenue expenditure on software and consumable items, staff costs, sub-contracted R&D costs and externally provided workers.

SMEs with losses can surrender them to the Revenue and receive a tax credit/ repayment.

The surrenderable amount is the lower of:
- Qualifying R&D x 150%
- Unrelieved trading losses

The tax credit will be the lower of:
- Surrendered amount x 16%
- The company's PAYE/NIC bill

Large companies can claim a tax deduction of 125% for qualifying R&D.

B9: TAX LAW AND ACCOUNTING PRACTICE

This chapter looks at the interaction of tax law and accountancy practice covering in particular:
- the importance of GAAP;
- Herbert Smith V Honour;
- the recognition of income.

B9.1 General principle

In general the tax treatment of a particular item will follow the accounting treatment, i.e. income shown in the P & L Account is taxable and expenses are deductible. This principle applies unless tax legislation or case law dictates otherwise. This principle has been around for years as the starting point for the measure of profit taxable under Schedule D Case I. However, recent legislative changes have actually made the accounting rules apply for tax purposes in many cases.

In Finance Act 1993 the foreign exchange gains and loss rules for tax purposes were aligned with the accounting treatment. Finance Act 1994 requires the recognition of gains and losses under the financial instruments rules to follow the accounting treatment. This was followed in Finance Act 1996 which applies the accounting treatment to all loan relationships, namely here the tax treatment of interest.

The Government went virtually the whole way towards aligning tax and accounting in **s.42 of the Finance Act 1998** which requires all accounts to be prepared using the true and fair basis. This effectively removed the cash basis for the recognition of income for all businesses and companies.

Recently we have seen many changes in the rules to deal with the adoption of international accounting standards (IAS). Most notably GAAP is now defined as including international accounting standards. The terminology used in statute has been amended to follow that used in IAS. For example, references to bad debt relief have been replaced with references to impairment losses.

B9.2 Accounting standards

As the tax treatment, in many cases, is dictated by the accounting treatment, it is important to ensure the proper adoption of **accounting standards.** The tax treatment should follow generally accepted accounting principles or **GAAP** as it is commonly shortened to. For accounting periods beginning on or after 1 January 2005 the definition of GAAP is extended to include adherence with International Accounting Standards (IAS) where required. The need to follow GAAP has been developed both in legislation **by s.42 Finance Act 1998** and in **case law**.

In the case of ***Gallagher v Jones***, a company entered into a four year finance lease with lease rentals are payable over this four year period. The rent actually paid was £397 in year 1 and a peppercorn rent i.e. £1 p.a. for the remainder of the lease and this was the treatment which was adopted in the accounts.

However, under **SSAP21** the correct accounting treatment should recognise the economic reality of the transaction. The asset is being leased for a four year period at an overall cost of £400, so therefore the correct accounting treatment is to recognise the cost evenly over the period of the lease as £100 per annum.

The Revenue disputed the accounting treatment and put forward the view that there is no rule in tax law stating that expenses are deductible when they are paid. The company was, through the accounting treatment, giving itself an up-front tax deduction to which the Revenue objected.

It was held in this case that the tax treatment should follow GAAP. Consequently the Revenue can successfully request that proper accounting principles are applied, at least in the tax computations, even if the item is not material to the accounts.

The decision in the ***Gallagher v Jones*** case reinforced SP 3/91 which requires the tax treatment of finance leased assets to follow correct accounting treatment.

B9.3 Importance of GAAP

Generally accepted accounting principles are very important when it comes to calculating taxable profits. If the correct accounting principles have been followed the Revenue cannot dispute the treatment unless statute or case law states otherwise. For instance, statute states that entertaining expenses are disallowed for tax purposes. This particular principle was established particularly in the case of ***Johnston v Britannia Airways.***

Britannia Airways fly a fleet of aeroplanes. Britannia matched the costs of overhauling the jet engines to the actual flying hours the fleet had flown during the year.

The Revenue disputed this provision, basically saying it did not relate to the costs actually incurred, but to costs which may have been theoretically incurred. They wanted the company to follow the accruals method of accounting by bringing forward an accrual from the previous year, accounting for the expenses actually incurred during the accounting period and accruing for expenditure committed to by the end of the year.

However, in the judgement to this case it was held that what Britannia was doing was perfectly acceptable under generally accepted accounting principles. The Court did not follow the argument put forward by the Revenue that something else might have been more acceptable.

Therefore, the conclusion that we can draw from this case is where there is a **choice as to how we apply a particular standard**, the **choice rests with the tax paying company**. We only need to prove what we have done is acceptable. It is not for the Revenue to argue that something else might be more acceptable.

Unfortunately **FRS 12** which deals specifically with the accounting for provisions, has **effectively prohibited a "Britannia style" provision in the future.** Britannia would now need to show that they have a present day obligation that is either contractual or legal, before they could provide for the overhaul costs in this way. This is examined in the next chapter.

B9.4 Herbert Smith v Honour (1999)

Herbert Smith is a solicitors practice. They opened up office number one in central London and soon expanded their operations to a second site. They expanded again and opened up a third and a fourth office, all in central London.

It was becoming logistically difficult to run the practice from four separate locations and consequently they made the decision to take out a lease on new larger premises, office five and moved everything under the same roof. All this happened back in December 1990, this date being very important for what was happening in the economy at the time.

The leases on offices one, two, three and four were taken out by the firm in the late 1980s when land prices, particularly in central London, were very high and therefore they had committed themselves to onerous rental payments. In December 1990 when they moved into site five, rental values on these properties had fallen considerably. As their landlords would not let them relinquish the leases, the only option that they had was to sub-let the premises until the head leases expired. As a result of this sub-letting, losses in excess of £5½ million would be created and the firm provided for the full amount in the 1990 accounts.

The Revenue sought to disallow this provision. They quoted **SP 3/90** which basically says that we are not allowed to anticipate losses for tax purposes. Their argument was that the firm should have accrued for the rental losses over the period that the head leases expired. The firm disagreed as they argued that what they had done was consistent with the concept of prudence. **SSAP 2** specifically says that the prudence concept overrides the accruals concept.

Consequently when the case came before the **High Court** the Judge **ruled in favour of the firm** on the basis that they could prove what they had done was acceptable on accounting grounds. As a result the Revenue were forced to withdraw SP 3/90.

B9.5 Review of the main accounting policies

The recognition of income

Currently we follow the **prudence** and **matching rules**, i.e. generally accepted accounting principles. However, a new financial reporting standard (FRS) is to be issued shortly and once this is applicable, we must follow it, not only for accounting purposes, but also for tax purposes.

If we fail to apply this new FRS the Revenue can argue successfully, as given by the ***Gallagher v Jones,*** case that we have not applied generally accepted accounting principles.

Finance leases

The treatment of leases under **SSAP 21** which the Revenue specifically refer to in **SP 3/91** as enforced by the ***Gallagher v Jones*** case.

Stock
Stock valuation is given under **SSAP 9**. This affects the profit figure, but of course, we have a choice as to how we value stock and provided that what we do is acceptable, i.e. we follow **SSAP 9** there is nothing the Revenue can do to challenge the figures.

Provisions
The treatment of provisions is given under **FRS 12.** This is covered in the next chapter.

Many disputes with the Revenue may centre on the interpretation and application of accounting standards, as we have seen from the three cases referred to already. Therefore, the Revenue are making increasing use of accountants, both in their investigations team and as expert witnesses in tax appeal hearings.

B9.6 Materiality

The concept of materiality is not recognised by the Revenue. For tax purposes all the figures in the accounts must be examined, not just the material ones, as the failure to apply generally accepted accounting principles is likely to lead to an adjustment being required.

For instance, let us say that we received a letter from the Revenue asking us to confirm whether a particular provision meets the requirements of **FRS 12.** When we open up the audit file we realise that we did not make any comments during the audit on this particular provision as it is immaterial to the accounts. Unless we can put forward sufficient evidence to show that we have applied **FRS12** correctly the Revenue have every right to ask for an adjustment to be made in the tax computation.

B9.7 GAAP and the FRSSE

The **Revenue will accept accounts prepared under the Financial Reporting Standards for Small Enterprises (FRSSE)** and cannot insist that a non-FRSSE standard is applied in a particular situation as the accounts as submitted for that size of organisation have followed the correct accounting treatment and therefore it cannot be challenged.

A company may choose not to adopt FRSSE, in other words to adopt the full array of standards. The Revenue's view on this is that if a company chooses to apply one particular standard which is not applicable to the FRSSE, they must apply all of the other standards and must do so in full. This view is yet to be challenged.

B9.8 Capital and revenue

The Revenue believe that the **accounting treatment cannot change the nature of an item,** be it **capital** or **revenue.** This view is expressed in their bi-monthly publication **Tax Bulletin, issue 39**.

Is this contrary to the principle established in the Herbert Smith case?

S.72 ICTA 1988 disallows capital expenditure specifically.

S. 74(f), disallows expenditure which **provides an enduring benefit to the business.** This has been subject to plenty of interpretation before the Courts.

S. 74(g) disallows the costs of improvement to business premises.

Consequently, the Revenue can rely on separate statutory rules so one can legitimately say that this is not contrary to the Herbert Smith principle which only requires the accounting treatment to be followed if tax statute or case law is silent on the matter.

B9.9 Income recognition

The critical area for tax purposes is the recognition of income. There is currently no accounting standard dealing with the recognition of income for accounting or indeed therefore tax purposes. However, where the Revenue can show that GAAP have not been followed in recognising income in the accounts, they can successfully request the appropriate adjustment.

This was given in the decision in the ***Gardner Mountain*** case. In this particular case, insurance commission agents sold policies and were entitled to an amount of commission which was paid to them at the time the policy was sold. However, if the policyholder cashed the policy in within the first two years some of that commission may have to be refunded back to the insurance company. The insurance company, Gardner Mountain, advised all of their agents to account for the commissions income to the Revenue as follows:

- 50% in Year 1
- 25% in Year 2
- 25% in Year 3

The argument being that at the time the commission is actually paid to them there is a risk some of it will have to be refunded and therefore it would be wrong to recognise all of it for tax purposes up front.

However, the Revenue successfully argued that this treatment did not accord with the underlying economic reality of the transaction. For tax purposes, the Revenue were of the view that all of the commission should be brought into charge in the accounting period in which it is received, as it is this accounting period in which the work has been done to sell the policy.

In the second and third years the Revenue would accept an expense of any commissions which the agent subsequently has to refund. In some situations, a provision might be acceptable, but of course nowadays we would need to follow **FRS 12.**

B9.10 Moving towards IAS

As stated above, for accounting periods beginning on or after 1 January 2005, compliance with GAAP includes compliance with International Accounting Standards (IAS). The main difference between the GAAP and IAS is the tendency towards fair value accounting.

IAS concentrate more on the balance sheet and recognising movements in the opening and closing balance sheet within the profit and loss account. IAS provide for recognition of anticipated profits. Accruals and prudence are still the basis for accounting however there is greater use of fair value accounting. Where there is a conflict between prudence and fair value, fair value will prevail.

In amending the legislation, in particular that relating to loan relationships and derivatives, to deal with IAS the Revenue have left themselves the right to issue regulations requiring that amounts recognised under GAAP are not brought in for tax and how these amount will be dealt with for tax.

We will have to wait and see how far the amounts recognised to tax will differ from the amounts recognised under IAS.

For accounting periods beginning on or after 1 January 2005, where in a group of companies one company uses IAS and another UK GAAP, then if there are transactions between the two and a tax advantage would arise as a result of the different accounting policies, they are both to be treated as using UK GAAP. s.51 FA2004

A group for these purposes is as defined for capital gains tax.

SUMMARY - TAX LAW AND ACCOUNTING PRACTICE

The Revenue is looking more and more towards Accounting Standards to determine the tax treatment of income and expenditure.

GAAP is very important. If the correct accounting treatment has been followed the Revenue cannot dispute the treatment unless statute or case law states otherwise.

Following the Herbert Smith case, which looked at the provision for losses on a lease, the Revenue had to withdraw SP 3/90 which prohibited anticipation of losses.

There is currently no accounting standard dealing with the recognition of income. However if the Revenue can show that GAAP has not been followed they can request the appropriate adjustment as they did in the Gardner Mountain case.

The inclusion of IAS in GAAP will result in a move towards fair value accounting and recognising movements in balance sheet values. The Revenue have the right to issue regulations requiring amounts recognised for GAAP to be adjusted in the tax computations.

C: Taxation of Limited Companies

C1: COMPUTATION OF CORPORATION TAX

This chapter will explain how a company calculates its corporation tax liability once PCTCT is known. In particular it will explain how the size of the company affects the rate of tax that is applied.

C1.1 Rates of tax

Companies pay Corporation Tax for a **chargeable accounting period** or CAP. The rules for determining the **CAPs** of a company were covered in the first chapter.

Corporation tax is calculated based on rates of tax set by the Chancellor of the Exchequer for each financial year. A financial year runs from 1 April to 31 March for companies and is denoted by the year in which it begins. For example, **financial year 2005 (FY 2005) runs from 1 April 2005 to 31 March 2006.**

The rates of tax applicable in the last few financial years are as follows and are given in the tax tables accompanying this course:

Financial Year	*2002 to 2005*
Full rate	30%
Small companies' rate	19%
Lower (or starting) rate	0%
Profit limit for lower/starting rate	£10,000
Profit limit for lower/starting rate marginal relief	£50,000
Profit limit for small companies' rate	£300,000
Profit limit for small companies' marginal relief	£1,500,000
Marginal relief fraction - small companies' rate	$\frac{11}{400}$
Marginal relief fraction – lower/starting rate	$\frac{19}{400}$

Companies pay **tax on** their profits chargeable to corporation tax **(PCTCT)**. The definition of PCTCT was covered in the first chapter – PCTCT is all of the company's income and gains, less any allowable deductions, e.g. charges and losses. However, the **rate of tax is determined** by a company's **"notional profit"** (NP).

For example, if a company has notional profit of £2m, it will be a "large" company and will pay corporation tax on the whole of its PCTCT at the full rate of 30%.

A company with notional profit of, say, £100,000 will be a "small" company and its PCTCT would be fully charged at the small companies rate of 19%.

A company with notional profit of, say, £5,000 is a "very small" company and its PCTCT is charged at the starting rate of 0%. The starting rate is also sometimes referred to as the lower rate.

Companies whose notional profit is between the limits are known as "marginal" companies and will receive "marginal relief". We will look at marginal relief later in this chapter.

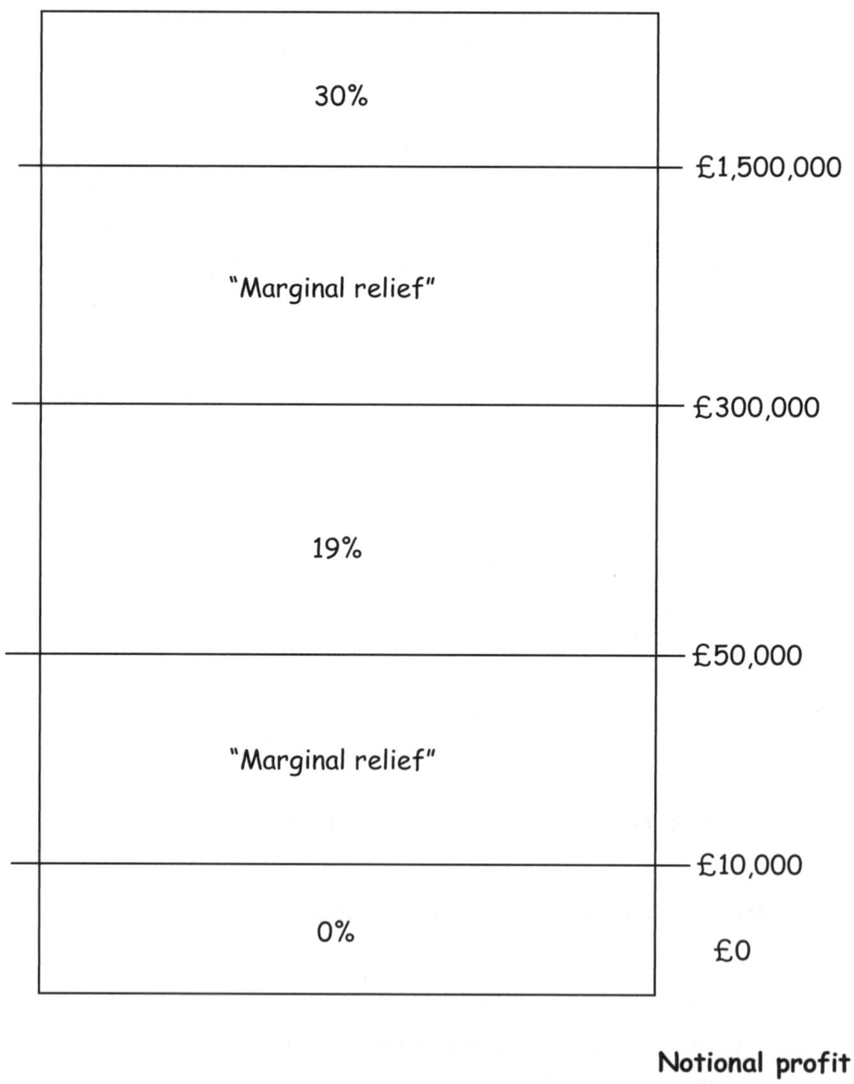

C1.2 Notional profit

The notional profit is obtained by taking PCTCT and adding to it dividends received, grossed up at a rate of 100/90.

This gross dividend figure is known as **franked investment income** and is commonly shortened to **FII**.

This gives us the notional profit and it is this figure which we compare with the limits in the tax tables to determine the rate of tax applicable to the particular company.

PCTCT	X
FII = Dividends received $\times \frac{100}{90}$	X
Notional profit	X

Remember that UK dividends received by a UK company are not charged to corporation tax.

We only consider **UK dividends received** in order to determine the **rate** at which the company will pay corporation tax. You should assume that dividends received are from other UK companies unless you are specifically told otherwise.

Furthermore we only consider UK dividends received from **non-group** companies. We will look at the definition of non-group companies later.

Illustration 1

Three separate companies, A, B and C make up accounts for the 12 months to 31 March 2006. Their PCTCTs for the period are:

A Ltd	£6,000
B Ltd	£200,000
C Ltd	£2,000,000

In each case they receive dividends of £1,800 from a UK company.

To compute each company's CT liability for the year the following method should be used:

1) Calculate the **notional profit** figure;

2) Consider the **limits** to determine **which rate** is to be applied to the PCTCT;

3) **Apply** the CT **rate to the PCTCT.**

	A	B	C
	£	£	£
PCTCT	6,000	200,000	2,000,000
FII £1,800 x 100/90	2,000	2,000	2,000
" Notional Profit"	8,000	202,000	2,002,000
Rate to be applied	0%	19%	30%
£6,000 x 0%	Nil		
£200,000 x 19%		£38,000	
£2m x 30%			£600,000

Remember that the dividends are **not** taxable income in the hands of a company, but they are included to decide what **rate** of tax will be payable on the taxable profits (PCTCT).

Example 1

Consider the following companies with a year end of 31 March 2006:

	A Ltd	B Ltd	C Ltd
	£	£	£
PCTCT	1,400,000	280,000	7,500
Dividends received	100,000	16,200	1,080

Calculate the corporation tax liability for each company.

C1.3 Marginal relief

Marginal relief applies where a company's **notional profit is between** the limits. This is between the **upper and lower limits** of £1.5 million and £300,000 and between the **starting rate limits** of £50,000 and £10,000. s.13

In computing the corporation tax liability, **PCTCT is initially taxed at the full rate of 30%** where profits are between the lower and the upper limits **or at the small companies' rate of 19%** where profits are between £10,000 and £50,000.

Marginal relief is then deducted.

Marginal relief is given by the formula:

$$\textbf{Fraction} \times \textbf{(Upper Limit - Notional Profit)} \times \frac{\textbf{PCTCT}}{\textbf{Notional Profit}}$$

When notional profits are between £300,000 and £1,500,000 the upper limit used in the formula is **£1.5 million**. In FY 2005 the fraction is $\frac{11}{400}$ and the marginal relief calculated is deducted from the initial calculation of corporation tax at **30%** to give the actual tax payable.

When notional profits are between £10,000 and £50,000 the upper limit used in the formula is **£50,000**. In FY2005 the fraction used here is $\frac{19}{400}$ and the marginal relief calculated is deducted from the initial calculation of corporation tax at **19%** to give the actual tax payable.

Illustration 2

A company has the following results for the year to 31 March 2006:

	£
PCTCT	500,000
FII	80,000
Notional Profit	£580,000

The notional profit is between the £300,000 and £1,500,000 limits and marginal relief will apply. The tax calculation will be:

	£
£500,000 x 30%	150,000
Less marginal relief	
$\frac{11}{400} \times (1{,}500{,}000 - 580{,}000) \times \frac{500000}{580000}$	(21,810)
Gross Corporation Tax (GCT)	£128,190

Example 2

Consider the following for the year ended 31 March 2006:

	G Ltd	H Ltd
	£	£
Schedule DI	250,000	15,000
Schedule A	60,000	8,000
Capital gain	180,000	7,200
Dividends received	18,000	2,520

You are required to calculate the Gross Corporation Tax payable.

Answer 1

	A Ltd	B Ltd	C Ltd
	£	£	£
PCTCT	1,400,000	280,000	7,500
FII (dividends $\times \frac{100}{90}$)	111,111	18,000	1,200
Notional profit	£1,511,111	£298,000	£8,700
	> 1.5m limit	< £300k limit	< £10k limit
Tax rate	30%	19%	0%
Corporation Tax (PCTCT x rate)			
£1,400,000 x 30%	**£420,000**		
£280,000 x 19%		**£53,200**	
£7,500 x 0%			**NIL**

Answer 2

	G Ltd	H Ltd
	£	£
Schedule DI	250,000	15,000
Schedule A	60,000	8,000
Capital gain	180,000	7,200
PCTCT	490,000	30,200
FII ($\frac{100}{90}$)	20,000	2,800
	£510,000	£33,000
	Between full limits	Between starting rate limits
Corporation tax:	£	£
£490,000 x 30%	147,000	
£ 30,200 x 19%		5,738
Less marginal relief:		
$\frac{11}{400} \times (1{,}500{,}000 - 510{,}000) \times \frac{490000}{510000}$	(26,157)	
$\frac{19}{400} \times (50{,}000 - 33{,}000) \times \frac{30200}{33000}$		(739)
GCT	**£120,843**	**£4,999**

SUMMARY - COMPUTATION OF CORPORATION TAX

Companies pay tax based on the level of their notional profits.

Notional Profits = PCTCT + FII (UK dividends received x 100/90)

"Marginal relief" applies to companies whose notional profits are between the relevant limits.

The formula for marginal relief is

$$\text{Fraction} \times (\text{Upper Limit} - \text{Notional Profit}) \times \frac{\text{PCTCT}}{\text{Notional Profit}}$$

The upper limit will be either £1,500,000 or £50,000 depending on which limits the profits are between.

The marginal relief amount is deducted from the initial calculation of corporation tax at either the full rate or the small companies rate to give the actual tax payable.

C2: ASSOCIATED COMPANIES

This chapter looks at the impact of associated companies when considering what rate of corporation tax a company should pay.

C2.1 Definition

Companies are **associated** with each other if **one company controls another company, or two companies** are **controlled by the same person** or persons.

The **definition of person** in the Taxes Act is very wide. It includes, for instance, a **company**, an **individual**, or **individuals, trustees** of a trust, or **partners** in a partnership. For instance if ICI plc has two subsidiaries, both of them 'controlled by' ICI, all 3 companies are associated.

Control means **more than 50%** of any of the following: s.416

(i) Voting power; or

(ii) Ordinary share capital (not fixed rate preference shares); or

(iii) Entitlement to distributable profits; or

(iv) Entitlement to assets on a winding up.

Example 1

Which of the following companies are associated with Mouse Limited, a company owned entirely by Mickey?

a) Rat Limited, a company in which Mickey owns 50% of the ordinary shares.

b) Cheese Limited, a company wholly owned by Mouse Limited.

c) Mole Limited, a company in which Mickey owns 40% of the shares which entitle him to 60% of the distributable profits.

d) Trap Limited, a company in which Mouse Limited owns 10% of the shares but has 55% of the voting power.

C2.2 Implications

The existence of associated companies means that:

- **When computing** FII (Franked Investment Income) we **ignore** any **dividends received from associated companies**.
- The **corporation tax limits**, that is the £1.5 million, £300,000, £50,000 and £10,000 limits, are **divided equally among all of the associated companies**.

Therefore in the last example, we would ignore any dividends received by Mouse Ltd from Cheese Ltd and Trap Ltd in computing notional profit for Mouse Ltd and when we compute Mouse Ltd's corporation tax liability, we would have to divide the limits by four as there are four associated companies (Mouse Ltd plus its three associates).

Note that it is these revised limits that are used in any marginal relief calculation.

Illustration 1

Iain Ltd has the following income for the year ended 31 March 2006

PCTCT	£120,000
Dividends from non-associated companies	£18,000
Dividends from associated companies	£45,000

We will assume that it has:

(a) one associated company

(b) two associated companies

(c) twelve associated companies

and will show how the corporation tax charge is calculated in each case.

To compute the CT liability:

Step One:
Consider the small company limits
How many associated companies are there?
Remember to include Iain Ltd itself!

	(a)	(b)	(c)
£300,000 & £1,500,000 divided by			
(a) 2	£150,000 & £750,000		
(b) 3		£100,000 & £500,000	
(c) 13			£23,077 & £115,385

Step Two:
Calculate the "notional profits"
Ignore dividends from associates

PCTCT	120,000	120,000	120,000
FII £18,000 x 100/90	20,000	20,000	20,000
Notional profits	140,000	140,000	140,000

Step Three:
Decide which tax rate applies:

	19%	Marginal	30%

Step Four:
Compute the liability:

a) £120,000 x 19%	**£22,800**		
b) £120,000 x 30%		36,000	
Less:			
$\frac{11}{400}$ x (£500,000 - 140,000) x $\frac{120,000}{140,000}$		(8,`6)	
		£27,514	
c) £120,000 x 30%			**£36,000**

Example 2

Plant Ltd and Flower Ltd each have 2 associated companies. Their profits in the year ended 31 March 2006 are as follows:

	Plant Ltd	Flower Ltd
	£	£
PCTCT	450,000	120,000
FII	60,000	30,000

Calculate the Gross Corporation Tax liability in each company.

C2.3 Associates s.417

When determining whether companies are associated, the holdings of an individual must be added to holdings of his associates. These include the individual and his spouse, plus also his brothers and sisters, children and remoter issue, i.e. grandchildren etc.

Individuals are also associated with parents and remoter forbear, i.e. grandparents etc. and any business partners trading in partnership. This does not extend to individuals who are directors in the same company. We also apportion the rights and powers of trustees, where the settlor is the individual or an associate of that individual. The settlor is the person who actually puts the money into the trust.

Example 3

Sam invites the following people round to dinner:

a) His brother

b) His brother's wife

c) His godson

d) His ex-wife

e) His business partner

f) His grandmother

g) His bank manager.

Who is associated with Sam?

C2.4 Other rules

Companies are **associated for a whole accounting period.** Therefore we include companies that join or leave the group during the year, even though they are only associated for part of the period. s.13(5)

We also **include all worldwide companies**. Although only UK companies are subject to corporation tax, existence of worldwide subsidiaries or holding companies will dilute the upper and lower limits.

Dormant companies are excluded. A dormant company is basically one that is not doing anything. In *Jowett v O'Neill v Brennan Construction Ltd,* a company simply holding funds in a bank deposit account and receiving interest income, was not an active company and counted as dormant for associated company purposes. s.513(3) Prior to this decision, the Revenue believed that a company was only dormant if it had no income. From this decision, the **company is dormant provided it has no activity.**

C2.5 Sub-subsidiaries

Sub-subsidiaries, i.e. where one company controls another, which in turn controls another, are **also included as associated companies**. The definition is a very wide one. Therefore if one company controls another, and that controls another, we **do not need to multiply the holdings downwards** to work out whether one company owns more than 50% of another. In other words, you do not need to use your calculator in determining whether companies are associated.

Example 4

Consider the following group structure:

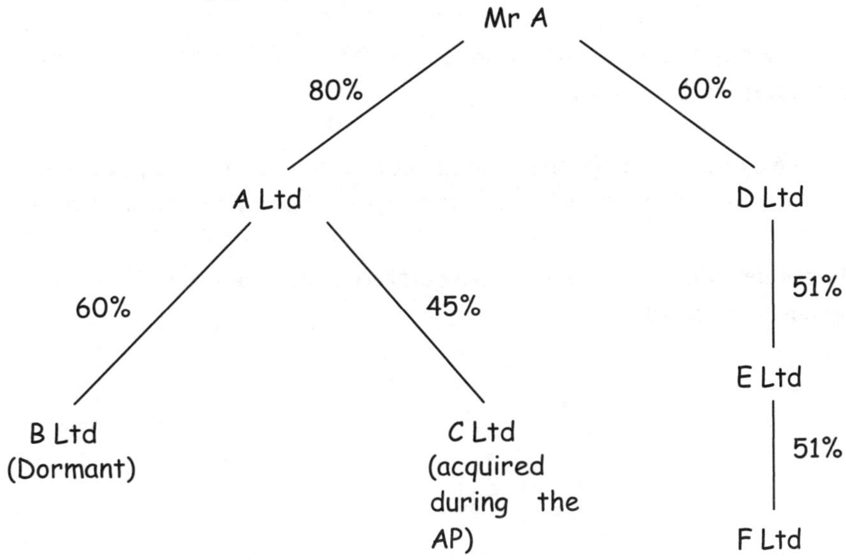

How many companies are associated with A Ltd for its accounting period to 31 December 2006?

Answer 1

(b), **(c)** and **(d)**

Note that the control condition is more than 50% hence in (a) Rat Limited is not associated with Mouse Ltd.

For the others we take the highest percentage of voting power, shares, profits or assets to determine whether the control condition is satisfied.

Therefore Mouse Ltd has 3 associated companies and there are 4 associated companies in total.

Answer 2

	Plant Ltd	Flower Ltd
	£	£
PCTCT	450,000	120,000
FII	60,000	30,000
	£510,000	£150,000
Adjusted profit limits		
(Each company has 2 associates)		
£1,500,000/3 = £500,000	>500k	Between limits
£300,000/3 = £100,000		
Corporation tax:	£	£
£450,000 x 30%	135,000	
£120,000 x 30%		36,000
Less marginal relief:		
$\frac{11}{400}$ (£500,000 - 150,000) x $\frac{120000}{150000}$		(7,700)
	£135,000	£28,300

Answer 3

(a), **(e)** and **(f)** only

Answer 4

A Ltd has **3 associates**: D Ltd, E Ltd and F Ltd

SUMMARY - ASSOCIATED COMPANIES

The profits limits are reduced for associated companies.

Dividends received from associated companies are ignored in determining FII.

Associated companies are companies under common control (i.e. >50%).

Common control can be by another company or an individual.

Dormant companies are excluded.

Overseas companies are included.

Companies which become associates or cease to be associates during the accounting period count as associates for the whole accounting period.

When looking at sub-subsidiaries there is no need to multiply through to find an effective interest - the sub-subsidiaries will be associated with the top company in the group provided there is control (i.e. > 50%) at each level.

C3: SHORT ACCOUNTING PERIODS

This chapter demonstrates how to calculate the tax liability of a company that has an accounting period of less than 12 months

C3.1 Apportioning the limits

The corporation tax limits apply to a twelve month period. Therefore, when the chargeable accounting period is less than 12 months long, the limits must be **time apportioned**.

Illustration 1

Duncan Ltd changed its year end from 31 December to 30 September. With this in mind, it makes up its accounts for the 9 months to 30 September 2005.

To determine the amount of tax payable it is necessary to know the small companies limits. These need to be **adjusted for the fact that there are only 9 month accounts** prepared.

The limits become:

£10,000 x 9/12	£7,500
£50,000 x 9/12	£37,500
£300,000 x 9/12	£225,000
£1.5m x 9/12	£1,125,000

The limits included in the marginal relief calculation should be these revised limits:

Lower limits:

$$\text{Fraction} \times £(37{,}500 - \text{Notional Profit}) \times \frac{\text{PCTCT}}{\text{Notional Profit}}$$

Upper limits:

$$\text{Fraction} \times £(1{,}125{,}000 - \text{Notional profit}) \times \frac{\text{PCTCT}}{\text{Notional Profit}}$$

Assume that Duncan Ltd's results for the 9 months ended 30 September 2005 are as follows:

	£
PCTCT	200,000
FII	50,000
Notional profits	250,000

As notional profits are between the limits, marginal relief applies:

GCT;	£
£200,000 x 30%	60,000
Less marginal relief	
$\frac{11}{400} \times (1{,}125{,}000 - 250{,}000) \times \frac{200000}{250000}$	(19,250)
Gross corporation tax	£40,750

Example 1

What will the limits be for an 8 month chargeable accounting period?

Upper Limit

Lower Limit

Starting rate upper limit

Starting rate lower limit

Example 2

George Limited and Zippy Limited make up accounts for the 8 months ended 30 November 2005 which show the following results:

	George Ltd	Zippy Ltd
	£	£
PCTCT	500,000	20,000
Dividends received	45,000	7,200

Calculate the gross corporation tax for each company.

C3.2 Short APs and associates

If a company had a short accounting period together with associated companies, the methodology remains the same i.e. ascertain the amended limits and calculate the tax accordingly.

Illustration 2

Ashdown Ltd has 3 subsidiaries. It draws accounts for a 6 month period ended 30 September 2005.

The limits become:

$£10,000 \times \frac{6}{12} \times \frac{1}{4}$	£1,250
$£50,000 \times \frac{6}{12} \times \frac{1}{4}$	£6,250
$£300,000 \times \frac{6}{12} \times \frac{1}{4}$	£37,500
$£1,500,000 \times \frac{6}{12} \times \frac{1}{4}$	£187,500

The results for the 6 months ended 30 September 2005 are:

PCTCT	160,000
FII	30,000
Notional profits	190,000

As notional profits exceed the upper limit, Ashdown Ltd is treated as a "Large" company and will pay corporation tax at the full rate: i.e.

£160,000 x 30% = £48,000

Example 3

Parasol Ltd draws up accounts for the period 1 January 2005 to 31 August 2005, showing PCTCT of £22,000 and FII of £12,000. Parasol Ltd has one associated company.

Calculate the gross corporation tax liability.

Example 4

Archer Limited draws up accounts for the period 1 January 2005 to 30 September 2005 showing PCTCT of £56,000 and dividends received from non-associated companies of £4,000. Archer Limited has four associated companies.

You are required to calculate the Gross Corporation Tax liability.

Answer 1

Upper limit (£1,500,000 × $\frac{8}{12}$)	**£1,000,000**
Lower limit (£300,000 × $\frac{8}{12}$)	**£200,000**
Starting rate upper limit (£50,000 × $\frac{8}{12}$)	**£33,333**
Starting rate lower limit (£10,000 × $\frac{8}{12}$)	**£6,667**

Answer 2

	George Ltd	Zippy Ltd
	£	£
PCTCT	500,000	20,000
FII (dividends × $\frac{100}{90}$)	50,000	8,000
Notional profit	£550,000	£28,000
Relevant limits:		
UL	1,000,000	
LL	200,000	
SRUL		33,333
SRLL		6,667
	Between limits	Between limits
Corporation Tax:	£	£
£500,000 × 30%	150,000	
£20,000 × 19%		3,800
Marginal relief:		
$\frac{11}{400}$ (1,000,000 − 550,000) × $\frac{500000}{550000}$	(11,250)	
$\frac{19}{400}$ (33,333 − 28,000) × $\frac{20000}{28000}$		(181)
	£138,750	**£3,619**

Answer 3

	£
PCTCT	22,000
FII	12,000
	£34,000

Profit Limits
(2 associates and an 8 month CAP)

$\frac{1500000}{2} \times \frac{8}{12}$	500,000
$\frac{300000}{2} \times \frac{8}{12}$	100,000
$\frac{50000}{2} \times \frac{8}{12}$	16,667
$\frac{10000}{2} \times \frac{8}{12}$	3,333

Small companies rate applies:	
£22,000 x 19%	**£4,180**

Answer 4

	£
PCTCT	56,000
FII (dividends x $\frac{100}{90}$)	4,444
Notional Profit	£60,444

Profit Limits
(5 associates and a 9 month CAP)

Upper limit: $\frac{1500000}{5} \times \frac{9}{12}$	225,000
Lower limit: $\frac{300000}{5} \times \frac{9}{12}$	45,000
	Between limits so marginal relief

	£
Corporation tax	
£56,000 x 30%	16,800
Less: Marginal relief	
$\frac{11}{400} \times (225{,}000 - 60{,}444) \times \frac{56000}{60444}$	(4,193)
GCT	**£12,607**

SUMMARY – SHORT ACCOUNTING PERIODS

Where a company makes up its accounts for less than 12 months, it is necessary to adjust the corporation tax limits on a pro-rata basis.

$$\text{Limits} \times \frac{n}{12}$$

where n = number of months in the short accounting period.

These adjusted limits are also used in the marginal relief calculations.

C4: LONG PERIODS OF ACCOUNT

This chapter demonstrates how to calculate the tax liability of a company that draws up accounts for a period more than 12 months long.

C4.1 Introduction

A chargeable accounting period **(CAP)** for corporation tax **cannot exceed 12 months**. However, under company law, accounts can be drawn up for periods as long as 18 months. The period for which accounts are made up is known as the period of account (POA). s.12

Where a period of account **exceeds 12 months**, it must be **split into two** separate CAPs for tax purposes. The first will be the **first 12 months,** because a CAP cannot exceed 12 months. The second will be the **balance of the period**, because a CAP always ends when a period of account ends.

Example 1

Longton Limited makes up a set of accounts for the 16 months ended 31 July 2005.

What are the chargeable accounting periods here?

C4.2 Splitting the profits

Once we have worked out the accounting periods, we **then split the company's income between the two separate CAPs**, as the accounts will have been drawn up showing profits for the entire period of account.

Trading profit is adjusted for the entire period for disallowed items, such as entertaining and depreciation. The adjusted result is then time apportioned to the two periods.

As far as **capital allowances** are concerned, we have to prepare **separate computations** for each CAP taking account of additions and disposals in each separate CAP. We claim a separate writing down allowance for each of the two CAPs, remembering that the **writing down allowance is time apportioned** for the second CAP. **First year allowances however do not need to be time apportioned.**

Illustration 1

Longton Limited prepares accounts for the 16 months ended 31 July 2005. The adjusted profit before capital allowances for the period is £480,000.

You are also given the following information in respect of capital allowances:

Plant pool b/f	1.4.04	£30,000
Additions:	1.1.05	£8,000
	1.6.05	£6,000
Disposals:	1.7.05	£(3,000)

Longton Limited is a medium sized company and is eligible for 40% first year allowances.

The Schedule DI profit for each CAP is as follows:

	12m to 31.3.05	4m to 31.7.05
	£	£
Adjusted profit before capital allowances	360,000	120,000
$£480,000 \times \frac{12}{16}, \frac{4}{16}$		
Less capital allowances (below)	(10,700)	(4,425)
Schedule D Case I profits	£349,300	£115,575

	FYAs	*General Pool*	*Claim*
Y/e 31.3.05:			
Pool at 1.4.04		30,000	
Addition:			
Machine (1.1.05)	8,000		
FYA @ 40%	(3,200)		3,200
WDA @ 25%		(7,500)	7,500
	4,800	22,500	£10,700
Transfer to pool		4,800	
TWDV c/f		27,300	
4 m/e 31.7.05			
Addition:			
Machine (1.6.05)	6,000		
FYA @ 40%	(2,400)		2,400
Disposal: Machine (1.7.05)		(3,000)	
	3,600	24,300	
WDA @ 25% $\times \frac{4}{12}$		(2,025)	2,025
		22,275	£4,425
Transfer to pool		3,600	
TWDV c/f		25,875	

Note how WDAs have been apportioned in the second CAP but FYAs have not.

C4.3 Splitting other income and charges

Schedules A, DIII, and DVI are split on a **time apportionment basis** as the accruals basis of accounting applies to these sources of income.

From 1 April 2004 management expenses for an investment company are split on accruals basis - previously they were deductible when paid.

Chargeable gains are split between the two separate accounting periods based on the **date of disposal** of the asset. This is the date of a binding contract of sale, which for property is the date of **exchange** of contracts.

Charges on income, are split between the periods based on the **date** that the amount was actually **paid.**

Franked investment income, is split between the accounting **periods based on the date of receipt** of the dividend.

We must be careful with the time apportionment of Schedule A, DIII or DVI income where the source is acquired part way through the accounting period. In this case, we must time apportion the income over the period in which it arose, rather than for the entire accounting period.

After all the income and charges have been allocated to the relevant CAP, two separate CT computations are prepared for the two separate periods.

As we shall see later, these two separate CT liabilities are paid at different times so there is never any point in adding them together.

It is also possible for a company to pay tax at different rates for the two periods.

For example, a company could pay tax at the small companies rate in the first (12 month) CAP, but then pay tax at the full rate in the other (short) CAP if, for example, a large capital gain fell into this latter period.

Illustration 2

Longton Limited (from Illustration 1) also received and paid the following:

Interest income (bank account opened in 1991)	£8,000
Schedule A rents (property acquired 1.1.05)	£14,000
Capital gains (asset sold 30.5.05)	£10,000
Annual gift aid donation (paid 1 July each year)	£1,000 pa

We split these amounts between the chargeable accounting periods for the 16 months to 31 July 2005 as follows:

	12m to 31.3.05	4m to 31.7.05
	£	£
Schedule DIII ($\frac{12}{16}$, $\frac{4}{16}$)	6,000	2,000
Schedule A		
1.1.05 - 31.3.05 ($\frac{3}{7}$)	6,000	
1.4.05 - 31.7.05 ($\frac{4}{7}$)		8,000
Chargeable gain		10,000
Charge on income (paid basis)	(1,000)	(1,000)

Note.
The Schedule A source commenced on 1.1.2005. The rents of £14,000 therefore arise over a 7 month period. Three months of rents are accrued in the first CAP and four months are accrued in the second CAP.

Example 2

If we also assume that Longton Limited received FII of £10,000 on 1 January 2005, the corporation tax computations for the 2 periods can now be shown as follows:

Longton Limited	12m to 31.3.05	4m to 31.7.05
	£	£
Schedule DI	349,300	115,575
Schedule A	6,000	8,000
Schedule DIII	6,000	2,000
Chargeable gain	-	10,000
Charges on income	(1,000)	(1,000)
PCTCT	360,300	134,575
FII	10,000	-
Notional profit	370,300	134,575

Assuming Longton Limited had one wholly owned subsidiary which was sold on 1 January 2005 calculate the gross corporation tax liability for each chargeable accounting period.

Example 3

Smith Ltd makes up its accounts for the 18 months to 30 June 2005. It owns 60% of the shares of Hague Ltd.

It has the following income and expenditure:

Adjusted profit before CAs	£240,000
Rental income £12,000 pa, increasing to £15,000 pa from 1 January 2005	£19,500
Bank interest (accruing evenly)	£3,600
Gain on disposal 14 May 2005	£110,000
Dividend received 14 September 2004	£9,000
Gift Aid donations:	
1 May 2004	£20,000
1 May 2005	£24,000

The TWDV of the capital allowances pool was £80,000 on 1 January 2004. During the year they had the following transactions:

1 May 2004	Bought P&M	£20,000
1 July 2004	Bought new car £16,000 (MD private use 20%)	
1 February 2005	Sold P&M	£8,000 proceeds
1 March 2005	Bought P&M	£12,000

Smith Ltd is a medium sized company

You are required to calculate the corporation tax liability for each chargeable accounting period.

Answer 1

CAP 1: **1.4.04 to 31.3.05**
CAP 2: **1.4.05 to 31.7.05**

The period of account begins on 1 April 2004 and so therefore, the first CAP will run through to 31 March 2005.

The second chargeable accounting period will start immediately afterwards on 1 April 2005 and will run through to the end of the period of account on 31 July. 2005.

Answer 2

	12m to 31.3.05	4m to 31.7.05
	£	£
PCTCT	360,300	134,575
FII	10,000	
Notional Profit	370,300	134,575

Profit Limits:
12m to 31.3.05 - one associate

$\frac{1500000}{2}$ £750,000

$\frac{300000}{2}$ £150,000

4m to 31.7.05 – no associates

$1,500,000 \times \frac{4}{12}$ £500,000

$300,000 \times \frac{4}{12}$ £100,000

	£	£
Corporation Tax:		
£360,300 x 30%	108,090	
£134,575 x 30%		40,373
Marginal Relief:		
$\frac{11}{400} \times (750,000 - 370,300) \times \frac{360300}{370300}$	(10,160)	
$\frac{11}{400} \times (500,000 - 134,575)$		(10,049)
GCT	**£97,930**	**£30,324**

Answer 3

Computation of corporation tax liability:

	12 months to 31.12.04	*6 months to 30.6.05*
	£	£
Adjusted profit (12:6)	160,000	80,000
CAs (W1)	(31,000)	(14,300)
Schedule DI	129,000	65,700
Schedule A	12,000	7,500
DIII (12:6)	2,400	1,200
Gain		110,000
	143,400	184,400
Less: charges	(20,000)	(24,000)
PCTCT	123,400	160,400
CT (W2)		
£123,400 x 19%	**23,446**	
£160,400 x 30%		48,120
Less: $\frac{11}{400}$ x (375,000 - 160,400)		(5,902)
		42,218

(W1) CAs

	FYA	General Pool £	Car > £12,000 £	Total allowances £
12 m to 31 December 2004				
TWDV b/f		80,000		
Addition – car (no FYAs)			16,000	
WDA 25%		(20,000)		20,000
Maximum £3,000			(3,000)	3,000
		60,000	13,000	
FYA purchases				
1.5.2004	20,000			
FYA 40%	(8,000)			8,000
		12,000		31,000
TWDV c/f		72,000	13,000	
6m to 30 June 2005				
Disposal		(8,000)		
		64,000		
WDA 6/12 x 25%		(8,000)		8,000
Maximum £3,000 x 6/12			(1,500)	1,500
		56,000	11,500	
FYA purchases				
1.3.2005	12,000			
FYA 40%	(			4,800
	4,800)	7,200		14,300
TWDV c/f		63,200	11,500	

(W2) Tax rates

	£	£
PCTCT	123,400	160,400
FII £9,000 x 100/90	10,000	
Profits	133,400	160,400
Limits – one associate	150,000/750,000	
Limits - 6 month accounting period		75,000/375,000
Tax rate:	19%	Marginal relief

SUMMARY – LONG PERIODS OF ACCOUNT

For a company with a period of account that exceeds 12 months, the period of account must be split into two chargeable accounting periods (CAPs) – the first CAP will be the first 12 months and the second CAP will be the balance (n months).

A separate tax computation must be performed for each CAP.

The adjustment of profits, before capital allowances, is done for the period of account as a whole.

The income and gains are then split between the two CAPs as follows:

Adjusted profit	Time apportionment
Capital allowances	Two computations required – one for each CAP Scale down WDA by n/12 in short CAP but not FYA
Sch A, DIII and DVI	Accruals basis
Gains	When realised
Charges	When paid
Dividends received	When received

Don't forget to time apportion the limits by n/12 when calculating corporation tax for the second CAP which will be less than 12 months long.

C5: CORPORATION TAX SELF ASSESSMENT (CTSA)

This chapter examines the Corporation Tax Self Assessment (CTSA) procedures, including:
- filing requirements;
- enquiries;
- claims;
- record keeping.

C5.1 Introduction

Corporation tax self assessment applies to all chargeable accounting periods ending on or after 1 July 1999. The regime deals with all of the administration areas of corporation tax which includes the payment of tax.

Corporation tax for smaller companies is **due 9 months and 1 day after the end of the chargeable accounting period**. Larger companies are required to pay tax under the quarterly instalment system.

The regime also deals with the filing of **tax returns (CT600)** which give details of the income a company has earned, together with the calculation of the corporation tax liability.

The submission of the tax calculation is compulsory for companies, unlike individuals who can shift the responsibility for calculating the tax to the Inland Revenue provided they file the return by an earlier date. This facility is not available to companies.

There is **a statutory liability for a company to notify chargeability to corporation tax.** s.55 FA 2004

Where a company has not received a notice to file a tax return (CT603) it must give notice to the Revenue within 12 months of the end of the accounting period that it is chargeable to tax.

When a company submits its **form CT600**, it will also send in a **set of accounts** together with any other detailed analysis and computations necessary to show that the return is complete and correct and answers all of the Revenue Officer's most obvious questions.

Normally a CT600 is due for submission to the Revenue 12 months from the end of the chargeable accounting period. For example if the chargeable accounting period ends 31 December 2005, the CT600 must be filed by 31 December 2006.

However, a later filing date may be appropriate as a company will always have a minimum of 3 months from the receipt of the filing notice. If this date is later than the 12 month date, then this date becomes the new filing date.

Illustration 1

A company makes its accounts for the 12 months to 30 June 2006. It receives its CT 600 for this period on 30 April 2007.

The normal filing date would be 30 June 2006 + 12m = 30 June 2007.
Notice received 30 April 2007 and 3 months after that is 31 July 2007.
The filing date is therefore 31 July 2007 as this is later than the normal filing date.

C5.2 Long periods of account

Where the company makes up its accounts for more than 12 months, it is required to split it into two accounting periods for the purposes of calculating the tax payable. However, for filing purposes, there is a single filing date that will be 12 months from the end of the period of account.

Two returns will be submitted - one for each CAP - but the due date for filing these returns is the same.

Illustration 2

A small company draws accounts for a 15 month period ending on 31 March 2006.

The period of account must be divided into two chargeable accounting periods for the purposes of calculating corporation tax:

CAP No. 1:	12 m/e 31 December 2005
CAP No. 2:	3 m/e 31 March 2006

The due dates for the payment of corporation tax and for the filing of the form CT600 are:

	CAP No. 1 *y/e 31.12.05*	*CAP No. 2* *y/e 31.3.06*
Tax due	1.10.06	1.1.07
CT600 due	31.3.07	31.3.07

Two forms CT600 will be submitted on 31 March 2007, together with financial statements and corporation tax computations covering both chargeable accounting periods.

Example 1

Complete the filing date in the following:

	CAP ends	Notice issued	Filing date
a)	31.3.06	12.11.06	
b)	31.5.06	24.3.07	

C5.3 Duty to notify chargeability

s.55 FA 2004

Companies have an obligation to notify the Revenue when their first accounting period begins or when they come back within the charge to tax. They will also have to provide certain prescribed information.

The company must give **written notice within three months of the start of the accounting period. The notice must state when the accounting period began.** s.55(2) FA 2004

The detailed information to be given in the notice is as follows: SI 2004/2502

(a) The company's name;

(b) The address of the company's registered office;

(c) The address of the company's principal place of business;

(d) The nature of the business being carried on by the company;

(e) The date to which the company intends to prepare accounts; and

(f) The full names and addresses of the directors of the company.

(g) In the case of a business formerly carried on by others:

- the name and address of that former business; and
- the name and address of the person from whom the business was acquired.

(h) In the case of a company which is in a group relief group:

- the name of the parent company and the address of its registered office.

(i) In the case of a company which, has been obliged to comply with the requirements of the Income Tax (Pay as You Earn) Regulations 2003:

- the date on which that obligation first arose.

The rules **do not apply to unincorporated associations or partnerships**. s.55(5) FA 2004

No failure to give notice will arise where the company has **a reasonable excuse,** so long as it gives notice within a reasonable time once the excuse has passed. s.55(4) FA 2004

C5.4 Processing of the returns

A form CT600 is submitted to the Revenue, and is processed by the corporation tax processing department. As part of the processing procedure the Revenue will have 9 months from the actual date of filing the return to correct any obvious errors in it. This would include, for instance, where a list of figures had been added incorrectly or the wrong rate of tax has been taken. Para 16 Sch 18 FA 1998

These errors will be identified when the Revenue type the figures from the return into their computer system, and find that there are differences between the two. In this case, the processor will write to the company and ask for the appropriate amendments to be made.

The **company has 12 months from the due filing date**, (not the actual filing date) **to make any amendments to the return**. This could be, for instance, revising a loss relief claim, amending a capital allowances claim, or any other amendments. Para 15 Sch 18 FA 1998

Once the return has been processed, it may then go to a Revenue Officer, who might give it a more detailed review. If the Officer looks at the return and the accompanying accounts, and he sees there is information that he would like to ask questions about, he has **12 months from the due filing date to start an enquiry.** It is very important that the Revenue stick to these enquiry deadlines, because once they have passed this deadline there is very little they can do if they disagree with something on the return. Para 24 Sch 18 FA 1998

If the chargeable accounting period ends on 31 December 2005, the CT600 must be filed by 31 December 2006 and any enquiry must commence by 31 December 2007.

For an enquiry to commence, the company must receive the notice of enquiry. The commencement date is not the date stated on the enquiry notice but the date that the company must reasonably be expected to receive it. Therefore allowing for first class post, this could take 3 days or second class post 6 days, so the Revenue try to make sure they post it well before the deadline.

If, however, the **return is filed late**, the **Revenue will have a minimum of 12 months to start their enquiries** and the enquiry deadline will move to the end of the next quarter day. This also applies to any amendments relating to that return which are filed after the normal filing date. The Revenue will have extra time to start an enquiry in respect of those amendments only.

The quarter days do not coincide with the usual quarter days of the year. They are 31 January, 30 April, 31 July and 31 October. These are the same quarter days which apply to income tax self assessment.

Illustration 3

Lazy Ltd drew accounts for the 12 months ending 31 May 2005. A notice to deliver a return was received by the company on 15 July 2005, but the company's CT600 is not submitted to the Tax Office until 14 August 2006.

The return should have been filed by 31 May 2006 - therefore it is late.

This extends the deadline by which the Officer can commence an enquiry into the return. The deadline for commencing an enquiry is the end of the calendar quarter following the anniversary of the return, i.e.

14 August 2006 + 12 months = 14 August 2007
14 August 2007 is in the q/e 31 October 2007

The Officer has until 31 October 2007 to start an enquiry into the return.

Example 2

Consider the following:

	(a)	(b)
CAP ends	31.3.06	31.5.05
CT600 filed	31.1.07	30.6.06

What are the dates by which the Revenue may correct obvious errors and the dates by which the Revenue may open an enquiry?

C5.5 Enquiries

CTSA enquiries take place to ensure that companies submit corporation tax returns which are both complete and correct. An enquiry can start for a number of reasons. The enquiry could be **"random"** - generated by the Revenue's computer. The return could be subject to a **"selected"** enquiry where the Officer has identified something on the return which he is not happy about, or wishes to ask further questions about.

There could also be **"routine"** enquiries. This will apply particularly to very large companies, where simply because of the amount of profits and tax involved, the return will be subject to an enquiry virtually every year.

C5.6 Claims

Claims must be made on **the tax return**. Examples of claims include losses, group relief and capital allowances. The claims themselves must be made on the CT600 and must be quantified in amount. Claims may be amended in the normal time limit, which is 12 months following the normal filing date. **The general time limit for claims is six years unless otherwise specified** in the Taxes Act. Supplementary claims can be made in the case of errors in claims. Para 54 Sch 18 FA 1998

C5.7 Group relief

Tutor note: It is best to come back and study this topic after you have studied group relief later in this course.

Clear instructions on group relief claims are set down in Paras 66 to 77 of Sch 18 FA 1998. The claim has to be made on the **claimant company's tax return.** Para 67 Sch FA 1998

It must **specify the amount** claimed, the **name of the surrendering company**, whether any of the companies are not resident in the UK during the accounting period of the surrendering company to which the surrender relates and the **accounting period** of the claimant to which the claim relates. Para 68 Sch FA 1998

A claim can be made for less than the amount available. The claim will be **ineffective if made for more than the amount available**. Where there is more than one claim and the total exceeds the amount available, the Revenue can determine which claims are ineffective. Para 69 Sch FA 1998

A claim requires the **written consent of the surrendering company** for a group relief claim and the written consent of each member of a consortium in the case of a consortium relief claim. Para 70 Sch FA 1998

Claims will be **ineffective unless they are accompanied by the written consent.** To be effective the written consent must specify: Para 71 Sch FA 1998

- The name of the surrendering company;
- The name of the claimant;
- The amount;
- The accounting period of the surrendering company to which the claim relates;
- The tax district references of the surrendering and claimant company.

Notices of consent can be withdrawn and replaced by another notice, **they cannot be amended.** The notice of withdrawal has to have the written consent of the claimant to the withdrawal unless it arises due to a reduction in the amount available for relief. The claimant must amend its tax return for the period of the claim to reflect the withdrawal. Para 73 Sch FA 1998

The surrendering company must amend its tax return if the notice of consent is given after it has filed the return. If, as a result a reduction arises in a future accounting period in respect of losses carried forward, that return must also be amended.

A claimant company can only withdraw a claim for group relief by amending its tax return. It cannot amend the claim. It can only be withdrawn and replaced.

The time limit for making and withdrawing group relief claims is whichever is the **latest** of the following dates: Para 74 Sch 18 FA 1998

- First anniversary of the filing date of the claimant;
- 30 days after completion of an enquiry into the return;
- 30 days after the issue of an amended self assessment following the completion of an enquiry;
- 30 days after the settlement of an appeal against such an amendment;
- such later time as the Revenue allow.

Where the amount available for surrender is reduced, the surrendering company has 30 days to withdraw and re-issue the consent to surrender, sending copies to the Inland Revenue and each claimant company. Para 75 Sch 18 FA 1998

If the surrendering company fails to do so, the Revenue can give notice to the surrendering company as to how the reduced group relief will be surrendered sending a copy of the notice to each claimant company. The surrendering company has 30 days in which to appeal in writing against any such notice issued by the Revenue. The claimant company on receipt of the new surrender or Revenue notice must amend their tax return.

Where the withdrawal of consent (or a new consent) results in a company becoming chargeable to tax, and that tax remains unpaid after six months after the time limit for claims by that company, the Revenue can issue an assessment in the name of that company or any company that has obtained group relief as a result of the surrender. The Revenue have two years to issue the assessment. The assessment cannot be more than the lower of the tax unpaid or the tax saved by the other company receiving group relief. The company so assessed is entitled to recover the amount plus interest on unpaid tax under s.87 TMA 1970 from the company that failed to pay the tax.

The Revenue can issue an assessment to recover any excessive group relief claimed. This does not affect their ability to issue a discovery assessment. Para 76 Sch 18 FA 1998

C5.8 Simplified arrangements for group relief

SI 1999/2975

Tutor note: Again it is best to come back and study this topic after you have studied group relief later in this course.

Under the simplified arrangements, the group makes an application to the tax office that deals with the **authorised company** identifying all the companies to be covered by the arrangements by giving tax references and the names of tax offices for each one and sufficient detail on each one to verify that they are a group company. The application is made by the authorised company and **signed by all the other companies (the authorising companies)**, stating that they will be bound by the arrangements. The application must include an example of the group relief schedule that the authorised company will use in the future.

Once the application is submitted, the authorised company cannot implement the arrangements for **three months** unless the Revenue give their consent at an earlier date. The Revenue can, within the three months, accept the application but exclude certain companies if they think they have not complied with all their obligations to file returns and pay tax.

The Revenue can refuse the application within three months if they think one or more companies is not a group company or they have not complied with their obligations to file returns and pay tax. The application can also be refused if it is not the case that all or substantially all the companies' tax returns are dealt with in the same tax office or the specimen group relief schedule is not adequate. At any time the Revenue can exclude companies which it believes are not group companies or have not complied with their obligations.

Under the arrangements, the **claim for group relief is made by the authorised company and does not have to include a consent to surrender** if the authorised company gives authority to the claim being made. This authority has to be included in the tax return of the authorising company for which the claim is made and be signed by the authorised person.

The authorised company must from time to time provide **a group relief schedule** to the Revenue containing sufficient information for the making of returns for itself and the authorising companies as regards making and withdrawing group relief claims. The statement must contain the same details as listed above concerning the details of the claim and the amount surrendered. It must also include details showing the effect on each company's self assessment and details of any of the company's tax returns that are under enquiry. If sufficient detail is not shown in the statement it is ineffective.

An authorising company remains liable for any errors in claims or tax returns. Both the authorised company and the Revenue can give notice in writing at any time to the other terminating the arrangements from the date of the notice. The authorised company can at any time give notice in writing excluding an authorising company from the arrangements from the date of the notice.

C5.9 Duty to keep and preserve records

Para 21&22 Sch 18 FA 1998

The company must keep such records required to allow it to file a **correct and complete return** and to preserve those records for **six years** from the end of the period for which the company may be required to deliver a tax return.

Where the company is required to deliver a tax return before the end of that six year period the records have to be kept until the later of:

(i) the date an enquiry into the return is completed

(ii) if there is no enquiry, the date the Revenue can no longer enquire into the return.

If the company is required by notice to deliver a return outside that six year period and it still has those records then to the later of the same above dates.

The records that must be kept are

(i) all receipts and expenses arising in the course of the trade and details of the matters to which they relate;

(ii) all sales and purchases of goods for a company dealing in goods;

(iii) all supporting documents must also be kept.

Answer 1

a) **31.3.07**

For the CAP ending 31 March 2006, the return must be filed by 31 March 2007. The notice was issued before the start of the 3 months leading up to the filing date and therefore the normal due filing date is relevant.

b) **24.6.07**

For the CAP ending 31 May 2006, the notice was issued within the 3 months leading up to the normal filing date of 31 May 2007. Therefore, as the company will always have a minimum of 3 months from the receipt of the notice, the due filing date is 24 June 2007.

Answer 2

	(a)	(b)
Correction of obvious errors	**31.10.07**	**31.3.07**
Enquiry deadline	**31.3.08**	**31.7.07**

In (a) the return is filed on time. Therefore, the Revenue has 9 months from the actual filing date to correct any obvious errors. That is 31 October 2007. The enquiry deadline runs exactly one year from the due filing date, which is 31 March 2008.

In (b) the return is filed a month late, the Revenue will have 9 months from the actual filing date to correct any obvious errors, which takes us to the 31 March 2007 and, will have one year from the next quarter date to start an enquiry. The next quarter date is 31 July 2006, add 12 months, that takes us to 31 July 2007.

SUMMARY – CORPORATION TAX SELF ASSESSMENT (CTSA)

Companies are required to file their return and statutory accounts 12 months after the end of the accounting period (or 3 months after the notice to submit a return has been issued, if later).

Where the company has a long period of account, there are two chargeable accounting periods and two returns, but both returns are due on the same date.

Companies have to self assess the amount of tax due.

There is a statutory obligation to notify chargeability where a company first comes within the charge to tax or comes back into the charge. Certain prescribed information must also be provided.

Schedule 18 FA 1998 lays down clear guidelines on how claims are to be made and amended.

There is a simplified procedure available for group relief claims.

Companies must keep records to support their tax returns.

C6: PAYMENT OF CORPORATION TAX

This chapter looks at the payment of corporation tax covering in particular:
- the due date for payment of a company's corporation tax liability;
- payment by instalments;
- group payment arrangements;
- group tax surrenders.

C6.1 Introduction

There are two types of company for payment purposes; those who pay tax at the full rate and those who do not.

Small companies (including marginal relief companies) are required to pay all of their corporation tax **9 months and 1 day** after the end of the chargeable accounting period.

For example, where a chargeable accounting period ends on 31 December 2005, the due and payable date for corporation tax is 1 October 2006.

Large companies are required to **pay their tax by quarterly instalments.** They had to make a balancing payment in the first 3 years of corporation tax self assessment, while the full system was phased in. This is no longer the case.

Large companies are defined as those who have notional profits (PCTCT + FII) in excess of £1,500,000. This figure is adjusted for short accounting periods and associated companies.

In summary, companies that pay tax at the full 30% rate pay tax by instalments. All other companies pay tax 9 months and one day after the chargeable accounting period.

C6.2 Payment of tax by instalments SI 1998/3175

Companies who **paid corporation tax at the full rate in the previous accounting period** will have an obligation to pay tax by instalments.

The **first year that a company is large, there is no need to pay tax by instalments, unless profits exceed £10 million**.

The £10 million is **divided among all the associated companies**, and is **reduced for accounting periods which are less than 12 months long**. However, the number of associated companies is arrived at by looking at the associated companies at the end of the **immediately preceding** accounting period.

Full rate companies whose CT **liability is below £10,000, are exempt** from quarterly payments. These could be companies that pay tax at 30%, but are part of a very large group, so their individual liability is relatively small.

The instalment payments are due as follows:

(i) The **first** payment is due **6 months plus 13 days from the start** of the accounting period;

(ii) **Subsequent** payments are due **3 months after** the previous instalment;

(iii) **Final** payment is due **3 months plus 14 days from the end** of the chargeable accounting period.

All tax due by instalments must be paid by the due date for the final payment, otherwise interest will run.

Illustration 1

Assume we have a chargeable accounting period for the year ending 31 March 2006.

The first instalment will be due 6 months plus 13 days from the start of this accounting period, i.e. 14 October 2005.

The next instalment is due 3 months later, i.e. 14 January 2006.

The following instalment is due 3 months after the previous, i.e. 14 April 2006.

The following instalment is due 3 months after the previous, i.e. 14 July 2006.

As this is the final instalment, it cannot be later than 3 months and 14 days from the end of the accounting period, i.e. 14 July 2006. For a twelve month accounting period the final instalment will fall 3 months and 14 days after the end of the accounting period.

Example 1

Assume we have a chargeable accounting period for the year ending on 31 July 2006. What are the instalment dates?

C6.3 Amount due by instalments

The amount of each instalment is based on the corporation tax liability of the **current year**, even though the company at the time of making the first instalment is only half way through the accounting period.

The system was initially **phased in**, such that in the first 3 years of CTSA not all of the tax was due by instalments. Since July 2002, companies pay 100% of their corporation tax by instalments.

The balancing payment was due 9 months and 1 day following the end of the chargeable accounting period.

Each instalment is calculated using the formula:

$$\frac{3}{N} \times \textbf{estimated corporation tax liability}$$

where N is the number of months in the accounting period.

The first thing we must do is to identify **how many instalments** there will actually be, using the $\frac{3}{N}$ formula. For a 12 month accounting period, the instalments will be $\frac{3}{12}$ths, $\frac{3}{12}$ths, $\frac{3}{12}$ths and $\frac{3}{12}$ths, of the tax due by instalments. This gives a total of four instalments, which are due.

For a 10 month accounting period, for example, the instalments will be as follows, $\frac{3}{10}$ths, $\frac{3}{10}$ths, $\frac{3}{10}$ths (which gives us $\frac{9}{10}$ths) and the final instalment will be just $\frac{1}{10}$th. If we pay another $\frac{3}{10}$ths we will actually have paid too much. This once again gives us four instalments.

For an 8 month accounting period the instalments due will be $\frac{3}{8}$ths, $\frac{3}{8}$ths and $\frac{2}{8}$ths, which gives only three instalments. For a 5 month period the instalments due will be $\frac{3}{5}$ths and $\frac{2}{5}$ths, which only gives two instalments.

Once we have established how many instalments are due we **then need to consider the amounts**. The important thing is to look at when the accounting period **ends**.

Illustration 2

Assume we have a chargeable accounting period for the year ending 31 March 2006, with profits of £2 million. This gives us a corporation tax liability at 30% of £600,000.

Each instalment amount will be £600,000 x $\frac{3}{12}$ = £150,000.

The first instalment will be due for payment on the 14 October 2005. The next 3 instalments will each be £150,000 due on 14 January, 14 April and 14 July 2006.

Example 2

Consider a chargeable accounting year ended 31 July 2006, with profits of £1.75 million. Show the amount of tax due on each of the appropriate dates.

Illustration 3

Consider an 8 month accounting period ended 31 December 2005 and a tax liability of £800,000. Our first step is to work out how many instalments there actually are. Here this will be $\frac{3}{8}$ths, $\frac{3}{8}$ths and $\frac{2}{8}$ths, which is the 3 instalments.

The first instalment is due 6 months plus 13 days from the start of the accounting period, which takes us to 14 November 2005. The next instalment is due 3 months later, which is 14 February 2006.

The final instalment cannot be **later than 3 months plus 14 days** from the end of the accounting period, which is 14 April 2006. If we were to use the three months rule we would go to 14 May 2006. This is not allowed so the final instalment falls on 14 April 2006.

Summary of Payments:

Instalment	*Due*	*Working*	*£*
1	14.11.05	£800,000 x 3/8	300,000
2	14.2.06	as above	300,000
3	14.4.06	£800,000 x 2/8	200,000
			£800,000

Example 3

Consider a 6 month accounting period ending on 30 June 2006, with a tax liability due of £100,000.

Calculate the amounts and due dates of the tax payable.

C6.4 Group payment arrangements

s.36 FA 1998

Where one or more companies in a 51% group (parent with 51% subsidiaries and their 51% subsidiaries) are liable to pay tax by instalments, they may nominate a company to deal with the group payment arrangements for the group. They complete a group payment arrangements document listing all the companies who are to participate and submit it to the Revenue two months before the first instalment payment is due by any group member.

"Group" is defined in section 36 FA 1998 as a company and all its 51 per cent subsidiaries, and their 51 per cent subsidiaries, and so on.

The application must state the start and end dates of the first period to which the arrangements are to apply. The arrangements will then apply automatically to subsequent periods of account unless and until the companies notify that they that wish to terminate it or the Revenue terminate it.

The nominated company undertakes to pay the corporation tax liabilities of the participating companies for accounting periods falling within the periods of account covered by the arrangements (the relevant accounting periods). It is up to the nominated company to determine how much to pay and when to make payments. Payment requests or reminders will not be issued.

For every period of account covered by a group payment arrangement, there is a "**Closing Date**". This is the date at which the nominated company's liabilities are fixed, and after which it must say how the payments it has made are to be allocated to the individual participating companies.

The nominated company then within 30 days irrevocably specifies in writing how payments made under the agreement should be apportioned amongst the participating companies. Payments to be apportioned will be net of any repayments made, and of any other apportionments already made (for example to a departing company).

C6.5 Group tax surrenders

s.102 FA 1989

This section relates to groups which have not entered into group payment arrangements.

A company that is due a refund can surrender it to a fellow group company. A group here is as for group relief. The companies must have the same accounting period and have been members of the group throughout the period from the start of the accounting period to the day the notice is given. The companies have to give joint notice in writing of the surrender, stating the name and tax reference of both companies and the type and amount of the refund surrender. The surrender can apply to the whole or part of a refund.

The recipient company is treated as having paid the amount surrendered on the later of the date it was paid or the due date of payment. The surrendering company is treated as receiving a refund on the same day. For instalment payments the tax is treated as being paid the later of the date it was paid by the surrendering company and the due date for the first instalment.

Interest paid by the surrendering company is treated as if it had been paid by the recipient company. Payments between the companies in respect of the surrender are ignored for tax and will not be treated as distributions.

Answer 1

14 February 2006
14 May 2006
14 August 2006
14 November 2006

Answer 2

Total tax due: £1,750,000 x 30% = £525,000

Each instalment will be

£525,000 x $\frac{3}{12}$ ths = £131,250

Due on	14.2.06	£131,250
	14.5.06	£131,250
	14.8.06	£131,250
	14.11.06	£131,250

Answer 3

How many instalments? 2 of $\frac{3}{6}$ ths each

Instalment	*Due*		£
1	**14.7.06**	£100,000 x 3/6	**50,000**
2	**14.10.06**	as above	**50,000**
Total			**£100,000**

SUMMARY - PAYMENT OF CORPORATION TAX

Companies paying tax at the full rate of 30% are required to pay their corporation tax by instalments.

Companies who do not pay tax at the full rate are not required to pay by instalments. Instead any tax is due 9 months and one day after the end of the accounting period.

Where the tax due is under £10,000, no instalments will be required.

A company is not required to pay in instalments for the first year it becomes large providing the profits are less than £10 million (twelve month limit).

For companies who do pay at the full rate the required instalments are due on the 14th of months 7,10, 13, and 16 counting from the start of the AP.

If the tax is not paid on the due date, interest will be charged from the due date to the date before it is paid.

Where there is a 51 % group the group can apply for the nominated company to make all payments of tax for the group and allocate the payments after the closing date.

If the group payment arrangements are not used amounts of tax overpaid can be surrendered within a group relief group.

C7: INTEREST ON LATE PAID TAX

> This chapter looks at interest and in particular it covers:
> - interest on late paid tax and repayments;
> - the effect of amounts carried back.

C7.1 Introduction

Interest runs **from the due date of payment to the day before the actual date of payment** of the tax where corporation tax is paid late. s.97A TMA 1970 s.826 ICTA 1988

This applies to all payments of corporation tax - whether the company pays by instalments or not. So small companies, who are required to pay their tax 9 months and 1 day after the end of the accounting period, will also be charged interest where they pay that tax late.

Problems are experienced particularly by larger companies, as **tax due by instalments is based on the tax liability of the current year**, yet the payments are made during the year. A company will therefore have the problem of **estimating its tax bill**, which could well change during the year, so what they pay may not reflect their actual liability. If they do not pay enough, interest will run. If they pay too much, they will get repayment interest, but at a lower rate.

Illustration 1

Guesswork Limited estimates its profits for the year ended 31 May 2006 to be £2 million when it makes its first instalment of corporation tax.

As this is a 12 month CAP each instalment will be 3/12 x 100% = 25%. The amount of tax due on 14.12.05 will therefore be:

£2,000,000 x 30% = £600,000 x 25% = £150,000

At the beginning of March the company wins a major new contract which is likely to increase the company's predicted profit for the year to £2.2 million. For its second instalment due on 14.3.06 the company would be advised to make a payment as follows:-

£2,200,000 x 30% = £660,000 x 50% =	£330,000
Less tax paid on 14.12.05	(150,000)
	£180,000

By the end of the accounting period the draft accounts reveal a taxable profit of £2.25 million. The company should therefore pay tax as follows on 14.6.06 in respect of its third instalment:

£2,250,000 x 30% = £675,000 x 75% =	£506,250
Less tax paid so far	(330,000)
	£176,250

By the end of August the company has been audited and the profit originally anticipated has been reduced to £2.15 million. The company should therefore pay tax as follows on 14.9.06 in respect of its fourth instalment:

£2,150,000 x 30% = £645,000 x 100% =	£645,000
Less tax paid so far	(506,250)
	£138,750

The company prepares its final corporation tax computations by the end of February 2007, which show a final taxable profit of £2,190,000.

The company therefore pays tax as follows on 1.3.07:

£2,190,000 x 30% =	£657,000
Less tax paid by instalments	(645,000)
	£12,000

It is normal for a company to **keep revising its estimated corporation tax liability** in this way.

Payments Summary:

	Paid £	*Cumulative* £	*Due* £	*Cumulative* £	*Underpaid/ (overpaid)*
14.12.05	150,000	150,000	164,250	164,250	14,250
14.3.06	180,000	330,000	164,250	328,500	(1,500)
14.6.06	176,250	506,250	164,250	492,750	(13,500)
14.9.06	138,750	645,000	164,250	657,000	12,000
1.3.07	12,000	657,000			
	657,000		657,000		

The Revenue will issue an interest statement once the return has been submitted and the final liability has been calculated.

Interest Summary:

14.12.05 to 13.3.06	Interest **charged** on £14,250 underpaid
14.3.06 to 13.6.06	Interest **credit** on £1,500 overpaid
14.6.06 to 13.9.06	Interest **credit** on £13,500 overpaid
14.9.06 to 28.2.07	Interest **charged** on £12,000 underpaid

Assuming a rate of interest on underpaid tax of 7% and a rate of interest on overpaid tax of 5% the interest position can be calculated as follows:

	£
$£14{,}250 \times 7\% \times \frac{90}{365} =$	245.96
$£(1{,}500) \times 5\% \times \frac{92}{365}$	(18.90)
$£(13{,}500) \times 5\% \times \frac{92}{365}$	(170.14)
$£12{,}000 \times 7\% \times \frac{168}{365}$	386.63
Interest due to the Revenue	**£443.55**

The Revenue will raise an **interest demand** which **must be settled within 30 days.** If it is settled late there will be interest charged on the interest.

The Revenue have confirmed that they will accept payments of corporation tax at any time so if the company calculates and pays its corporation tax earlier this will stop the interest running.

Any interest received will be taxed under Schedule DIII. Any interest paid by the company will be treated as interest paid on a non-trading loan and can be deducted from DIII income. s.100 FA 1996

C7.2 Effect of carry backs

Where losses are carried back under s.393A(1) and result in a repayment of tax, then for calculating the interest on this repayment **it is treated as tax repaid for the accounting period of the loss unless the repayment arises in respect of an accounting period that falls wholly within the twelve months prior** to the one in which the loss arose.

If the carry back reduces an amount of unpaid tax, **interest will cease to run from the due date of the period in which the loss was made** for the amount of tax unpaid that the carry back negates. Apart from this it is ignored in calculating the interest on unpaid tax except for an accounting period falling wholly within the 12 months before the one in which the loss arose.

For carry back of **non-trade deficits** on loan relationships the calculation of interest on underpaid or overpaid corporation tax is not affected except that in the case of underpayments **the amount met by the carry back is treated as paid on the due date for the accounting period in which the deficit arose**. Otherwise it is treated as a repayment of corporation tax for the accounting period in which the deficit arose.

SUMMARY – INTEREST ON LATE PAID TAX

Interest runs on tax paid late from the due date to the day before payment.

Interest will be paid on overpaid tax from the due date/date paid to the day before the repayment.

Tax repaid as a result of a loss carry back is treated as tax repaid for the year giving rise to the loss unless the accounting period of the carry back falls wholly within the twelve months before that of the loss.

Tax repaid as a result of a DIII deficit carry back is treated as a repayment of corporation tax for the year in which the deficit arose.

C8: CTSA PENALTY REGIME

This chapter examines the Corporation Tax Self Assessment (CTSA) procedures relating to penalties.

C8.1 Introduction

The CTSA penalty regime has been introduced to ensure compliance with the various CTSA administrative requirements. The penalty regime aims to penalise various misdemeanours. These include **late filing** of returns, **failure to notify** chargeability, **record-keeping** failures and **fraudulent or negligent** returns.

C8.2 Late filing of returns

All companies are **required to file their return within 12 months of the end of the period of account (POA)** which is the company's financial reporting period i.e. the period for which the company has made up its set of accounts. In most situations the period of account and the chargeable accounting period will be the same.

There are two types of penalties for the late filing of a return; **a flat rate penalty** and a **tax geared penalty**.

A **flat rate** penalty of **£100** will be levied automatically by the Revenue (subject to a **7 working day period of grace**) where the return is **up to three months late**. The £100 penalty stands regardless of the level of profits. Para 17 Sch 18 FA 1998

The penalty itself increases to **£200** where the return is **more than 3 months late**. These penalties are increased to **£500 and £1,000** if this is the **company's third consecutive offence**.

As for the **tax geared** penalties, a **10%** penalty will arise if the return is **filed more than 18 months** after the end of the chargeable accounting period. The 10% will be taken on any corporation tax owing at that 18 month point. This penalty doubles to **20%** where the return is **filed more than 24 months** after the chargeable accounting period but this is based on the **tax owing at the 18 month point**. Para 18 Sch 18 FA 1998

Remember that the end of the **period of account** is the trigger in respect of the **flat rate penalties** as these are based on the **filing date** but the end of the **chargeable accounting period** triggers the **tax geared** penalties.

Illustration 1

Harris Limited makes up accounts for the 16 months ended 31 August 2005. This is a long POA for tax purposes and must be split into two separate CAPs - one for the first 12 months and then the balance of the period.

The company will have 2 CAPs, 2 payment dates and 1 filing date which we can remember by calling this the "2-2-1" rule.

The CAPs are the 12 m/e 30 April 2005 and the 4 m/e 31 August 2005. This leads to two separate payment dates: the liability in respect of the 12 m/e 30 April 2005 is due on 1 February 2006 and the liability in respect of the 4 month period is due on 1 June 2006.

This is on the assumption that the company is a small company and not liable under the CTSA instalment regime.

There is only one filing date because this is triggered by the POA. Both returns are due within 12 months of the end of the POA so the due date for the filing of both the returns is 31 August 2006.

There will be penalties if Harris Ltd fails to comply with CTSA requirements. The £100 penalty will be triggered if either of the returns is filed more than 7 working days after 31 August 2006. This applies per return, so two returns filed late means £200. Each penalty itself increases to £200 if either of the returns are filed after 30 November 2006, in other words are over 3 months late.

Note: The Revenue allows a 7 day period of grace for filing the return, however this is by concession.

The penalty of 10% of the tax outstanding is triggered if either of the returns are filed more than 18 months after the end of the relevant CAP:

y/e	30.4.05 + 18m	=	31.10.06
4m/e	31.8.05 + 18m	=	28.2.07

The penalty of 20% of tax outstanding is triggered if either the returns are filed more than 24 months after the end of the relevant CAP and will be chargeable on any tax outstanding at the 18 month point - not the 24 month point.

y/e	30.4.05 + 24m	=	30.4.07
4m/e	31.8.05 + 24m	=	31.8.07

C8.3 Failure to notify chargeability

For accounting periods beginning on or after 22 July 2004 a penalty will arise for companies failing to notify chargeability within three months of the start of their first accounting period or of them coming back within the charge to tax.

The penalty will be £300 for initial failure with a potential penalty of £60 a day for continued failure once the initial penalty has been levied. s.98 TMA 1970

A penalty of £3,000 can be charged if incorrect information is provided **fraudulently or negligently.** s.98 TMA 1970

For accounting periods beginning before 22 July 2004, a company which was chargeable to corporation tax and had not received a notice requiring a return had to notify the Revenue of its chargeability within 12 months from the end of its accounting period. Para 2 Sch 18 FA 1998

The penalty for late notification is the **tax due** and unpaid at that 12 month point. Therefore, if the tax has been paid, there will be no late notification penalty.

C8.4 Record keeping failures

Companies are required to **keep certain records** for **at least 6 years** by the end of the chargeable accounting period. These are the same as the Companies Act requirements and will include: Para 21 Sch 18 FA 1998

(i) records of receipts and expenses, and the matters to which they relate;

(ii) details of all sales and purchases made in the course of trade, where the trade involves dealing in goods; and

(iii) supporting documents, such as accounts, books, vouchers, contracts, deeds etc.

The penalty for failing to keep these records is **£3,000 per chargeable accounting period.** Para 23 Sch 18 FA 1998

C8.5 Fraudulent or negligent returns

Negligent for these purposes includes any innocent error that the company fails to correct without "unreasonable delay". The penalty also extends to fraudulent or negligent claims made on the return or amendments to it. Para 20 Sch 18 FA 1998

The penalty is **up to 100% of the tax avoided** as a result of the negligence or fraud on the return, i.e. the difference between the tax that should be payable and the tax that actually was paid based on that return. This penalty is subject to mitigation based on the size of the offence, the degree of co-operation and voluntary disclosure of the error giving rise to the under-declaration of tax.

C8.6 Not producing documents

A company failing to produce documents for the purpose of an enquiry is liable: Para 29 Sch 18 FA 1998

(i) £50 penalty
(ii) Where there is continuing failure after the above penalty further penalties of £30 a day if the penalty is imposed by a Revenue Officer £150 a day if it is imposed by the Commissioners.

C8.7 Multiple penalties

Where the company receives more than one penalty that is determined by the tax payable for the accounting period, the second and subsequent penalties are reduced so that they do not exceed the maximum of such penalties. s. 90 Sch 18 FA 1998

C8.8 Failure to pay by instalments

If a company deliberately and recklessly fails to pay its instalments or makes a claim for repayment of instalments, there is a penalty of twice the amount of interest charged on the tax unpaid. Para 13 SI 1999/3175

SUMMARY - CTSA PENALTY REGIME

Penalties will apply where a return is late.

The flat rate penalties are:

£100 up to 3 months late;
£200 more than 3 months late;

Tax geared penalties are charged if the return is filed more than 18 months after the end of the CAP. The penalties are:

10% of tax unpaid at 18 months if return > 18 months after CAP
20% of tax unpaid at 18 months if return > 24 months after CAP

An initial penalty of £300 will be charged where a company fails to notify chargeability in accordance with s.55 FA 2004. An additional penalty of £60 a day can be charged.

A £3,000 penalty can be charged where incorrect information is provided negligently or fraudulently in relation to notification of chargeability.

Penalties will also be applied where there has been a failure to keep records or the return is incorrect due to fraudulent or negligent conduct.

C9: INCOME FROM PROPERTY

This chapter will consider the taxation of income from property.

C9.1 Introduction

Income from **UK situated property** is taxed on companies under **Schedule A**.

Income from **overseas property** is taxed under **Schedule D Case V**.

Income from all property is treated as a single source of business income. A single source means that all profits and losses **are pooled together**. Where the pool creates a profit, we tax it under Schedule A; where the pool creates a loss, we relieve it under the Schedule A loss relief rules.

We bring the income into charge to tax using accounting principles as applied for Schedule D Case I, ie the basis of taxation will be an accruals basis for the recognition of income.

Example 1

Renton Limited acquires an investment property on 1 July 2005 and lets it out immediately on an annual rent of £24,000, payable on the first day of each month in advance.

How much rental income will be taxable in Renton Limited's accounting period for the year ended 31 March 2006?

C9.2 Expenses

As rental income is treated as business income, deduction of expenses follows the normal rules. **Relief** is given for **expenses** which have been incurred **wholly and exclusively for the purposes of the rental business.** This is the same as deduction for trading expenses as given by Section 74 ICTA 1988.

The detailed rules on allowable expenses are covered within the Income Tax course.

Common deductible expenses include:

(i) Maintenance and repairs but not improvements - redecoration would therefore qualify but not anything to actually improve the fabric of the building. For instance, a complete refurbishment when the property is first purchased would not be an allowable deduction against rental income. If a window gets broken and a new pane is fitted, that is deductible as a maintenance or repair cost.

(ii) Insurance

(iii) Management and agents fees

(iv) Rent collection costs

(v) Advertising for tenants

(vi) 10% wear and tear allowance - this is only available for furnished property and is calculated as 10% x (rents less council tax and water rates).

Example 2

Comlet Limited lets a furnished property on commercial terms. The rental income charged for the period to 31 December 2005 was £20,000 rising to £22,000 for the period to 31 December 2006.

Expenses relating to letting included:

	£
Water rates	1,000
Insurance	500
Ground rent	700

Agent's fees amounted to 15% of rental income. In November 2005 the tenant accidentally damaged the ceiling in the living room. Comlet Limited took the opportunity to refurbish the whole room at a total cost of £4,000. The cost relating to rectifying the damage amounted to only £500.

Comlet Limited makes up accounts for the year ended 31 March 2006. What is the Schedule A income?

C9.3 Loan interest

For companies, **interest on a loan taken out to purchase a rental property is not an allowable expense** in arriving at the income taxed under Schedule A. Instead the loan interest is treated as a non-trading loan relationship debit under the loan relationship rules. These are covered in a later chapter.

C9.4 Schedule A losses

The relief for Schedule A losses is covered later in the chapter entitled Relief for Other Losses.

Answer 1

The rental income accrues for the period 1 July 2005 to 31 March 2006, which is a period of nine months.

£24,000 x 9/12 = **£18,000**

Answer 2

	Y/e 31.3.06 £
Rental income accrued:	
£(20,000 x $\frac{9}{12}$) + (22,000 x $\frac{3}{12}$)	20,500
Expenses:	
Agent's fees: £20,500 x 15%	(3,075)
Redecoration	Nil
Water rates	(1,000)
Insurance	(500)
Ground rent	(700)
Wear and tear: 10% x (20,500 – 1,000)	(1,950)
Schedule A income	**£13,275**

SUMMARY – INCOME FROM PROPERTY

Schedule A income is taxed on an accruals basis.

Relief is given for expenses incurred wholly and exclusively for the Schedule A business.

Interest on loans taken out to buy properties is never a Schedule A expense for companies, it is instead relieved under the loan relationship rules.

C10: LOAN RELATIONSHIPS

This chapter looks at loan relationships covering in particular:
- the meaning of loan relationship;
- trade v non trade;
- relief for non trade deficits;
- connected parties.

C10.1 Definition

s.81 FA 1996

A loan relationship is **any transaction involving** the **borrowing or lending of money.** For a loan relationship to exist there must be a transaction for the lending of money.

This will include **interest received** on **bank accounts**, interest received on **loan stock** or debentures or even interest paid to the company by the government on a tax repayment.

The loan relationship rules also cover **interest paid** by a company - for example; interest on a **bank overdraft**, debenture interest paid to loan stockholders or **interest on a loan** taken out by the company to buy a new building or to purchase trading stock.

Example 1

Which of the following constitute a loan relationship?

a) Debentures in a company

b) Government gilts

c) Bank deposit account

d) Bank overdraft

e) Debtors ledger

f) Loan to an employee

C10.2 Debits and credits

s.84 -s.85 FA 1996

Debits and credits on loan relationships follow the accounting treatment, i.e. the profit and loss account definition, in that **debits are expenses and credits are income.** The rule introduced in Finance Act 1996 is that the **amounts put through the profit and loss account** or income statement in accordance with UK generally accepted accounting practice or international accounting standards, are the amounts that are tax deductible (if expenses) or that are taxable (if income).

The amounts put through the profit and loss account and other statements for accounting purposes are interest **receivable** and interest **payable**.

It is not just interest that comes within the loan relationship rules. **All debits and credits in relation to the debt liability** are taxed under the rules.

Example 2

Which of the following are eligible for tax relief under the loan relationship rules?

a) Interest payable

b) Early redemption penalties

c) Bank arrangement fees

d) Amounts written off loans (bad debts)

e) Loss on disposal of loan stock

C10.3 Trading v non-trading s.82 FA 1996

A company can be either a debtor or a creditor in terms of a loan relationship. In either case the tax treatment is determined by looking at whether the loan relationship is **trade or non-trade**.

Looking at the position where the company is the borrower, we ask "why did the company borrow the money"?

A **trading purpose** is defined as a loan taken out for the purposes of the trade. Generally speaking, this is where the **funds are used to generate income** which is **taxed under Schedule DI**. An example could be a loan to buy stock used in the trade.

The loan equally may have been entered into for a **non-trading purpose**. This is where the **funds are used to generate income** which is **not taxed under DI**. A good example of this could be a loan taken out to buy units in a unit trust, which generates investment income rather than trading income.

Example 3

Classify the following loans between trading and non-trading:

a) Loan to buy a factory

b) Loan to buy rental premises

c) Loan to buy shares on the stock market

d) Loan to buy shares in a trading subsidiary company

e) Funds lent to a subsidiary for the purpose of its trade.

When we look at loans where the company is the creditor, we define trade and non-trade slightly differently. This time we ask was the lending of the money done as an integral part of the company's trade? Here the answer will only be "yes" in the case of banks and financial institutions.

C10.4 Tax treatment

This can best be summarised by a flowchart:

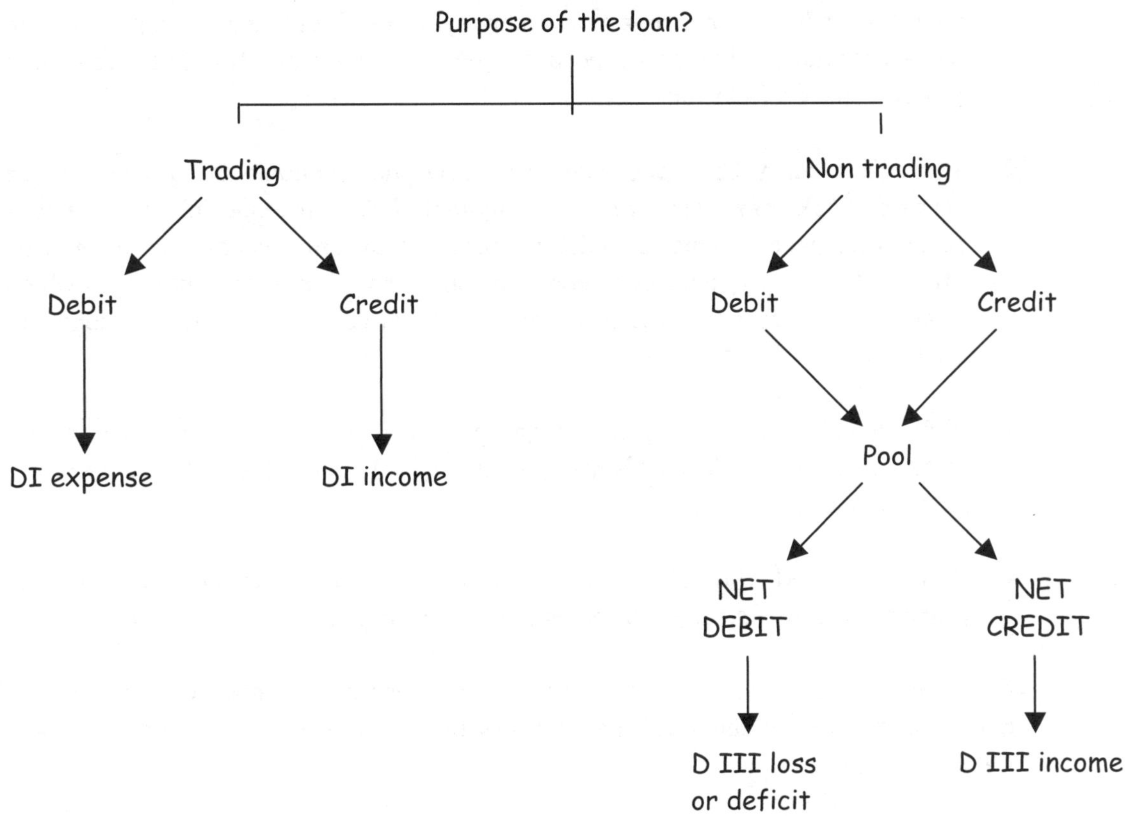

C10.5 DIII loss relief

The rules for relief for Schedule D Case III deficits (or "DIII losses") are very similar to the rules relating to Schedule D Case I losses, which will be covered in a later chapter. s. 83(2) FA 1996

Illustration 1

Assume a company takes out a loan of £100,000 to buy a portfolio of quoted shares. Interest payable on the loan is £10,000 per annum.

This is quite clearly a non-trade loan as the income generated by the quoted shares will be dividend income which is not taxed under Schedule DI.

Assume the company has a bank deposit account which earns interest of £6,000 per annum. This interest is taxable under Schedule DIII.

Interest payable on non-trading loans is deducted from DIII income as follows;

Schedule DIII credits	6,000
Schedule DIII debits	(10,000)
DIII loss	£(4,000)

The next step to consider is what the company can do with this DIII loss?

1. Relief is allowed in the **current year against other income** before charges including capital gains. This is given in priority to Schedule D Case I current year loss relief. Therefore if a company makes DIII and DI losses in the same year, and makes two separate current year claims, the DIII loss claim will be relieved first; or s.83(2)(a) FA 1996

2. There is a carry back provision, whereby the Schedule DIII loss can be **carried back one year** and set **against DIII income** in the previous accounting period. This is DIII as reduced by any charges on income or other losses, in the previous year's computation. This is the only claim which is determined by a set formula and is not entirely open to the company to decide; or s.83(2)(c) FA1996

3. DIII deficits are available for **group relief** by allowing the loss to be transferred to a fellow 75% group company. These rules will be covered in detail in a later chapter; or s.403 ICTA 1988

4. **Carry forward** the DIII loss, and set it **against future non-trading profits**. This is basically any income and gains in the future year, except DI. s.83(3A) FA1996

It should be appreciated that all of these claims are **independent** and we can make a current year claim before we carry back or a group relief claim whenever we want to, etc.

What we generally must remember is the **two key rules** for relieving losses:

(i) set them off against the income subject to tax at the **highest marginal rate**; and

(ii) try to relieve them **earlier rather than later**.

In the claim, we must **specify the amount that we wish to relieve** and therefore, it does gives us flexibility to use part of the loss in say, the current year, and part of it by say group relief, if that is what we want to do.

To the extent that the DIII deficit is not used by group relief current year claim or carry back it will go forward to be used against non-trading profit of the succeeding accounting period. The company will have **two years to make a claim not to have the deficit set off against non-trading profit** in the succeeding accounting period. Para 4 Sch 8 FA 1996

Example 4

Which of the following is not available to relieve a Schedule D Case III deficit?

a) Set off against general income in the current year

b) Set off against general income in the preceding 12 months

c) Group relief

d) Carry forward against non-trading profits in future periods

C10.6 Late interest

Where the parties to a loan relationship are **connected** and the interest is **not paid within 12 months of the end of the accounting period,** a debit for that interest **will not be allowed** until it has been paid if the creditor is not within the charge to corporation tax in respect of the loan - for example where the creditor is the overseas parent of the debtor. Para 2 Sch 9 FA 1996

Example 5

When is interest deductible on a **paid** basis?:

a) If the interest remains unpaid 12 months after the year end; or

b) Where the borrower and lender are connected; or

c) Where the lender is not chargeable to corporation tax; or

d) Where all of the above apply;

Answer 1

All but the debtors ledger (e) - this is not a loan relationship as it has not arisen through the lending of money but through the company selling goods or providing services to a customer.

Answer 2

All items are tax deductible as they are all amounts put through the accounts relating to a loan.

Answer 3

(a) The loan taken out to buy the factory is a **trading loan**, providing the factory is used by the company for the purpose of its trade.

(b) The loan taken out to buy rented premises generates Schedule A income, therefore, as this is not DI, it is a **non-trading loan**.

(c) The loan taken out to buy shares on the stock market produces dividend income, again this is not DI, so is a **non-trading loan**.

(d) Equally the loan taken out to buy shares in the trading subsidiary, is also a **non-trading loan** because, again these shares will generate dividend income. It doesn't matter what the subsidiary actually does, what is important is that we are buying shares and shares do not generate trading income (unless the company is a share dealing company).

(e) The loan taken out to lend money to a subsidiary for the purposes of its trade is again a **non-trading loan**, because the loan is not taken out to fund the trade of the lending company. This of course is on the assumption that the lending company is not a bank.

Answer 4

The answer is **(b)**

The set off is against DIII income (not general income) of the preceding 12 months.

Answer 5

The answer is **(d)**

SUMMARY - LOAN RELATIONSHIPS

A loan relationship arises when there is the lending of money

Interest payable on trading loans is deducted from DI income.

Interest payable on non trading loans (e.g. interest on a loan to buy an investment property) is deducted from DIII income.

Interest receivable will be treated as DIII in most cases.

DIII debits and credits are pooled if the DIII debits exceed the DIII credits then loss relief is available for the resulting deficit.

A DIII deficit can be set off against other income in the current year, group relieved, carried back or carried forward

C11: RELIEF FOR TRADING LOSSES

This chapter examines the relief available to a company when it makes a trading loss in particular:

- the availability of relief for trading losses in the current and earlier accounting periods;
- the effect of carrying forward the trading loss to a later period.

C11.1 Introduction

A company makes a loss when its income is less than its expenses. The loss per the accounts is adjusted for the normal tax deductions, such as disallowed expenditure (e.g. entertaining, depreciation) and can be increased by claiming capital allowances. A company may not wish to claim all of the capital allowances in order to reduce the amount of loss.

Where the adjusted Schedule D Case I figure is a loss, the Schedule D Case I assessment in the corporation tax computation will be nil. The loss itself is relieved by making a number of separate claims.

C11.2 Relief for trading losses

There are a number of options available:

(i) Set against total profits before charges in the current accounting period. s.393A(1)(a) ICTA 1988

(ii) **Carry back** and **set against total profits before non-trade charges** in the preceding **12 months**. s.393A(1)(b) ICTA 1988

(iii) **Carry forward** and set against next available **future profits from the same trade.** s.393(1) ICTA 1988

(iv) **Surrender** the loss **to** a **fellow 75% owned group company**. This type of relief is known as group relief. These rules will be covered in a later chapter. s.402 ICTA 1988

C11.3 Current year relief

The loss is set against total **profits before charges** of the current year.

The claim must be for the lower of the available loss or the available profit. In other words, no partial claims are allowed, the claim must either use all of the loss, or eliminate all of the available profits. s. 393A(1)(a

Illustration 1

Lossington Ltd has the following results for the year to 31 March 2006:

	£
Trading loss	(70,000)
Chargeable gains	15,000
Schedule A	21,000
Charge on income	(3,000)

The current year claim under s.393A(1)(a) will be as follows:

	12m to 31.3.06
	£
Schedule DI	Nil
Schedule A	21,000
Chargeable gains	15,000
Total profits	36,000
s.393A(1)(a) Current year loss	(36,000)
	-
Charge on income	Unrelieved
PCTCT	-

As the loss is offset before the deduction for charges on income, the charge here is unrelieved.

The unrelieved trading loss of £34,000 will be carried forward against future profits from the same trade.

This is summarised in a loss memorandum as follows:

Loss memorandum	£
Loss (y/e 31.3.06)	70,000
Current year claim s.393A(1)(a)	(36,000)
Unrelieved loss to carry forward	£34,000

C11.4 Unrelieved charges

Unrelieved **trade charges** may be carried forward and set against future profits of the same trade i.e. they are **added to the s.393(1)** loss carry forward.

However, following the introduction of the **IFA** rules with effect from 1 April 2002, trade charges became very rare, and, looking forward, trade charges no longer exist. Therefore, it makes sense to ignore them for the rest of this session.

Non-trade charges, such as Gift Aid payments, are **lost** if there is no profit in the current year to set them against. They cannot be carried forward.

C11.5 Carry back of losses

The claim to **carry back** a loss under s.393A(1)(b) may **only** be made **once a current year claim has been made**, under s.393A(1)(a) - i.e. (a) before (b). s. 393A(1)(b)

The loss carried back is set against profits in the **previous 12 months**, before any non-trade charges.

As with the current year claim, the carry back claim must be for the lower of the available loss or the available profit.

Illustration 2

Assume in the last illustration that Lossington Limited had the following income in the previous 12 month accounting period, the year ended 31 March 2005:

	£
Schedule D Case I	10,000
Schedule A	21,000
Gift Aid payment	(1,000)

As a current year claim to use the loss in the year ended 31 March 2006 has already been made, we can now carry the loss back to the year ended 31 March 2005.

The carry back claim under s.393A(1)(b) will be

	12m to 31.3.05
	£
Schedule D Case I	10,000
Schedule A	21,000
Total	31,000
Current year loss (nil as there is no loss in this year)	-
	31,000
s.393A(1)b Losses carried back	(31,000)
	Nil
Non-trade charges (Gift Aid)	Unrelieved
PCTCT	Nil

This further use of the loss can again be shown in the loss memorandum as follows:

Loss Memo:	£
Total loss	70,000
Current year claim (from Illustration 1)	(36,000)
	34,000
Carry back claim s.393A(1)(b)	(31,000)
Loss to carry forward	£3,000

If a company wishes to make a claim under s. 393(A) to use its losses in the current year/preceding year, it must **notify the Revenue within two years** of the end of the accounting period in which the loss was made.

In this example a claim must be made no later than 31 March 2008. The Revenue may extend this time limit at their discretion.

C11.6 Losses carried forward

The losses are set against the first available future profits from the same trade under s.393(1) i.e. **against DI income only**. s. 393(1)

No claim is required as the relief is given **automatically.** The relief is compulsory - if we have a loss brought forward, it will automatically be set against the next available future profits from the same trade.

Illustration 3

In the Lossington Limited illustration there is an unrelieved loss of £3,000.

Assume the company has the following results in the year ended 31 March 2007:

Schedule D Case I	£15,000
Schedule A	£21,000

The relief available under s.393(1) will be as follows:

	£
Schedule D Case I	15,000
s.393(1) loss brought forward	(3,000)
	12,000
Schedule A	21,000
PCTCT	£33,000

Finally here let's show the computations of PCTCT for all three years here in columns next to each other, as you would probably set it out like this in an examination question:

	Year ended 31 March		
	2005	*2006*	*2007*
	£	£	£
Schedule D Case I	10,000	nil	15,000
Less losses b/fwd	-	-	(3,000)
	10,000	nil	12,000
Schedule A	21,000	21,000	21,000
Chargeable gains	-	15,000	-
	31,000	36,000	33,000
Less current year loss		(36,000)	
	31,000	nil	33,000
Less carried back loss	(31,000)		
	nil	nil	33,000
Less non trade charges	Lost	Lost	-
PCTCT	nil	nil	33,000

Example 1

X plc has the following results:

	Y/e 31.3.05	*Y/e 31.3.06*	*Y/e 31.3.07*
	£	£	£
Schedule DI profit	100,000	nil	14,000
Trading loss		(150,000)	
Schedule DIII	10,000	12,000	5,000
Chargeable gain	12,000	-	-
Non trade charge	(500)	(500)	(500)

You are required to:

(a) Show how the trading loss will be relieved assuming relief is required as early as possible

(b) List any amounts to be carried forward, indicating the relief available

(c) Calculate the repayment of tax due to X plc as a result of the loss relief.

C11.7 Carry back complications

Remember that the carry back of a loss is for a full 12 month period. If the previous accounting period is less than 12 months, you can carry back to the period before that one by **applying time apportionment to the profits before charges of the previous period.**

Example 2

Losster Limited has the following results in recent years:

	Y/e 30.9.04	*6m/e 31.3.05*	*Y/e 31.3.06*	*Y/e 31.3.07*
	£	£	£	£
Schedule D Case I	26,000	12,000	nil	6,000
Trading loss			(50,000)	
Schedule A	10,000	5,000	10,000	10,000
Non-trade charges	(1,000)	(1,000)	(1,000)	(1,000)

(a) What will the S. 393A(1)(a) claim be?

(b) What will the S. 393A(1)(b) claim be?

(c) How much loss will be relieved under S. 393(1)?

Answer 1

(a) X plc

	Year ended 31 March		
	2005	*2006*	*2007*
	£	£	£
Schedule D Case I	100,000	nil	14,000
Less losses b/fwd	-	-	(14,000)
	100,000	nil	nil
Schedule DIII	10,000	12,000	5,000
Chargeable gains	12,000	-	-
	122,000	12,000	5,000
Less current year loss		(12,000)	
	122,000	nil	5,000
Less carried back loss	(122,000)		
	nil	nil	5,000
Less non trade charges	Lost	Lost	(500)
PCTCT	Nil	Nil	4,500

(b) Loss Memo:

	£
Loss y/e 31.3.06	150,000
Used current year 31.3.06	(12,000)
Used previous year 31.3.05	(122,000)
Available to carry forward	16,000
Used following year 31.3.07	(14,000)
Loss available to c/fwd	2,000

(c) Tax repayment y/e 31 March 2005

Original computation:

	£
DI profit	100,000
DIII	10,000
Gain	12,000
	122,000
Less: non trade charge	(500)
PCTCT	121,500
GCT @ 19%	£23,085

The whole of the tax of £23,085 will be repaid as PCTCT is reduced to nil after the carry back of losses.

Answer 2

(a) Current Year Claim

	Y/e 31.3.06
	£
Schedule D Case I	Nil
Schedule A	10,000
Total Profits	10,000
s.393A(1)(a) current year loss	**(10,000)**
	Nil
Non-trade charges	Unrelieved
PCTCT	Nil

Loss Memo:

	£
Total loss	50,000
Current year claim	(10,000)
	£40,000

The unrelieved non trade charges will be lost.

(b) Losses Carried Back

	Y/e 30.9.04	6m/e 31.3.05
	£	£
Schedule D Case I	26,000	12,000
Schedule A	10,000	5,000
	36,000	17,000
s.393A(1)(b) loss brought back	**(18,000)***	**(17,000)**
	18,000	Nil
Non-trade charges	(1,000)	Unrelieved
PCTCT	£17,000	Nil

* The time apportioned carry back is calculated on profits before charges i.e. £36,000 x $\frac{6}{12}$ = £18,000.

(c) Loss Carried Forward

	Y/e 31.3.07
	£
Schedule D Case I	6,000
Losses brought forward	**(5,000)**
	1,000
Schedule A	10,000
	11,000
Non-trade charges	(1,000)
PCTCT	**£10,000**

Loss memo:

	£
Total loss	50,000
Current year	(10,000)
Carried back to 6m/e 31.3.05	(17,000)
to 12m/e 30.9.04	
$£36,000 \times \frac{6}{12}$	(18,000)
Carried forward	5,000
Offset in y/e 31.3.07	(5,000)
Carried forward	Nil

SUMMARY - RELIEF FOR TRADING LOSSES

When a company makes a trading loss it can relieve it against the profits of:

(i) the same accounting period, then

(ii) the previous 12 months, and any unused loss is then automatically

(iii) c/fwd against future trading profits only.

A carry back claim can only be made after a current year claim has been made.

Both claims are all-or-nothing - partial claims are not permitted.

The time limit for these claims is two years from the end of the loss making accounting period.

Care needs to be taken if there is a short accounting period, as the carry back must be against 12 months worth of profits, if the loss is large enough.

When a loss is carried back it will generate a repayment of CT paid for the earlier accounting period.

C12: RELIEF FOR OTHER LOSSES

This chapter examines the relief available to a company when it makes other losses, covering in particular:

- Schedule A losses;
- Management expenses;
- Capital losses;
- Terminal loss relief;
- Schedule DIII losses;
- Schedule DVI losses on IFAs.

C12.1 Other losses

Other losses include:

(i) Schedule A losses, on property income;

(ii) Excess management expenses, for companies with investment business;

(iii) Capital losses.

(iv) Schedule D Case III losses, being deficits on non trading loan relationships;

(v) DVI losses on IFAs

C12.2 Schedule A losses

A company may rent out a number of different properties, some may make a profit, some a loss. All of the **results of each property are pooled together** into a Schedule A pool, very similar to the rules for pooling debits and credits for loan relationships.

Where the pool produces a net profit, this is simply taxed under Schedule A as income. Where the pool produces a net loss, relief will be available.

Initially **Schedule A losses must be set against other profits in the current accounting period**. No claim is required as the relief is automatic. The set off is compulsory and when we make a Schedule A loss, we simply include a negative figure in the corporation tax computation. s.392A ICTA 1988

The relief is **given in priority** to any **DI losses** of that year. The excess Schedule A loss, i.e. the amount of the Schedule A loss that exceeds profits the current year, will be **available for group relief** by surrendering it to fellow 75% group companies. A claim is required under S. 402 ICTA 1988.

If group relief does not relieve the rest of the loss or is not available, the **loss is automatically carried forward** and treated as a Schedule A loss of the next period and thus it is possible to set it against other profits in that future period.

Losses on overseas properties (Schedule DV Losses) are pooled together with profits on overseas properties. Any resulting loss is then carried forward and set against Schedule DV profits of future accounting periods.

s.392B

There is no "mixing and matching" of DV losses with Schedule A profits.

Remember that a Schedule A loss is automatically set against current year income (which could include income taxed under DV).

C12.3 Management expenses

Management expenses are **set against investment income and gains** in the **current** accounting **period**. This relief, like that for Schedule A losses, is automatic and compulsory.

To the extent that the management expenses exceed current year income and gains, they are "excess". Like Schedule A, they may be **group relieved** or, failing that, they are **carried forward against future income and gains** of any description.

C12.4 Capital losses

Capital losses may only be carried forward against future capital gains. There is no current year relief against income, there is no carry back and no group relief. However, group companies can make notional transfers to ensure gains and losses in different group companies are set off against each other. This is covered in more detail in a later chapter.

C12.5 Terminal loss relief s.393A(7)

When a company ceases to trade, and it makes a loss in the final period, it is not possible to carry the loss forward, as there will be no future profits (and no future trade).

In this situation, the loss of the final 12 months of trade can be carried back against the profits of the previous 3 years. This effectively extends the claim under s393A(1) beyond the normal 12 month carry back.

Losses are relieved first against any profits of the final period (before charges), then are carried back for a maximum of 36 months against later periods before those of earlier periods.

C12.6 Schedule DIII losses

s.83 FA 1996

Interest paid and interest received on non-trading loan relationships is pooled together to give a Schedule DIII credit ("profit") or a Schedule DIII deficit ("loss").

The possible claims a company can make to use a DIII loss are:

(i) Set against any profits of the same accounting period; or

(ii) Set against DIII profits of the previous 12 months; or

(iii) Surrender to a company in the same group ("group relief").

DIII losses are very flexible - i.e., the company can carry back the loss without first having to use the loss in the current year.

DIII losses are used in priority to DI trading losses and Schedule A losses:

	£
Income for period	X
Less DIII deficit	(X)
Less Schedule A loss	(X)
Less trading losses	(X)
PCTCT	X

To the extent that a DIII deficit has not been used by group relief, a current year claim or a carry back claim, it will go forward to the succeeding accounting period to be set against non DI income and gains. If the company does not want this automatic set off in the next accounting period then they have two years to make a claim so that all or part of the deficit carried forward is not so set off. s.83(3A) Para 4 Sch 8 FA 1996

C12.7 The carry back of a DIII deficit

The carry back claim is an all or nothing claim as it has to be made for the lower of: Para 3 Sch 8 FA 1996

(i) the DIII deficit available for carry back and

(ii) the profits available to set it off against.

The DIII deficit available to carry back is the deficit of the current year to the extent that it has not been relieved by a current year or group relief claim.

C12.8 DVI losses on IFAs

Para 35 Sch 29 FA 2002

Where a company incurs a non-trading loss on IFAs, it has two years from the end of the accounting period of the loss to make a claim to set the whole or part of the loss against total profits of that period. Alternatively excess DVI losses can be group relieved.

Otherwise the loss is carried forward and treated as a non-trading debit arising in the next accounting period.

C12.9 Losses summary

	DI trading losses	**DIII deficits**	**Schedule A losses/ Management Expenses/DVI losses on non trade IFAs**
CURRENT YEAR	Profits before Charges	Profits before Charges (in priority to both DI and Sch A losses)	Profits before Charges (compulsory offset for Sch A and management expenses)
CARRY BACK	12 months - against profits before non-trade charges (must do current year claim first)	12 months - against DIII only (no need to current year claim first)	N/A
CARRY FORWARD	Future profits of same trade (automatic)	Any future profits except DI (can claim for this not to occur)	Any profits
GROUP RELIEF	Whole loss	Whole deficit	Excess amount only (i.e. must use in CY before group relieve)

SUMMARY – RELIEF FOR OTHER LOSSES

Schedule A losses must be set-off against any profits of the current period. If excess losses remain these can be carried forward against future profits. Excess Schedule A losses can be also be group relieved.

Management expenses for an investment company must be set-off against any profits of the current period. If excess management expenses remain these can be carried forward against future profits. Excess management expenses can be also be group relieved.

Capital losses can only be used to relieve capital gains of the same or later accounting periods.

Where the company ceases to trade, the trading loss of the last 12 months can be carried back against profits before non trade charges of the last 36 months rather than the normal 12 months.

Schedule DIII losses can also be offset against any profits in the period, although a 12 month carry back against DIII income is also possible. They can also be group relieved. These claims can be done in any order and are very flexible. Unused DIII losses are automatically carried forward against future non trading income and gains unless the company elects for them not to be offset in this way.

DVI losses on IFAs can be used in the current period against other income, group relieved (if excess) or carried forward.

C13: CORPORATE CAPITAL GAINS

This chapter explains how companies pay corporation tax on capital gains covering in particular:
- how we calculate the gain chargeable;
- what relief is available against a capital gain.

C13.1 Introduction

A **company pays corporation tax on capital gains** arising on the disposal of chargeable assets. Most capital assets are chargeable with a number of minor exceptions, e.g. cars. The definition of a car does not extend to vans and other commercial vehicles which may give rise to chargeable gains where they are sold at a profit.

Individuals pay capital gains tax (CGT) on disposals, whereas companies pay corporation tax. The rules for computing gains for companies are very similar to the rules that apply to individuals. However, companies continue to claim indexation allowance beyond 5 April 1998 when it was frozen for individuals. Companies are not eligible for taper relief, nor are they entitled to an annual exemption.

C13.2 Computation of gains

The proforma for computing gains for a company is shown below. We start with sale proceeds from which we can deduct any incidental costs such as solicitor's or surveyor's fees, etc.

We deduct the cost of the assets which will also include any enhancement expenditure and other incidental costs of acquisition. That gives us the unindexed gain.

We then deduct indexation allowance, which is an allowance for inflation, to give the indexed gain, which is the gain we subject to corporation tax.

	£
Proceeds	X
Less: cost	(X)
Unindexed gain	X
Indexation allowance	(X)
Indexed gain	X

Illustration 1

Viscount Limited sold a factory for £1,200,000 on 30 September 2005. Solicitors fees amounted to £2,000. The factory had been purchased in May 1990 at a cost of £350,000.

The capital gain will be computed as follows:

	£
Proceeds	1,200,000
Less incidental selling costs	(2,000)
	1,198,000
Cost	(350,000)
Unindexed gain	848,000
Indexation (£350,000 at, say, 50%)	(175,000)
Indexed gain	£673,000

C13.3 Indexation allowance

The indexation factor is calculated by taking the movement in the **Retail Price Index** (RPI) **between the date of acquisition of the asset and the date of sale.** Where there is enhancement expenditure, we also look at the movement in the Retail Price Index between the date the enhancement expenditure was incurred and the date of disposal.

The RPIs are given in the tax tables accompanying this course.

The indexation factor is computed using the formula:

$$\frac{\textbf{RPI at sale} - \textbf{RPI at acquisition}}{\textbf{RPI at acquisition}}$$

The result of this is rounded to three decimal places or can be expressed as a percentage.

Illustration 2

In the previous illustration, Viscount Limited, we assumed the indexation factor was 50%.

The correct indexation factor for May 1991 to September 2005 is:

$$\frac{191.0 - 133.5}{133.5} = 0.43071 = 0.431 \text{ (or 43.1\%)}$$

The correct gain is therefore:

	£
Unindexed gain	848,000
Indexation (£350,000 x 43.1%)	(150,850)
Indexed gain	£697,150

Example 1

Cresta Limited purchased a warehouse in May 1988 for £425,000 and incurred solicitor's and surveyor's fees on this purchase amounting to £2,000. Stamp Duty was charged at 1% on the purchase price and this was payable by Cresta Limited. The warehouse is sold in January 2006 for £1.5 million and solicitor's fees of £3,000 were incurred.

You are required to calculate the indexed capital gain assuming the RPI in January 2006 is 188.9.

C13.4 Enhancement expenditure

Enhancement expenditure is added to the "base cost", or allowable cost, of the asset. It may need to be indexed separately if the enhancement occurs in a month other than the month of acquisition of the asset.

Illustration 3

Assume in the Viscount Limited example that the factory was extended in November 1995 at a cost of £200,000. For simplicity we will ignore the incidental selling costs now.

	£
Proceeds (Sept 2005)	1,200,000
Cost (May 1991)	(350,000)
Enhancement (Nov 1995)	(200,000)
Unindexed gain	650,000
Indexation on cost May 1990 to Sept 2005 $\frac{191.0 - 133.5}{133.5}$ = 43.1% x £350,000	(150,850)
Indexation on enhancement Nov 1995 to Sept 2005 $\frac{191.0 - 149.8}{149.8}$ = 27.5% x £200,000	(55,000)
Indexed gain	**444,150**

C13.5 Capital losses

Capital losses are computed in the same way as capital gains, except that indexation cannot create or increase a capital loss, it **can only reduce a gain to zero.**

Illustration 4

Assume in Illustration 2 that the asset was actually sold for just £400,000.

	£
Proceeds	400,000
Cost	(350,000)
Unindexed gain	50,000
Indexation allowance:	
43.1% x £350,000 = £150,850 restricted to	(50,000)
Indexed gain	**nil**

Illustration 5

Assume now that the asset was actually sold for just £250,000.

	£
Proceeds	250,000
Cost	(350,000)
Allowable loss	**£(100,000)**

No indexation is claimable as it cannot increase this loss.

The capital loss may be utilised against capital gains in the same year, or carried forward against future chargeable gains. The relief for capital losses is dealt with later.

C13.6 Assets purchased before 31 March 1982

Capital gains and losses can be computed by comparing the calculation based on cost with the calculation based on the value of the asset on 31 March 1982.

Consequently, if the value of the asset has risen from the time of purchase to March 1982, it will be advantageous to use the March 1982 value.

We will prepare **two calculations; one based on cost and one based on the March 1982 value.** Where this produces **two gains**, we **take the lower gain**. If this gives us **two losses** or any other result, we take the **lower loss.** Where we produce **one gain** and **one loss**, the answer will be **zero.**

Indexation allowance runs from March 1982 and is based on the higher of the cost or March 1982 value in both calculations.

If the company has submitted a "global rebasing election", the cost calculation need not be performed, as the election means that the company will only use March 1982 values in the computations.

Illustration 6

Ventura Limited purchased a factory in June 1970 for £80,000. It was worth £190,000 on 31.3.82. The factory is sold in January 2006 for £500,000 when you should assume the RPI factor was 191.8.

	Cost	March 1982
	£	£
Proceeds	500,000	500,000
Cost/March 1982 value	(80,000)	(190,000)
Unindexed gain	420,000	310,000
Indexation		
March 1982 to January 2006		
On higher of cost or March 1982 value		
$\frac{191.8 - 79.44}{79.44}$ = 141.4% x £190,000	(268,660)	(268,660)
Indexed gain	**£151,340**	**£41,340**

As the two columns both produce gains, the lower is taken i.e. £41,340

Illustration 7

Assume now that instead the asset was sold for £400,000.

	Cost	March 1982
	£	£
Proceeds	400,000	400,000
Cost	(80,000)	(190,000)
Unindexed gain	320,000	210,000
Indexation: £190,000 x 141.4%	(268,660)	(210,000)*
Indexed gain	**£51,340**	**nil**

* The indexation is restricted so as not to produce a loss.

The **lower amount** is taken i.e. nil.

C13.7 Rollover relief

Where a company sells one qualifying asset and purchases another qualifying asset, within a specified period, the **gain** on the **sale of asset 1** can be **deducted** from the **base cost of asset 2** upon the company making an election. This will ensure that the company does not pay corporation tax on the sale of the first asset.

These rules only apply when the company is selling assets used for the purposes of a trade. The Government is keen to encourage companies to reinvest in their trading activities without having to pay corporation tax on gains along the way.

Eligible assets include:

(i) Land and buildings (used in the trade)

(ii) Goodwill bought or created prior to April 2002

(iii) Fixed plant and machinery - "Fixed" means bolted to the floor or building.

Goodwill bought or created after 1 April 2002, is not within the CGT rules as explained in the chapter on IFAs.

The **specified period** during which asset 2 must be purchased, is **one year before the disposal of asset 1 to three years afterwards.**

Further details regarding the calculation of chargeable gains and the operation of rollover relief can be found in the Capital Gains Tax part of this course.

C13.8 Disposal of substantial shareholding

From 1 April 2002, disposals by a company of "substantial shareholdings" in other companies will be exempt from tax. Consequently gains will not be taxable and losses will not be allowable when dealing with disposals of substantial shareholdings.

The rules apply to shareholdings in both UK resident and non-resident companies.

A substantial shareholding is defined as **10% or more** of a company's ordinary share capital. The ordinary shares held must also give entitlement to at least 10% of the company's distributable profits and 10% of assets on a winding up. For these purposes the holdings of other group members are taken into account.

To qualify

(i) A substantial shareholding must have been held for **at least 12 months** in a period beginning not later than two years before the sale takes place.

(ii) the investing company must either be a sole trading company or the member of a trading group. For these purposes the definition of trading company is the same as that used for taper relief.

(iii) the shares must be in a qualifying company which is a defined as a trading company or a member of a trading group.

Conditions (ii) and (iii) must apply in the latest 12 month period in which the substantial shareholding test has been satisfied and ending with the time of the disposal AND immediately following the disposal.

Answer 1

	£	£
Proceeds	1,500,000	
Incidental costs	(3,000)	
Net sale proceeds		1,497,000
Cost	425,000	
Incidental costs	2,000	
Stamp duty £425,000 x 1%	4,250	
Total cost		(431,250)
Unindexed gain		1,065,750
Indexation		
May 1988 to January 2006		
$\frac{188.9 - 106.2}{106.2}$ = 77.9% x £431,250		(335,944)
Indexed gain		**£729,806**

SUMMARY – CORPORATE CAPITAL GAINS

Indexation allowance did not cease for companies on 6 April 1998.

Companies do not get taper relief or an annual exemption.

Rollover relief is available when qualifying assets are disposed of and the proceeds are reinvested in other qualifying assets.

Goodwill bought or created after 1 April 2002 is not an eligible asset for rollover relief for companies.

From 1 April 2002, gains on the disposal of substantial shareholdings will be exempt.

Substantial is defined as 10% or more. A 10% holding must have been held for at 12 months in the preceding two years. The company making the sale and the company whose shares are being sold must both be trading companies.

C14: ROLLOVER RELIEF

In this chapter you will look at the general principles of rollover relief including:
- how the relief operates;
- proceeds not fully reinvested;
- conditions for the relief;
- qualifying assets;
- time limits.

C14.1 Introduction

You will sometimes see rollover relief referred to as "replacement of business assets" relief, for the simple reason that the legislation gives a Company relief when it **sells a business asset and replaces it with another**. s. 152

Illustration 1

A Company is using a building for the purposes of its trade. It sells the building for £200,000 making a capital gain - before any reliefs - of £80,000. The reason the Company has sold the old asset, is because it wishes to replace it with a new one. The Company may be expanding and need larger premises.

The Company replaces the old office building with a new office building costing £250,000. Where a Company disposes of a business asset and reinvests the proceeds in buying another business asset, it can make a claim to defer the gain it has made. In this example, the Company sells the old asset for £200,000 and reinvests the whole of the proceeds in buying a new asset for £250,000. The Company has therefore not retained any of the sale proceeds.

As all proceeds are reinvested, full rollover relief is given as below. s. 152(1)

	£
Proceeds	200,000
Cost	(100,000)
Indexation (say)	(20,000)
Gain	80,000
Roll over relief	(80,000)
Gain	Nil

Rollover relief is a deferral relief as it pushes the capital gains back to a later period in time. The way rollover relief works, is that the amount of the **gain deferred** - in this instance £80,000 - is **rolled over and reduces the base cost of the new asset purchased**. s. 152(1)(b)

New building:

	£
Cost	250,000
Rolled over gain	(80,000)
Base cost of new asset	£170,000

Therefore when the Company comes to sell the second building, because its base cost has been reduced by £80,000, the capital gain on the sale of that building will be uplifted by £80,000. Therefore the **capital gain** of £80,000 on the sale of building number 1, has been **deferred until the sale of building number 2.** The advantage of making a rollover relief claim, is that the Company can elect to pay corporation tax on this £80,000 several years later, therefore obtaining a cash flow advantage.

C14.2 Proceeds not fully reinvested s.153

Illustration 2

Assume a Company sells a business asset for £200,000 realising a capital gain of £80,000. The Company uses the money to buy a replacement asset which costs £180,000. You will see therefore, that the Company has not fully reinvested its proceeds of sale.

Cash retained = £200,000 - 180,000 = £20,000

Where the Company does not spend all of the sale proceeds, the amount of **cash retained** (£20,000) is **immediately chargeable** to capital gains tax. This amount is the gain before taper relief. This means that having made a capital gain of £80,000, the Company is immediately charged on £20,000. The **balance** - here being £60,000 - **is the rollover relief** that the Company can claim.

	£
Proceeds	200,000
Cost	(100,000)
Indexation	(20,000)
Gain	80,000
Roll over relief	(60,000)
Chargeable Gain (£200,000 - 180,000)	£20,000

The £60,000 will be rolled over and reduces the base cost of the new asset.

	£
Cost	180,000
Rolled over gain	(60,000)
Base cost of new asset	£120,000

Illustration 3

Assume a Company sells a business asset for £200,000, realising a capital gain of £80,000. It uses part of the sale proceeds to buy a replacement asset. The new building is considerably smaller and costs £110,000. Where a Company has not fully reinvested its proceeds of sale, we must identify the amount of cash retained.

Cash retained = £200,000 - 110,000 = £90,000

However it is not possible for the Revenue to charge the Company on a gain of £90,000, as his actual gain is only £80,000. Therefore the whole of this gain of £80,000 will be immediately charged to tax, and no rollover relief will be available. The base cost of the new asset will remain at £110,000.

This demonstrates that when the **cash retained by the Company exceeds the capital gain**, the whole of the gain is chargeable and **no rollover relief can be claimed.**

	£
Proceeds	200,000
Cost	(100,000)
Indexation	(20,000)
Gain	80,000
Roll over relief	Nil
Chargeable Gain	80,000

C14.3 Conditions for the relief

Rollover relief can only be claimed by a **company** sells an asset and reinvests the proceeds in a replacement asset. s. 152(1)

The **old asset** - i.e. the asset being sold - must be **used for the purposes of a business** carried on by the Company. Rollover relief is also available where an individual owns an asset, but the asset is used by his personal company. (i.e. where the individual owns at least 5% of the voting shares).

The **new asset** - i.e. the asset being acquired - must be **immediately taken into use for the purposes of the trade.** It is not possible for a Company to buy an asset, and use it for non-trading purposes if rollover relief is to be claimed. ESC D24

C14.4 Qualifying assets

Rollover relief is only available to a Company that makes a disposal of a "qualifying asset", and reinvests all or part of the proceeds in another "qualifying asset". The legislation contains a list of qualifying assets at s.155 TCGA 1992. s. 155

The most common type of qualifying assets is **land and buildings** used for the purposes of a trade. These will typically include shops, offices, factories, warehouses etc.

The **goodwill** of a business is also a qualifying asset. When a trader sells his business, a major part of the value of the business will often be the reputation of the business and the customer contacts. This is what we mean by "goodwill".

Fixed plant and machinery are qualifying assets for rollover relief. Note the word "fixed". Fixed means immovable, so assets such as tractors or combine harvesters used by a farmer, or vehicles used by Companies, will not be eligible for rollover relief.

Ships, aircraft and hovercraft are qualifying assets as are satellites, space stations and spacecraft. Milk, potato and fish quotas will also qualify for rollover relief, as will ewe and cow suckler premiums.

The qualifying assets you are most likely to see in practice are the top three in the list - land and buildings, goodwill, or fixed plant and machinery.

It is important to note that the **old and the new assets do <u>not</u> need to fall within the same category**. If a Company makes a gain on the sale of a building, it will obtain rollover relief if it purchases either another building, or any of the other qualifying assets. Therefore a Company that sells a milk quota and reinvests the proceeds in space travel, will obtain rollover relief.

One asset you will **not** find on the list of qualifying assets is **shares. ** If a Company either **buys or sells shares, it will not be able to claim rollover relief**. Shares can never be used for the purposes of a trade. A share is simply an investment in a company, and is not used for any specific purpose.

C14.5 Statutory time limits

Rollover relief is only available if the new asset is acquired within a certain period of time. The **new asset must be acquired** within a four year time window, running **from 12 months before the sale of the old asset, to 36 months afterwards**. These time limits can be extended at the discretion of the Revenue. s. 152(3)

Rollover **relief must be claimed** by the Company within a certain time limit. That time limit is **six years from the end of the company's accounting period**. s. 43(1) TMA 1970

For example, let us assume that a Company sells the old asset in its year ended 31 December 2006. A rollover relief claim should therefore be made no later than 31 December 2012.

Provisional claims for rollover relief will be allowed. Therefore if the above Company sells an asset in 2006, but has not bought the new asset by 31 December 2007, but is intending to buy the asset before the three year reinvestment period has expired, the Revenue will allow it to defer the capital gain, even though proper computations cannot be prepared. s. 153A

Rollover relief is not automatic, and if a Company does not wish to defer a capital gain, it will simply not make a rollover relief claim. This may be the case if the gain is covered by losses.

Q	Now test your understanding by attempting the examples which follow.

Example 1

Which of the below assets are qualifying assets for rollover relief purposes?

(a) Goodwill
(b) Freehold office
(c) Lease on a factory
(d) Tractor
(e) Shares in a personal company
(f) Painting

Example 2

X Ltd bought a shop in May 1994 for £180,000. It sold it in May 2005 for £275,000. In June 2004 X Ltd had bought a hovercraft for use in its trade for £255,000. It sold the hovercraft in March 2006 for £265,000.

Assuming all claims are made calculate X Ltds chargeable gains in the year ended 31 March 2006.

Answer 1

	Qualifying Asset?	
	Yes	*No*
a) Goodwill	✓	
b) Freehold office	✓	
c) Lease on factory	✓	
d) Tractor		X (Not fixed)
e) Shares in Personal Co.		X
f) Painting		X (Not used in trade)

Answer 2

May 2005	Gain on shop	- £
	Proceeds	275,000
	Less: Cost	(180,000)
	Less: Indexation	
	180,000 x 0.314	(56,520)
	Indexed gain	38,480
	Rollover relief	(18,480)
	Chargeable Gain (275,000-255,000)	20,000
	Hovercraft	£
	Cost	255,000
	Rolled over gain	(18,480)
	Base cost of new asset	236,520
March 2006	Gain on Hovercraft	£
	Proceeds	265,000
	Less: base cost (above)	(236,520)
	Less: Indexation	
	236,520 x 0.011	(2,602)
	Chargeable Gain	37,680
	Add:	
	Gain on shop	20,000
	Chargeable gains year ended 31 March 2006	**£57,680**

SUMMARY – ROLLOVER RELIEF

Rollover relief applies when a company sells one business asset and replaces it with another.

If all the proceeds from the sale of the old asset are reinvested in the new asset, the gain on the old asset is not charged but instead is deducted from the base cost of the new asset. There will therefore be a bigger gain in the future when the new asset is sold.

If proceeds are not fully reinvested a gain equal to the cash retained must be left chargeable.

Rollover relief is available to companies and persons carrying on a trade. The old and the new asset must both be used in the trade.

Qualifying assets include:

- Land and buildings
- Goodwill (for individuals only)
- Fixed plant and machinery
- Ships/aircraft/hovercraft
- Satellite/space stations/space craft
- Milk/potato/fish quotas

Shares are not a qualifying asset for rollover relief.

The new asset must be acquired 12 months before to 36 months after the sale of the old asset.

A claim must be made for rollover relief within six years from the end of the company's accounting period.

C15: SHARES AND SECURITIES: MATCHING RULES

In this chapter you will cover the rules that apply when an individual sells shares including:
- the six matching rules;
- calculating gains for non-pooled shares;
- application of taper relief.

C15.1 Introduction

In this chapter, we shall examine how we calculate capital gains on shares sold in 2005/2006, which were acquired after 6 April 1998. When the Government froze indexation and introduced taper relief on 6 April 1998, they also took the opportunity to change the rules with regard to shares and securities.

Before we examine the special rules for shares, let us spend a few moments discussing why we need them in the first place. Consider a taxpayer who has been buying shares in a quoted company called XYZ Plc for a number of years. The share purchases have been as follows:

Date	*Shares*	*Cost*
December 1975	1,000	£1,000
June 1986	3,000	£6,000
September 1990	2,000	£8,000
December 1999	4,000	£20,000
Total	10,000	£35,000

The taxpayer currently has 10,000 shares, **which have been acquired in four tranches** between 1975 and 1999 and the total cost of the taxpayer's shareholding is £35,000. In August 2005, the taxpayer sells 6,500 of the XYZ Plc shares for total proceeds of £39,000. In order to calculate the chargeable gain arising on the sale of these 6,500 shares, we **need to identify exactly which shares the taxpayer has sold**. Until we know exactly which shares have been sold, we cannot identify the base cost of the shares, and we cannot therefore work out the indexation allowance or the taper relief.

The **share "matching" rules** determine the exact order in which shares are deemed to have been sold. These "matching" rules are extremely important, and we will revisit them many times over the course of the next few chapters. The "matching" rules we are about to study, **apply for individuals only.** There are slightly different matching rules for disposals of shares by companies. Also note that the "matching" rules **only apply to shares in the same class in the same company**. We should never mix up different types of shares in different companies.

IR 218 Tax Bulletin No. 52 (April 2001)

C15.2 The share matching rules

There are 6 matching rules, and we shall cover them in their order of priority: s. 106(A)

(1) If an individual disposes of shares, he is **first** deemed to have sold any shares he acquired on the **same day**. s. 105

(2) Next, the shareholder is deemed to have sold any shares he acquired in the **following 30 days**. This rule was introduced in April 1998, to prevent the common tax planning practice known as "bed and breakfasting". s. 106A(5)

(3) Next the taxpayer is deemed to have sold any shares he acquired **after 5 April 1998.** Acquisitions of shares after April 1998 are kept separate, and are deemed to have been sold on a **"last in first out** basis". This means that more recent shares will be deemed to have been sold before any earlier shares. s. 106A(6)

(4) Next the disposal will be matched with share acquisitions between **April 1982 and April 1998**. Shares bought in this period, are pooled together and form one asset for CGT purposes. Shares acquired between these dates, are held in what we call the **"Finance Act 1985 pool".** We will examine share pooling in the next chapter. s. 106A(8)(a

(5) Next the taxpayer is deemed to have sold shares which he bought between **April 1965 and April 1982**. Shares bought between these two dates are pooled together in what we call the **"1982 pool"** or the **"1982 holding".** Once again, "1982 share pooling" will be examined in a later chapter. s. 106A(8)(b

(6) Finally the taxpayer is deemed to have sold shares which he acquired **before 6 April 1965**.

Illustration 1

Geoff has acquired shares in a company called XYZ Plc as follows:

Date	*Shares*	*Cost*
		£
1 December 1992	6,000	6,000
1 July 2001	4,000	8,000
1 February 2006	2,000	5,000
1 March 2006	500	2,000
	12,500	21,000

On 15 February 2006, Geoff sold 4,500 of the XYZ Plc shares for gross proceeds of £13,500.

To calculate Geoff's capital gain, we must first identify which shares Geoff has sold, by applying the share matching rules. Geoff sold the shares on 15 February 2006. Our first question is "did Geoff buy any shares on the **same day**" - i.e. did he buy any shares on 15 February 2006? If he did, these shares will be sold in priority to any others. The answer to this question is "no" .

We then move down to the second matching rule, and ask ourselves whether Geoff bought any shares in the **30 days following** the date of disposal. The 30 days following the disposal, runs from 16 February 2006 to 18 March 2006. The answer to this question is "yes" - Geoff did buy some shares in this period - he bought 500 shares on 1 March 2006. We therefore have a "match". What we are saying here, is that of the 4,500 shares sold on 15 February 2006, the **first** ones to be sold were those bought on 1 March 2006.

We now move down to matching rule number 3. The third match, is with any shares acquired **since 6 April 1998**. Geoff has bought two lots of shares since April 1998 - some in July 2001 and some others in February 2006. Where different shares have been bought since April 1998, we match on a **"last in first out basis"** - i.e. with later shares in priority to earlier shares. This tells us that the **second** lot of shares to be sold, are the 2,000 shares bought for £5,000 on 1 February 2006.

At this point, we have accounted for 2,500 out of the 4,500 shares sold on 15 February 2006. The **final** lot of shares to be sold, are those purchased on 1 July 2001. Of the 4,000 shares bought in July 2001, 2,000 are deemed to have been sold on 15 February 2006. We have now accounted for all of the shares sold in February 2006.

Once we have a "match", the next step is to calculate the resulting chargeable gain. In this question, we have **three matches,** which means we will need to prepare **three different capital gains computations**.

At first sight this seems a very complicated exercise, but you will quickly become familiar with the process once you have done a few practice questions.

Let us now calculate Geoff's capital gain on the sale of the 4,500 XYZ Plc shares in February 2006.

The first match is with 500 shares, bought on 1 March 2006:

		£
Disposal 1:	Proceeds	
	$13{,}500 \times \frac{500}{4500}$	1,500
	Less: cost (1.3.06)	(2,000)
	Loss	£(500)

The second match is with 2,000 shares bought on 1 February 2006:

		£
Disposal 2:	Proceeds	
	$13{,}500 \times \frac{2000}{4500}$	6,000
	Less: cost (1.2.06)	(5,000)
	Gain	£1,000

Finally, the third match is with 2,000 of the 4,000 shares bought on 1 July 2001:

		£
Disposal 3:	Proceeds	
	$13{,}500 \times \frac{2000}{4500}$	6,000
	Less: cost (1.7.01)	
	$8{,}000 \times \frac{2000}{4000}$	(4,000)
	Gain	£2,000

In summary:

		£
Disposal 1	Bought 1 March 2006	(500)
Disposal 2	Bought 1 February 2006	1,000
Disposal 3	Bought 1 July 2001	2,000

The final step in this example, is to look at how we deal with taper relief.

In arriving at Geoff's gain of £2,500, we have added together gains and losses on three separate assets. This is a very important principle as far as shares are concerned.

Shares bought after April 1998, are always **treated as separate assets** for CGT purposes, and should not be pooled together. Because the shares are treated as separate assets, and have been acquired at different times, the gains on those shares will **qualify for different rates of taper relief.**

There is a loss of £500 arising from the sale of shares bought in March 2006, a gain of £1,000 from shares bought in February 2006, and a gain of £2,000 from shares bought in July 2001.

If we consider the gain of £1,000, this will not qualify for any taper relief because the shares were bought in February 2006, and sold a couple of weeks later on 15 February 2006. These shares have not been held for one year, so no taper relief will be available.

If we consider the shares bought in July 2001, they were sold in February 2006, so these shares have been held for four complete years. As Geoff is selling shares in a quoted company, the shares will be non-business assets. The appropriate percentage for taper relief, will therefore be 90%.

We now need to consider the capital loss of £500. We will set the capital loss against whichever of the gains qualifies for the lowest amount of taper relief.

The loss of £500 will therefore be set against the gain of £1,000, to leave a gain before taper relief of £500. We will not set any of the loss against the gain on the shares bought in July 2001, as to do so would waste taper relief.

	Taper rates	
	100%	*90%*
	£	£
Disposal 2	1,000	
Disposal 3		2,000
Loss on Disposal 1	(500)	
Gain before taper	£500	£2,000
Gains after taper relief @ 100%/@ 90%	£500	£1,800
Total gains	£2,300	

Q	Now test your understanding by attempting the examples which follow.

Example 1

Rufus sold 2,000 shares in Widget Co Ltd, an unquoted trading company, for £16,000 on 1.10.05. The shares are business assets for taper relief. His shares had been acquired as follows:

Date	*No.*	*Cost*
		£
1.12.02	1,000	4,000
1.12.03	1,000	5,000
1.12.04	1,000	6,000
1.12.05	1,000	8,500

Calculate Rufus's chargeable gain.

Example 2

Anna had the following share transactions in ABC plc:

Date	*Event*	*No.*	*Cost*	*Proceeds*
			£	£
1.3.06	Buy	10,000	15,000	
21.3.06	Sell	8,000		16,000
21.3.06	Buy	4,000	10,000	
29.3.06	Buy	6,000	18,000	

Calculate Anna's gain/(loss) on the sale in March 2006.

Answer 1

2,000 shares sold 1.10.05		
Same day?	X	
Next 30 days?	X	
Post April 1998	✓	1,000 bought 1.12.04
		1,000 bought 1.12.03
		2,000

	£	£
Disposal 1		
Proceeds		
$16{,}000 \times \frac{1000}{2000}$	8,000	
Less: cost (1.12.04)	(6,000)	
Gain before taper relief	£2,000	
Gain after taper relief		
1.12.04 – 1.10.05 = < 1 year ∴100%		2,000
Disposal 2		
Proceeds		
$£16{,}000 \times \frac{1000}{2000}$	8,000	
Less: cost (1.12.03)	(5,000)	
Gain before taper relief	£3,000	
Gain after taper relief		
1.12.03 – 1.10.05 – 1 year ∴50%		1,500
Total chargeable gains:		£3,500

Answer 2

8,000 shares sold 21.3.06

Same day? ✓	4,000 bought 21.3.06
Next 30 days ✓	4,000 bought 29.3.06
	8,000

Disposal 1 – sale of 4,000 shares bought 21.3.06

	£	£
Proceeds		
$16,000 \times \frac{4000}{8000}$	8,000	
Less: cost (21.3.06)	(10,000)	
Loss	£(2,000)	(2,000)

Disposal 2 – sale of 4,000 shares bought 29.3.06

	£	
Proceeds		
$16,000 \times \frac{4000}{8000}$	8,000	
Less: cost (29.3.06)		
$18,000 \times \frac{4000}{6000}$	(12,000)	
Loss	£(4,000)	(4,000)

Total loss		**£(6,000)**

SUMMARY - SHARES AND SECURITIES - MATCHING RULES

The current rules for share disposals were introduced in April 1998.

When shares that have been bought in tranches over time are sold, we use matching rules to identify which shares are being sold.

The matching rules for individuals are:

1st	Shares acquired on same day
2nd	Shares acquired in following 30 days
3rd	Shares acquired after 5 April 1998 (LIFO basis)
4th	Shares acquired between 6 April 1982 and 5 April 1998 ("1985 pool")
5th	Shares acquired between 6 April 1965 and 5 April 1982 ("1982 pool")
6th	Shares acquired before 6 April 1965

Once the disposals have been matched with the acquisitions, a gain is calculated for each match and taper relief is applied in the normal way.

C16: SUBSTANTIAL SHAREHOLDING EXEMPTION

In this chapter you will look at the exemption that applies to substantial shareholdings held by companies in more detail, including:

- the definition of "substantial" for these purposes;
- the 12 month period during which the holding must have been substantial;
- the conditions for the investing company;
- the conditions for the investee company;
- the interaction of these rules with other areas including the group rules.

C16.1 Introduction

With effect from 1 April 2002 gains arising on disposals of qualifying shareholdings on or after that date **are tax-free** and **losses are not allowable.**

C16.2 Outline of the relief

Sch 7AC TCGA 1992

Gains are not chargeable and losses are not allowable where:

(i) an investing company;

(ii) which has held a substantial shareholding in an investee company (referred to by Sch 7AC TCGA 1992 as 'the company invested in') throughout a 12-month period;

(iii) disposes of any shares in the investee company.

There is no requirement for the proceeds from the sale of this shareholding to be used in any particular way.

C16.3 The substantial shareholding requirement

The exemption is dependent on the investing company having held a substantial shareholding in the investee company throughout a 12-month period beginning no more than two years prior to the disposal. Para 7 Sch 7AC TCGA 1992

The investing company must hold at least 10% of the ordinary share capital of the investee company and must also be beneficially entitled to at least 10% of: Para 8 Sch 7AC TCGA 1992

(i) the profits available for distribution to equity holders; and
(ii) the assets available for distribution to equity holders on a winding up.

The definition of 'equity holder' and the determination of profits or assets available for distribution broadly follow the approach in Sch 18 ICTA 1988.

The purpose of the time limit referred to above is to allow subsequent disposals out of what was once a substantial shareholding to continue to qualify for exemption for a further 12 months, notwithstanding the fact that the 10% threshold may have ceased to be satisfied.

Illustration 1

Vaughan Ltd has owned 15% of Key Trading Ltd since 1997.

On 1 June 2005, Vaughan Ltd sold a 10% stake in the company at a profit. The gain on this disposal clearly qualifies for the substantial shareholding exemption. However, some months later, the directors of Vaughan Ltd are considering the possibility of selling the remaining 5% shareholding.

Even though the shares in Key Trading Ltd no longer constitute a substantial shareholding, the exemption is still available for disposals in the 12 months following 1 June 2005. Thus, if the second sale is also expected to realise a gain, it will be sensible for Vaughan Ltd to effect the disposal on or before 1 June 2006. However, if the value of Key Trading Ltd has recently declined such that a share sale would now crystallise a loss, the company should wait until after 1 June 2006 so that the loss will be allowable.

If a group's shareholding in the investee company is split between various group members, the shares can be aggregated in order to determine whether the substantial shareholding requirement is satisfied. For the purposes of these rules, a group comprises a principal company and its 51% subsidiaries – note that the s.170 TCGA 1992 definition of a group is used, the only difference being the substitution of '51%' for '75%'.

Illustration 2

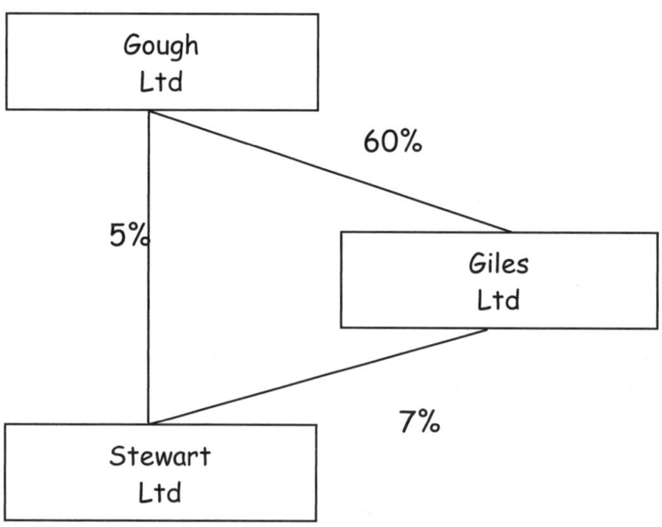

In this diagram, Gough Ltd does have a substantial shareholding in Stewart Ltd (5% + 7% = 12%). Because Gough Ltd controls Giles Ltd the shares in Giles Ltd are treated as though they are held by Gough Ltd. Note that there is no need to work out an indirect interest.

C16.4 Liquidations

When a company goes into liquidation, it loses beneficial ownership of its assets as a result of those assets being vested in the liquidator. However, the rules protect an investing company from this outcome as far as the substantial shareholding rules are concerned so that it can continue to satisfy the necessary conditions for exemption. Para 16 Sch 7AC TCGA 1992

C16.5 Conditions for the investing company

Para 18 Sch 7AC TCGA 1992

The investing company must be either:

(i) a 'sole trading company'; or

(ii) a member of a 'trading group'

beginning with the start of the latest 12-month period in relation to which it passed the substantial shareholding test and ending with the time of the disposal.

It must also be a sole trading company or a member of a trading group immediately after the disposal.

A sole trading company means any trading company which is not a member of a group. 'Trading company' and 'trading group' are defined in much the same way as they are for business asset taper relief purposes.

Illustration 3

Poulter Ltd acquired 2,500 ordinary shares in Rose Ltd on 30 April 2000. This represented a 25% stake.

On 30 April 2005 Poulter Ltd sold 2,000 of these shares and 11 months later on 31 March 2006 the remaining 500 were disposed of.

In respect of the sale on 30 April 2005, Poulter Ltd must be a trading company or a member of a trading group for 12 months from 1 May 2004 until 30 April 2005.

However, for the sale on 31 March 2006, the qualifying period runs for 23 months from 1 May 2004 until 31 March 2006.

C16.6 Conditions for the investee company

Para 19 Sch 7AC TCGA 1992

The investee company must have been a trading company or the holding company of a trading group throughout the period referred to in Illustration 3.

It must also be a trading company or the holding company of a trading group immediately after the disposal.

However, where the investee company ceases to trade on being put into liquidation or following an intra-group transfer of its trade (so that it would no longer satisfy the test above), a special rule means any gain accruing to the investing company on a disposal of shares in the investee company to continue to be exempt for a further two-year period. Para 3 Sch 7AC TCGA 1992

C16.7 Negligible value claims

If an investment proves to be worthless, it is not permitted to make a negligible value claim under s.24(2) TCGA 1992 and backdate the disposal to before 1 April 2002 so as to give rise to an allowable loss.

C16.8 Holdover relief

Where a gift of shares is made to a company and holdover relief is claimed under s.165 TCGA 1992, it is not possible for the company subsequently to dispose of those shares with the benefit of the substantial shareholding exemption. An amount equal to the held over gain will still be chargeable. Para 37 Sch 7AC TCGA 1992

C16.9 Investments in non-UK resident companies

The substantial shareholding exemption is not restricted to disposals of shares in UK-based companies. Gains arising on the sale of non-UK resident subsidiaries and other investments are also covered.

C16.10 Intra-group transfers

The substantial shareholding exemption does not apply to s.171 transfers within a capital gains tax group. Effectively the s.171 provisions override the substantial shareholding rules where shares in trading companies are transferred between group companies. Para 6 Sch 7AC TCGA 1992

When an investing company acquires shares under a s.171 transfer and subsequently disposes of those shares to an unrelated company, the holding period is extended to include the period for which the transferor held those shares (and any period for which the transferor was treated as holding those shares as a result of the same provisions). Para 10 Sch 7AC TCGA 1992

C16.11 Degrouping charge

Where a degrouping charge arises under s.179 TCGA 1992 in relation to a holding of shares that, at the time of the company leaves the group, would qualify for the substantial shareholding exemption on an actual disposal of the shares, the substantial shareholding rules effectively override the s.179 provisions. Para 38 Sch 7AC TCGA 1992

SUMMARY - SUBSTANTIAL SHAREHOLDINGS EXEMPTION

From 1 April 2002 gains on shares held by companies are exempt from corporation tax provided that at least a 10% stake has been held for 12 out of the last 24 months of ownership.

Both companies must be trading companies (or members of a trading group) as defined for taper relief purposes throughout the 12 month holding period AND immediately after the disposal.

Losses on the sale of a "substantial shareholding" are not allowable and negligible value claims made on or after 1 April 2002 cannot be backdated to trigger a loss.

Substantial shareholdings are transferred within a capital gains group on a no gain/no loss basis. Ownership periods of all group companies are aggregated to determine whether the conditions have been satisfied.

Where a company leaves a group taking a "substantial shareholding" with it a degrouping charge under s.179 will not arise. The base cost of the shares will become the market value at the time of leaving the group.

C17: THE PRINCIPLES OF GROUP RELIEF

This session will consider the relief that is available to a group of companies where one of them makes a trading loss. In particular it will look at:

- how a group is constituted;
- the rates at which a loss can be relieved;
- how a company will decide where the loss should be relieved bearing in mind the amount of tax saved;
- the timing of the relief.

C17.1 Introduction

Group relief allows losses to be transferred to profit making companies in the same **75% group**.

Illustration 1

A Ltd £100,000

75%

B Ltd (£60,000)

Under the group relief provisions, we can surrender the loss of £60,000 from B to A reducing A's taxable profit and its corporation tax liability.

The maximum claim is the lower of the **available loss or the available profit**.

Illustration 2

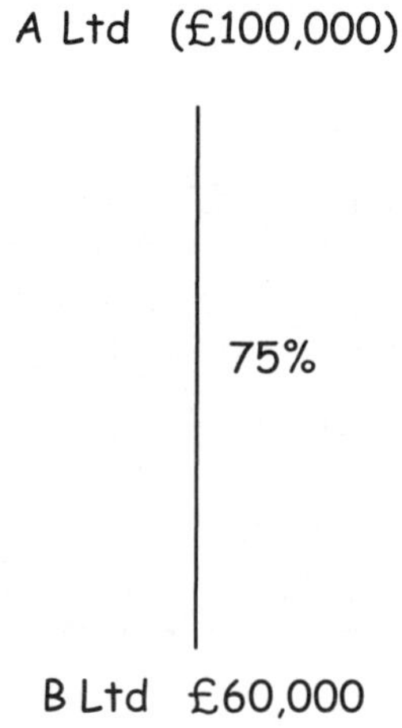

The group relief claim here will be a maximum of £60,000. A Ltd will have the remaining loss of £40,000 which it may be able to set off in the current year, carry back, or carry forward. Losses that are unutilised can only be carried forward in the company that originally sustained them.

C17.2 The 75% definition s.413 Sch 18 ICTA 1988

For **group relief** to apply, **one company must own at least 75% of the other.** For example if A Limited owns 75% of B Limited, that means that losses can flow from A to B or from B to A.

Note that the provisions **only apply to company ownership**, therefore, if Mr A owned 75% of B Limited, losses could not flow between Mr A and B Limited, as Mr A pays Income Tax and B Limited pays Corporation Tax.

Group relief **also applies between two companies** that are **each owned to** the extent of **75% by the same parent company**.

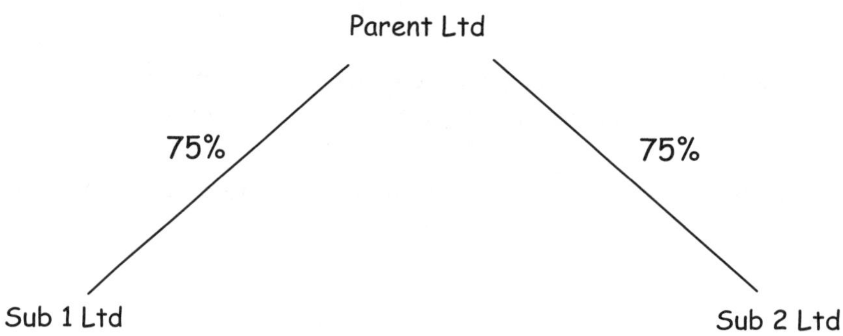

Losses can flow between the parent and the two subsidiaries **in either direction** and losses can also flow between the two subsidiaries.

If the two subsidiaries are owned by Mr P instead of Parent Ltd, losses could not flow either between Mr P and the two companies, or indeed between the two subsidiaries. Corporate ownership must apply for group relief of losses.

The **75% test** applies to all three of the following:

(i) There must be 75% **ownership of ordinary share capital** of the company; and

(ii) Those shares must entitle the shareholders to at least 75% of the **available distributable profits**; and

(iii) Those shares must entitle the shareholder to at least 75% of the company's **assets on a winding up.**

These three together form the definition of **"equitable ownership"**.

Illustration 3

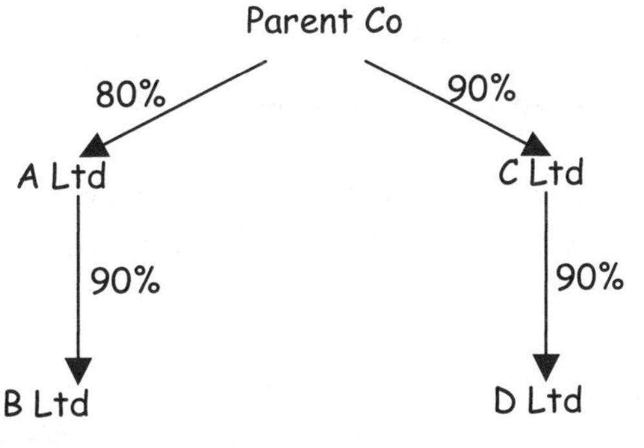

In the above scenario, Parent Co and A Ltd are in a 75% group.

However to determine whether Parent Co and B Ltd are in the same group relief group, we multiply 80% and 90% to give 72%. This is less than 75% so a group is not formed. If B Ltd has a loss, it cannot surrender it to Parent Co. or vice versa. B Ltd and A Ltd are in a 75% so trading losses can be surrendered between them.

Contrast this with the relationship between Parent Co and C Ltd and D Ltd. In this instance the 3 companies <u>are</u> in a group relief group as Parent Co's effective interest in D Ltd is 81% (i.e. 90% x 90%).

The group relief groups are therefore:

Parent Co + A Ltd + C Ltd + D Ltd

and

A Ltd + B Ltd

It can be seen, therefore, that a company can participate in more than one group relief group.

Note that all 5 companies are associated with each other so the corporation tax limits for each of the companies are divided by 5.

C17.3 Available amounts

The surrendering company (i.e. the loss making company) may surrender: s.403 ICTA 1988

(i) trading losses

(ii) DIII losses

The total amount of these losses may be surrendered before the surrendering company is required to consider any loss offset in its own computation.

Furthermore the surrendering company may also surrender

(iii) excess management expenses

(iv) excess Schedule A losses

(v) excess DVI losses on non trade IFAs

(vi) excess charges (trade and non-trade)

The amount of "excess" available for group relief is found by comparing gross income before any loss set offs to charges, management expenses, Schedule A losses and DVI losses on IFAs as appropriate.

The surrendering company surrenders to the claimant company (i.e. the profit making company) who must **set the losses against profits chargeable to corporation tax.**

The claimant company must set the losses against profits chargeable to corporation tax in the same accounting period.

The claimant company **must use the losses in its current accounting period** - any losses claimed under group relief cannot be carried back, carried forward or given to another group member.

The offset against PCTCT will be made after charges and any current year or brought forward losses. However the offset is made before losses brought back from a future period i.e. losses carried back do not displace group relief already claimed.

Illustration 4

Two 75% group companies have the following results:

	Claimton Ltd	*Surrton Ltd*
	£	£
Schedule D Case I	(6,000)	(80,000)
Schedule D Case III	20,000	(4,000)
Schedule A	-	10,000
Charges on income	(1,000)	-

The available loss of Surrton Ltd is as follows:

	Surrton Ltd
	£
Schedule D Case I	(80,000)
Schedule D Case III	(4,000)
Available loss	(84,000)

The available profit of Claimton Ltd is as follows:

	Claimton Ltd	Surrton Ltd
	£	£
Schedule D Case I	Nil	(80,000)
Schedule D Case III	20,000	(4,000)
Current Year Loss	(6,000)	
	14,000	
Charges on income	(1,000)	
	13,000	(84,000)
Group relief from Surrton Ltd – lower of PCTCT or loss available	(13,000)	13,000
		(71,000)
Current year claim in Surrton (if made)		10,000
Remaining loss		£(61,000)

C17.4 Effective use of losses

When using losses, it is important to obtain relief at the highest marginal rates of tax and secondly to use the losses up sooner rather than later.

From a timing perspective our preference would be for claims in the following order:

(i) **current year** and then **carry back**;

(ii) **group relief**;

(iii) **carry forward**.

However, the primary objective for the companies is to save the maximum tax possible on a group wide basis. To appreciate how this is done, we must consider the effective **marginal rates** of tax of all of the companies in the group.

C17.5 Marginal rates of tax

We have various marginal rates of tax, depending on the level of the company's notional profit.

By "marginal" rate we mean the rate of corporation tax effectively payable on the final £1 of a company's PCTCT.

Tax rates:	FY 2002 to 2005	FY 2001
£0 - £10,000	0%	10%
£10,001 - £50,000	23.75%	22.5%
£50,001 - £300,000	19%	20%
£300,001 - £1,500,000	32.75%	32.5%
> £1,500,000	30%	30%

The **limits** would obviously be **divided amongst the number of associates in the group.**

The marginal rates of 23.75% and 32.75% are calculated as follows:

23.75% rate:

£		£
50,000	x 19%	9,500
(10,000)	x 0%	-
40,000		9,500

$$\frac{9500}{40000} = 23.75\%$$

32.75% rate:

£			£
1,500,000	X 30%		450,000
(300,000)	X 19%		(57,000)
1,200,000			393,000

$$\frac{393000}{1200000} = 32.75\%$$

Illustration 5

Hill Ltd owns 100% of the shares of Collis Ltd. As the companies are associated, the corporation tax limits will be as follows:

	£
Starting rate limit	5,000
Lower rate limit	25,000
Small companies limit	150,000
Upper limit	750,000

Assuming Hill Ltd has PCTCT of £1m it will be a "large" company and will pay corporation tax at the full rate of 30%, i.e.

£1,000,000 x 30% = £300,000

Another way to arrive at this CT liability is to consider the marginal tax rates which apply within each of the 5 tax bands:

	£
First £5,000 @ 0%	-
Next £20,000 @ 23.75%	4,750
Next £125,000 @ 19%	23,750
Next £600,000 @ 32.75%	196,500
Remaining £250,000 @ 30%	75,000
Total tax on PCTCT of £1m	£300,000

Diagramatically these marginal rates can be illustrated as below:

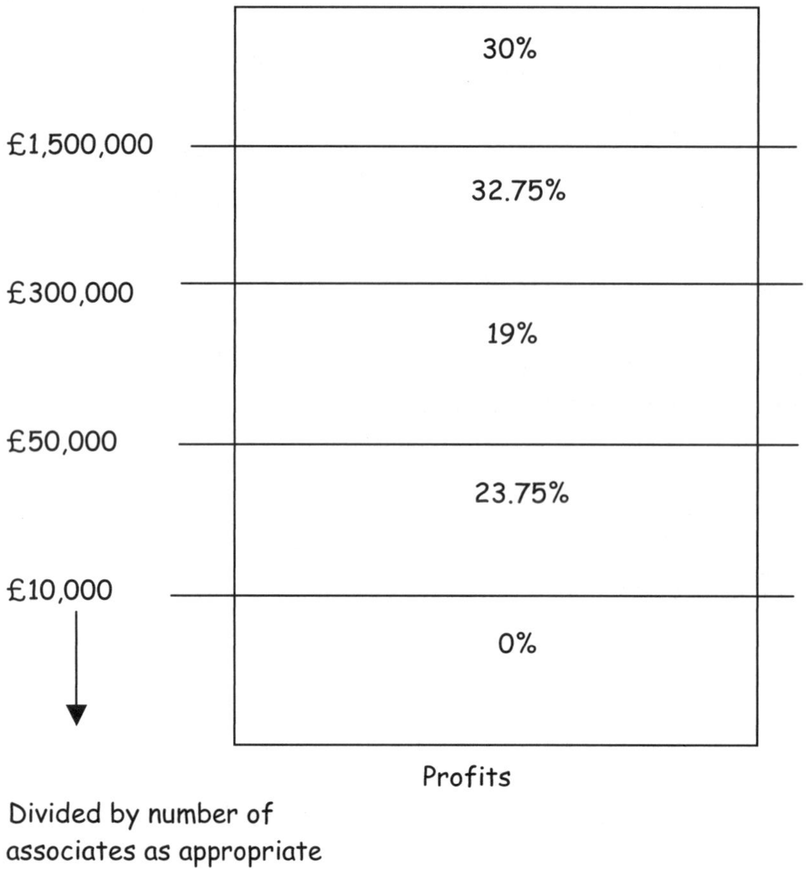

This diagram illustrates that if a company had profits between the upper limit and the small companies limits (i.e. between £300,000 and £1,500,000 in this example), and it were given an **extra £1** of income it would pay corporation tax at a rate of **32.75%** on that "marginal" £1.

This 32.75% rate is an effective **marginal** rate and should **not** be used when calculating MCT liabilities.

Therefore when making group relief claims, we will try to eliminate profits taxed at the highest marginal rate, i.e. 32.75%.

To achieve this we need to **specify** the amount of group relief required in order to bring the profit down to the **exact level** of the small companies limit. This ensures that **all** of the loss will be relieved at an effective rate of 32.75%. As group relief claims can be specified, this is very easy to do.

We would then start eroding profits taxed at 30%, then profits taxed at 23.75%, again specifying the claim to reduce the profit down to the starting rate lower limit and no further. Next we erode profits taxed at 19%, we should avoid eliminating profit that is taxed at 0%.

Illustration 6

X Ltd is a parent company with two wholly-owned subsidiaries Y Ltd and Z Ltd.

The results in the year ending 31 March 2006 are as follows:

	X Ltd	*Y Ltd*	*Z Ltd*
	£	£	£
Schedule D Case I	600,000	(40,000)	(20,000)
Schedule D Case III	50,000	121,000	10,000

In order to calculate the optimum loss relief we need to carry out the following steps.

First we build up the corporation tax computations so that we can work out what rates of tax the profits are being charged at.

	X Ltd	Y Ltd	Z Ltd
	£	£	£
Schedule D Case I	600,000	Nil	Nil
Schedule D Case III	50,000	121,000	10,000
Profit	650,000	121,000	10,000

Next we need to calculate the upper and lower limits:

Limits $\frac{£300000}{3} = £100{,}000$ $\frac{£10000}{3} = £3{,}333$

$\frac{£1.5m}{3} = £500{,}000$ $\frac{£50000}{3} = £16{,}667$

We can see that X is paying tax at 30%, Y is paying tax at 32.75% on the top part of its profits and Z is paying tax at 23.75%.

We want to save tax at the highest marginal rate.

Y has a loss of £40,000. The optimum claim will be to use £21,000 of loss to reduce Y's profits down to the lower limit and then to use the balance of the loss in X by way of group relief.

Z has a loss of £20,000 and the best place to use this loss will again be in X by way of group relief.

Therefore, in Y, as we cannot specify the amount to offset under a current year claim (it is an all or nothing claim), the group relief claim of £19,000 must be made first before submitting an all-or-nothing current year claim under s.393A(1)(a) for the balance, being £21,000.

	X Ltd	Y Ltd	Z Ltd
	£	£	£
Schedule D Case I	600,000	Nil	Nil
Schedule D Case III	50,000	121,000	10,000
Profit	650,000	121,000	10,000
Current year claim		(21,000)	
Group relief: Y Ltd	(19,000)		
Z Ltd	(20,000)		
PCTCT	**£611,000**	**100,000**	**10,000**

Example 1

Consider the following:

	Fog Ltd	*Mist Ltd*
	£	£
Schedule D Case I	80,000	10,000
Schedule A	-	(100,000)
Charges on income	(5,000)	-

What is the maximum loss that can be surrendered from Mist Ltd to Fog Ltd?

Example 2

Consider the group below:

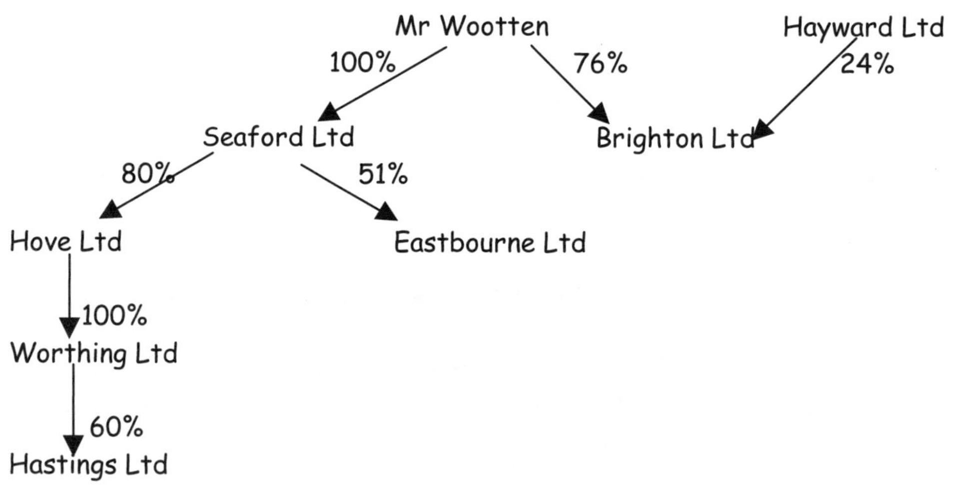

You are required to:

(1) Identify the companies which are associated with Seaford Ltd for corporation tax purposes.

(2) Identify the groups which exist for group relief purposes.

Example 3

Houllier Ltd has two wholly owned subsidiaries Owen Ltd and Heskey Ltd, and 60% of the shares in Gerrard Ltd. The results for the year ended 31 March 2006 are as follows:

	Houllier Ltd	*Owen Ltd*	*Heskey Ltd*	*Gerrard Ltd*
	£	£	£	£
Schedule DI	100,000	40,000	nil	90,000
Trading loss			(60,000)	
Schedule DIII	10,000	4,000	6,000	2,000
Chargeable gain	20,000	-	-	4,000

You are required to calculate the corporation tax liability for each company, assuming the loss relief is taken in the most efficient way.

Answer 1

	Fog Ltd	Mist Ltd
	£	£
Schedule D Case I	80,000	10,000
Schedule A		(10,000)
Charge on income	(5,000)	___
Profit	75,000	Nil
Group relief	**(75,000)**	
PCTCT	**Nil**	

The excess Schedule A loss is £90,000 of which £75,000 can be surrendered. The remaining £15,000 will be carried forward.

Answer 2

(1) Associated companies:

Seaford Ltd Hove Ltd Eastbourne Ltd Worthing Ltd Hastings Ltd Brighton Ltd	Limits for corporation tax are therefore divided by 6

Seaford Ltd is associated with Brighton Ltd as they are controlled by the same person – i.e. Mr Wootten.

To determine whether Seaford Ltd and Hastings Ltd are associated, we do <u>not</u> multiply the effective interests – it is sufficient that each company in the chain is controlled by its parent.

(2) Group relief group:

There is only one group for group relief purposes, i.e.

Seaford Ltd + Hove Ltd + Worthing Ltd.

Seaford Ltd and Brighton Ltd are not in the same group as they are not under the 75% control of the same <u>company.</u>

Answer 3

Small companies limits – 4 company group	
£10,000 × ¼	£2,500
£50,000 × ¼	£12,500
£300,000 × ¼	£75,000
£1.5m × ¼	£375,000

	Houllier Ltd	Owen Ltd	Heskey Ltd	Gerrard Ltd
	£	£	£	£
Schedule DI	100,000	40,000	-	90,000
Schedule DIII	10,000	4,000	6,000	2,000
Chargeable gain	20,000			4,000
PCTCT before loss relief	130,000	44,000	6,000	96,000
Tax rate prior to relief	*Marginal*	*19%*	*Small marginal*	*Marginal*
Current year			(3,500)	
Group relief	(55,000)	(1,500)		n/a
PCTCT after group relief	75,000	42,500	2,500	96,000
CT @ 19%	14,250	8,075	-	
CT @ 30%				28,800
11/400 x (375,000 – 96,000)				(7,673)
CT payable	14,250	8,075	-	21,127

Notes:

1. Gerrard Ltd is not a 75 % subsidiary and so cannot participate in the group relief claim (it is however an associate)
2. Houllier Ltd's profits are in the highest marginal band – i.e. 32.75%. Therefore we first use sufficient losses to bring Houllier Ltd's profits down to the small companies limit of £75,000.
3. Heskey's Ltd's profits are in the lower marginal band – i.e. 23.75%. Therefore we have used sufficient losses to bring Heskey Ltd's profits down to the starting rate limit of £2,500.
4. It would have been equally correct to allocate the £1,500 balance of losses to Houllier Ltd instead of Owen Ltd, as it saves 19% tax in both cases, and in fact would save administrative work as a signatory for each company has to sign a group relief claim.
5. The order of claims will be as follows:

	£
Loss in Heskey Ltd	60,000
Less: group relief in Houllier Ltd	(55,000)
Less: group relief to Owen Ltd	(1,500)
Balance	3,500
Less: s.393(A)(1)(a) current year Claim in Heskey Ltd	(3,500)
Loss remaining	Nil

SUMMARY - THE PRINCIPLES OF GROUP RELIEF

When a company makes a trading loss it can surrender it to another member of the same 75% group.

The maximum amount that can be surrendered is the lower of:

(i) the loss of the surrendering company, and

(ii) the PCTCT of the claimant company

There is no requirement for the surrendering company to use the loss against its own income before surrender but it may do if it so chooses.

Schedule DIII deficits may also be group relieved in the same way.

Excess Schedule A losses, excess charges (trade or non trade), excess management expenses and excess DVI losses on non trade IFAs can also be included in a group relief claim.

The loss is allocated to relieve income taxed at the highest (marginal) rates.

The marginal rates are:

£0 - £10,000	0%
£10,001 - £50,000	23.75%
£50,001 - £300,000	19%
£300,001 - £1,500,000	32.75%
over £1.5m	30%

C18: GROUP CAPITAL GAINS

This chapter covers the definition of a gains group and looks at how it differs from a losses group. Once we have established the group we will then consider:
- the effect of transferring assets between group companies;
- the loss relief which is available;
- the availability of rollover relief in a gains group;
- the transfer of assets to stock within a group.

C18.1 Definition

Companies are in the same capital gains group when one company owns at **least 75%** of the ordinary shares of another company or two companies are 75% owned by the same parent. s. 170 TCGA 1992

This 75% definition is similar to the rules for group relief but, for group gains purposes, we **only need 75% of the ordinary shares** and not 75% of distributable profits nor 75% of assets on a winding-up.

The group gains regime also has slightly different rules for sub-subsidiaries.

For group gains, the direct relationship must be at least 75% but **the indirect relationship need only be above 50%.** We refer to this as the effective 51% subsidiary test. s. 170(3) TCGA 1992

In addition, for group gains a company can only be a member of one group. s. 170(6) TCGA 1992

Illustration 1

Consider the following structure:

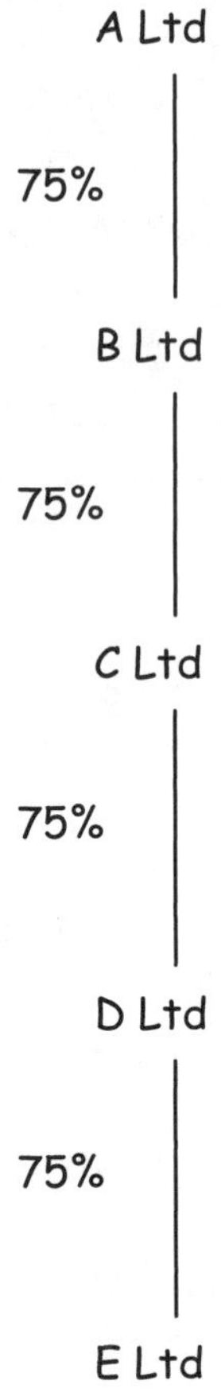

Group relief group:

For group loss relief we need a **75% direct and indirect relationship**.

Therefore, for group relief we can transfer losses between A and B, between B and C, between C and D and between D and E.

The indirect relationship between A and C is 56.25%. For group relief we need at least 75%; no losses can flow between A and C nor between A and any other companies further down the group.

Group gains group:

When considering a capital gains group we must look at the A group as A is the ultimate holding company. Thus we call A the principal company. A owns 56.25% of C and, consequently, C can be included in A's gains group.

However, A only owns 42% of D (75% of 56.25%), and therefore as this is below 50%, D is not part of A's group. Consequently, the A capital gains group comprises companies A, B and C.

We cannot link C and D for the group gains purposes - the reason for this is that a company which is a 75 % subsidiary of another company cannot be a principal company unless it fails the effective subsidiary test. In other words a company cannot be a member of more than one group for group gains purposes.

As C is a member of A's gains group, it cannot form a sub-group with D. This rule does not apply to group relief so for group relief we can link C and D, but for group gains we cannot.

However, D can be a principal company and form its own group and, consequently, we can link D and E together for group gains purposes as D becomes a new holding company. So, for group gains, we have two groups, the A group comprising A, B and C, and the D group comprising D and E.

Transfers of assets:

C and D are clearly connected companies and consequently any transfers between these companies will be at market value.

Transfers of assets within the **same capital gains group** however will all take place at **no gain no loss** - we shall study this in more detail shortly. s. 171 TCGA 1992

Example 1

Consider the following structure:

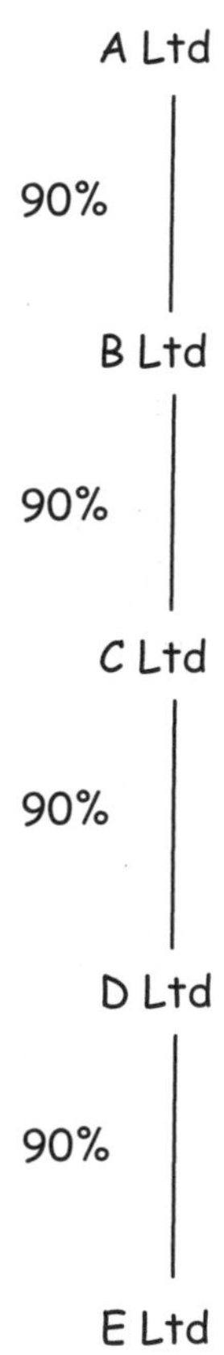

Identify which companies are in A's group relief group and capital gains group.

C18.2 Intra group transfers of assets

s.171 TCGA 1992

Transfers between **members** of the **same group** are treated as **no gain no loss transfers**. This rule applies automatically and is compulsory. This is the same rule that applies to transfers of assets between a married couple.

The rules apply where:

a) the transferring company is UK resident at the time of the disposal or the asset is a chargeable asset in relation to the company immediately before that time and
b) the transferee company is either UK resident at the time of the disposal or the asset is a chargeable asset in relation to that company immediately after that time.

Illustration 2

Beckham Limited owns 100% of Posh Limited. In September 1991 Beckham Limited purchased a property at a cost of £500,000. In January 2006, Beckham Limited decided to transfer this property to Posh Limited. The transfer will take place at no gain no loss.

We have a cost of £500,000, indexation of say £250,000 therefore, our proceeds are deemed to be £750,000 in order to give us no gain no loss.

	£
Proceeds	750,000
Cost	(500,000)
Indexation at, say 50%	(250,000)
	nil

In other words the proceeds are cost plus indexation to the date of transfer.

Consequently, Posh Limited will have a base cost of this particular property of £750,000 which it will index in a future disposal calculation from January 2006, the date of the intra-group transfer.

Example 2

Thompson Ltd has one wholly owned subsidiary, Murphy Ltd. Murphy bought a property for £180,000 in July 1986. In December 1997 it transferred the property to Thompson Ltd when its market value was £250,000.

Thompson Ltd sold the property in August 2006 for £380,000.

You are required to calculate the gain chargeable on Thompson Ltd in its accounts for the 12 months to 31 December 2006.

Assume (for illustration purposes) the following indexed rises:

July 1986 – December 1997:	0.641
December 1997-August 2006:	0.186

C18.3 Notional transfers

s.171A TCGA 1992

A notional transfer is where we **pretend** that an asset or part of it has been **transferred within the group prior to it being sold**.

This is to **utilise capital losses** and also to ensure **gains are taxed at the lowest marginal rate** possible.

Illustration 3

Bush Limited owns 100% of Blair Limited. They have income in the year ended 31 March 2006 of £500,000 and £75,000 respectively. Blair Limited has capital losses brought forward of £90,000.

In the year ended 31 March 2006, Bush Limited sold a property and realised a capital gain of £150,000. What we must do is ascertain in which company it would be better for the gain to arise.

As there are two companies in the group, the corporation tax lower and upper limits must be divided by two giving us £150,000 and £750,000 respectively. The marginal rates of tax are 19% below £150,000, 32.75% between the limits and 30% above £750,000.

As Bush has other profits of £500,000, if we were to add the gain to Bush's profits, the gain would be taxed in full at the marginal 32.75% rate of tax. The extra tax would be:

£150,000 x 32.75% = £49,125

If however we were to do a notional transfer, transferring the property from Bush Limited to Blair Limited (by electing on the CT600), we might find we get a better result.

Blair Limited has other income of £75,000. We would utilise Blair Limited's capital losses brought forward of £90,000 reducing the taxable capital gain to £60,000. The gain will all be taxed at 19% so the extra tax this time would be:

£(150,000 - 90,000) x 19% = £11,400

So effecting the transfer will save the group corporation tax of:

£49,125 - £11,400 = £37,725

Clearly this would be worthwhile.

C18.4 Making a notional transfer claim

s.171A TCGA 1992

The claim to treat an asset or any part of it as being transferred to a fellow group company immediately before its sale can only be made if the no gain no loss transfer rule would apply between the two companies who make the election.

It has to be a **joint election made in writing within two years** of the end of the accounting period of the company who sells the asset. s. 171A(4) TCGA 1992

Any incidental cost incurred by the company making the actual disposal will be deemed to be incidental cost of the other company. s. 171A(2) TCGA 1992

Any payments made between the companies in relation to the notional transfer will be ignored to the extent they do not exceed the chargeable gain or allowable loss that arises on the company making the deemed disposal. s. 171A(5) TCGA 1992

Example 3

Calf Limited is a wholly owned subsidiary of Bull Limited. Bull Limited does not have any other subsidiaries. During the year ended 31 March 2006, the predicted profits of each company are £100,000 and £700,000 respectively. Calf Limited has capital losses brought forward of £30,000 and in February 2006 Bull Limited sold a property realising a capital gain of £100,000.

Assuming that they are going to make the most beneficial elections, calculate the minimum corporation tax payable on this gain.

C18.5 Group wide rollover relief

A **capital gains group** is **treated as one unit for rollover relief purposes.**

Assume that A and B are part of the same capital gains group and that A has sold an asset for £900,000 which has realised a capital gain of £350,000. s. 175 & s. 152 TCGA 1992

Remembering the normal rules of rollover, provided that **within one year prior to the sale and three years after,** A reinvests all of the £900,000 proceeds, the capital gain can be rolled over and deducted from the base cost of a replacement asset.

Assume B invested £1 million into a new asset. This will enable the gain in A to be rolled over against the base cost of the asset purchased by B under the group wide rollover provisions. This gives a base cost of the replacement asset in B of £650,000.

C18.6 Transfers within a group: trading stock

s.173 TCGA 1992

Special rules apply where an asset held as capital is transferred to another member of a capital gains group which will hold the asset as stock and vice versa.

Where an asset held as **capital** is transferred by company A **to** company B in the same gains group who will hold the asset as **trading stock,** the **transfer will take place under the no gain/ no loss rules**. Once B receives the asset, it will be immediately **taken to trading stock at its market value.**

Illustration 4

Cap Ltd, a trading company, transfers a property to Hat Ltd, a property-dealing company. The companies are in the same gains group. Cap Ltd had bought the property many years ago for £550,000. The indexation factor up to the date of transfer is 0.225. The market value of the property at the time of the transfer was £740,000

Firstly, the property will go from Cap Ltd to Hat Ltd at no gain no loss. The deemed disposal proceeds for Cap Ltd will be:

	£
Cost	550,000
IA 0.225 x 550,000	123,750
	673,750

This will also be the base cost of the property for Hat Ltd.

The asset will then be taken to stock in Hat Ltd at its market value of £740,000 and so a gain will arise in Hat Ltd as follows:

Deemed proceeds	740,000
Indexed cost	(673,750)
	66,250

If Hat Ltd now sells the property from stock at its market value there will be no trading profit.

Hat Ltd, a property-dealing company, has therefore ended up with a capital gain. The company normally has DI income or losses from property sales.

Hat Ltd can make use of the election in s.161 TCGA 1992 - this election allows a trader who is appropriating a capital asset to stock to **elect for the asset to be taken to stock at its indexed cost.** The election has to be **made within two years** of the end of the accounting period in which the asset is taken to stock.

If Hat Ltd makes this election, at the time of the transfer from Cap Ltd the building will be taken to stock at a value of £673,750 and there will be no capital gain. On a future sale of the property at market value, a DI profit of £66,250 will arise.

This election will be especially useful where the property-dealing company has trading losses brought forward or the transferred asset is standing at a capital loss.

If an asset is transferred by a company that holds it as trading **stock, to** a company that will hold the asset as a **capital** asset, then the company that holds the asset as trading stock is treated as making a **disposal from trading stock** at market value prior to the transfer.

Illustration 5

Paper Ltd and Tray Ltd are two companies in a gains group. Paper Ltd is a property dealing company, Tray Ltd is a trading company. Paper Ltd has a property which it bought for £370,000. The market value of the property is £400,000. It is to be transferred to Tray Ltd.

Paper Ltd will be treated as taking the property out of trading stock at its market value and so will make a DI profit of £400,000 - £370,000 = £30,000.

Tray Ltd will receive the property at its market value of £400,000. Indexation allowance will begin to run from the date the property is transferred.

Answer 1

Group relief group:

Clearly for group relief we can transfer losses between A and B and between B and C. A indirectly owns 81% of C (90% of 90%). Consequently, losses can also be transferred between A and C.

A indirectly owns 72.9% of D (90% of 81%). This is below 75% and consequently losses cannot flow between A and D.

Therefore the group relief group relevant to A includes companies **A, B and C.**

Group gains group:

For group gains A indirectly owns 81% of C, 72.9% of D and 65.61% of E (90% of 72.9%). So, going all the way down the chain, we find that A's indirect relationship in E is above 50% so consequently all of the companies are in A's gains group.

Therefore the group gains group relevant to A includes companies **A, B, C, D and E.**

Answer 2

Transfer from Murphy Ltd to Thompson Ltd in December 1997:

	£
Cost to Murphy Ltd	180,000
IA from July 1986 - December 1997	
0.641 x £180,000	115,380
Cost to Thompson Ltd	295,380

Disposal by Thompson Ltd in August 2006:

Proceeds	380,000
Less: cost December 1997	(295,380)
	84,620
Less: IA Dec 1997 - August 2006	
0.186 x £295,380	(54,941)
Gain y/e 31.12.2006	**29,679**

Answer 3

The upper and lower limits are £750,000 and £150,000 respectively.

Bull Ltd has other income of £700,000.

If the gain was taxed in Bull Ltd it would increase corporation tax liability by:

£(50,000 x 32.75%) + £(50,000 x 30%) = £31,375

Calf Ltd has other income of £100,000.

If we notionally transfer the asset to Calf Ltd to trigger the gain in Calf Ltd, the position would be improved as Calf has some capacity in the 19% band and also has capital losses brought forward.

	£
Gain	100,000
Capital losses b/f	(30,000)
	70,000

The corporation tax liability would be:

(£50,000 x 19% + £20,000 x 32.75%) = **£16,050**

Electing for the notional transfer has therefore saved tax of £15,325 for the group.

SUMMARY – GROUP CAPITAL GAINS

A gains group requires a 75% relationship between companies. However, unlike group relief groups it is possible to include sub-subsidiaries of 75% subsidiaries, providing the effective holding is more than 50%.

Assets transferred between members of a gains group automatically move on a no gain no loss basis, i.e. the new company inherits the indexed cost of the old one.

Companies can elect to treat assets as if they were transferred intra group prior to sale.

Gains groups can claim rollover relief on a group wide basis.

If a fixed asset held by one group member is transferred to another who will take it to stock then a gain will arise on the transferee when the asset is appropriated to stock. An election is however available to allow the asset to be appropriated to stock at indexed cost.

C19: CLOSE COMPANY DEFINITION

This chapter looks at the following areas:
- the definition of a close company;
- the definition of associate;
- exceptions to being a close company.

Statutory references in this chapter are to ICTA 1988 unless stated otherwise.

C19.1 Introduction

A close company is a company which is **resident in the UK** and is **controlled by either** s. 414

- **five or fewer participators** (shareholders); or
- **any number of directors who are also shareholders**.

Consequently, in the UK, **most private companies are close.**

C19.2 Directors

In this context a director is anyone who acts as a director by whatever name called (e.g. Chairman). In addition, we include any manager of the company, who, with their associates, owns 20% or more of the voting shares of the company.

C19.3 Associates

When **determining the level of ownership** by **one particular shareholder** we **must also include shares owned by his or her associates**. The rules for associates are very similar to those which apply in determining whether companies are associated with each other. s. 417

For close company purposes associates include:

- the **individual's immediate family**,

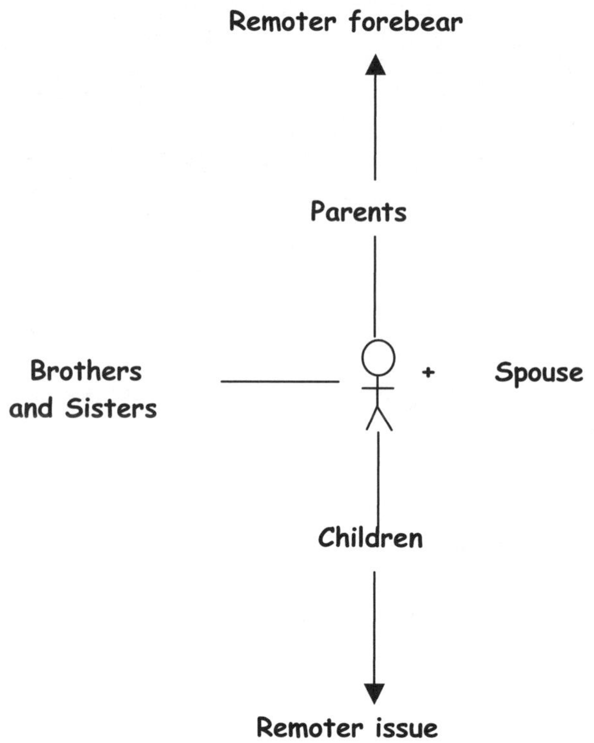

- **business partners** (but not co-directors)
- **trustees of trusts** set up by the individual or any of his immediate family
- **nominees** (a nominee is simply an individual who owns shares on behalf of someone else).

Example 1

Julie invites the following people round to dinner. Which of them are associated with her?

	Yes	No
Her brother		
Her brother's wife		
Her godson		
Her ex-husband		
Her business partner		
Her grandmother		
Her bank manager		

Example 2

Reynolds Limited is owned as follows:

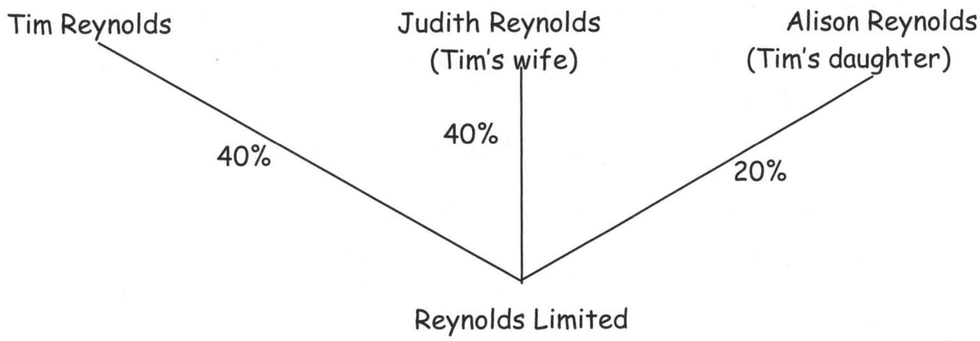

Is Reynolds Limited a close company?

Example 3

Eastenders Limited is owned as follows:

* Phil Mitchell	11%
* Pauline Fowler	11%
* Dorothy Cotton	11%
* Pat Evans	11%
* Terry Raymond	6%
Gary Hobbs	5%
Others – owing less than 5%	45%
	100%

* = Director

Is Eastenders Limited a close company?

Does your answer change if Gary Hobbs is appointed a director?

Example 4

Trotters Independent Traders Limited is owned as follows:

Derek Trotter	20%
Rodney Trotter (Derek's brother)	7%
Albert Trotter (Derek's uncle)	5%
Boycee	10%
Marlene (Boycee's wife)	3%
Trigger	6%
Cassandra (Rodney's girlfriend)	4%
Others (1% each)	45%
	100%

Is the company close?

C19.4 Exceptions

s.414(1)

Certain companies will not be close companies. These are:

1) non resident companies;
2) registered friendly or industrial societies building societies and life assurance companies;
3) companies controlled on or behalf of the crown;
4) companies controlled by open companies;
5) quoted companies with substantial public interest.

Answer 1

	Yes	No
Her brother	✓	
Her brother's wife		✓
Her godson		✓
Her ex husband		✓
Her business partner	✓	
Her grandmother	✓	
Her bank manager		✓

Answer 2

Reynolds Limited is a close company as over half of the shares (in this case all of the shares) are owned by 5 or fewer participators.

Answer 3

The 5 "largest" shareholders are:

Phil	11%
Pauline	11%
Dot	11%
Pat	11%
Terry	6%
	50%

This is not control by five or fewer shareholders (not more than 50%) so the company is not close.

If Gary is appointed as a director, then 55% of the shares are owned by the directors. This is control by any number of director shareholders so the company would become close.

Answer 4

The top 5 shareholders in the company are as follows:

Derek (including Rodney)	27%
Boycee (including Marlene)	13%
Trigger	6%
Albert	5%
Cassandra	4%
	55%

This is control so the company is close.

SUMMARY – CLOSE COMPANY DEFINITION

A close company is a company that is resident in the UK and controlled by either 5 or fewer participators or any number of participator directors.

In looking at a person's shareholding we consider shares held by their associates.

For close company purposes associate includes: Spouse, parents and remoter forbears, children and remoter issue and siblings.

There are exceptions which include;

- registered industrial societies, friendly societies, building societies and life assurance companies
- companies controlled on behalf of the crown
- companies controlled by open companies
- quoted companies with substantial public interest.

C20a: CLOSE COMPANY IMPLICATIONS – PART 1

This chapter looks at the following areas:
- the impact of being a close company on the company and its shareholders;
- the impact of a company making a loan to one of its shareholders.

Statutory references in this chapter are to ICTA 1988 unless stated otherwise.

C20a.1 Introduction

Close company rules exist to prevent shareholders and directors of close companies from using those companies as an extension to their own private banking facilities without paying any tax! Rules exist with regard to:

- **loans to participators** and
- **benefits provided to participators**.

C20a.2 Loans to participators

Jack is both a director and shareholder of Vine Limited. Within the company's books Jack is likely to have a current account, where amounts he is entitled to from the company are credited and amounts he takes out are debited. s. 419

Jack is entitled to a salary, after tax, of £80,000. The company will debit salary costs and credit Jack's current account. The salary itself is taxed as earnings using the PAYE system.

Jack is also entitled to dividends from the company of £50,000. The company will debit dividends and credit Jack's current account. The dividends themselves will be taxed on Jack at the usual dividend rates and higher rate tax may be due.

We can see that Jack is entitled to withdraw a total of £130,000 from the company. Assume that Jack actually takes out £150,000. Jack has borrowed an extra £20,000 from the company by way of a "loan to a participator".

It is this loan that the close company rules seek to tax under the provisions of s.419 ICTA 1988.

C20a.3 S.419 tax

Close companies which are not liable to pay their corporation tax by instalments will be required to pay **s.419 tax on their normal due date, i.e. 9 months and 1 day** following the end of the chargeable accounting period. s. 419(3)

The **tax is calculated as 25% of the loan** and is payable by the company.

The **amount of the loan** is taken as the **lower of the amount outstanding on**

- **the last day of the chargeable accounting period** or
- **the normal due date.**

For larger close companies s. 419 tax is added to the amount of tax due by instalments which adds a horrendous complication to the instalments system!

Example 1

Jack borrowed £20,000 from Vine Limited (a small close company) on 30 September 2004. He will repay it as follows:

30.9.05	Repaid £10,000
30.9.06	Repaid £5,000
30.9.07	Repaid £5,000

Vine Limited has a 31 December accounting date.

How much tax is due under s.419 and when is it due?

C20a.4 Repayment of s.419 tax

Where the loan is either repaid by the participator or waived by the company (in other words written off, with the participator being released from any further repayments), tax previously paid under section 419 will be refunded back to the company.

The **refund** is **made by reducing the company's tax liability for the chargeable accounting period in which the loan is repaid or waived.** As most close companies are small, this will normally be nine months and one day from the end of the accounting period in which the repayment or release of the loan is made. s. 419(4)

Example 2

In the previous example, Vine Limited paid s.419 tax of £2,500 on 1.10.05 in respect of a loan outstanding of £10,000.

The loan is repaid as follows:

30.9.06	£5,000
30.9.07	£5,000

How much s.419 tax will be refunded to Vine Limited and when?

C20a.5 Implications for the participator

If a company waives a loan to a participator the company will receive a repayment of the s.419 tax. The individual has received real money from the company. The **participator** therefore **will be treated as receiving a dividend equal to the amount of the loan waived**. s. 421(1)

The date of receipt of the dividend will be the date of the loan waiver. An individual will pay higher rate tax via self assessment if he is a higher rate taxpayer.

Illustration 1

Heppel Limited, a small close company, advanced £15,000 to Fred, who is a director and shareholder, on 31 December 2003.

On 31 December 2005 Fred repaid £5,000 and Heppel Limited waived a further £9,000.

Heppel Limited has a 31 March year end.

Implications for Heppel Limited:

The loan is advanced on 31 December 2003, which is in the company's accounting period ended 31 March 2004.

S.419 tax is due nine months and one day later, on 1 January 2005:

25% x £15,000 = £3,750

This tax is refunded when the loan is either waived or repaid. A total of £14,000 is released from the loan on 31 December 2005, which is during the company's year ended 31 March 2006.

Any refund is made nine months and one day later, on 1 January 2007:

25% x £14,000 = £3,500

Implications for Fred:

Fred is deemed to receive a dividend of £9,000 on 31 December 2005, which is in tax year 2005/06. Assuming that Fred is a higher rate taxpayer, he will be taxed on that dividend. The dividend itself is grossed up for the tax credit of 10%.

	£
$£9,000 \times \frac{100}{90}$	10,000
Tax at 32.5%	3,250
Tax credit: £10,000 x 10%	(1,000)
Higher rate tax due	2,250

This tax will be due on 31 January 2007.

A simpler way of calculating this higher rate tax would be to take the net dividend of £9,000 and multiply it by 25% which leads us to the same figure of £2,250.

Answer 1

Loan advanced 30.9.04 which is during the company's year end 31.12.04

Amount outstanding:
At end of CAP i.e. at 31.12.04 = £20,000
At due date of payment for CT i.e. at 1.10.05 = £10,000

So the s.419 tax due on 1.10.05 is:

£10,000 x 25% = £2,500

Answer 2

First repayment on 30.9.06 is during the company's year ended 31.12.06

Refund made on 1.10.07 is:

£5,000 x 25% = £1,250

Second repayment on 30.9.07 is during the company's year ended 31.12.07

Refund made on 1.10.08 is:

£5,000 x 25% = £1,250

SUMMARY - CLOSE COMPANY IMPLICATIONS (1)

Where a close company makes a loan to a shareholder it is first necessary to see if it is exempt. If not, there will be a s.419 charge on the company equal to 25% of the amount of the loan.

This will be payable with the CT liability for the period, unless the loan has been repaid before the tax is due.

Where the tax is payable, it can be reclaimed by the company if the loan is repaid.

If the loan is written off, the company can reclaim the tax but the recipient will become liable to income tax as though the loan written off was a dividend.

C20b: CLOSE COMPANY IMPLICATIONS – PART 2

This chapter looks at:
- the impact of close companies providing benefits to shareholders who are not employees;
- the consequences of being a close investment holding company.

Statutory references in this chapter are to ICTA 1988 unless stated otherwise.

C20b.1 Loans excluded from s.419 Charge s. 420

Loans **made in the ordinary course of business of the company** are excluded from the s.419 charge. Under this exclusion the close company must be a bank or similar moneylender.

There is also an exclusion for the supply of goods or services in the ordinary course of the trade unless the credit period is longer than normal. s.420(1)

There is an exclusion for loans of no more than £15,000 made to a full-time director or employee who is entitled to no more than 5% of the company's assets on a winding-up. When calculating this 5%, we must also take account of holdings owned by his associates. s.420(2)

If the borrower acquires a 5% holding at a time when the whole or part of the loan remains outstanding, then he will be treated as receiving a loan at that time. s.420(2)

Illustration 1

Green Ltd a close company with a December year end makes a loan of £12,000 to Jim who is a full time working director and holds 3% of the share capital on 1 October 2005. On the 1 January 2006 Jim repays £5000 of the loan. On the 31 March 2006 Jim increases his shareholding to 6%.

At the time the loan is made it is covered by the exception as it is for less than £15,000, and to a full-time working director who does not hold a material interest in the company. No s.419 tax is payable. The repayment of £5,000 has no implications for s.419.

On 31 March 2006 Jim acquired further shares and now holds more than 5%. Thus Green Ltd is treated as having made a loan on 31 March 2006 equal to the loan outstanding which is £12,000 - £5,000 = £7,000.

S.419 tax is payable in respect of the accounting period ended 31 December 2006. If the company is not large it will be due on 1 October 2007.

C20b.2 Beneficial loan interest s. 418

Where a **company makes a loan to a participator**, and either **charges no interest, or** charges interest **below the official rate**, a **benefit in kind is levied on the participator**. Where the participator is an employee or director this will need to be reported on his P11D and will be taxed under the earnings rules.

Illustration 2

Campbell Limited, a close company, lends £10,000 to Ted who is a shareholder and employee in the company. The loan is advanced on 1 October 2004 and Ted repays it to Campbell Limited on 30 September 2005. Assuming that the beneficial interest rate is 7.25%, Ted's benefit in kind will be as follows.

For the tax year 2004/05, we look at the period 1 October 2004 to the 5 April 2005 which is 187 days and therefore the benefit will be:

$$£10{,}000 \times 7.25\% \times \frac{187}{365} = £371$$

For the next tax year 2005/2006, we look at the period 6 April 2005 to the 30 September 2005, that is a period of 178 days, and therefore the benefit will be:

$$£10{,}000 \times 7.25\% \times \frac{178}{365} = £354$$

These figures will need to be reported on Ted's P11Ds for those separate tax years.

C20b.3 Benefits to participators s. 418

Where a shareholder is an employee or director of a close company, any benefits he receives are taxed under the earnings rules. Therefore, in the absence of any special rules, where shareholders are not directors or employees, they would not pay any tax on benefits they receive. This is the reason for **S.418 which will treat those benefits as net dividends paid to those shareholders**. The net dividend is calculated using the normal benefit rules for earnings.

Illustration 3

Joan receives a company car from Morley Limited, a close company. The car has a list price of £21,000, and CO_2 emissions of 188g/km. She is a shareholder in the company but not an employee or a director. In tax year 2005/06, she will be treated as receiving a net dividend calculated using the benefit in kind rules.

	£
Car Benefit [185 - 140]/5 = 9 + 15 = 24% £21,000 x 24% = £5,040	
Deemed gross dividend £5,040 x $\frac{100}{90}$	5,600
Tax at 32.5%	1,820
Tax credit: £5,600 x 10%	(560)
Higher rate tax due	1,260

That gives us a net dividend of £5,040 which we gross up at 100/90 to £5,600.

The tax will be added to Joan's tax liability for 2005/06 and the tax must be paid by 31 January 2007.

C20b.4 Close investment holding companies

All close companies are Close Investment Holding Companies (CIHCs) unless they exist wholly or mainly for one of the permitted purposes which basically are to be a trading company or a member of a trading group or to make investments in land. s.13A

Where the company is a CIHC, it **cannot use the small and marginal company rates of tax.** Instead such companies will **always be taxed at the full rate** of corporation tax (currently 30%), regardless of the level of its profits.

C20b.5 Jointly held property

From 6 April 2004 where shares in a close company are held jointly by a husband and wife any **income from the shares will be taxed according to actual ownership**. Previously the income was taxed 50:50 unless an election was made for taxation according to actual ownership.

C20b.6 Summary

Where a **benefit is paid to an employee or director**, as far as the recipient is concerned, the benefit is taxed in the usual way under the earnings rules and reported on **form P11D**. As far as the company is concerned, the cost of providing that benefit is tax deductible in the usual way.

As far as a non-working participator recipient is concerned, the individual will be **treated as receiving a dividend on any s.418 benefits received.** The value of the dividend will be calculated using the normal benefit rules and will be subject to higher rate tax where appropriate.

As far as the company is concerned, the cost of providing that benefit will **not be deductible** as it is treated as an appropriation from profit.

The exception to this rule is **the write off of a loan to a participator**. A loan write off **is always treated as a distribution**.

SUMMARY - CLOSE COMPANY IMPLICATIONS (2)

If a close company provides a benefit to an employee/shareholder, it is taxed under the normal earnings rules. If the shareholder is not an employee, the value of the benefit is treated as a dividend paid to the shareholder.

The write off of a loan to a participator is always treated as a dividend.

Close Investment Holding Companies, are companies whose main activity is making investments, rather than trading. A CIHC is always taxed at the full CT rate, currently 30%.

The income from jointly held shares will be taxed according to actual ownership of each spouse from 6 April 2004.

C21: INVESTMENT COMPANIES

This chapter explains the basic rules in relation to the taxation of companies with investment business including:

- definition of an investment company and a company with investment business;
- treatment of management expenses pre and post 1 April 2004;
- change in ownership provisions for companies with investment business;
- definition of CIHC;
- relief available for investment companies for losses on sale of shares.

C21.1 Definition

A **company with investment business** is defined in the legislation as a "company whose business consists **wholly or partly** in the making of investments". s .130

This definition was introduced by FA 2004 with effect from 1 April 2004 and is particularly relevant in relation to claiming relief for management expenses.

A company with investment business is not simply a company that holds investments or receives investment income. It is a company that has a **business** of making investments.

Prior to FA 2004, a company had to be an **investment company** in order to obtain relief for management expenses. An investment company is a "company whose business consists **wholly or mainly** in the making of investments **and the principal part of whose income is derived therefrom**".

It can be seen that the definition of a company with investment business is wider than that of an investment company and that all investment companies are also companies with investment business.

The term investment company is now only relevant when considering which companies may claim relief against income for capital losses on sales of certain shares. More on this later. s.573

The Revenue, in Tax Bulletin 19, tell us to look at the totality of the company's functions and activities to identify a business wholly or partly in the making of investments.

Consider a flat management company that owns the freehold of a block of flats and all the flat owners have a share in the company. This type of company would **not** be treated as a company with investment business as its business is not that of making investments; its business is the provision of management services.

In the case of *Cook v the Medway Housing Society Limited* in 1997, it was held that a Housing Association purchasing property from a Local Authority, and receiving rental income, with the aim of applying any profits to either buy more property or pass it to charity, **was an investment company** because it had a business of making investments and had an intention of making a profitable return. It did not matter that the return was never going to be paid to the shareholders. The intention was enough for investment company status to apply.

We can contrast this with the case of *Tintern Close Residents Society Ltd.* In 1995 this company owned and managed an estate that consisted of 21 houses 1 flat and 22 lock up garages. The company's income consisted of members' subscriptions and ground rents. It was held that the main function and activity of the company was the management and maintenance of the property. Although it had been formed to purchase land, it was not for the purpose of turning the land to profit.

In the case of *Jarrett v O'Neill and Brennan Construction Limited*, it was held that a company depositing funds into a bank account and receiving interest, did not constitute a business and therefore, for associated company purposes, it was treated as dormant.

C21.2 Management expenses post 1 April 2004

From 1 April 2004, the ability to claim management expenses has been extended to **include companies with an investment business** - not just those qualifying as investment companies - and also to include **non UK resident companies**.

The extension to companies with an investment business will be important for companies who hold shares in subsidiaries as well as having their own trade.

FA 2004 replaced the existing rules relating to management expenses with a **new s.75** that applies to all accounting periods beginning on or after 1 April 2004. Where an accounting period straddles this date the company will be treated as having two notional accounting periods.

Management expenses are deductible against the total profits of a company with an investment business. **The expenses will be deducted based on when they are debited in the accounts.** The accounts must be drawn up in accordance with GAAP. Where the period of account exceeds twelve months, management expenses will be time apportioned. s.75A

No expenses can be deducted as management expenses if they are **otherwise deductible for tax.** s.75(2)

Expenses of a capital nature are not management expenses, unless they relate to capital allowances. Thus for the first time there is statutory authority to exclude capital expenditure from management expenses. This has arisen as a result of case law in this area, as we shall see below. s.75(3)

Expenses will only qualify for a deduction to the extent that they are made in respect of the company's investment business and to the extent that they are **not made for an unallowable purpose**. s.75(4)

An investment is held for **an unallowable purpose** to the extent that it is not held for a business or other commercial purpose, or is held for activities outside the charge to corporation tax. This will exclude investments held for social or recreational purposes and investments of a non resident company with a permanent establishment in the UK, if the investment is not part of the business of the PE.

Surplus capital allowances are added to management expenses.

Examples of management expenses include:

(i) **Commissions paid to agents**, such as stockbrokers who manage the portfolio of shares;

(ii) **Capital allowances on plant used to manage the investments**, such as computer equipment used to monitor the progress of the investments;

(iii) **Reasonable salaries**, which includes redundancy costs. The Revenue may seek to disallow excessive directors' remuneration where it cannot be justified given the amount of input the directors have in managing the investments against the return derived from them. If the Revenue feel the amount is excessive, they will seek to disallow some management expenses. However, they will still tax the director's full salary and subject the company to Class 1 secondary National Insurance on the salary being paid;

(iv) **Premises costs**, for instance relating to the offices used to manage the investments;

(v) **Audit and accountancy costs**.

Remember that **commitment fees and guarantee commissions**, are part of the cost of raising loans, and so are not management expenses - they will be deductible from DIII under the **loan relationships** rules.

Any expenses relating to specific income must be set against that source only, for example under Schedule A. Expenses relating specifically to properties being let out must be set against the Schedule A income, not treated as a management expense.

All Intangible Fixed Assets held will be held for **non-trading purposes**. Thus from 1 April 2002 royalty payments and receipts will go into the **DVI pool**.

C21.3 Management expenses prior to 1 April 2004

Many of the rules we looked at above applied prior to the FA 2004 changes hence we will just concentrate on the differences here.

In accounting periods beginning **before 1 April 2004**, management expenses could only be deducted by **UK resident** investment companies.

They were deductible in the accounting period in which they were **disbursed.**

There are **transitional provisions** to ensure that amounts are **not deducted twice or missed,** as we move to deduction according to when the expense is debited in the accounts.

The old s.75 did not include any reference to capital expenditure or to investments held for unallowable purposes.

C21.4 Relief for management expenses

Management expenses are **automatically set against investment income and gains in the current accounting period**. This relief is automatic and compulsory.

Management expenses are deducted **before charges on income** and before any **loss relief** claims under section 393A.

Where the management expenses **exceed the gross income and gains in the current period**, they are **"excess"**. If the company is part of a group they **may be transferred to a fellow 75% owned company**, upon making a claim.

s. 75(8)

Failing that, excess management expenses are **carried forward** and set against future income and gains of the company.

C21.5 Loan interest

Interest paid by companies with investment business on loans taken out to purchase investments is a **Schedule D Case III debit**. The tax treatment and relief for DIII debits was covered in the earlier chapter on loan relationships.

Remember such interest is never treated as a Schedule A expense or a management expense.

Commitment fees and guarantee commissions, are part of the cost of raising loans, and not management expenses. They will be covered by loan relationship rules.

C21.6 Losses on sale of shares

Where an investment company makes a capital loss on the disposal of shares in certain qualifying companies, it may claim to **set that loss against income**.

On making a claim within two years of the end of the accounting period of the loss, the loss can be set against income for the **accounting period of the loss**, and if necessary any **previous accounting period ending in the 12 months before** the start of the accounting period of the loss. This loss relief is claimed before any other deductions including management expenses and charges. However claims under the CVS rules take priority. s. 573

To be able to make the s. 573 claim, the company **must be an investment company** and have been so throughout a continuous period of six years. If this is not the case it must not previously have been a trading company. The company must have **subscribed for shares in a qualifying trading company** (as defined by the EIS rules), which has not been associated with it from the date of subscription to the date of disposal. Associated here is the wide meaning of control.

Note that this relief can **only be claimed by investment companies**. It does **not extend to companies with an investment business.**

SUMMARY - INVESTMENT COMPANIES

A company with investment business is a company deriving its income wholly or partly from the making of investments.

The PCTCT of a company with investment business is found by adding together investment income and gains and deducting management expenses.

Management expenses include agent's commissions, professional fees, premises costs and reasonable director's salaries, but exclude expenses of a capital nature or for an unallowable purpose.

Since 1 April 2004 management expenses are deductible based on when they are debited in the accounts.

If management expenses exceed profits, a company has "excess management expenses". These excess management expenses can either be group relieved or carried forward.

An investment company is a company where business consists wholly or mainly in the making of investments and the principal part of whose income is derived therefrom.

When an investment company has a capital loss on the disposal of shares that it subscribed for in a qualifying company, it can claim to set that loss off against income of that period or the previous period.

C22: CORPORATE VENTURING SCHEME

This chapter outlines the reliefs available for investments under the CVS scheme covering in particular:
- the corporation tax relief;
- what happens on sale of the shares;
- conditions for the relief;
- capital gains relief including relief for losses.

C22.1 The Corporate Venturing Scheme (CVS) Sch 15 FA 2000

The scheme gives tax relief to companies who invest in small unquoted trading companies. The intention is to encourage larger companies to invest in smaller companies – the tax relief is an incentive for them to do so.

Tax relief is given as a **tax reducer** – i.e. the relief reduces the amount of corporation tax payable by the investing company. The tax reducer is usually **20% of the amount invested** (or a lower amount if the tax relief reduces the CT liability to zero). There is **no upper limit.**

Illustration 1

On 1 May 2005, Generous Ltd subscribes for £200,000 of new shares issued by Start-Up Ltd, a company which satisfies the conditions of the Corporate Venturing Scheme. Generous Ltd has taxable profits of £1.8m in the year ended 31 March 2006.

The corporation tax payable will be:

	£
£1.8m x 30%	540,000
Less CVS relief	
£200,000 x 20%	(40,000)
Gross corporation tax	£500,000

Note that the CVS relief could reduce a company's tax liability to zero but it cannot create a tax repayment.

If the company **sells the new CVS shares within 3 years, relief is withdrawn**.

The relief withdrawn will either be:

(i) The **original relief** given if the shares are **sold at a profit**; or

(ii) **20% x proceeds** if the shares are **sold at a loss**.

Illustration 2

Assume in the above example that Generous Ltd sold its shares in Start-Up Ltd for £125,000 on 1 December 2006.

As the CVS shares have been sold within 3 years of issue, corporation tax relief is withdrawn. To **withdraw the relief**, the Revenue will issue an **assessment** (under Schedule DVI) in the period in which the relief was **originally given** (i.e., the year of the original subscription of the shares).

The revised CT computation for the year ended 31 March 2006 will be:

	£
£1.8 m x 30%	540,000
Less CVS relief originally given	
£200,000 x 20%	(40,000)
CT originally due	500,000
Add: CVS relief withdrawn	
£125,000 x 20%	25,000
Revised gross corporation tax	£525,000

Note that as the shares were sold at a loss, the withdrawal of relief is restricted to 20% of proceeds.

C22.2 Conditions for CVS relief

Certain conditions must be satisfied throughout the **qualification period** of the shares both by the **investing company** (i.e. the company acquiring the CVS shares) and the **issuing company** (i.e. the company issuing the new shares to the investors). Para 3 Sch 15 FA2000

The qualification period is a period starting with the issue of the shares and ending:

- Immediately before the **third anniversary of the issue date** where the qualifying trade is already being carried on or,
- Immediately before the third anniversary of the date on which the **trade commences.**

The investing company must **not** either: Para 5&8 Sch 15 FA2000

- have **more than 30%** of the ordinary shares or voting rights of the issuing company, or
- be able to **control** the issuing company (i.e. with its associates).

The investing company must carry out a **non-financial trade** (e.g. it must not be an investment company etc). The investing company can be the parent company of a group, as long as the group carries out non-financial trades. Para 10 Sch 15 FA2000

The investing company must subscribe for new shares in the CVS company.

In their judgement the House of Lords stated that

> "...if it is to be the subject of an assessment, it must arise **from the employment.** It is not sufficient to render a payment assessable that an employee would not have received it unless he had been an employee ...it is assessable if it has been paid to him in return for acting or being an employee".

The Lords held that the compensation payment was made to the individual in his capacity as a homeowner rather than "in return for acting or being an employee". As the payment was not made by reference to any services performed, it was not an emolument of the employment.

[Note: this was a 1959 case and such payments are now dealt with under s.271 to s.289 concerning removal expenses].

To illustrate the subtle complexities of case law, a different decision was arrived at in the case of *Hamblett v Godfrey (1987).* In this case, an employee of a government agency (GCHQ in Cheltenham) was offered £1,000 as compensation for agreeing to give up her rights to join a trade union. The employee contended (citing *Hochstrasser v Mayes)* that the payment was not an emolument from her employment as it was not being made in return for services.

In this case the Courts disagreed and found the payment to be a taxable emolument. The right to join a trade union is part and parcel of "**acting or being an employee**". The payment was too closely linked to the employer-employee relationship for it to be treated as anything other than an emolument.

In *Shilton v Wilmshurst (1991),* a footballer (England goalkeeper Peter Shilton) transferred from Nottingham Forest to Southampton football club. As the player was under contract to Nottingham Forest, the club agreed to pay Mr Shilton £75,000 to agree to the transfer. Again the question arose as to whether this payment arose "from the employment".

Mr Shilton contended that the payment was made to him by his former employer in connection with the termination of his employment (such termination payments being tax free up to £30,000). The Revenue argued that the payment was a reward or inducement flowing from the services he was about to offer to Southampton FC.

The Courts agreed with the Revenue and found the payment to have arisen **from Mr Shilton's employment** (therefore fully taxable). Mr Shilton had received payment "**to remain or become an employee**" - the payment was to **induce** the player to become an employee of Southampton FC and for no other reason.

D2.4 Amount of employment income charged to tax

S.9 ITEPA 2003 deals with **how much** of a taxpayer's income is chargeable to income tax for a particular tax year. s.9

In the case of "general earnings", the amount charged to tax is the "**net taxable earnings**" from the employment in the tax year. "Net taxable earnings" are "taxable earnings" less any **deductions allowed from those earnings** under the "expenses provisions" within the Act. Essentially employees receive tax relief in respect of any expenses "**wholly, exclusively and necessarily**" incurred in doing their job. We shall look specifically at employment expenses in a later chapter. s.11

Net taxable earnings can therefore be broadly summarised as:

	£	£
Cash remuneration:		
Salary, bonus etc		X
Other emoluments which have direct monetary value		X
Non cash remuneration:		
Benefits		
		X
Less: exempt income		(X)
Taxable earnings		X
Less: allowable deductions:		
Employment expenses	X	
Other deductions		
		(X)
NET TAXABLE EARNINGS		**X**

D2.5 The "receipts" basis

S.15 ITEPA 2003 deals with general earnings (cash plus benefits) of an employee resident ordinarily resident and domiciled in the UK and tells us that... s.15

> "The **full amount** of any earnings ...which are **received** in a tax year is an amount of "**taxable earnings**" from the employment in that tax year".

Therefore the way we tax an individual's employment income is on a "**receipts basis**". This means that employees and directors will be taxed on their employment income **when it is received**.

The rules for taxing earnings are slightly different for employees who are either resident, or ordinarily resident or domiciled outside the UK, and these will be covered in a later session.

The date of receipt of earnings consisting of money is the earlier of two dates: s. 18

1) the time when **payment is made** Rule 1

2) the time when a person becomes **entitled to payment** Rule 2

Therefore if an employee or director becomes **entitled** to a payment before he or she is physically paid the money, the date of entitlement is treated as the date of receipt and the payment is taxed at that point. In practice this distinction is not particularly important, as for most of us the date of entitlement and the date of physical receipt are usually the same.

Where the receipts basis becomes important is with regard to the taxation of **bonuses**. Consider a company which draws up accounts for the year ended 31 December 2004. On the 28 April 2005, the annual general meeting is held and the board of directors of the company sign off the accounts and agree the profits of the year just ended. At this point the company are in a position to determine the bonuses due to their employees.

An employee receives a bonus at the end of April 2005 in respect of work carried out by him in the year which ended in December 2004. For employment income purposes, the employee is taxed on his bonus not in the period in which the bonus was earned, but instead **on the date the bonus is physically received**.

As such this bonus is taxable at the end of April 2005 and therefore goes into the employee's tax computation for the 2005/06 tax year.

This is a general principle and there are always occasional exceptions. Certain **special rules exist for company directors** but in most cases the normal receipts basis will apply.

In relation to company directors, the date of receipt is the **earliest** of either of the above two dates, and; s.18 Rule 3

a) when sums on **account** of his earnings are **credited** in the company accounts; or
b) at the **end** of the company's accounting period if the earnings have been determined **by the end** of that period; or
c) at the date the earnings are **determined** if that date falls **after** the end of the company's accounting period.

Illustration 1

Mr Matthews is a company director earning £60,000 per annum. He is entitled to an annual bonus based on the company's results for each year ending on 31 December.

At their Board Meeting on 25 March 2006, the Board agree the draft accounts and determine Mr Matthews' bonus in the sum of £25,000. This is paid to Mr Matthews on 30 April 2006.

Although the date of physical receipt is 30 April 2006, as Mr Matthews is a director, we need to consider Rule 3 in s.18 ITEPA 2003. Mr Matthews' earnings were determined after the end of the company's accounting period, therefore rule (c) above applies. The date of "receipt" for employment income purposes is therefore 25 March 2006 and the bonus will be taxable in 2005/06.

D2.6 Taxable benefits

Benefits are very important as far as your exam is concerned. By benefits we mean non-cash remuneration. Many employees receive such benefits as part of their overall remuneration package. s.63

These benefits often include the use of a **company car**, the use of company provided **accommodation**, or a cheap **loan.** **Private medical insurance** or contributions by the employer to the employee's **pension scheme** are also very common benefits, as is the provision of a **mobile phone** along with associated telephone calls. The majority of these benefits are taxable in the hands of the employee. There are certain benefits which are exempt from tax and we shall deal with these later.

For taxable benefits, we need to determine the **"cash equivalent"** of each particular benefit. Essentially we are allocating a cash figure to each taxable benefit and thereafter we will tax that cash equivalent as if it was an additional amount of earnings.

D2.7 Measuring the benefit

Benefits are chargeable to tax if they are either:

(i) specifically charged within the Benefits Code; or
(ii) "employment-related" benefits under s.201 onwards ITEPA 2003.

We shall look at specific benefits within the Benefits Code in later sessions, but first we will examine the rules for taxing **employment related benefits.**

An employment related benefit is a benefit provided either for an **employee,** or for a member of the employee's **family or household**, by reason of the employee's employment. Therefore, a taxpayer cannot avoid being taxed on the provision of a benefit simply by directing his employer to provide the benefit to, say, his wife rather than himself. s.201

This means, for example, if by reason of Jack's employment, Jack's wife or son are provided with a company car or other benefit, it is Jack who will be charged to income tax on the cash equivalent of that benefit.

S.203 ITEPA 2003 tells us that "the **cash equivalent** of an employment related benefit **is to be treated as earnings** from the employment for the tax year in which it is provided", and .. s.203

> "The cash equivalent of an employment-related benefit is the **cost of the benefit** less any part of that cost **made good by the employee** to the persons providing that benefit".

Under s.204 ITEPA 2003, "the cost of an employment related benefit is the **expense incurred in, or in connection with, the provision** of that benefit". s.204

This means that, for example, if an employer wishes to provide a benefit to an employee in the form of, say, private medical insurance, and the cost to the employer of paying the premium is £500, the cash equivalent - i.e. the amount charged to tax - is £500. The fact that it might cost the employee more than £500 to obtain the same level of medical cover is irrelevant - we simply look at **what it cost the employer to provide the benefit**.

Amounts **paid by the employee** to the employer towards the provision of the benefit can be **deducted** from the cash equivalent. Therefore if the employee reimburses the employer's full cost, the taxable benefit will be zero.

Every benefit provided by an employer to an employee which has a cash equivalent, must be **reported to the Revenue** by the employer on a **special form** called a **P11D**. The employer should complete a form P11D for each employee who has received taxable benefits, and these forms should be **submitted** to the Revenue **no later than 6 July after the end of the tax year.** The P11D tells the Revenue the amount of the cash equivalent of each benefit. A copy is given to the employee to enable him to complete his own tax return.

In the case of certain benefits, it is very difficult to establish exactly what is the cost to the employer of providing the benefit. In such cases special rules exist to help us calculate the cash equivalent. Special rules are in place for calculating company car and fuel benefits, accommodation benefits, cheap loans and instances where an employer lends an asset to an employee. We shall take a look at these various special rules later.

D2.8 Pepper v Hart

The concept of the **"cost of providing"** a benefit was the subject of a leading and extremely important tax case heard by the House of Lords in 1993. The case of ***Pepper v Hart*** concerned a private, fee-paying school. Just before the start of term, the school had some surplus places, which it had been unable to sell. The school therefore allowed some of the **schoolmasters** to **send their own children to the school** to be educated at a **subsidised price**.

The Revenue and the schoolmasters both agreed that a benefit had arisen. This was because an employee or members of his family or household were being provided with a benefit (i.e. cheap education) by reason of the schoolmasters' employment. There was no dispute that a benefit had arisen.

The argument was about how to determine the "cost to the employer" in providing the education to the children involved. Each side put forward an alternative way of establishing the cost to the school of providing the benefit.

The **Revenue** argued that we should first take the total cost of running the school for the year. This figure should then be divided by the number of pupils in the school to give an average cost of providing education per student. From this average cost, we deduct the fees actually paid by the schoolmasters and the difference is the taxable benefit. The Revenue therefore **argued that "cost of providing"** as per the legislation **actually meant the "average" cost**.

The taxpayer put forward an alternative suggestion. He argued that we first calculate the cost of running the school for its **normal fee paying pupils** (i.e. not counting those students receiving subsidised education). Next we calculate the cost of running the school for **all the pupils**, this time including the additional children who had paid reduced fees. The **difference** between these two figures is the additional cost incurred by the school in providing these extra places.

Therefore the cost of providing each additional place is this figure divided by the number of extra places. From this we deduct the fees paid by the schoolmasters and the difference is the taxable benefit. What the **taxpayer** was advocating was a **"marginal" cost method** as opposed to the Revenue's average cost method.

The House of Lords on a majority decision found in favour of the **taxpayer** and decided that the **marginal cost method** was the correct way of calculating the cash equivalent in this instance.

The case of *Pepper v Hart* has particular relevance when it comes to calculating the benefit in respect of **"in-house benefits"** as we shall now illustrate.

Illustration 2

A flight is about to leave from London Heathrow airport to JFK New York. The flight will cost the airline £20,000. The plane has 100 seats. This means that the average cost to the airline is £200 per seat. Assume that all but one of the seats have been sold to normal fee paying passengers. A few minutes before the flight is due to leave, the airline offers this spare seat to one of its employees for the bargain price of £10.

There is a benefit arising to the employee because the employee is receiving a benefit - i.e. a very cheap flight - by reason of his or her employment. The cash equivalent will be the cost to the airline of providing that one heavily subsidised seat to one if its employees.

Following *Pepper v Hart* we do not take the average cost per passenger of £200. Instead we consider the marginal cost. This will be the extra cost to the airline of flying that one extra passenger over to New York.

This extra cost should be negligible - presumably it costs more or less the same to fly 100 passengers to New York as it does to fly 99. There will be a few additional costs such as one extra in-flight meal or an extra newspaper which should be covered by the £10 paid by the employee.

As a result following the principle established by *Pepper v Hart*, where an employee is using goods or services manufactured or provided by his employer, the marginal cost is effectively zero giving rise to a taxable benefit of nil.

D2.9 Lower paid employees s.216

Certain chapters of the Benefits Code do not apply if those benefits are provided to an employee who defined as a **lower paid employee** and who is **not a director of a company**. These excluded benefits include company cars and vans, cheap loans, certain share related benefits and certain expenses payments.

A lower paid employee is one earning less than £8,500 in the tax year.

In order to establish whether an employee earns more or less than £8,500, we need to take account of **cash earnings** (including expense reimbursements) and any payments **treated as earnings**, for example under the **Benefits Code**. We also need to add in any amounts received under the special rules for intermediaries (see Chapter 27). We then need to deduct "authorised deductions" as listed in s.217(4) which include payroll giving and certain pension contributions: s.217

	£
Cash earnings (including reimbursed expenses)	X
Payments treated as earnings (eg Benefits)	X
Earnings from intermediaries	
Less: authorised deductions	
TEST HERE	X

Note that for the purposes of the test, we include expense reimbursements but do not deduct general business expenses (eg travel etc) which are allowable under the expenses rules as these are not in the list of authorised deductions.

If the resulting figure at the bottom is £8,500 or more, we do not have a lower paid employee. In this instance, all benefits and expenses payments will be taxed in the normal way. The above test is designed in this way to prevent a company paying an employee a cash salary of £8,499 and "topping-up" his remuneration package with a number of non-cash benefits and expenses.

If an employee is a lower paid employee, taxable benefits will still need to be reported to the Revenue but this time on a form P9D as opposed to form P11D.

It is more common for an employer to provide benefits to employees who are not lower paid employees nor directors, and we will concentrate on these for the rest of this course.

D2.10 Pension income and social security income

Parts 9 and 10 of ITEPA 2003 deal with the taxation of pension income and social security income.

Income from pensions is generally taxable. This will include the State Pension and any pension income paid by a former employer whether in the UK or abroad.

If a taxpayer is resident and domiciled in the UK and receives income from an overseas pension, only 90% of the pension income arising is taxable. This "10% deduction" rule also applies to overseas government pensions paid in the UK. s. 65(2) ICTA 1988 s.617

Many social security benefits paid to UK taxpayers are exempt from tax. Such exempt sources include bereavement payments, child benefit, council tax benefit, housing benefit, disability living allowances and the new working tax credits and child tax credits. s.677

There are however, still a significant number of social security benefits which are taxable under ITEPA 2003. These include incapacity benefit, income support, job seekers allowances, statutory maternity pay and statutory sick pay. s.660

Q	Now test your understanding by attempting the examples which follow.

Example 1

Bruno works for Online Tutors Limited (OTL). Which of the following are taxable under ITEPA 2003?

a) Salary
b) Performance Related Bonus
c) M&S voucher from employer
d) Dividend on shares in OTL
e) Interest free loan from OTL
f) Profit from one-off consulting job for a local business

Example 2

Chris and Dean work for Online Tutors Limited. Their earnings are as follows:

	Chris	*Dean*
	£	£
Salary	6,000	5,000
Bonus	1,000	Nil
Benefits (cash equivalent)	1,400	2,800
Business expenses reimbursed	200	600

Which of them is a lower paid employee?

a) Chris only
b) Dean only
c) Both of them
d) Neither of them

Answer 1

	Employment income?
a) Salary	✓
b) Performance Related Bonus	✓
c) M&S voucher from employer	✓
d) Dividend on shares in OTL	X (Dividend income)
e) Interest free loan from OTL	✓
f) Profit from one-off job	X (Miscellaneous income)

Answer 2

The answer is B

	Chris	Dean
	£	£
Salary	6,000	5,000
Bonus	1,000	Nil
Benefits	1,400	2,800
Expenses	200	600
TEST	8,600	8,400
"Lower paid"	NO	YES

Dean would therefore not be taxable on the benefits.

SUMMARY - EMPLOYMENT INCOME & BENEFITS

The Income Tax (Earnings & Pensions) Act 2003 taxes income from employment including cash and non-cash remuneration. It also taxes pensions received, termination payments and profits on share options.

The receipts basis applies so a bonus is taxed when received, not when earned.

Non-cash benefits are also taxable. Their cash equivalent is equal to the cost to the employer in providing the benefit and is reduced by any contribution made by the employee. Benefits are reported on the P11D due by 6 July following the tax year.

The case of Pepper v Hart established the principle that cost to the employer should be marginal cost.

Lower paid employees earning < £8,500 p.a. who are not directors are not taxable on some benefits.

D3: COMPANY CAR & FUEL BENEFITS

In this chapter you will learn the rules for the taxation of company car and fuel benefits including:
- how to find list price;
- how the cash equivalent is based on CO_2 emissions;
- non availability;
- fuel benefit.

All statutory references are to ITEPA 2003 unless stated otherwise.

D3.1 Introduction

One of the most common benefits offered by employers to their employee is the provision of a company car and fuel for private motoring. s.114 - s.172

If a car is provided to a lower paid employee who is not a director, **the benefit is tax free.** s.216(4)

For other employees, special rules exist to enable us to calculate the cash equivalent on the provision of a company car. If a car is made available by an employee for the exclusive use of a particular employee, it doesn't matter whether the car is owned by the employer or leased by the employer from a third party, the **employee will have a taxable benefit in respect of the private use of the car.** The cash equivalent depends on a number of factors. s.120 & s.121

The starting point in calculating car benefits is the **list price** of the car when it is first registered (i.e. when brand new). This is not necessarily the same as the price actually paid by the employer for the car. s.122

The cash equivalent also depends on the vehicle's **carbon dioxide (CO_2) emissions**. Essentially, the **lower the emissions, the lower the benefit.** This is an attempt by the government to be responsible with regard to the protection of the environment. s. 139

Also the benefit depends on **whether the car was available for the whole of the year.** As is the case with most benefits, if the employee does not have the benefit for the whole of the year, we need to do an apportionment to arrive at the cash equivalent. s.143

Later on in this chapter we will look at the separate benefit that arises when an employer provides the employee with fuel for his or her private motoring. s.149

D3.2 List price

We will now put all of these variables together into a company car proforma:

	£
List price when new	A
Accessories	B
Less: capital contributions (max £5,000)	(C)
Revised list price (capped at £80,000)	D

We start with the **list price of the car** when new and to this we **add on the cost of any accessories** provided with the car. For example if you buy a new car, the garage will charge you extra if you want leather seats or a CD player etc, so we need to add these items on. s.121 s.125

The next step is to **deduct any capital contributions** made to the employer by the employee. A capital contribution is a one-off payment made by the employee to enable the employer to provide a better car. s.132

List price, plus accessories, minus capital contributions gives a revised list price which in the proforma we have called "D". This list price **cannot exceed £80,000** for tax purposes. s.121

If an accessory is added to the car after it was first made available to the employee, we only need to add on the cost to the list price if the accessory cost more than £100. If not, we can ignore it. s.126

With regard to **capital contributions,** the **maximum deduction** from the list price is **£5,000**. If an employee makes a capital contribution of £1,000, this amount is deducted from the list price. However if an employee makes a capital contribution of £6,000, the list price is reduced by £5,000 only. s.132(3)

D3.3 Cash Equivalent

The basic cash equivalent is the **list price,** multiplied by a certain percentage. This percentage will depend on the amount of CO_2 emitted by the car. The minimum charge is **15%,** rising to a maximum charge of **35%.** s.139(2) & (3)

We can see two things here. Firstly the benefit depends on the **type of car** we have - the more expensive the car, the higher the benefit. Secondly, employees who drive around in large cars with **high CO_2 emissions** will pay more tax than those who are more environmentally friendly and have use of cars with low emissions.

The list price, multiplied by the appropriate percentage gives us the **basic cash equivalent**.

The benefit is reduced **if the car has not been available** to the employee **for the whole of the tax year**. For example, the employee may have been given use of the car part way through the year or he may have returned the car to the employer before the end of the year. We do a **pro-rata apportionment** by removing the number of months during which the car was not available to the employee. s.143(1)

For example, if a taxpayer joined a company on, say, 1 January 2006 and was given use of a car on that date, that person will have had the car for only 3 months of 2005/06. We therefore remove nine twelfths of the car benefit.

As is the case for the vast majority of benefits, if the employee is required to make a contribution towards the benefit and actually does so, these contributions reduce the cash equivalent. This is quite common in practice as with many car schemes, employees make monthly contributions to their employer for the use of the car. These reduce the taxable benefit. s.144

Here is the rest of the proforma to find the car benefit for the tax year. The final cash equivalent will be entered by the employer on to the employee's P11D:

	£
Revised list price	D
Basic cash equivalent	E
D x %	
- depends on CO_2 emissions	
- minimum 15%, maximum 35%	
Less: non availability ($\frac{n}{12}$)	(F)
	G
Less: employee contributions	(H)
Car Benefit	I

D3.4 Determining the percentage s. 133

The next step is to determine the relevant percentage. List price is multiplied by a percentage which depends entirely on the car's recorded CO_2 emissions. The higher the emissions, the higher the percentage.

Carbon dioxide emissions are measured in terms of the **grams per kilometre (g/km)** of gas emitted from the car.

For 2005/06 there is a "**baseline**" **figure of 140 g/km.** This means that all cars emitting CO_2 at a rate of **140 g/km or less** will be taxed at the **minimum rate of 15%.** This "baseline" was 145g/km in 2004/05.

The relevant percentage will **increase by 1 for each additional 5 g/km of CO_2 emitted above 140** for 2005/06. For example, a car with recorded CO_2 emissions of 145 grams per kilometre, will be taxed using a percentage of 16%, and so on. s.139(3)

The formula for calculating the percentage is:

$$\% = [(\text{Emissions} - 140) \div 5] + 15\%$$

We take the CO_2 emissions of the car and deduct the baseline figure of 140. We divide the result by 5 and add it to the minimum of 15% to give the relevant percentage. This is then multiplied by the list price of the car to give the basic cash equivalent.

Illustration 1

An employee has use of a company car with a list price of £20,000. Accessories are added to the car at a cost of £2,000. The employee made a one-off capital contribution of £4,000 for the use of the car. The car has recorded CO_2 emissions of 195 g/km.

	£
List price	20,000
Add: Accessories	2,000
Less: Capital contribution	(4,000)
Revised list price	£18,000
Cash equivalent	£
£18,000 x 26% [(195-140) ÷ 5 = 11 + 15]	**4,680**

D3.5 Further points

In reality, CO_2 emissions figures are **exact numbers** and are not rounded to the nearest whole multiple of 5. For tax purposes, we are allowed to **round down to the nearest 5 g/km.** s.139(5)

For example, if a car has a CO_2 emissions figure of 199 g/km, we would round this down to 195 to determine the percentage.

The percentage can **never exceed 35%.** This rate will therefore apply for all cars with an emissions figure of 240 g/km or above.

There is a **3% supplement** for cars which run on **diesel** - i.e. an additional 3% is added to the relevant percentage. This is because diesel engines are less environmentally friendly than petrol engines. The **minimum percentage** which can therefore be applied to a diesel vehicle **is 18%.** The 3% supplement **cannot** take the relevant percentage **above 35%.** s.141

Electric cars produce **no CO_2 emissions** and receive **a 6% discount**. The percentage to be applied in these cases will therefore be **9%.** There are also discounts for cars running on road fuel gas (e.g. liquid petroleum gas or LPG). SI 2001/1123 s.146

D3.6 No emissions figure s. 140, s.142

Certain vehicles, particularly old ones, will have no recognised or recorded CO_2 emissions figure. In these cases, the percentage we use to calculate the benefit will be **based on the engine size** of the vehicle. The engine size is measured in terms of the vehicle cylinder capacity in cubic centimetres.

The percentages for cars registered **before 1 January 1998** are shown in the table below and rise from a minimum of **15%** for small cars to **32%** for larger vehicles.

The percentages are slightly different for cars registered on or **after 1 January 1998**. Again the minimum is **15%,** this time rising to the usual upper limit of **35%.**

Once again, a **3% supplement** is added for **diesel** cars, again capped at a maximum of 35%. These percentages are given in the Tax Tables provided with this course.

Engine Size	*Pre 1.1.98*	*Post 1.1.98*
0 - 1,400 cc	15%	15%
1,401 - 2,000 cc	22%	25%
over 2,000 cc	32%	35%

D3.7 Non-availability s.143

The benefit is reduced if the employee does not have use of the car throughout the whole of the tax year. This will apply if an employee **joins** a company part way through the year and is given use of a car, or if an employee **leaves** the company and has to return the car.

Apportionment is done on a monthly basis by removing the benefit arising in the period in which the employee did not have use of the car.

If a car is being repaired or serviced, or having its MOT, a non-availability deduction can only be made if the car is off the road for a continuous period of **at least 30 days**. s.143(2)

So, if the car is in the garage for one week having a few minor repairs, this will have no effect whatsoever on the car benefit calculation. However if the car is involved in a serious accident and is off the road for, say, 2 months, we would take a non-availability deduction of 2 out of 12 months.

Illustration 2

An employee has use of a company car with a list price of £12,000. The car has a CO_2 emissions level of 152 g/km. The employee is given use of the car for the first time on 1 July 2005. The employee makes contributions of £40 per month to the employer for the use of the car.

During the year, the car was off the road for 3 weeks having some minor repairs after an accident.

To calculate the benefit for 2005/06 the starting point is the list price of £12,000. We multiply this by a percentage based on the car's CO_2 emissions, which we know to be 152 g/km. As this is not exactly divisible by 5, we round down and use an emissions figure of 150 in the formula.

As the car was only available to the employee from 1 July 2005 - i.e. for 9 months of the tax year - we must take a non-availability deduction for 3/12ths of the benefit. Note that no reduction has been made for the 3 weeks during which the car was being repaired as this period is less than 30 days.

The employee is required to make a contribution of £40 per month for the use of the car. As is the case for the majority of benefits, employee contributions act to reduce the cash equivalent.

	£
List price	12,000
Cash equivalent	
12,000 x 17% [(150 - 140) ÷ 5 = 2 + 15]	2,040
Less: non-availability	
$\frac{3}{12}$ x 2,040	(510)
Less: contributions	
40 x 9	(360)
Benefit	£1,170

D3.8 More than one car

An employee may have use of two company cars or he may have one car himself and a second car for a member of his family or household.

In this instance, the employee simply has **two benefits**, each calculated in the same way - i.e. using list price and CO_2 emissions. Note that if a car is made available by an employer for a member of the employee's family, it is the **employee who will have the benefit, not the family member.**

D3.9 Classic cars s.147

A "classic car" is one that is more than 15 years old and whose market value at the end of the tax year is more than £15,000.

If an employee is provided with a classic car, to work out the **cash equivalent** we **use the market value of the car** when it was given to the employee instead of the list price when new.

D3.10 Pool cars and emergency vehicles s.167

No benefit will arise if the employee has some incidental private use of a pool car. A pool car is essentially a shared vehicle which is mainly used for business purposes.

As long as private use is **incidental** and the **pool car is not normally kept overnight at the employee's residence,** no benefit will arise. Many employers have a small fleet of pool cars which are normally kept somewhere on the premises and which are used for business journeys.

There is also no taxable benefit when emergency service vehicles used by fire, police or ambulance workers are taken home when on-call. s.248A

D3.11 Administration

Employers have to file quarterly returns to the Tax Office on form P46 (car) giving details of any changes in cars provided to employees.

D3.12 Fuel benefits

A **separate benefit** will arise where **private petrol costs** are reimbursed. If the employer only pays for fuel for business purposes, no benefit will arise. s. 149, s.151(3)

If an employee is provided with fuel for private motoring, the taxable benefit is identified by using the formula below:

£14,400 x % based on CO_2 emissions s. 150

To calculate the appropriate percentage, we use exactly the same rules as above for car benefit purposes.

No fuel benefit will arise if an employee is required to reimburse the whole of the expense incurred by the employer in providing private fuel and actually does so. If the employee only makes a partial reimbursement, this will have no effect and the benefit will be calculated as above. Therefore an employee contribution towards the costs of private fuel will not result in a "pound-for-pound" reduction in the taxable amount as is the case for other benefits. s. 151(2)

The fuel benefit will be reduced if private use fuel is not provided to the employee for the whole of the tax year. However, if private fuel is withdrawn but then reinstated in the same tax year, the benefit charge will apply for the whole tax year. So it is not possible to opt in and out of the car fuel benefit, for example during holidays. s. 152

Illustration 3

Ralf is provided with a car by his employer on 1 October 2005. The car has a list price of £15,000 and CO_2 emissions of 168g/km. All fuel costs are met by the company. The costs of private fuel amounted to £2,000 of which Ralf reimbursed £750.

The taxable benefits in 2005/06 are:

	£
Car:	
£15,000 x 20% [(165 - 140) ÷ 5 = 5% + 15% = 20%]	3,000
Less: non-availability	
£3,000 x 6/12	(1,500)
Car benefit	1,500
Fuel benefit	
£14,400 x 20% x 6/12	1,440
Total	£2,940

No reduction for partial reimbursement of private fuel. Note a reduction would have been made if Ralf had contributed £750 towards the general running costs of the car itself (rather than the fuel directly), provided that this was a condition stipulated by the employer.

Q	Now test your understanding by attempting the examples which follow.

Example 1

Eddie is provided with use of a Jaguar car for the whole of 2005/06. The list price is £32,000 and CO_2 emissions are 233 g/km.

Eddie pays £50 per month for the use of the car. All his petrol costs are met by the company.

Calculate Eddie's taxable benefit for 2005/06.

Example 2

Jensen has use of a Volvo car (list price £12,000 and CO_2 emissions 148g/km). On 1 July 2005 his employer exchanged the Volvo for an Audi (list price £14,000 and CO_2 emissions 139 g/km). The Audi runs on diesel. The company reimburse Jensen for business fuel costs only.

Calculate Jensen's taxable benefit for 2005/06.

Answer 1

List price	£32,000
Cash equivalent	£
£32,000 x 33% [(230-140) ÷ 5 = 18 + 15]	10,560
Less: employee contributions	
(12 x £50)	(600)
Car Benefit	9,960
Add: Fuel benefit - £14,400 x 33%	4,752
Taxable Benefits	**£14,712**

Answer 2

Volvo (3 months)		
List price £12,000		
Cash equivalent	£	£
£12,000 x 16% [(145-140) ÷ 5 = 1 + 15]	1,920	
Less: non availability		
$£1,920 \times \frac{9}{12}$	(1,440)	
		480
Audi (9 months)		
List price £14,000		
Cash equivalent		
£14,000 x 18% [15% + 3%]	2,520	
(<145g/km plus diesel supplement)		
Less: non availability		
$£2,520 \times \frac{3}{12}$	(630)	
		1,890
Total benefit		**£2,370**

SUMMARY - COMPANY CAR & FUEL BENEFITS

Company car benefit is not chargeable on lower paid employees who are not directors

Company car benefit is based on a number of factors including list price and CO_2 emissions.

List price includes accessories and is reduced by capital contributions of up to £5,000. There is an overall cap of £80,000.

A percentage is applied to the list price. The percentage will be between 15% and 35%.

The "baseline" figure for CO_2 emissions for 2005/06 is 140g/km.

The relevant percentage is calculated as

$$\% = [\text{emissions} - 140] \div 5 + 15\%$$

The emissions figure is rounded down to the nearest 5g/km.

There is a 3% supplement for cars which run on diesel.

As electric cars produce no emissions a percentage of 9% only is used.

Older cars with no recorded emissions figure use percentages based on engine size which vary according to whether the car was registered before or after 1 January 1998.

If the employee has had the car for less than a year, the benefit is time apportioned.

Non-availability deductions only apply if the car is off the road for 30 days.

Classic cars are those over 15 years old and worth more than £15,000 at the end of the tax year. Market value is used instead of list price.

Where fuel is provided for private motoring, the taxable benefit is:

£14,400 x % (based on CO_2 emissions)

Fuel benefits cannot be reduced by employee contributions but can be time apportioned if appropriate.

D4: LIVING ACCOMMODATION – TAXABLE BENEFITS

In this chapter you will cover the way in which taxable benefits for living accommodation provided by the employer are calculated including:
- job related accommodation;
- rented accommodation;
- employer owned accommodation;
- accommodation costing > £75,000;
- the 6 year rule;
- household expenses.

Statutory references are to ITEPA 2003 unless stated otherwise.

D4.1 Introduction

If a house, flat or any property that is owned or rented by the employer is made available for use by an employee, there will be a taxable benefit for the employee as he is occupying a property provided to him by his employer.

The provision of **living accommodation is a taxable benefit for all employees** even lower paid employees.

The way that the benefit is taxed depends on whether the accommodation is "job related" or "non job related".

D4.2 "Job related" accommodation s.99

If an employer provides an employee with job related accommodation, there is no benefit arising to the employee on the use of that accommodation.

Job related accommodation is accommodation which is **"necessary"** for the job or is provided for the "better performance" of the employee's duties. Employees such as **publicans** or **caretakers** will live in job related accommodation. Typically these are employees who are normally required by their employers to live on site in order to do their job.

Job related accommodation also covers situations where accommodation is provided **"customarily"** for the better performance of the job. So for example it is customary to provide a **vicar** with a vicarage in the parish. This would constitute job related accommodation.

D4.3 Rented accommodation

For the rest of this chapter we are going to look at how we calculate the benefits where the accommodation provided to the employee is not job related. We will start by looking at how we calculate the cash equivalent where the **property is rented by the employer**.

The benefit - i.e. the cash equivalent - is **the higher of the rents paid by the employer** for the use of the property, **and the annual value of the property**. s.105(4)

The "annual value" of living accommodation is defined as the **rent** which might **reasonably be expected to be obtained on letting the property** if the tenant paid all the usual household bills and the landlord met all repair and maintenance costs. The "annual value" will be provided for you in the examination. s.110

In practice, however, the Revenue will use the **gross rateable value** of the property under the old rating system as the annual value. This will be much lower than the annual value as defined in the Act. If the property has no rateable value (for example because it was built recently), an estimate must be made. Any disputes as to the amount of the annual value will be referred to the General Commissioners for ruling.

We then deduct any **employee contributions** – i.e. any rents paid by the employee to the employer for the use of the property. This will give us the cash equivalent.

Higher of:	
Rents paid by employer } *Annual value of property*	*X*
Less: employee contributions	(X)
Taxable benefit	X

Remember that this method of calculating the benefit only applies where the employer is **renting** the accommodation from another landlord.

D4.4 Employer owned accommodation

There are similar rules where the **employer owns the accommodation** being made available to the employee.

Once again, the starting point in calculating the benefit is the annual value. If the **accommodation cost the employer less than £75,000,** then the benefit is equal to the annual value. s. 105(2)

If the house cost the employer **more than £75,000**, there will be an additional benefit to the employee called the additional yearly rent – this **extra benefit** will be **added to the annual value** to give the total benefit. s. 106

To calculate the additional yearly rent we start by taking the cost of the accommodation - here "cost" means the original cost plus any improvements. From this we **deduct £75,000,** and **multiply** the difference by the **"ORI"** which is the Revenue's official interest rate at the **start of the tax year**.

When calculating the "cost" of the property, only improvements carried out before the beginning of the tax year are taken into account. Improvements undertaken during the year will affect the "cost" used in calculating the benefit for the following year. s. 104

If the employee makes a contribution towards the benefit, this can be deducted in arriving at the taxable cash equivalent.

If employee contributions exceed the amount of the benefit, no loss will arise. The result is simply a benefit of zero.

Annual Value	X
Add:	
Additional yearly rent if Cost > £75,000	
£(Cost - £75,000) x ORI at start of year	X
	X
Less: employee contributions	(X)
Taxable Benefit	X

Illustration 1

An employee lives in accommodation that is owned by his employer. The house cost the employer £100,000 and has an annual value of £1,000. The employee pays rent to the employer of £100 per month for the use of the house. Assume the Revenue's official rate of interest is 5%.

The calculation the taxable benefit that will be entered onto the employee's form P11D will be as follows:

	£
Annual Value	1,000
Additional yearly rent:	
(100,000 - 75,000) x 5%	1,250
	2,250
Less: employee contributions:	
(£100 x 12)	(1,200)
Taxable Benefit	**£1,050**

D4.5 The "6 year" rule s. 107

The "6 year rule" applies when a house was bought by an employer and is made available for use by the employee more than 6 years after it had been first acquired. The additional yearly rental in respect of accommodation will not be based on cost. Instead, the charge will be based on the market value of the house on the date the property was made available to the employee.

In effect we are substituting market value in place of original cost. Note that this rule only applies where there are more than 6 years between the property being acquired by the employer and it being made available to the employee.

Illustration 2

An employee was provided with a house by his employer in June 1998. He pays £100 a month for use of the house. The house had been purchased £100,000 in 1990 and has an annual value of £1,000. The house had a market value of £120,000 in June 1998. Assume an official rate of interest of 5%.

The benefit will be calculated as follows:

	£
Annual Value	1,000
Additional yearly rent £(120,000 - 75,000) @ 5%	2,250
Less: employee contributions	(1,200)
Taxable Benefit	**£2,050**

As house prices normally rise over time, we would expect the original cost to be **less** than a later market value. However, if property prices fall such that when the employee moves in more than 6 years later, the market value is less than original cost, **this market value of the property will still be used to calculate the benefit** even though it is less than original cost.

If the original cost of the accommodation is **less than £75,000**, there will **not be additional yearly rent**, regardless of current market value. For example, if a company buys a house in London in the 1960s for, let's say, £20,000, and the employee is given use of the property today when the house is worth, say, one million pounds, there is no additional charge because the original cost is below the £75,000 threshold. s. 107(1)(b)

If the **house is not made available** to the employee **for the whole of the tax year** - i.e. the employee moves in or moves out during the year - the benefit needs to be apportioned. Apportionment can be done on a monthly basis.

If the same living accommodation is provided for more than one employee at the same time, the cash equivalent of the benefit (as calculated above) is apportioned between the employees on a "just and reasonable" basis. s. 108

D4.6 Household expenses

If the **employer pays** any household bills on behalf of the employee, for example **gas, electricity** and **telephone bills** etc, this will give rise to an additional and **separate benefit**. This benefit is calculated by taking the cost to the employer of paying these particular bills.

There is a special rule relating to expenses paid on behalf of employees who live in **job related accommodation**.

Illustration 3

Assume a vicar is living in job related accommodation. The vicar will not have a benefit on the provision of the house, as the accommodation is job related.

The vicar has a salary of £20,000 and his employer pays for the gas, electricity and telephone bills relating to the house. These come to £2,300. As the employer discharges these bills, this gives rise to an additional benefit.

The special rule says that where such expenses are paid on behalf of employees in job related accommodation, the amount on which the employee will be taxed in respect of this **benefit cannot exceed 10% of his other earnings from that employment for the year.** s. 315(3) & (4)

Here the vicar's earnings for the year is his salary of £20,000, so the amount on which the vicar will be taxed in respect of these reimbursed expenses cannot exceed 10% of this - ie £2,000.

This 10% restriction rule only applies to expenses provided for employees in job related accommodation. **Where the accommodation is not job related, the full amount of the expenses are taxable.**

Q	Now test your understanding by attempting the examples which follow.

Example 1

Neil lives in a company owned flat. The flat cost the company £150,000 in 2001. The annual value is £800 and Neil pays rent of £150 per month. Neil moved out of the flat on 1 January 2006 and bought his own house.

Calculate Neil's taxable benefit assuming that the official interest rate is 5%.

Example 2

Alf is the manager of the Golden Lion Public House. He is employed on a salary of £18,000 and is required to live in the flat above the pub. His benefits for the year are as follows:

	£
Private medical insurance	500
Gas and electricity bills for flat	2,200

Calculate Alf's taxable employment income for the year.

Answer 1

	£
Annual value	800
Additional charge:	
£(150,000 - 75,000) @ 5%	3,750
	4,550
$\times \frac{9}{12}$ (6.4.05 - 1.1.06)	3,412
Less: employee contributions	
(£150 x 9)	(1,350)
Taxable Benefit	**£2,062**

Answer 2

	£
Salary	18,000
Medical Insurance (amount treated as earnings)	500
	18,500
Living expenses £2,200	
Restricted to	
10% x £18,500	1,850
Total employment income	**£20,350**

Accommodation is job related so the restriction in s.315 applies.

SUMMARY - LIVING ACCOMMODATION - TAXABLE BENEFITS

Job related accommodation is a tax free benefit. This is where the accommodation is:

a) necessary for the job; or
b) customary or provided for the better performance of the job; or
c) provided because of a threat to the employee's security

Non-job related accommodation is a taxable benefit for all employees.

The benefit for rented accommodation is the higher of rents paid by the employer and the annual value.

If the employer owns the property, the benefit is the annual value.

Additional yearly rent is calculated if the property cost > £75,000 as:

(Cost - £75,000) x ORI at start of year

ORI is the official rate of interest.

If there was more than 6 years between the purchase of the property and the employee moving in, the market value of the property at the date the employee moved in is substituted for cost in the above formula.

Any household expenses paid by the employer also lead to a benefit for the employee. If the employee is in job related accommodation, the benefit is limited to 10% of the other earnings from this employment for the year.

D5: LOANS TO EMPLOYEES & USE OF ASSETS

In this chapter you will cover taxation of the following benefits:
- the provision of a taxable cheap loan;
- use of a company owned asset;
- transfer of an asset from employer to employee.

Statutory references in this chapter are to ITEPA 2003 unless stated otherwise.

D5.1 Loans to employees s.173 - s.191

When a company lends money to an employee, this is likely to give rise to a taxable benefit called a taxable cheap loan. The cash equivalent of the benefit is calculated using the Revenue's official rate of interest. If no interest is charged or the interest rate is less than the official rate of interest, the cash equivalent is the difference between the interest that would have been payable at the official rate of interest and any interest which is paid. s.175

There are two ways in which we can calculate the cash equivalent. The first is by using the **average method,** and the second uses the **strict method.** The average method is perhaps more commonly used although either the taxpayer or the Revenue can insist that the strict method is used instead. s.182 s.183

The employee will have no taxable benefit if the aggregate of all loans outstanding throughout the tax year is £5,000 or less. Therefore if the employee makes one loan to the employee and throughout the tax year this **loan never exceeds £5,000, the taxable benefit is zero.** s.180

This provision is intended to exempt such things as season ticket loans, so for those of you who travel to work on public transport and have an annual travel card obtained via a loan from your employer, as long as the travel card costs **£5,000 or less** (and you don't have any more loans), you will not have a taxable benefit.

Note here that the **£5,000 rule refers to the aggregate of all loans** in the year - this is to prevent an employer abusing the rules by offering a series of loans to the same employee, each of just under £5,000. s.180(2)

D5.2 Average Method s.182

Under the average method we start by taking the loan outstanding at the **start** of the tax year - i.e. at 6 April - and to this we will add on the loan outstanding as at the **end** of the tax year - i.e. at the following 5 April. Having added these together, we divide by two to give the **average loan outstanding** during the year.

If there is no loan outstanding at the start of the tax year - for example the employer makes the loan to the employee part way through the year - we start by using the amount of the loan **at the point it was made**. Similarly if the loan outstanding at the end of the year is nil - for example if the loan is completely repaid during the year - we add on the amount of the loan **at the point it was repaid**.

Having arrived at the average loan for the year, we multiply this by the Revenue's average official rate of interest (ORI) for the year.

$$\frac{\text{Loan at 6 April + Loan at 5 April}}{2} \times \text{average ORI for tax year}$$

If the employee is required to make some sort of contribution - i.e. if the **employee** pays some interest to the employer on the loan - these **contributions reduce the cash equivalent**.

D5.3 Strict method s.183

Under the strict method we **simply calculate interest on a daily or monthly basis** on the exact amounts of the loan outstanding during the tax year.

Either the taxpayer or the Revenue has the right to insist that the strict basis be used instead of the average basis. s.183(1)

If the strict basis gives a lower cash equivalent than the average basis, the taxpayer would be advised to elect for this strict basis to apply. Alternatively, if the strict basis gives rise to a higher benefit, you would expect the Revenue to insist that we use this strict basis.

However the Revenue will only insist on the strict basis if the average basis gives a **significantly distorted result** - if there is only a few pounds difference between the two, the Revenue will not insist on the strict basis.

Illustration 1

Paul borrows £100,000 from his employer in 1999 and uses the money to buy a house. The loan is interest free so Paul is not required to make any employee contributions. Paul repays £20,000 of the loan on 1 December 2005.

In order to find the cash equivalent we must calculate the benefit using both the average and the strict basis then compare the results. We will assume an official rate of 5%.

Average basis:

$$\frac{100{,}000 + 80{,}000}{2} = 90{,}000 \times 5\% \qquad \underline{\underline{£4{,}500}}$$

Strict basis:

$$100{,}000 \times \frac{8}{12} \times 5\% \qquad 3{,}333$$

$$80{,}000 \times \frac{4}{12} \times 5\% \qquad \underline{1{,}333}$$

$$\underline{\underline{£4{,}666}}$$

Either the Revenue or the taxpayer can insist on the use of the strict basis. It makes no sense for Paul to make an election here as the strict basis gives a higher benefit. The Revenue will only insist on using the strict basis - i.e. on taxing the £4,666 - if they feel that the average basis had significantly distorted the benefit.

Here, the Revenue would not bother so the average basis would be used. The taxable cash equivalent would therefore be £4,500.

If the loan remains reasonably constant throughout the year, when preparing the P11D the average basis is usually used.

However if the loan outstanding is changing - i.e. amounts are being repaid or additional loans are being taken out - it will be more usual to prepare the P11D using the strict basis.

D5.4 Use of employer's assets s.205

If an **employer lends an asset** to one of his employees, this will give rise to a **taxable benefit**. Note that the employer is allowing the employee to use the asset - ownership of the asset remains with the employer and does not transfer to the employee.

The benefit in this instance is the higher of:

a) the annual value of the use of the asset; or
b) the sums paid by the employer in providing the asset by way of rent or hire charge.

The "annual value" referred to above is **20% of the market value** of the asset at the time it was first made available to the employee.

If the **employee makes a contribution** - i.e. he pays some sort of rent to the employer for the use of the asset - we can **deduct** this to arrive at the taxable cash equivalent.

If the asset is lent to the employee part way through the year, having calculated the basic cash equivalent, we must then **apportion** this for the number of months in the year in which the employee had use of the asset.

This rule will often apply in relation to furniture provided by the employer in living accommodation made available to the employee.

Because the asset remains the property of the employer, at some point the employee will be required to give it back. If the employee doesn't return the asset to the employer – i.e. the employer allows the employee to keep the asset - there will be a taxable benefit on this transfer.

D5.5 Transfer of assets

The benefit will be the higher of: s.206

a) The market value of the asset at the date it was transferred to the employee.

b) The market value of the asset at the date it was originally lent to the employee reduced by any amounts which have been charged to tax in respect of the employee's use of the asset.

S.206 ITEPA 2003 contains a "step-by-step" approach in how to compute this benefit.

The Revenue will take whichever is the **higher** and will tax this figure. Any payments made by the employee to the employer for the transfer of the asset can be deducted.

Illustration 2

An employer lends a painting to an employee on 1 January 2003. At this date the painting was worth £100,000.

On 30 September 2005, the employer allows the employee to keep the painting. It is worth £40,000 at this point.

Benefit for use of painting:				£
2002/2003:	$£100,000 \times 20\% \times \frac{3}{12}$			5,000
2003/2004:	£100,000 x 20%			20,000
2004/2005:	£100,000 x 20%			20,000
2005/2006:	$£100,000 \times 20\% \times \frac{6}{12}$			10,000
				55,000
Benefit on gift is higher of:				
a) MV @ transfer			40,000	
b) Original MV		100,000		
Less: already charged for use		(55,000)		
			45,000	i.e. 45,000

Benefit for use in 2005/06 (from above)	10,000
Benefit on transfer	45,000
Total Benefit in 2005/06	**£55,000**

D5.6 Transfers of cars or houses

The rules above on transfers of assets **do not apply** when assets such as **cars** or **houses** are given to employees.

Where an employee has use of a company car and at a later date that car is transferred to the employee, the benefit is the **market value of the car** at the date of the transfer minus any payments made by the employee for the transfer of the car. The rules regarding amounts previously charged to tax do not apply here.

This arrangement commonly applies as part of a termination agreement. If an employee is made redundant, to soften the blow the employer may allow the ex-employee to keep his company car.

The same rule applies to transfers of houses.

D5.7 Use of computers s.320

If computer equipment is lent by an employer to an employee and the employee uses that equipment for private purposes, this will give rise to a taxable benefit. However, the **first £500** of this benefit is **exempt** from tax.

Therefore if an employer has a computer worth £2,500, if this is lent to an employee, the benefit will be 20% of the £2,500 being £500. This benefit would then be completely exempt from tax.

It is very common in practice for an employer to allow an employee to use a desk top or a lap top for some private purposes. The £500 rule means that employees are unlikely to have a benefit in respect of their private use.

If the computer is subsequently transferred to the employee, the benefit is calculated by using the market value of the computer at the date of transfer. The original acquisition cost calculation is not used in this case.

"Computer equipment" includes printers, scanners, modems and other peripheral devises including the right to use software. The exception does not however extend to access to telecommunications systems such as the Internet.

Q	Now test your understanding by attempting the examples which follow.

Example 1

Ron borrowed £50,000 from his employer to buy a house on 1 May 2005. The loan is interest free. On 1 August 2005 Ron borrowed a further £40,000 to add an extension.

Calculate Ron's taxable benefit assuming an official interest rate of 5% throughout.

Example 2

Lesley borrows a wide screen TV and DVD player from her employer on 30 September 2004. The equipment was worth £800 at that date.

On 1 July 2005, Lesley bought the equipment from her employer for £200. It was worth £450 at that date.

Calculate Lesley's taxable benefit for 2005/06.

Answer 1

Average method:

$$\left[\frac{50,000 + 90,000}{2}\right] = 70,000 \times 5\% \times \frac{11}{12} \qquad \underline{\underline{£3,208}}$$

Strict method:

	£
$50,000 \times 5\% \times \frac{3}{12}$	625
$90,000 \times 5\% \times \frac{8}{12}$	3,000
	£3,625

The Revenue may elect for the strict basis as the average basis distorts the benefit.

Answer 2

	£	£
Benefits for use		
2004/05:		
$800 \times 20\% \times \frac{6}{12}$		80
2005/06:		
$800 \times 20\% \times \frac{3}{12}$		40
		120
Transfer of equipment		
Higher of:		
a) MV at transfer	450	
b) Original MV	800	
Less: charged already for use	(120)	
	680	

2005/06	£
Use of asset	40
Transfer of asset	680
Less: paid by employee	(200)
Total taxable benefit	**£520**

SUMMARY - LOANS TO EMPLOYEES & USE OF ASSETS

If a cheap loan is made to an employee by his employer, it only leads to a taxable benefit if the aggregate of all loans outstanding throughout the tax year exceeds £5,000.

There are two methods to calculate the benefit. The average method is as follows:

$$\frac{\text{Loan at 6 April + Loan at 5 April}}{2} \times \text{average ORI for tax year}$$

The strict method calculates interest on a monthly basis using the exact loan outstanding during the year.

The taxpayer can elect for the strict basis if it is lower, the Revenue will insist on the strict basis if the benefit would otherwise be significantly distorted.

If an employee has the use of an asset owned by his employer the benefit is:

20% x MV of asset when first provided to the employee

If the employer allows the employee to keep an asset, the benefit is the higher of:

a) MV when given;
b) MV when originally provided less amounts already charged for use of the asset.

These transfer rules do not apply to cars nor houses given to an employee, the benefit here is just MV less any amount paid by the employee.

The first £500 of benefit calculated for use of a computer is tax free.

D6: MISCELLANEOUS BENEFITS

In this chapter you will learn about some miscellaneous benefits including:
- company vans;
- vouchers;
- mileage allowances;
- tax exempt benefits.

Statutory references in this chapter are to ITEPA 2003 unless stated otherwise.

D6.1 Company vans

Where an employer allows an employee exclusive use of a company owned van, there will be a taxable benefit. A "van" in this context is a mechanically propelled road vehicle which is a goods vehicle weighing less than 3.5 tonnes. As a van is not a car, we do not use the company car rules to calculate the benefit. The van rules are very simple. s.115(1)

If an employee has use of a **new van**, the benefit is a flat **£500 per annum.** If the employee has use of an **old van**, the benefit is **£350**. A van is **new** if it is **less than 4 years old at the end of the tax year**. s.155

These charges are **apportioned** if the van is not available for the whole of the year. Where the van is "shared" - i.e. concurrently available to more than one employee – **the cash equivalent is split between the employees** based on the days it was available. The benefit charge covers the provision of fuel for private use, unlike the benefit charge for cars. s.158

The van rules will **change from 2007/08**. A van with unrestricted private use will have a **flat rate benefit of £3,000** regardless of the age of the van. In addition there will be a scale charge of **£500** where fuel for private use is provided by the employer.

D6.2 Mobile phones s.319

If an employer provides an employee with a **mobile phone,** this is a **tax exempt** benefit even if the employer is paying for the employee's personal telephone calls.

It is quite common in practice for employees, particularly those who are not office based, to be provided with a company mobile phone. The Revenue recognises that there will inevitably be some personal calls made by the employee but they have chosen not to treat this as a taxable benefit.

The exemption only covers the "**provision for an employee**.....of a mobile phone". Therefore if an employee has his own mobile phone and the employer reimburses any private calls or standing charges there will be a taxable benefit equal to the cost to the employer of reimbursing such expenses.

D6.3 Vouchers

If an employer provides vouchers to an employee - for example a high street store voucher - there will be a taxable benefit. The cash equivalent will be the **cost to the employer of providing the voucher** to the employee. This is common at Christmas where employers often give bonuses to employees in this form. s.87

Where an employer provides **meal vouchers** to an employee, this is also a **taxable benefit** except that the **first 15 pence per day of vouchers** provided is **exempt** from tax. So, if the employer gives a one pound meal voucher to an employee, only 85 pence of this is taxable. s.89

Similarly if an employee is provided with some form of "credit token" - for example, a credit card, debit card or other token or document giving the employee the right to obtain goods or services - the cost of providing such a token will be a taxable benefit for the employee. s.90

D6.4 Mileage allowances s.229

Mileage allowances will be paid when an **employee uses his own car for work** purposes. When an employer pays a mileage allowance to the employee, he is reimbursing that employee at a fixed amount per mile for using his own car. The mileage allowances rules do not therefore apply to company vehicles. s.229(4)

The Revenue want to make sure that the employee is not making a profit from the mileage allowance paid to him. If there is a **profit** - i.e. the cost to the employee of using his car is less than the allowance paid - the Revenue will **tax that profit** as employment income.

To work out the profit, the Revenue has **tax-exempt limits** which we need to apply. If allowances are paid above these limits the employee will be making a profit - if allowances are paid below these limits, the employee will be making a loss.

The tax-exempt limits **depend on the employee's business mileage** in the year. Remember that business mileage does **not include travelling from home to work**. If an employer reimburses an employee's travel costs from home to work, this will be a fully taxable benefit. The limits are given in the Tax Tables provided with your course and are also reproduced below.

Vehicles	*First 10,000 Business miles*	*Additional Business miles*
Cars	40p	25p
Motorcycles	24p	24p
Bicycles	20p	20p

You will note from the table that the tax-exempt limits change once the business mileage threshold of 10,000 miles has been exceeded.

Remember that the point of **this scheme** is to **determine whether the employee is making a profit or loss from using his own car for work.**

To determine the profit, we simply take the allowance reimbursed and deduct the tax-exempt limit. **Profits are taxable** whilst **losses are deductible**.

Illustration 1

An employee owns his own car for occasional business journeys. In the tax year the employee did 15,000 business miles. His employer reimburses him at a fixed rate of 60 pence for every business mile travelled. The calculation is as follows:

	£
Reimbursed	
15,000 x 60p	9,000
Less: tax exempt limits	
10,000 x 40p	(4,000)
5,000 x 25p	(1,250)
Taxable profit	**£3,750**

Illustration 2

If the employee in the illustration above was reimbursed at a lower rate of 20 pence per mile, the calculation is as follows:

	£
Reimbursed	
15,000 x 20p	3,000
Less: tax exempt limits	
10,000 x 40p	(4,000)
5,000 x 25p	(1,250)
Loss (deductible from earnings)	**£(2,250)**

The taxpayer is allowed to deduct this loss from his other taxable earnings for the year. s.231

In practice, many employers make sure that they reimburse their employees at a rate **exactly equal to the tax exempt limits**, so year on year employees using their own cars for business purposes will neither have a profit nor a loss.

D6.5 Passenger payments s.233

In an attempt to encourage drivers to share business journeys wherever possible, the Revenue has introduced a scheme whereby **payments can be made free of tax** and NIC to **an employee carrying one or more passengers**.

"Passenger payments" can be made tax exempt to an employee if:

- the driver and passenger(s) are **fellow employees** making the same business journey; and
- the "passenger payments" do not exceed the "approved amount" of **5p per business mile**; and s.234
- the employee **physically receives the passenger payment** from the employer (i.e. an employee who is not paid extra for carrying passengers cannot claim an additional 5p per mile allowance).

Only payments in respect of **business mileage** are tax-free - the passenger payment scheme does not extend to private mileage such as home to office travel.

The "passenger allowance" applies per passenger (eg 10p per business mile for 2 passengers etc) and applies to both company vehicles and for employees using their own cars for business purposes.

D6.7 Tax exempt benefits

There is a long list of benefits which are completely exempt from tax. Here we will pick up a dozen or so of the more familiar **tax exempt benefits.**

One of the most valuable benefits that employees receive from their employers, is an **employer's contribution to the employee's pension** scheme. This is exempt from tax as long as the pension scheme has Revenue approval. s.307

Therefore if an employer pays into either the employee's occupational pension scheme or into the employee's personal pension scheme, no taxable benefit will arise. The level of employer's contributions is irrelevant.

The provision of a **mobile phone** and **associated calls** is a tax-exempt benefit. s.319

The **reimbursement of removal expenses is exempt, up to** a maximum amount of **£8,000**. For example, if an employee is transferred to another office and the employer pays the relocation expenses, no taxable benefit will arise as long as the cost of the move is less than £8,000. s.287

The exemption applies to "removal benefits" and to the "payment or reimbursement of removal expenses". Such expenses will qualify if they are "reasonably provided in connection with a change in the employee's residence" - i.e. in respect of a change in the duties and/or location of the employment or on the employees becoming employed.

Qualifying removal expenses will include:

- legal fees in connection with the acquisition of a new residence (including stamp duty land tax);
- any such abortive acquisition costs;

- legal fees in connection with the disposal of a former residence;
- costs of transporting belongings (including temporary storage costs);
- travel and subsistence for the employee (and family) to visit the new area.

A detailed breakdown of allowable costs is given at s.277 – s.283 ITEPA 2003.

Qualifying removal expenses will also include the additional interest paid on a bridging loan taken out between buying a new property and disposing of an old one. s.284

The provision by the employer of a **crèche or nursery** for employee's children is a tax-exempt benefit. The facilities must usually be exclusively for the employer. s.318

There is a partial exemption of up to £50 a week for childcare vouchers. This also applies to other childcare where the employer contracts directly with the childcare provider such as a commercial nursery. s. 318A

The provision of "**workplace parking**" is a tax-exempt benefit. This covers not just a space in the employer's car park but would also extend to the costs of a season ticket at a public car park close to work. Similarly the provision of **motorcycle or bicycle spaces** at or near work is a tax-exempt benefit. s.237

Subsidised staff canteens are tax-exempt benefits as long as the canteen facilities are available to all employees. Therefore if a company has a canteen or restaurant that is reserved for use by senior executives only, those executives will have a taxable benefit on the costs of the free or subsidised meals provided. s.317

Incidental expenses paid by an employer to employees working away from home are tax exempt up to a daily limit. These limits are £5 per night while working in the UK and **£10 per night** whilst **working abroad**. s.240 & s.241

Costs incurred by the employer in providing **full time, day release or block release training** are tax-exempt benefits. SP4/86

The provision by the employer of a **Christmas party** or other similar function for the employees, will not give rise to a taxable benefit for the employees as long as the costs of the party did not exceed **£150 per head**. This will mean that for most office parties, there will be no corresponding tax charge on the employees. However, if the employer throws a particularly lavish party which costs, say, £200 per head, the taxable benefit for each employee will be the full £200 and not just the excess over £150. It is an all or nothing benefit. s.264 SI 2003/1361

Awards by an employer to an employee from a **staff suggestion scheme** are generally tax exempt provided that the award does **not exceed £5,000**. s.321 & s.322

Long service awards of up to **£50 per year of service**, as long as the **employee** had **at least 20 years service** with the same employer are also exempt. This exempts **gifts** such as gold watches etc to a **long serving employee on retirement.** s.323 SI 2003/1361

Employers can make tax-exempt payments to an employee in respect of **reasonable additional costs incurred for working at home. This must be** under a **homeworking arrangement** where the employee regularly works at home. s.316A

There is no limit to such payments stated in statute. However, the Revenue has stated that **no records need to be kept by employers for payments up to £2 per week or £104 per year**. If payments exceed these limits, the employer should keep records to provide evidence that the higher payments were wholly in respect of additional household expenses incurred by the employee in working from home.

This covers the most common tax exempt benefits but it is by no means a definitive list.

Other benefits which are tax exempt include:

- workplace sports or recreational facilities for use by staff generally s.261
- "third party benefits" – ie benefits from someone other than one's employer – not exceeding £250 per year. s.324 SI 2003/13
- late night taxis etc when the employee is occasionally required to work late (ie after 9 pm) s.248
- hospitality or entertaining if provided by someone other than the employer s.265

Q	Now test your understanding by attempting the examples which follow.

Example 1

Which of the following benefits are tax exempt in 2005/06?

a) Use of company van
b) £500 loan to buy annual travelcard
c) £40 per week childcare vouchers
d) Car park voucher near work
e) Employer payment to work pension scheme
f) Loan of computer costing £1,000

Example 2

Rodney uses his own car for work. In 2005/06 he did 25,000 miles, half of which were for business purposes. His employer reimbursed Rodney at 40p for each business mile.

Calculate Rodney's taxable benefit.

Answer 1

		Tax exempt	Taxable
a)	Use of company van		✓
b)	£500 travelcard loan	✓	
c)	£40 per week childcare vouchers	✓	
d)	Car park voucher	✓	
e)	Payment to pension scheme	✓	
f)	Loan of computer	✓	

Answer 2

	£	£
Mileage reimbursed		
12,500 @ 40p		5,000
Less: tax exempt limits		
10,000 @ 40p	4,000	
2,500 @ 25p	625	
		(4,625)
Taxable profit		**£375**

SUMMARY - MISCELLANEOUS BENEFITS

If an employee is provided with a company van, the benefit is £500 for the year. If the van is ≥ 4 years old at the end of the tax year the benefit is £350. These rules are changing from April 2007.

If an employee is given vouchers, the cost of providing these is taxable as a benefit. However the first 15p per day of meal vouchers is exempt from tax.

If the employer reimburses the employee for business mileage incurred using his own car, the amount reimbursed must be compared with the tax exempt limits set by the Revenue.

If the amount reimbursed exceeds the limits this excess is taxable. If it is less than the limits, the shortfall is deductible.

There are a number of tax exempt benefits including:

- Employer contributions to an approved pension scheme
- Mobile phones
- Removal expenses up to £8,000
- Exclusive nursery up to £50 per week childcare vouchers/other directly provided childcare
- Car parking at or near the place of work
- Staff canteens provided available to all employees
- Incidental expenses for working away from home (£5 in UK, £10 if abroad)
- Training costs
- Christmas party or other functions costing below £150 per head
- Staff suggestion scheme awards up to £5,000
- Long service awards up to £50 per year of service if served at least 20 years
- Additional costs of working from home under a homeworking arrangement

D7: EXPENSES OF EMPLOYMENT

> In this chapter you will learn how to treat payments received from the employer in respect of expenses including:
> - expenses that are 'wholly, exclusively and necessarily' incurred;
> - qualifying traveling expenses
> - professional fees and subscriptions;
> - payroll deduction scheme.

D7.1 Introduction

In this chapter we shall look at the expenses that are allowed as a deduction in arriving at net taxable earnings. Before we do so, let's remind ourselves where they fit into the earnings proforma.

Cash remuneration	X	
Benefits	X	
	X	
Less: exempt income	(X)	
Taxable earnings	X	
Less: allowable deductions	(X) ←	
Net taxable earnings		X

We start with cash remuneration such as salary and bonuses. We also need to add any expenses reimbursed to the employee by the employer. All expenses paid by an employer to an employee are treated in the first instance as cash earnings – i.e. money received by the employee. To this we add any benefits.

At this point we can take a deduction for any allowable deductions. Taxable earnings less allowable deductions gives net taxable earnings for the year. It is this figure that goes into the income tax computation as non-savings income.

Allowable deductions broadly fall into five main categories.

a) Expenses deductible under **s.336 ITEPA 2003**.

b) Travel expenses (s.337 – s.340 ITEPA 2003).

c) Payments made by an employee **to an occupational pension scheme** - the detailed rules with regard to pension contributions will be dealt with in a later chapter.

d) **Professional fees or subscriptions** paid to an organisation approved by the Revenue.

e) **Donations** made by an employee to **charity** under the Payroll Deduction Scheme.

D7.2 Section 336 – "deductions for expenses: the general rule"

Section 336 lays out the general rules for deductions to be made from taxable earnings. A deduction under the general rules is allowed if: s.336

a) the employee is **obliged to incur and pay the expense** as holder of the employment; and
b) the amount is incurred "**wholly, exclusively and necessarily**" in the performance of the duties.

In order to ascertain whether an expense is deductible, we therefore need to look closely at the terms **"wholly, exclusively and necessarily"**.

The word "necessarily" is the biggest obstacle to us when trying to persuade the Revenue that expenses are allowable. The question the Revenue will ask us is "could the employee do his job without incurring that particular expense?".

If the answer to this question is "yes" – i.e. he could do his job if that expense had not been incurred – the Revenue will argue that the expense is **not absolutely necessary and is not therefore deductible** from taxable earnings.

However, if the answer is "no" – i.e. he **cannot do his job without incurring that expense** - the expense will be necessary for the performance of the duties and will therefore be allowable.

The Revenue are very strict in applying this rule and it is **notoriously difficult for employees to get relief for expenses under Section 336**. Later on we will have a look at a couple of tax cases, and you will see that the Revenue have been successful more often than the taxpayer and most disputed claims for expenses have been disallowed.

D7.3 Travel expenses

Sections 337 and 338 deal with the deductibility of travel expenses. Under general principles a deduction for the employee's travel costs will be allowed if the expenses are: s.337-338

(i) **necessarily incurred** on travelling in the performance of the duties of the employment; or
(ii) attributable to the employee's **necessary attendance** at any place in the performance of the duties of the employment.

Section 338 specifically denies a deduction for "**expenses of ordinary commuting**". "Ordinary commuting" in this context is defined as travel between either:

a) the employee's **home and a permanent workplace**; or
b) a place that is not a workplace (eg a hotel or someone else's home) and a permanent workplace.

This means that if an employee incurs travel expenses in going from his **home** to his **normal place of work,** these expenses will **not** be allowable, as they constitute expenses of ordinary commuting. You will be aware of this already as your employer does not reimburse you for home to office travelling and you do not get tax relief for these costs.

No deduction is allowed for travel between any two places that is, for practical purposes, **substantially ordinary commuting**. This means that if an employee, for instance, is required to attend a training college and the journey to the college is substantially the same as that to the usual place of work (and at a similar expense), no deduction will be allowed for travel costs to the college.

However, once at work, if an employee incurs expenses in travelling from his normal place of work to **visit a client**, that is not "ordinary commuting" but is instead travel in the performance of the duties and as such these expenses will be deductible. Therefore, **office to client travel is allowable**.

But what if the employee travels directly from his home to a client's premises and doesn't go into the office first? The Revenue have accepted that these travel expenses are allowable as they are not ordinary costs of commuting but only providing that the client's premises constitute a "**temporary workplace**".

A "temporary workplace" is defined as a place which the employee attends in the performance of his duties in order **to perform a task of limited duration** or for some other temporary purpose. s.339

A workplace will **not** be "temporary" if **the employee attends for a period of continuous work lasting more** than 24 months. Therefore if an employee is visiting a client for a day, or a few days or even a few months, the client premises will be a "temporary workplace" and travel to and from that workplace will be deductible expenses.

A "temporary workplace" may become a "permanent workplace" if either:

a) the employee has worked at that location for a continuous period of 24 months; or
b) it becomes apparent that the absence from the original permanent workplace will exceed 24 months.

In these instances, travel costs up to the point of "change" are deductible, but costs after that date are not.

An "area" could be regarded as a permanent workplace and travel costs to and from that area would not be deductible. An "**area based employee**" is one whose employment duties are defined by reference to an "area" (rather than a specified site or building) and where the employee attends different places in the area in the course of his job. s.339(8)

Certain **"site based" employees** will have no permanent workplace and will travel to various different "sites" to perform their duties. Providing that a job at a particular site is not expected to last more than 24 months, costs of travelling from home to site (and back again) will be deductible.

Finally, the Revenue do not accept that an employee whose employment contract is for less than 24 months is by definition travelling to and from a temporary workplace. Deductions for travel costs in these instances will be denied. IRPR 16.5.95 s.339(5)(a)(ii)

D7.4 Professional fees and subscriptions

A deduction from taxable earnings is allowed for an amount paid by an employee in respect of a **professional fee**. The deduction is allowed provided that the **employment involves the practice of the profession to which the fee relates** and the payment of the fee is a **condition** which must be met if that profession is to be practiced. s.343

Section 343 contains a list of deductible fees and these include practice fees for doctors, dentists, opticians, vets, lawyers, architects and teachers.

A deduction from taxable earnings is also allowed for **annual subscriptions** paid to an "approved body". The Revenue has a published list of such bodies. The subscription will be deductible as long as the activities of the body are of direct benefit to, or concern the profession practiced in, the performance of the duties. s.344

For example, a subscription by a company director to the Institute of Directors would be deductible because the subscription relates to the employment and is to an approved body. However if the same director then paid a subscription to his local golf club, this would not be deductible as this has nothing to do with the employment.

The Revenue would not accept an argument that it is "necessary" for this employee to be a member of the golf club, even though he may meet clients and do some business at the club. This was tested in the tax case of *Brown v Bullock* where a bank manager's Gentleman's Club fees were disallowed by the courts on the grounds that they were not absolutely necessary. He could do his job as a bank manager without being a member of the club. The fact that his club membership occasionally won him some business was held to be irrelevant.

D7.5 Charitable donations s. 713

There are two methods of obtaining tax relief on charitable donations.

As we have seen already, the first is via the **Gift Aid scheme.** Gift Aid payments are made net of basic rate tax and we give higher rate relief by extending the basic rate band by the gross amount of the donation.

The second way in which a taxpayer can get tax relief on a donation to charity is by using the Payroll Deduction Scheme. You may also see this referred to as the **Give As You Earn (GAYE) scheme**.

Donations are made **gross** - i.e. there is no withholding of basic rate tax at source. This gross donation is **deducted from taxable earnings** for the year.

In practice, the gross donation is deducted by the payroll department before PAYE is applied thereby giving the employee tax relief as he goes along. The employer will then pass on the amounts withheld to the relevant charity.

D7.6 Reimbursed expenses

Most business expenses incurred by employees will be reimbursed by their employers at a later date when the employee makes an expense claim. As far as the tax computation is concerned, we need to do two things.

First we **treat the expenses reimbursed by the employer to the employee as earnings from the employment** - i.e. we include this payment to the employee's taxable earnings. As such, the amount reimbursed should be reflected by the employer as a benefit on the employee's P11D.

Having treated the reimbursed expense as income, we need to **determine whether that expense can be deducted** to arrive at next taxable earnings.

It will be allowable if it is either **wholly, exclusively & necessarily incurred** in the performance of the duties, or if it is a **qualifying travelling expense** or it is a professional fee or subscription. In these cases, the expense can be deducted from taxable earnings.

In the case of genuine business expenses, the amount which goes into the computation as income and the amount that is deducted as an allowable expense, will cancel out leaving nothing taxable.

This will not be the case however if the expense is not wholly, exclusively & necessarily incurred in the performance of the duties. In this case, no deduction will be allowed for the expense and the amount reimbursed by the employer will be taxed in the same way as a benefit. This will be the case if personal expenses are reimbursed by the employer.

D7.7 Dispensations s.65

A "dispensation" is a notice provided by the Revenue to an employer agreeing that **no additional tax will be payable** by an employee who receives certain payments or benefits. The payments in question will be **genuine business expenses** reimbursed by the employer to the employee.

In the absence of a dispensation, expenses reimbursed to an employee will be treated as **earnings** in the first instance and entered on form P11D. The employee will then be left to claim relief for the expense via his self assessment return.

If an employer makes an application for dispensation, this unnecessary "paper chase" can be avoided.

Illustration 1

Chris makes a business trip to Edinburgh and his return train ticket costs £75. When he returned to the office, he made an expense claim and his employer, Online Tutors Ltd, reimbursed this £75.

Chris is employed on a salary of £25,000. Strictly what should happen is that the expenses reimbursed of £75 should be treated as income, and the employer should produce a form P11D for Chris including this £75 as a benefit. Chris's total earnings for the year will now be £25,075.

As far as Chris is concerned, the £75 is a qualifying travelling expense and is therefore deductible from his taxable earnings. He will make a claim under s.337 on his tax return and the £75 will be deducted, leaving Chris with taxable s.337
income of £25,000. This is exactly the same as the salary figure so you will see that the two entries of £75 have cancelled each other out.

	£
Salary	25,000
Add: reimbursed expense	75
Taxable earnings	25,075
Less: travel expenses	(75)
Net taxable earnings	£25,000

What we have achieved is to create a lot of paperwork with no end result. The company has to prepare a P11D to show a benefit of £75, and Chris has to prepare a tax return to claim this amount as an expense of his employment.

This is a waste of time, so in these circumstances the Revenue will issue a notice of nil liability or dispensation to the employer in respect of the business travelling expenses. This means that the employer here can ignore these travel expenses when preparing P11Ds.

Employers **must apply to their local Tax Office for dispensations**, and dispensations are issued by the Inspector in respect of specific categories of expenditure – business travel being the most common.

Note that if an employer does **not** have a dispensation for a particular type of expense, such expenses reimbursed to employees **must be reflected on the P11D** and the employee will then make a claim via his tax return if he thinks the expense is deductible.

D7.8 Round Sum Allowances

A round sum allowance is a general allowance - usually a fixed amount of cash - paid to the employee in advance to cover his or her expenses for a particular period. For example, Online Tutors Ltd could pay a round sum of £1,000 to Chris to cover forthcoming expenses.

A **round sum allowance** should be treated in the first instance as salary and the employer should **withhold tax under PAYE**. This will normally happen automatically as the payment is often made via the payroll system. There is no way around this as the Inland Revenue will not issue dispensations for round sum allowances.

Chris will spend the money on various items and will claim a deduction, via his end of year tax return, for any amounts spent for business purposes - i.e. any expenses incurred wholly, exclusively & necessarily in the performance of his duties.

One important thing to be aware of here is that the Revenue **do not regard expenses incurred in entertaining customers or clients as genuine business expenses**. Therefore if Chris spends part of his round sum allowance on client entertaining, no deduction will be allowed. s.356

However, relief for the entertaining expense **will be allowed if the amount falls to be disallowed** in computing the employer's taxable trading profits as will be the case for client entertaining. In this case, the employee will be able to take a deduction for the entertaining costs in calculating net taxable earnings. s.357

The above restriction for "client" entertaining does not apply to expenses of entertaining **fellow employees**. These costs are generally fully deductible. s.358

Q	Now test your understanding by attempting the example which follows.

Example 1

Mr Broker (a City analyst) incurs the following expenses:

a) Tube fare to work
b) Taxi fare from office to client
c) Payment to company pension scheme
d) Financial Times to read on the tube
e) Subscription to the Institute of Stockbrokers
f) Pinstripe suit and braces for office.

Which of these expenses are deductible in arriving at net taxable earnings?

Answer 1

		Allowable	*Not Allowable*
a)	Tube fare to work		X
b)	Taxi fare to client	✓	
c)	Pension payment	✓	
d)	Financial Times (see Note 1 below)		X
e)	Subscription to Institute of Stockbrokers	✓	
f)	Pin stripe suit and braces (see Note 2 below)		X

Note 1

Mr Broker's newspaper costs will not be allowed by the Revenue. Mr Broker would argue that, as a stockbroker, it is necessary for him to read the Financial Times on a daily basis, but a similar claim has already been heard and rejected by the courts.

In the case of **Smith v Abbott**, a journalist for a national daily newspaper argued that it was necessary for him to buy and read the daily newspapers of his competitors in order to do his job.

The courts agreed with the Revenue and disallowed this expense as it was held not to be absolutely necessary as it was possible for this journalist to do his job without incurring that expense.

The courts said that the expenditure simply enabled the employee to do his job better and this was not enough to pass the stringent tests laid down in s.336.

Note 2

The Revenue have again been successful before the courts in arguing that the costs of suits etc are not allowable on the grounds that the expense is not exclusively for the performance of the duties.

The courts have said that we buy clothing not just for business purposes but also to provide us with warmth and decency and hence the expense has a duality of purpose and is not allowable.

Deductions will only be available for such things as protective clothing or costumes or uniforms - i.e. clothing which could not be worn in an everyday context.

SUMMARY - EXPENSES OF EMPLOYMENT

Any amounts received from an employer in respect of expenses incurred are included as part of taxable earnings.

A deduction will then be given if the expense was 'wholly, exclusively and necessarily' incurred which is a strict test.

Qualifying travelling expenses are also deductible but these exclude ordinary commuting (ie home to work). Travel from the office or from home to a temporary workplace (less than 24 months) will be deductible.

Professional fees and subscriptions are deductible provided they are paid to an approved body.

Payments to charity can be made via the Payroll Deduction Scheme whereby the payment is made gross and is deducted from salary before applying PAYE to give relief. This is an alternative to obtaining relief via Gift Aid.

Reimbursed expenses are brought in as taxable earnings unless the employer has a dispensation which saves including them on the P11D only for them to be claimed as a deduction later.

Round sum allowances will always be taxable in the first instance but a deduction can be claimed for what is spent on allowable expenses. This however excludes any amount spent on client entertaining, unless the amount has been disallowed in the employer's tax calculation.

D8: CALCULATING THE INCOME TAX LIABILITY

In this chapter you will learn how to use a proforma for calculating income tax on non savings income including:
- the personal allowance;
- the rates of tax for non savings income;
- tax deducted at source.

References in this chapter are to the Income & Corporation Tax Act 1988 (ICTA 1988) unless otherwise stated.

D8.1 Introduction

The first step in calculating an individual's tax liability for the tax year 2005/06, is to arrive at taxable income for the year. Having arrived at taxable income, we then apply 2005/06 tax rates to that income to give a tax liability for the year.

The proforma for calculating an individual's tax liability is very important.

The income tax proforma differentiates between **three different types** of income. The first type of income is **non-savings income**. Non-savings income essentially means income from employment, income from self employment and rental income.

The second form of income is bank or building society **interest** and the third and final form of income received by individuals is **dividend income**.

We separate these three forms of income within the computation because they are taxed in different ways and at different rates.

D8.2 Proforma income tax calculation

	Non savings	*Interest*	*Dividends*
Earnings	X		
Trading income	X		
Property income	X		
Interest		X	
Dividends			X
Foreign income	X	X	X
Total income	T	T	T
Less: Charges on income	(X)	___	___
Statutory total income	STI	STI	STI

Foreign income could be non-savings income if it arose from rents in a villa in Spain. It could also be interest income if it was bank interest on a Jersey bank account. It could also be dividend income if it was dividends on shares in an American company. Entries could therefore be made in the non-savings column, the interest column or in the dividend column.

Income from all sources is then added together to give total income. Certain expenses incurred by individuals can be deducted in order to arrive at taxable income. These expenses are called **charges on income**.

Charges on income are deducted from **non-savings income first**, although if there is insufficient non-savings income, charges can be deducted from interest and then from dividends as appropriate. **Total income** less **charges on income** gives us "Statutory Total Income" or **STI**.

Statutory total income (STI) is not the same as taxable income. From statutory total income we **deduct the personal allowance** for the year in order to arrive at taxable income.

	Non Savings	***Interest***	*Dividends*
Statutory Total Income	X	X	X
Less: Personal Allowance	(PA)	—	—
Taxable Income	X	X	X

As with charges on income, the personal allowance is deducted from non-savings income in priority to interest and in priority to dividend income. Having deducted the personal allowance from the STI, this gives us taxable income from all sources.

The **personal allowance** for the tax year **2005/06** is **£4,895**. s. 257

The personal allowance is available to all individuals who are resident in the UK, and certain individuals who are resident abroad. A personal allowance is given to everybody, even to children.

Illustration 1

Mr Brown has the following income and expenditure for 2005/06:

	£
Salary from his job	30,000
Benefits from his employment	8,000
Rents from flat in Brighton	7,000
Rents from chateau in France	4,500
Charge on income paid	(1,000)

Mr Brown's taxable income is calculated as follows:

	Non Savings
	£
Income from earnings (30,000 + 8,000)	38,000
Property income	7,000
Foreign income	4,500
	49,500
Less: Charge on income	(1,000)
Statutory Total Income (STI)	48,500
Less: Personal Allowance	(4,895)
Taxable Income	£43,605

D8.3 Calculating the tax liability

To calculate an individual's tax liability, we start by looking at how non-savings income is taxed for the tax year.

Three rates of tax apply to non-savings income.

We have a lower rate of 10%, a basic rate of 22% and a higher rate of 40%.

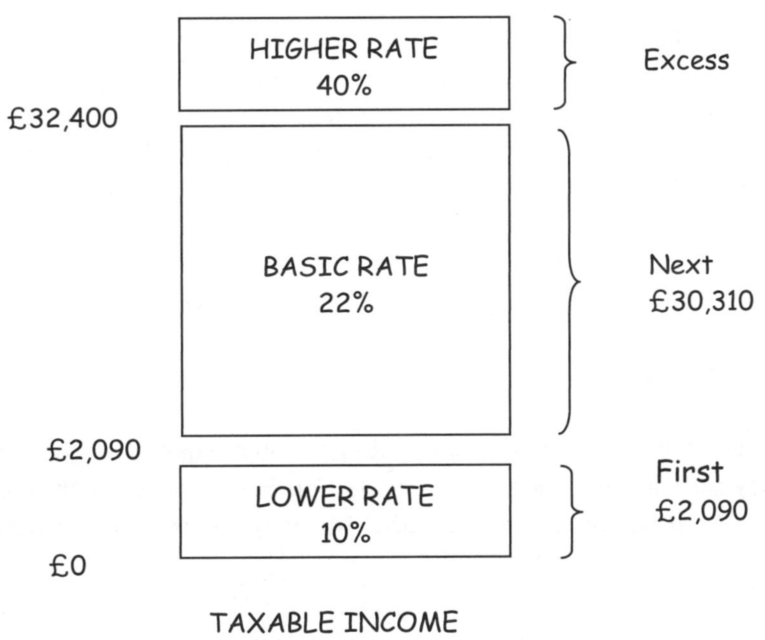

The first £2,090 of an individual's taxable income is charged to tax at the lower rate of 10%.

The next chunk of an individual's income is charged at the basic rate of tax, which is 22%. The basic rate applies to taxable income between £2,090 and £32,400. As you will see, this gives us a basic rate band of £30,310.

For individuals with taxable income in excess of £32,400, the higher rate of tax applies. This is currently 40%. This applies to all taxable income in excess of the basic rate threshold.

Remember that the **10%, 22% and 40% rates** apply to **non-savings income** only. Different rates apply to interest and dividends, as we shall see later.

Illustration 2

Continuing the previous illustration, Mr Brown's tax liability is calculated as follows:

Taxable Income	£43,605
Tax	£
2,090 @ 10%	209
30,310 @ 22%	6,668
11,205 @ 40%	4,482
43,605	
Tax liability	£11,359

D8.4 Tax already paid

Any income tax which Mr Brown has already paid during the course of the year can be deducted from tax liability to give a final figure of tax due and payable to the Revenue. The tax due will be collected by the Revenue under the self assessment regime.

If the tax paid at source in the tax year exceeds the tax liability, the taxpayer will be due an income tax repayment from the Revenue.

Illustration 3

Assume that Mr Brown from the previous illustration had paid tax on his employment income under the Pay As You Earn (PAYE) system of £9,000. This £9,000 can be deducted from the tax liability to give a figure of tax due as follows:

	£
Tax liability	11,359
Less: PAYE	(9,000)
Tax due	£2,359

Q Now test your understanding by attempting the examples which follow.

Example 1

Mrs White has the following income/expenses in 2005/06:

	£
Earnings from employment	32,000
(PAYE deducted £6,000)	
Rent from apartment in New York	9,500
Charge on income paid	(1,200)

Calculate her Income Tax due.

Example 2

Mr Green has the following income in 2005/06:

	£
Salary (PAYE £3,000)	12,000
UK rental income	3,500
Premium bond winnings	2,000

Calculate his income tax due/repayable.

Answer 1

	Non Savings
	£
Earnings	32,000
Foreign income	9,500
Less: Charge on income	(1,200)
STI	40,300
Less: Personal allowance	(4,895)
Taxable Income	£35,405

Tax	£
2,090 @ 10%	209
30,310 @ 22%	6,668
3,005 @ 40%	1,202
Tax liability	8,079
Less: tax paid under PAYE	(6,000)
Tax due	**£2,079**

Answer 2

	Non savings
	£
Earnings	12,000
Property Income	3,500
Premium bond winnings	***Exempt***
STI	15,500
Less: Personal allowance	(4,895)
Taxable Income	£10,605

Tax	£
2,090 @ 10%	209
8,515 @ 22%	1,873
Tax liability	2,082
Less: PAYE deducted	(3,000)
Tax repayable to Mr Green	**£(918)**

SUMMARY - CALCULATING THE INCOME TAX LIABILITY

Taxable income is calculated by combining all sources of income, deducting charges on income paid and finally deducting the personal allowance which is £4,895 for 2005/06.

Non savings income is then taxed as follows:

First £2,090 at 10%
Next £30,310 at 22%
Rest at 40%

Finally any tax paid at source, such as PAYE, is deducted to find the tax due or repayable for the year.

D9: INTRODUCTION TO PAYE

In this chapter you will learn about the PAYE system which collects tax from employment income including:
- what PAYE applies to;
- how the system works;
- tax codes;
- under payments of tax;
- K codes.

Statutory references in this chapter are to ITEPA 2003 unless stated otherwise.

D9.1 Introduction

The Pay As You Earn (or PAYE) system is a method by which tax is deducted from **employment income** at source. **PAYE** is not a tax in itself - it is simply a system under which tax on employment income and National Insurance is taken from salaries at the point of payment and handed over to the Revenue. s. 684 SI 2003/2682

PAYE schemes are operated by employers. The Revenue use employers as unpaid tax collectors on their behalf. If employers fail to operate PAYE correctly there are penalties for these failures.

The PAYE system aims to recover tax and National Insurance wherever "PAYE income" is paid to an employee. National Insurance Contributions are paid by both employers and employees and we shall take a detailed look at NIC in a separate chapter.

The PAYE regulations also contain detailed provisions with regard to the collection and recovery of tax and NIC, the retention and production of records, interest and penalties for compliance failures and PAYE appeal procedures.

PAYE must be applied at the "time of payment". The date at which PAYE income is "paid" is defined in Section 686 as the earlier of: s. 684 (2) s. 686

(i) the time when payment is made; and
(ii) the time when the person becomes entitled to the payment.

There are special rules for directors as discussed in Chapter 15.

Employers pay the PAYE tax and NIC to the Revenue on a monthly basis on the 19th of each month. The **due date** for payment is **14 days after** the **end of the tax month** of payment, and each tax month ends on the **5th** of the month.

There is one exception to this. If the total tax and National Insurance Contributions payable by the employer are less than £1,500 per month on average, the employer has the option to make payments under PAYE on a quarterly basis. For this purpose, the four tax quarters end on 5 July, 5 October, 5 January and 5 April, so PAYE payments are due 14 days after each of those quarter ends. SI2003/2682 Reg. 70

D9.2 PAYE income

ITEPA 2003 defines "PAYE income" in s.683. It consists of:

(i) PAYE employment income (see below).

(ii) PAYE pension income (e.g. payments by employers to former employees under pension schemes); and

(iii) PAYE social security income (e.g. Statutory Sick Pay and Statutory Maternity Pay paid by employers to relevant employees).

We are mostly concerned with PAYE employment income which consists of:

(i) any taxable earnings from an employment in the year; and

(ii) any taxable specific income from an employment in the year. s.696 s.702

This definition therefore covers most cash payments made by employers to employees including salaries, bonuses and termination payments.

There are some cash payments made by an employer to an employee that will not be subject to PAYE. The main example is the payment of excluded business expenses. These are expenses which would not give rise to a taxable benefit which the Inland Revenue has authorised the employer to ignore.

PAYE is not just restricted to payments in cash. Payments to employees in the form of **"readily convertible assets"** are also subject to PAYE. A "readily convertible asset" is an asset which is tradeable on a recognised Stock or Commodities Exchange. These assets will include quoted shares - i.e. shares listed on a recognised Stock Exchange - or gold bullion.

For example, if an employee works for Marks & Spencer plc, and as part of his remuneration he is given shares in Marks & Spencer plc, as these shares are listed on the UK Stock Exchange, they are readily convertible assets and tax at source under PAYE would have to be deducted from the payment.

A readily convertible asset also includes any asset for which trading arrangements exist. A trading arrangement basically means that the employer has arranged for the employee to be able to sell the asset which has been awarded to him - ie, the employer arranges for the employee to receive cash from a third party in return for the asset.

For example, let us say that as part of an employee's remuneration, his employer gives a brand new Ferrari. There is no recognised Commodities Exchange for Ferraris, but if, as part of the deal, the employer has arranged with a third party for the employee to be able to sell that Ferrari and receive cash in return, the asset is a readily convertible asset and PAYE will have to be applied to the payment.

Normal benefits such as the use of a **company car** or a **taxable cheap loan** or **living accommodation**, are not generally subject to deduction of tax at source under PAYE. These benefits are usually entered on **form P11D** and tax is paid on these benefits at the end of the year under Self Assessment.

However, as we shall see later, in order to prevent there from being a large underpayment of tax on benefits at the end of the year, the Revenue usually tax benefits via the employee's tax code. We shall deal with tax codes later on in this chapter.

D9.3 How the PAYE system works

Once the employer has arrived at the employee's PAYE income for a particular earnings period - the most common earnings period being that of one month - this income is entered on to a PAYE deduction card. The employer then calculates tax on the income using the employee's **tax code**.

The purpose of a tax code is for the Revenue to tell the employer what allowances etc., are due to the employee. All of us will be entitled to the basic personal allowance so we can earn a certain amount of tax free pay every month. This tax free pay is deducted from the PAYE income and the excess is charged to tax.

The employer calculates the precise amount of tax due using tax tables. These tables are provided by the Revenue and there are separate tables for tax and National Insurance Contributions.

The employer looks at the monthly gross pay, then looks at the employee's tax code and where these two points meet on the tax tables, that is the income tax to be deducted for that particular month. What the tables effectively do is to take **gross pay, deduct some personal allowances**, and charge the **excess** at **10%,** at **22%** and, if relevant, at **40%.**

Once the employer has arrived at the tax and the National Insurance to be deducted, this is withheld from gross pay and the net amount is paid to the employee.

It is the employer's responsibility to keep records of all PAYE income paid to employees and of the tax and National Insurance deducted from that income. These pay and tax details will be recorded on various returns sent to the Revenue at the end of the year. PAYE Returns will be dealt with in the next chapter.

D9.4 Tax Codes

The **tax code** is issued by the Revenue to **employers** on **form P6**.

A detailed breakdown of how the Revenue has arrived at the **tax code** is given to the **employee** on a different form - **form P2**. Note here that the employer only receives the "bottom line" figure - i.e. the employer does not receive the detailed breakdown of the code as this is confidential information given to the employee only.

The purpose of the tax code is to tell the employer **how many allowances or reliefs** the employee is entitled to. These allowances will include personal allowances, age allowances and any other reliefs such as qualifying interest or EIS relief etc.

The tax code will also take account of any benefits to which the employee is entitled. The tax code takes the employee's allowances for the year, deducts any benefits the employee has for the year and the difference is the net allowances due to the employee.

Allowances for year	X
Benefits	(X)
Net allowances due	X

These net allowances are the employee's tax free pay. By restricting an employee's allowances by the amount of his benefits, what the Revenue are doing is effectively taxing benefits on a monthly basis as they go along. The Revenue do this to prevent the employee having a large tax bill at the end of the year.

Illustration 1

Mr Jones is entitled to a personal allowance in 2005/06 of £4,895. In the tax year he also receives some benefits from his employer. He has a company car with a benefit of £1,690. He is also provided with private fuel for that car, giving rise to a benefit of £2,240.

Tax code:	£	£
Personal allowance		4,895
Benefits:		
Car benefit	1,690	
Fuel benefit	2,240	
		(3,930)
Net allowances		**£965**

Tax Code

The Revenue will convert this tax free pay of £965 into a tax code. To do this they will simply knock off the end figure - i.e. remove the 5 - and replace that number with the letter L. So the tax code here is 96L. The suffix L simply means that Mr Jones is entitled to the normal Personal allowance.

In practice you may be asked by your client to check the detailed breakdown of the code to make sure that the allowances and the benefits within the tax code are correct.

What you are doing is simply checking that the Revenue are deducting more or less the correct amount of tax each month under PAYE. Any extra tax owed to the Revenue, or any repayments due to the taxpayer, will be dealt with once the Self Assessment return has been submitted.

Notices of Coding can take account of allowances other than the basic personal allowance. For example, they can take account of tax reducers such as subscriptions to EIS companies and any married couples relief due to older taxpayers. The codes can also take account of Gift Aid donations and any contributions to pension schemes which attract tax relief. Tax codes are also very commonly used to deal with tax under or over payments from previous years.

The tax code can also be used to tax small amounts of other income likely to arise in the tax year, such as rental or investment income. However, a taxpayer can object to this income being encoded.

D9.5 Underpayments of tax

PAYE is not an exact science, so the amount of tax deducted at source under PAYE will not always be exactly the same as the tax liability for the year. Most taxpayers in the UK will either have small under or over payments at the year end.

If the tax due for the year is less than £2,000, the Revenue do not require this tax to be paid under Self Assessment on 31 January. Instead they are happy to collect this tax a later tax year under PAYE. For example, if the underpayment occurs in 2005/06, the Revenue will usually adjust the tax code in 2007/08.

The idea is that the employee will pay slightly more tax in the later year to cancel out the tax underpayment from the earlier year.

Illustration 2

Mr Wood is employed on a salary of £20,000 per annum and has benefits of £500. In 2003/04 Mr Wood had a tax underpayment of £150.

Mr Wood's tax code for the tax year 2005/06 is calculated as shown:

	£
Personal allowance	4,895
Benefits	(500)
Tax underpaid 2003/04	
$£150 \times \frac{100}{22}$	(682)
Net allowances	**£3,713**
Tax Code	**371L**

This calculation requires some explanations. We will start with Mr Wood's allowances. He has a normal Personal allowance of £4,895.

Mr Wood's benefits for the year are £500, so these are deducted. In 2003/04 Mr Wood had a small underpayment that we need to deal with via his tax code. What we need to do here is to restrict Mr Wood's allowances by such an amount so as to create an extra tax liability of £150 in 2005/06.

As Mr Wood is a basic rate taxpayer, we do this by multiplying by 100 over 22 giving £682. We are effectively pretending that in 2005/06 Mr Wood has extra income of £682. When multiplied by the basic rate of 22%, this will create an extra tax liability of £150. This is the tax that he owes for the previous year.

The net allowances due for the year are the total allowances less the benefits, giving £3,713. We then knock off the final 3 and replace that with the letter L for normal personal allowances to give Mr Wood a tax code for the year of 371L.

D9.6 K Codes

A "K" code is a negative code and will arise where benefits **exceed allowances for the year**. So whereas in the case of a normal code an employee has an amount of tax free pay each month, where an employee has a **"K" code this will actually increase the taxable pay**.

If an employee has a normal Personal allowance and total benefits of £8,000 for the year his code will be as follows:

	£
Personal allowance	4,895
Benefits	(8,000)
Negative allowance	£(3,105)
Tax code	K309

A "K" code is so-called because the code is prefixed by the letter K. Here we take £3,105, we remove the final 5 to give us 310, and then the Revenue **deduct one** to give 309. The Revenue then put a "K" on the front so that the code becomes **K309.**

This will be notified to the employer by the Revenue on form P6. This tells the employer to increase the employee's PAYE income by a certain amount each month, so as to effectively tax the benefits at source. This prevents a large tax underpayment from arising at the end of the year.

When a **K code** is used, the **maximum amount of tax that can be deducted in any period cannot exceed 50% of gross pay**. For example, if an employee has gross cash pay of £3,000 in a month, the maximum amount of tax that can be deducted under PAYE is £1,500. This is to prevent hardship - i.e. to prevent an employee's cash pay from being totally wiped out in tax.

The sole purpose of the code is to determine how much tax an employee pays each year under PAYE. If you think back to your income tax computation, you always tax gross earnings and then deduct tax already paid under PAYE at the bottom to give you a figure of tax due or tax repayable. As far as is possible, the Revenue will try to make the tax deducted under PAYE more or less equal to the employee's tax liability for the year by using the tax code system. However they understand that PAYE codes cannot be totally accurate, so small under or over payments are inevitable.

If on receiving his form P2, an employee thinks that his tax code is incorrect, the employee can make an appeal to the Revenue. The appeal can be made in writing or, the employee can telephone the Tax Office and ask them to change the tax code.

Q	Now test your understanding by attempting the examples which follow.

Example 1

Which of the following are PAYE income?

a) Performance related bonus
b) Statutory sick pay
c) Company car
d) Non taxable business expenses
e) Bonus paid in silver bullion
f) Compensation for loss of office.

Example 2

Albert was 72 on 1 February 2005. He is married to Elsie who is 68.

Albert has a part time job paying £12,000 per annum

He has no benefits and no other income.

Calculate what his tax code for 2005/06 will be.

Answer 1

		PAYE income?
a)	Performance related bonus	✓
b)	Statutory sick pay	✓
c)	Company car	X
d)	Non-taxable business expenses	X
e)	Bonus in silver bullion	✓
f)	Compensation for loss of office	✓

Answer 2

	£
Personal age allowance	7,090
Married couples relief	
£5,905 x 10% = £591	
Given as	
$591 \times \frac{100}{22}$	2,686
Total allowances	**£9,776**
Tax Code	**977V**

Albert is 72 and so is entitled to Personal Age allowances. He is married so he is also entitled to Married Couples relief as he was born before 6 April 1935. Albert has a salary of £12,000 and no other income. This means that as his STI is less than £19,500, these allowances are given in full with no restriction.

Albert's Married Couples relief will be £5,905 at 10%. Married Couples relief is given as a tax reducer so we need to factor this in to Albert's tax code. We therefore need to increase Albert's allowances by such an amount that it saves Albert tax of £591. As Albert is a basic rate taxpayer we do this by multiplying by 100 over 22.

This has the effect of giving Albert additional allowances of £2,686. The idea is that by increasing Albert's allowances by £2,686, we save him tax at 22% giving rise to a tax saving of £591.

Adding these together gives Albert total allowances of £9,776. We remove the last digit to give us a tax code of 977 and this time we add the suffix "V" which denotes age related Married Couples allowances. So Albert's tax code will be 977V.

(Note: the various coding suffixes ("L", "V" etc) are not important for examination purposes).

SUMMARY - INTRODUCTION TO PAYE

PAYE is the system by which employers collect tax on employment income paid to their employees and pass it on to the Inland Revenue.

PAYE is due on the 19th of the month, but can be paid quarterly if the amount is less than £1,500 per month on average.

Most cash payments are subject to PAYE but it also applies to readily convertible assets being assets tradeable on a recognised exchange or where trading arrangements exist.

The employer uses the employee's tax code and some tax tables to calculate the tax and NIC due each month.

The tax code represents the personal allowances that the employee is entitled to, and is reduced by benefits.

A reduction in the tax code can also be made to collect tax underpaid in an earlier year.

K codes occur when benefits exceed allowances. The maximum tax that can be collected via such a code is 50% of gross pay.

D10: PAYE END OF YEAR RETURNS

In this chapter you will learn about the PAYE end of year returns including:
- forms sent to the Revenue;
- forms given to the employee;
- due dates;
- interest;
- penalties for a late return;
- penalties for an incorrect return.

D10.1 Introduction

A number of end of year return forms have to be filed by the employer to the Revenue. It is the employer's responsibility to provide certain details to the Tax Office at the end of the year, and there are a variety of specific forms to enable the employer to do so.

The form P60 contains details of taxable earnings paid by an employer to an employee in the year along with details of any tax and National Insurance deducted from those earnings. The P60 will also contain basic details such as the employer's name and address and the employee's National Insurance number.

The **P60 is given by the employer to the employee no later than 31 May following the end of the tax year**. The employee will then use the details on the P60 to prepare his own Self Assessment tax return.

The employer will also complete a **form P14 for each employee**. The details on the P14 are the same as those on the P60. The difference here is that the P14 is **given by the employer to the Revenue**.

All the forms P14 are effectively rolled together to form an **end of year summary** which is called the form **P35**. The P35 summarises all the individual deduction sheets for each and every employee.

Forms P14 and P35 must be submitted by the employer to the Revenue no later than 19 May following the end of the tax year. SI 2003/2682 Para 73

A form **P11D** is provided to every **higher paid employee** who receives benefits in the tax year. A higher paid employee is any employee who earns more than £8,500 per annum. If benefits are provided to **lower paid employees,** these are summarised on **form P9D**.

Each of these forms contains details of the cash equivalent of each benefit provided. The deadline for the submission of forms P11D and P9D to the Revenue is 6 July following the end of the tax year. The employer will give a copy of the P11D to the employee to enable the employee to put together his Self Assessment Return. SI 2003/2682 Para 85

A form **P45** is given by the employer to every **employee who leaves that particular employment.** P45s are also provided in respect of employees whose employment terminates as a result of death.

The form P45 has four parts. The employer will send the first part of the form to the Revenue and give the other three parts of the form to the employee. The employee will keep one part of the P45 for his own record purposes and give the other two parts of the form to his new employer. The new employer fills in details of the new employment, then keeps one part of the P45 for his own record purposes. The employer sends the final part to the Revenue.

The P45 contains details of pay and tax from the start of the tax year to the date the employment terminated. The P45 also contains the code number operated by the previous employer. This code number will then be operated by the new employer until a new one is issued by the Revenue.

In certain circumstances, an employee will be asked to fill in a form P46. A P46 is completed by employees who join an employer but do not have a P45. This will be the case if this is the employee's first job since leaving education or if the employee has another job and does not have a form P45.

The form **P46** will ask the employee to certify one of two things.

a) If the employee certifies that this is his first or main job the employer will operate an "emergency code". This emergency code for 2005/06 will be 489L, which means that when the employer deducts tax under Pay As You Earn, the employee will simply be given the normal Personal allowance as his tax free amount.

b) If the employee certifies on form P46 that this employment is neither his first job nor his main job, the employer will operate code BR. This means that tax will be deducted from earnings at the basic rate of 22% without any personal allowances being given.

D10.2 Interest

Tax and National Insurance should be paid over to the Revenue no later than the **19th of each month**. If an employer makes these payments late, the Revenue will charge the employer interest on the late paid tax. The rules here however are quite generous in that **interest does not start to run until 19 April following the end of the tax year**.

So in respect of tax due for the tax year 2005/06, if the employer still owes the Revenue some tax for this tax year then interest will run from 19 April 2006 to the date before the tax is actually paid. This means that as long as the employer has paid all of his tax and National Insurance due under PAYE 19 April following the end of the tax year, then no interest charge will be levied.

If tax has been overpaid by the employer and a repayment of tax is due, then repayment supplement will run for the same period.

D10.3 Penalties

It is the employer's obligation to operate Pay As You Earn correctly and if he fails to do so, the Revenue has the right to charge a penalty. Penalties will be charged either if the employer sends in his end of year Returns late, or if those Returns are incorrect.

D10.4 Late Returns

s. 98A TMA 1970

Forms P35 and P14 are due for submission on 19 May following the end of the tax year. However the Revenue has confirmed that, by concession, they **will not charge a penalty if the P35 or P14 is submitted within 7 days of the normal due date.**

If the P35 or P14 is more than 7 days late, the penalty will be **£100 per month** (or part month) **for each group of up to 50 employees**. So for example, if a form P35 is one month late and the company has 110 employees, the penalty will be £100 multiplied by 1 month multiplied by 3 - 110 employees constituting 3 separate groups of 50 employees. This penalty is fixed and cannot be mitigated at the discretion of the Inspector.

If the returns are **more than 12 months late, a further penalty of up to 100% of the tax unpaid at that time may also be levied.**

Forms **P11D** or **P9D** should be submitted **no later than 6 July following the end of the tax year**. If these forms are late, the Revenue can charge an **initial penalty** of up to **£300 per late form** and can **thereafter** charge a further penalty of up to **£60 per day** for each day that the failure continues. These penalties can be mitigated at the discretion of the Revenue.

D10.5 Incorrect Returns

s. 98A TMA 1970

If an employer files an incorrect form P35 or P14, the maximum penalty that may be charged is up to 100% of any tax or National Insurance lost as a result of the error. This is not a fixed penalty and it can be reduced by the Revenue depending on the facts and circumstances of each case.

The **penalty** for submitting an **incorrect form P11D or form P9D** is up to **£3,000 for each incorrect form**. This means that if an employer provides benefits to 100 employees and gets each of the forms P11D wrong, the Revenue could charge a penalty of £3,000 times 100 - i.e. a total penalty of £300,000.

D10.6 Recovery of tax

SI 2003/2 Reg 80

Where an **employer fails to operate Pay As You Earn correctly**, and this results in an underpayment of tax, the Revenue can either recover the tax from the employer or from the employee. In the majority of instances the Revenue will choose to recover the tax from the employer by using a **Regulation 80 determination**.

Having quantified the tax underpaid, the Revenue will issue a notice under Regulation 80 of the PAYE Regulations. The employer has a right to appeal this determination if he thinks it is incorrect but if no appeal is lodged, the determination becomes final and conclusive within 30 days.

If the Revenue are satisfied that the employer took reasonable care to comply with the PAYE Regulations and any underpayment of tax arose due to an error made in good faith, the Revenue will instead seek recovery of the tax from the employee. Reg 72

The Revenue will also seek collection of the tax from the employee if they have reason to believe that the employee accepted his earnings in the full knowledge that the employer had under deducted tax. Remember that interest will always run on late paid tax from 19 April following the tax year to the date before payment is made.

D10.7 Electronic filing

Tax Bulle No. 63

The Revenue has stated that all employers will be required to file their End of Year returns (P14s, P35s, P11Ds, etc) electronically by 2010. This can be done either directly by the employer or via an intermediary such as a payroll bureau or agent.

"Larger" employers (those with 250 or more employees) are required to "e-file" their year end returns by May 2005. Many were doing so already, so for larger employers this should not be an additional burden.

The compulsory electronic filing date will thereafter depend on the number of employees the employer has: s.135 & s.1 FA2002

Number of employees	*First compulsory electronic Return*	*Deadline*
250+	Tax year 2004/05	May 2005
50-249	Tax year 2005/06	May 2006
Under 50	Tax year 2009/10	May 2010

A penalty will be levied for a failure to comply with these deadlines. This will be £3,000 per annum per PAYE scheme for an employer's failure to make an electronic return. This penalty is in addition to the usual array of penalties for late filing.

"Small" employers (those with fewer than 50 employees) will be offered financial incentives to encourage them to make an early transition to e-filing. These are as follows:

End of year return	*Incentive*
	£
2004/05	250
2005/06	250
2006/07	150
2007/08	100
2008/09	75

This income is not taxable.

Q	Now test your understanding by attempting the examples which follow.

Example 1

By what date must the employer file his form P35 for 2005/06 to avoid a penalty being charged?

Example 2

Tardy Ltd has 63 employees.

The Finance Director sends the form P35 for 2005/06 to the Revenue on 27 July 2006.

What will the penalty charged on Tardy Ltd be?

Answer 1

The normal due date for the submission of a P35 is 19 May following the end of the year. However the Revenue allow a 7 day period of grace, so long as the P35 is submitted by 26 May no penalty will be charged.

Answer 2

Due date for P35 was 19 May 2006
Filing date was 27 July 2006
So P35 was just over 2 months late – this equals 3 months

Penalty
£100 per month per group of up to 50 employees
63 employees is 2 groups

£100 x 3 months x 2 = £600

SUMMARY - PAYE END OF YEAR RETURNS

The main end of year returns to be submitted are as follows:

P60	Given to employee, details of total pay and deductions	Due by 31 May
P14	As P60 but given to Revenue	Due by 19 May
P35	Summary of all the P14s given to the Revenue	Due by 19 May
P11D	Given to employee and Revenue, summary of benefits given to a higher paid employee	Due by 6 July
P9D	As above but for lower paid employee	Due by 6 July

The P45 is prepared when an employee leaves. One part is given to the Revenue, three parts are given to the employee who keeps one and gives the other two to the new employer.

A new employer fills in details of the new employment on the P45 and sends one part to the Revenue and keeps the other.

If no P45 is available, a P46 is completed by the new employee. The employer will use the emergency code if it is the employee's first job, or the BR code if it is a second job.

Interest runs on late paid PAYE and NIC from 19 April following the tax year.

Late returns attract penalties. For the P14 and P35 there is a grace period of 7 days.

P14/P35	> 7 days late	£100 per month per 50 employees
	> 12 months late	100% of the tax unpaid
P11D/P9D	if late	Initially £300 per form or £60 per day if failure continues

Incorrect P14/P35 attracts a penalty of 100% of the tax lost. Incorrect P11D/P9D penalty is £3,000 per form.

If PAYE is operated incorrectly any underpayment can be collected from the employer via a Regulation 80 determination. This becomes final if not appealed within 30 days.

The Revenue are encouraging businesses to move to electronic filing for year end returns. All employers must e-file returns for the tax year 2009/10 onwards.

D11: CLASS 1 NATIONAL INSURANCE CONTRIBUTIONS

In this chapter you will learn about Class 1 NIC including:
- an overview of the six classes of NIC;
- definition of earnings;
- Class 1 primary contributions;
- rules for directors;
- Class 1 secondary contributions.

References in this chapter are to Social Security Contributions & Benefits Act (SSCBA) 1992 unless stated otherwise.

D11.1 Introduction

NIC is a very important money-raising tool for the Treasury and, year on year, National Insurance Contributions bring in around 20 to 21 per cent of total Government revenue. Collection of NIC is administered by the National Insurance Contributions Office (NICO) which is now part of the HM Revenue and Customs. Other parts of the HMRC assist NICO in the collection of National Insurance Contributions, particularly via the PAYE system.

The purpose of National Insurance Contributions is to provide certain retirement benefits such as the State Pension, as well as to fund certain Social Security benefits such as Job Seekers Allowance and Incapacity Benefit. If the amount raised by NICO by way of National Insurance Contributions is insufficient to cover these benefits, any deficit is made up by a grant from the Treasury.

At present there are six classes of National Insurance:

a) Class 1 - paid by both employees and employers on earnings from employment. s. 1

b) Class 1A - paid by employers only on benefits awarded to employees.

c) Class 1B - paid by employers only on Pay As You Earn Settlement Agreements (PSAs).

d) Class 2 - paid by self-employed persons on the profits from their trade.

e) Class 3 - voluntary contributions paid by taxpayers who wish to top-up their contribution record in order to preserve their entitlement to State benefits.

f) Class 4 - paid by self-employed persons on the profits from their trade. Classes 2 and 4 will be covered in the business tax section of your course.

This gives us an overview of National Insurance. In this chapter we shall concentrate solely on Class 1 NIC.

D11.2 Class 1 NIC

s. 2

Class 1 National Insurance Contributions are broken down into **primary** contributions or **secondary** contributions. **Primary** contributions are paid by **employees** whilst **secondary** contributions are paid by **employers**.

Class 1 NICs are paid on earnings from the employment. If an employee receives earnings, that employee will pay Class 1 primary contributions whilst if an employer pays earnings to an employee, the employer makes a secondary Class 1 contribution.

Both primary and secondary contributions are accounted for under the PAYE system and are paid over to the Revenue, along with income tax, on the **19th of each month.**

Every time an employer makes a payment of earnings to an employee, that employer will have to account for Class 1 secondary NICs currently at a rate of 12.8%. This is a very substantial additional cost borne by employers and the majority of NICs raised by the Treasury are collected from employers rather than employees.

D11.3 Earnings

s. 3

Class 1 contributions are paid on "earnings". It is very important that we establish what constitutes **"earnings"** for National Insurance purposes. **Any cash payment** made by an employer to an employee is likely to be earnings for NIC purposes. This will include salaries and bonuses but will not include the reimbursement of genuine business expenses.

If an employer makes a non-cash payment to an employee - i.e. some form of payment in kind - and that **payment in kind** can be **surrendered for cash**, that payment will **also be earnings** for NIC purposes.

A payment in the form of a premium bond for example, will constitute earnings for NIC because the employee can take the premium bond to the Post Office and has a legal right to be able to exchange the premium bond in return for cash.

Note here the specific use of the word "surrender". This is very different to the word "sale". For example, if an employee were given a yacht as a bonus by his employer, this would not constitute earnings for NIC purposes as he could not take the yacht back to the shop and demand cash from the shop owner. This is not an asset that can be "surrendered" for cash in the same way as a premium bond.

Payments in the form of "**readily convertible assets**" are earnings for NIC purposes. You will recall from the PAYE chapter, that a readily convertible asset is an asset that is traded on a recognised Stock or Commodities Exchange or an asset for which trading arrangements exist. The definition of a readily convertible asset for NIC is exactly the same as the definition we looked at for PAYE. The readily convertible assets legislation was put in relatively recently as many employers had introduced imaginative NIC avoidance schemes to reduce their NIC liabilities.

s. 702 ITEPA 2003

If an **employer settles an employee's personal liability**, this payment will also constitute earnings for National Insurance. For example, if an employee makes a visit to the supermarket and spends £100 on goods, and that £100 is subsequently reimbursed by the employer, the employer has paid for an employee's personal bill, and that payment will constitute earnings for NIC. As such, the £100 will be charged to National Insurance.

Vouchers are earnings for NIC. Most commonly these will include High Street store vouchers. Childcare vouchers given to employees are specifically excluded and are not earnings for NIC.

Finally, **certain share option rewards** will constitute earnings for NIC.

The vast majority of common benefits will not be earnings for NIC purposes. For instance, if an employee is given use of a company car or has a taxable cheap loan, that benefit will be charged to income tax but it will not then be charged to National Insurance Contributions in the hands of the employee.

D11.4 Class 1 Primary contributions s. 5

Primary contributions are paid by employees on earnings in an "earnings period". Most UK employees have a monthly earnings period - i.e. we receive our salary etc on a monthly basis. Some employees, typically in manufacturing industries, still receive their earnings weekly. s.6

The current rates of National Insurance are given in the tax tables. For employees who receive their remuneration **weekly, no National Insurance is charged on the first £94 per week** of an employee's earnings. This is called the "earnings threshold" (ET). On **earnings between £94 per week and £630 per week,** the main rate of Class 1 NIC is **11%.** The weekly limit of £630 is called the "upper earnings limit" (UEL).

Employees also pay Class 1 NICs at the additional rate of **1% on earnings in excess of the upper earnings limit i.e. above £630** per week.

The tables also give us the annual limits. Most employees have a monthly earnings period, so to convert the annual limits into monthly limits, we simply divide by 12. For employees with a **monthly earnings period**, for earnings up to £408 per s.8
month, NIC is charged at zero percent. For earnings between £408 and £2,730 per month, the rate is 11% and there is a further NIC liability of 1% on earnings in excess of £2,730 per month.

You will see that the monthly and weekly limits have been specifically chosen by the Government to equate to an earnings threshold of £4,745 per annum, which coincides with the personal allowance. This is illustrated by the diagram below:

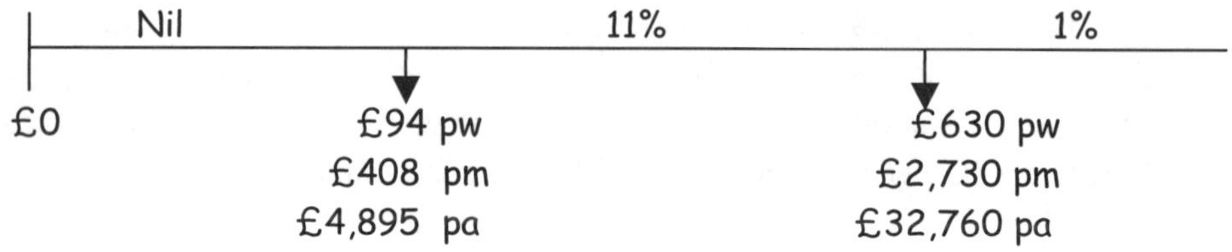

An employee will start to pay Class 1 primary contributions with effect from his 16th birthday and will stop paying NIC at the date of retirement, which for a man is currently 65 and, for a woman, is 60.

NICs are calculated for earnings periods. An employee who is paid monthly will have 12 earnings periods in any particular tax year, so to calculate his NIC for the year, we do 12 separate NIC calculations and add them together.

Illustration 1

An employee has a salary of £18,000 per annum which is paid monthly. The employee has use of a company car giving rise to a benefit of £2,500. The employee gets a cash bonus at Christmas of £5,000.

The salary and the Christmas bonus constitute earnings for Class 1 NIC but the company car benefit does not.

The monthly limits are:

Earnings threshold:	£4,895 / 12 = £408
Upper earnings limit:	£32,760 / 12 = £2,730

For 11 months of the year his earnings will be 18,000/12 = £1,500.
In December his earnings will be 1,500 + 5,000 = £6,500.

The calculation will therefore be as follows:

	£
Class 1 primary NIC	
11 months with earnings of £1,500	
£(1,500 - 408) x 11% x 11 months	1,321
1 month with earnings of £6,500	
£(2,730 - 408) x 11% x 1 month	255
£(6,500 - 2,730) x 1% x 1 month	38
NIC payable	£1,614

The effect of this is that part of the £5,000 bonus paid in December 2005, will only have been charged to NIC at 1%.

D11.5 Directors

The above rules do not apply to directors. **All directors** have an **annual earnings period**. This means to calculate a director's NIC we look at their earnings in the whole of the tax year, irrespective of whether the director was paid on a weekly or monthly basis. This is to prevent a company director from manipulating the NIC rules by paying himself in such a way as to minimise his NIC for the year.

Illustration 2

Let us take the figures in the previous illustration but this time assume that the salary, the car benefit and the Christmas bonus are accruing to a director rather than a normal employee.

To calculate the director's NIC we need to aggregate his earnings for the whole of the tax year and compare to the annual limits.

Annual earnings
£(18,000 + 5,000) = £23,000

Class 1 primary NIC
£(23,000 - 4,895) @ 11% **£1,992**

What you will see here is that, unlike as with the employee in the previous illustration, none of the director's earnings will attract the 1% rate of NICs and for this reason it tends to be more expensive from an NIC perspective to be a director rather than a normal employee.

D11.6 Class 1 Secondary contributions

Class 1 secondary contributions are paid by employers on any earnings paid to employees. The current rate of Class 1 secondary contributions is zero percent on earnings up to the earnings threshold and 12.8% on the excess. The weekly, s.9
monthly and annual earnings thresholds are the same for employers as they are for employees.

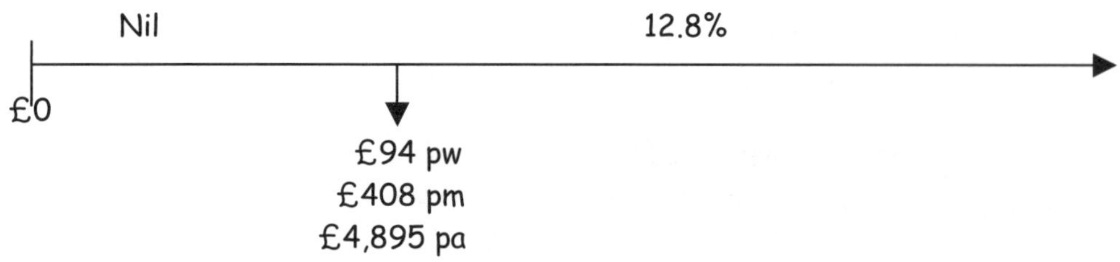

You will also note two things here. The first is that the **rate of NIC is higher for employers than for employees – i.e. 12.8% as opposed to 11%.** The second thing to note is that there is **no upper earnings limit** for employer's contributions, i.e. the 1% rate does not apply for employers. So for every one pound of earnings paid to an employee above the earnings threshold, the employer will have to pay 12.8 pence in National Insurance Contributions.

This is a substantial cost for employers to have to bear and, effectively, adds nearly another 12.8% to their total wages bill.

In the case of an employee or director earning £23,000 per year, the secondary liability to be paid by the employer is:

£(23,000 - 4,895) @ 12.8% = £2,317

Employer secondary contributions begin with effect from the employee's 16th birthday but there is no upper age limit. So if a salary is paid to an employee who is 68 years old, the employee will have no Class 1 primary liability but the employer will still have to pay Class 1 secondary contributions at 12.8%.

D11.7 NIC administration

NICs are dealt with on a day to day basis by the **National Insurance Contributions Office (NICO)**.

The collection and payment of Class 1 NICs is the responsibility of the employer under the PAYE regulations. If an employer fails to comply with the regulations, notices under Sch 4 SI 2001/1004 can be issued to recover any NICs underpaid. SI 2001/1004 Reg 67

S.203

Class 1 NICs are due for payment within **14 days** of the end of the income tax month. **Quarterly payments** can be made if the income tax and NIC to be accounted for is **less than £1,500 per month on average**. Sch 4 Para 10

Interest is charged on Class 1 contributions paid late. The rules for charging interest are generous in that interest will only start to accrue from the "reckonable date" which is 14 days after the end of the tax year for which the NICs were due. Therefore for NICs paid late in 2005/06, interest will only start to run from 19 April 2006. Sch 4 Para 17

Details of Class 1 primary and secondary NICs payable must be included on the employer's end of year summary (form P35). Penalties for late or incorrect forms P35 are as for income tax (see Chapter 22). **Penalties cannot be charged twice for tax and NIC failures in respect of the same form(s).**

Q	Now test your understanding by attempting the examples which follow.

Example 1

Which of the following forms of remuneration are earnings for Class 1 NIC purposes?

a) Interest free loan
b) £5,000 of premium bonds
c) £20,000 of gold bullion
d) John Lewis store voucher
e) Reimbursement of home telephone calls
f) Reimbursement of business expenses

Example 2

Harry is an employee earning £26,000 per year. He is paid weekly and in March 2006 he received a bonus of £1,000.

Calculate his Class 1 NIC due for 2005/06.

Answer 1

		Earnings?	
a)	Interest free loan	X	(No NICs on benefits)
b)	£5,000 of premium bonds	✓	(Surrendered for cash)
c)	£20,000 of gold bullion	✓	(Readily convertible asset)
d)	John Lewis store voucher	✓	
e)	Home telephone bill	✓	(Settlement of employee's liability)
f)	Reimbursed business expenses	X	

Answer 2

Earnings:
51 weeks @ £500
1 week @ £1,500

	£
NIC:	
£(500 - 94) @ 11% x 51	2,278
£(630 - 94) @ 11% x 1	59
£(1,500 - 630) @ 1% x 1	9
Total	**£2,346**

SUMMARY - CLASS 1 NATIONAL INSURANCE

Class 1 contributions are paid by both employees (primary contributions) and employers (secondary contributions) on earnings from employment.

Earnings include:

- Cash payments (other than reimbursement of genuine business expenses)
- Payments in kind that can be surrendered for cash
- Readily convertible assets
- Settlement of employee's personal liability
- Vouchers (except childcare)
- Certain share option rewards

The calculation of Class 1 primary contributions is done for an earnings period for employees. The weekly limits are:

First £94	no NIC
£94 - £630	11%
Above £630	1%

Monthly limits are obtained by multiplying by dividing the annual limits by 12.

The contributions start at age 16 and stop at retirement age (65 for men, 60 for women).

For a director an annual earnings period must be used.

Class 1 secondary contributions are at 12.8% on the excess above the earnings threshold.

The contributions start at 16 but there is no upper age limit.

NICO is part of HM Revenue and Customs and is responsible for the administration of NIC. The due dates, interest and penalty position essentially mirrors that for PAYE.

D12: CLASS 1A AND 1B NATIONAL INSURANCE CONTRIBUTIONS

In this chapter you will cover the two further classes of NIC payable by employers including:
- Class 1A NIC;
- Class 1B NIC;
- PAYE settlement agreements.

All references in this chapter are to SSCBA 1992 unless otherwise stated.

D12.1 Introduction

Class 1A NIC is paid by **employers only**. Employees do not pay Class 1A National Insurance. s. 10

Class 1A NIC is paid by employers on the **cash equivalent of benefits** as they appear on the form P11D. As Class 1A NIC is the liability of the employer, it is charged at the employer's rate of 12.8%. Payment is made in one sum on 19 July following the end of the tax year. This is deliberately timed so as to be two weeks after the submission of the form P11D to the Revenue. So having arrived at the cash equivalent of the benefit, it is easy for the employer to then go ahead and calculate his Class 1A NIC liability.

Class 1B is also paid by **employers only**. Class 1B NIC is charged on earnings which are included within a Pay As You Earn Settlement Agreement (PSA). We will look at PSAs later in this session. The rate of NIC is 12.8%. Class 1B NIC is collected annually on 19 October following the end of the tax year. s. 10A

D12.2 Class 1A

There is no Class 1A charge if there is no associated income tax liability. This means that exempt benefits such as a mobile phone, a work car parking space, or exclusive nursery etc, will not be charged to Class 1A NIC. The £50 exemption for other types of childcare applicable to income tax also applies to Class 1A NICs.

Similarly, if **benefits** are provided **to lower paid employees** - i.e. employees earning less than £8,500 per annum - no P11D will be prepared by the employer so accordingly there is **no liability to Class 1A** National Insurance Contributions.

If a payment in kind is categorised as earnings, and as such is charged to NIC under the normal Class 1 rules, that benefit will not be charged on the employer under Class 1A.

Therefore if an employer provides an employee with benefits such as premium bonds or readily convertible assets or High Street store vouchers, the employer will have to pay Class 1 secondary contributions on those benefits because they are classified as earnings. The employer will not have to pay Class 1A as well.

As we shall see later, if a benefit is charged to National Insurance under Class 1B, this also takes priority over Class 1A.

Finally, if an employer reimburses genuine business expenses to an employee, as this is not a taxable benefit, it will not give rise to a Class 1A NIC charge.

Illustration 1

An employee receives the following remuneration package for 2005/06:

	£
Salary (paid monthly)	24,000
Company car benefit	4,200
Medical insurance benefit	600
High street store voucher (awarded December 2005)	200
Cash bonus (March 2006)	10,000

To calculate total National Insurance Contributions payable for the tax year, we first calculate the Class 1 primary contributions payable by the employee on his earnings. We then move on to calculate the Class 1 secondary contributions paid by the employer on earnings given to the employee. The final National Insurance will be the Class 1A NIC's payable by the employer on the benefits awarded to the employee.

We start with the Class 1 primary contributions. The employee is paid monthly so he has a monthly earnings period. For 10 months of the year he earns a salary of £2,000.

In December 2005, he is given a High Street store voucher. This is regarded as earnings for Class 1 NIC purposes so his earnings for December 2005 go up to £2,200. Due to the cash bonus of £10,000 paid in March 2006, for this month his earnings in the period go up to £12,000.

Earnings:

10 months @ £2,000

1 month @ £2,200

1 month @ £12,000

Employees pay Class 1 National Insurance Contributions at 11% on monthly earnings between the earnings limits and at 1% above the upper earnings threshold. The monthly earnings threshold for 2005/2006 is £408 and the monthly upper earnings limit is £2,730.

	£
Class 1 primary	
£(2,000 - 408) @ 11% x 10 months	1,751
£(2,200 - 408) @ 11% x 1 month	197
£(2,730 - 408) @ 11% x 1 month	255
£(12,000 - 2,730) @ 1% x 1 month	93
	£2,296

Next we move on to Class 1 secondary contributions. Total earnings for the year are the salary of £24,000, the store vouchers of £200 and the bonus of £10,000. Total earnings, subject to secondary contributions in the year, are therefore £34,200. As there is no upper earnings limit for secondary contributions, all earnings in excess of the earnings threshold will be charged to NIC at the rate of 12.8%.

Class 1 secondary	
£(34,200 - 4,895) @ 12.8%	**£3,751**

Finally, we calculate the Class 1A liability. The car benefit is £4,200. The only other benefit which will appear on the P11D for the year is the medical insurance of £600. We add this on to give us total taxable benefits for the year of £4,800.

Class 1A	
£4,800 @ 12.8%	**£614**

In summary the following NICs are due:

Class 1 primary	**£2,296**	Collected monthly via PAYE system
Class 1 secondary	**£3,751**	Collected monthly via PAYE system
Class 1A	**£614**	Paid directly to NICO on 19 July 2006

This example demonstrates the interaction between Class 1 primary and secondary contributions and Class 1A NIC. What it also shows is that the NIC burden is much heavier on employers than on employees. This is partly because there is no upper earnings limit for employers and also because employees do not have the burden of Class 1A contributions.

D12.3 Class 1B contributions

To understand Class 1B contributions we first need to discuss exactly what we mean by the term **Pay As You Earn Settlement Agreement (PSA).** For those of you who have access to the tax statutes, it is certainly worth taking a look at Statement of Practice Number 5 of 1996 (SP 5/96) in which the Inland Revenue very clearly set out what can and what cannot be included within a PAYE Settlement Agreement. s.703 ITEPA 2003

The whole idea of a PSA is to **allow an employer to settle an employee's tax liability on minor or irregular benefits.** A common example of an irregular benefit which could be encompassed within a PSA, would be a staff Christmas party costing in excess of the tax-free threshold of £150 per person.

If an employer provides a Christmas party to an employee, and the cost of the party is less than £150 per employee, this is an exempt benefit. However, if the cost exceeds £150, the employee has a taxable benefit on the whole cost. It is therefore customary, as a gesture of goodwill, for the employer to meet any tax liabilities arising to employees. The employer will do this by negotiating a tax settlement with the Revenue.

The Revenue has also confirmed that PSAs are acceptable in instances where it is impractical for the employer to be able to apply Pay As You Earn to a particular emolument.

SP 5/96 clearly states that Pay As You Earn Settlement Agreements should not be used as a vehicle for settling tax liabilities on cash payments or on major benefits such as company cars or low interest loans etc.

If tax on a particular benefit is included within a PSA, that benefit does not then have to be entered on to form P11D. Similarly, the employee will not have to enter the cash equivalent of such benefits on to his own Self Assessment Tax Return. This is because someone else – ie, the employer - will pay the tax.

Having agreed that items can be included within the PSA, the Revenue will then negotiate the tax liability with the employer and the employer will pay the tax on a grossed up basis.

Illustration 2

A company has 100 employees. It holds a Summer Ball and the total cost of that function is £20,000, ie exactly £200 per head. Technically each employee will therefore have a benefit of £200 as the cost of the party exceeds the £150 per head threshold. However, as a gesture of goodwill, the company agrees to meet the tax liabilities via a Pay As You Earn Settlement Agreement. Of the employees, 50 of them pay tax at the basic rate of 22%, whilst 50 of them pay tax at the higher rate of 40%.

In order to work out the amount of tax to be paid by the employer under the PSA, consider the basic rate employees first. Each employee will have a benefit of £200. This is a "net" benefit because the employee is deemed to have received a benefit of £200 **after** the tax has been settled by the employer.

To calculate the tax on this net benefit, as we are dealing with a basic rate employee, we need to multiply the net figure of £200 by 22 over 78. This gives us tax of £56 and gives rise to a gross benefit of £256. If you work this back, you will see that the gross benefit of £256 multiplied by the basic rate of tax of 22% gives a tax charge of £56.

Basic rate employee:	£
Net benefit	200
Tax @ $\frac{22}{78}$	56
Gross benefit	**£256**

For each higher rate employee, again we start with the net benefit of £200. This time we arrive at the tax by multiplying the net benefit by 40/60 to give tax of £133. The gross benefit in this instance is £333. Again we can check this by taking the gross benefit of £333 and multiplying it by the higher rate of 40% to give tax of £133.

Higher rate employee:	£
Net benefit	200
Tax @ $\frac{40}{60}$	133
Gross benefit	**£333**

To finish the example, we need to calculate the total tax to be included in the PSA:

Tax in PSA	£
50 employees @ £56	2,800
50 employees @ £133	6,650
	£9,450

Whenever tax is settled under a PAYE settlement agreement, the employer also needs to consider the impact of Class 1B National Insurance. Class 1B NIC is charged on benefits included within a PSA. Included within the PSA is the total cost of the staff function - i.e. £20,000. We then need to add on any income tax that has been included within the PSA – i.e. any income tax paid by the employer on behalf of its employees. Class 1B National Insurance is charged at the employer's rate of 12.8%.

	£
Earnings within PSA	20,000
Income tax payable	9,450
	29,450
Class 1B NIC @ 12.8%	**£3,770**

Class 1B is the **employer's liability only** and the **due date for payment is 19 October following the end of the tax year**.

At first sight this may appear a little harsh, in that as well as paying income tax of £9,450, the employer also has to pay National Insurance at 12.8% on the income tax paid. This is because the income tax of £9,450 is strictly the liability of the employees, so what the employer is doing is settling the employees' personal liability. We know that if an employer settles an employee's liability under normal circumstances, there will be a charge to Class 1 secondary contributions. Here the charge is under Class 1B instead.

Q	Now test your understanding by attempting the examples which follow.

Example 1

Norman receives the following non-cash benefits from his employer, Techno plc. Techno plc is a company listed on the UK stock exchange.

a) Company car and fuel
b) Interest free loan of £4,000
c) 500 shares in Techno plc
d) £100 high street store voucher
e) Contributions to company pension scheme
f) Membership of local gym.

Which of the above are subject to Class 1A NIC?

Example 2

Brian is awarded a holiday to Florida by his employer. The holiday cost £3,000 and the company agree to pay the tax on Brian's behalf via a PSA. Brian is a salesman earning £20,000 per annum.

Calculate the Class 1B NIC liability for the employer.

Answer 1

		Class 1A?	
a)	Company car and fuel	✓	P11D item
b)	Interest free loan of £4,000	X	Exempt as <£5,000
c)	500 shares in Techno plc	X	Class 1 applies
d)	High street store voucher	X	Class 1 applies
e)	Pension contributions	X	Exempt
f)	Local gym membership	✓	P11D item

Answer 2

	£
Earnings covered by PSA	3,000
Tax @ $\frac{22}{78}$ (basic rate taxpayer)	846
	£3,846
Class 1B NIC @ 12.8%	**£492**

SUMMARY - CLASS 1A AND 1B NATIONAL INSURANCE

Class 1A is paid by employers on benefits that are on the P11D. The rate is 12.8% and the due date is 19 July following the tax year.

Class 1A is not paid on benefits which have already been charged to Class 1 secondary NIC. Also Class 1B takes priority over Class 1A.

Class 1B is payable on benefits included in and tax settled under a PAYE settlement agreement (PSA). The rate is 12.8% and the due date is 19 October following the tax year.

PSAs are used by employers to settle the tax on minor or irregular benefits or where it would be impractical to apply PAYE. A grossing up exercise must be done to find the tax payable.

D13: TERMINATION PAYMENTS

In this chapter you will cover the way in which termination payments are taxed including:
- fully taxable payments;
- fully exempt payments;
- partially taxable payments;
- foreign service;
- statutory redundancy pay;
- employees approaching retirement age;
- payments in lieu of notice;
- NIC implications.

Statutory references are to ITEPA 2003 unless stated otherwise.

D13.1 Introduction

Typical termination payments will include **compensation for loss of office**, **redundancy** payments, **damages** for dismissal, **payments in lieu of notice** – "PILONs" – and certain payments made on retirement. s.401-s.416

Termination payments will either be fully taxable, partially taxable, or fully exempt depending on the nature of the payment.

The statutory rules concerning termination payments are contained at Sections 401 onwards ITEPA 2003. To understand the taxation of termination payments we must first remind ourselves of a couple of basic principles.

ITEPA 2003 differentiates between "general earnings" and "specific employment income". "General earnings" are defined in s.7(3) as **earnings and any amount treated as earnings** (such as benefits under the benefits code). "Earnings" are broadly defined in s.62 ITEPA 2003 as salaries, wages and benefits (in money or money's worth), or anything else that constitutes an emolument of the employment.

In a number of decided tax cases it has been held that emoluments are "of the employment" if they are given to the employee **in return for services** performed under the employment contract. Therefore, in general terms, payments made by an employer to an employee which are **not** in return for services performed, will **not be classed as "general earnings"** under ITEPA 2003.

This general principle is important as far as termination payments are concerned, because a termination payment will generally compensate the employee for loss of office rather than being any sort of reward for services performed.

As such, **most termination payments are not regarded as earnings** from an employment and are therefore **taxed in a completely different way** to other earnings such as salaries and bonuses.

Instead, termination payments will generally fall into the category of "specific employment income" and will be taxed under the provisions of s.401 onwards ITEPA 2003.

D13.2 Does Section 401 apply?

This is an important question because there are certain **exemptions and reliefs** available within the legislation dealing with termination payments which would not apply if the payment were to be treated as "general earnings" under s.62.

Your starting point should be to **ask yourself whether the termination payment is contractual.** If the employment contract contains a clause under which the employee has a legal right to receive a termination payment, the termination payment will be regarded as earnings from the employment and will be taxed in full.

When there is any doubt about the taxation of a termination payment, the Revenue will ask to see the employment contract to see if any reference is made to termination payments. If there is, the payment will be regarded as being made in return for services and will be fully charged to tax.

If the contract is silent and makes no mention of termination payments, if the Revenue can prove that there was "**reasonable expectation**" on the part of the employee that he would receive a termination payment, the payment will be taxed in full. It can be difficult for the Revenue to prove that an employee expected to receive a termination payment. The Revenue Officer will look back at past practice and previous policy of the employer to see if other employees in a similar position received termination payments.

If a **termination payment is made outside the employment contract** and is totally voluntary - ie, the employee had no expectation whatsoever that he was to receive such a payment - this does **not** mean that the **payment is tax free.** It simply means that the payment will be **taxed under Section 401** which is the section that specifically deals with the taxation of genuine termination payments.

S.401(3) says that "this chapter does not apply to any payment or other benefit chargeable to income tax apart from this chapter". This means that if a payment is charged to tax **somewhere else** in the legislation, Section 401 will **not** apply. For example, if a payment is treated as general earnings from the employment it will be taxed as earnings under the definition in Section 62 which will take priority over Section 401.

This means that Section 401 only applies to non-contractual or "**ex gratia**" payments. Ex gratia here literally means "thank you" - ie, the payment is entirely **voluntary and without any obligation** on the part of the employer.

D13.3 Fully exempt payments

Certain payments falling within Section 401 are fully exempt from tax.

A **termination payment** made **on the death of an employee** is fully exempt from tax. Similarly, where the employment has been terminated due to the **injury or disability** of the employee, any subsequent compensation payment is exempt from tax. s.406

If an **employer** makes a **payment to a tax-exempt pension scheme** or approved personal pension arrangements as part of the termination package, this is also **completely free of tax.** Making a termination payment to such pension schemes, rather than to the employee directly, is very effective tax planning and is commonly used in practice. s. 408

Finally full exemption from tax is given in instances where the employee has a substantial amount of foreign service. We shall look at foreign service exemptions later on in this chapter. s.413 s.414

D13.4 Partially taxable payments

The most important rule as far as termination payments are concerned is the £30,000 rule. Section 403(1) says that termination payments are only charged to tax to the extent they exceed £30,000. This means that the **first £30,000 of a genuine termination payment is tax free.** s. 403(1)

The £30,000 exemption only applies to payments which are taxable under Section 401. This means that this tax free amount only applies to genuine ex gratia compensation payments such as redundancy or compensation for loss of office. It does not apply where the employee has a contractual right to receive the termination payment.

If more than one termination payment is made to the same employee, the £30,000 exemption applies to the aggregate of all payments. If termination payments are staggered so that the employee receives them in different tax years, the £30,000 exemption applies to the earlier payment first. s.404(4)

If a termination payment exceeds £30,000 so that some of it will be chargeable to tax, that excess must be taxed at source under PAYE. If the termination payment is made **before the employer issues the form P45**, income tax must be deducted from the excess under PAYE using the employee's **tax code**.

If, however, the termination payment is made **after the form P45 has been issued** to the employee, tax is deducted on the excess over £30,000 at the **basic rate of 22% only**.

If an employer is uncertain as to whether the £30,000 exemption applies, he can **apply to the Inland Revenue for clearance**. It is extremely important that the employer operates PAYE correctly as it is the employer, and not the employee, who is primarily responsible for paying any tax which has been under deducted.

D13.5 Foreign service

s.413 & s.41[illegible]

Exemption from tax can apply to termination payments where the employee has foreign service. Where an employee has worked overseas and that employee receives an "ex gratia" termination payment, one of two things will happen. The termination payment will either be fully exempt from tax, or it will be partially exempt.

The **full exemption** rules are quite complex. If **foreign service is at least three quarters of total service,** the termination payment is **completely tax free**. Therefore, if an employee has been in service for 10 years, and has spent 8 of those 10 years abroad, foreign service comprises more than three-quarters of total service so the termination payment is fully exempt. s.413(1)

If this rule is not satisfied we move down to test number 2. This says that **if total service has exceeded 10 years and the last 10 years of the employee's service has been spent abroad**, the whole of the termination payment is **exempt from tax**.

If neither test 1 nor test 2 have been satisfied, we finally move on to test number 3. This says that **if total service has exceeded 20 years**, any termination payment is **tax free if at least half of total service has been spent abroad, including 10 of the last 20 years**. These three rules are difficult to remember but they are listed in S.413(1).

If none of the three tests has been satisfied, then only the foreign service part of the termination payment will be exempt from tax. s.414

Illustration 1

William was made redundant in March 2006 and he received an ex gratia termination payment of £150,000. William had worked for the company for the last 30 years as below:

		Years
March 1976 to March 1982	London	6
March 1982 to March 1998	Paris	16
March 1998 to March 2006	London	8
Total		30

In order to work out how much of the termination payment is chargeable to tax, we need to apply the three foreign service tests to see whether the termination payment is fully exempt.

The first test is whether foreign service exceeds three quarters of total service. Here the answer is quite clearly "no" because foreign service is 16 years and total service is 30 years.

The second test says that the payment will be fully exempt if total service exceeded 10 years and the whole of the last 10 years was spent outside the UK. Again, this is quite clearly not the case as the last 8 years of William's service was spent in London.

The third test only applies if total service exceeds 20 years which is the case here. There are two more conditions to satisfy, the first being that foreign service must be at last 50% of total service. Foreign service here is 16 years and total service is 30 years so this 50% condition is satisfied. Finally here, we need to check whether foreign service makes up 10 of the last 20 years. If you look back at the last 20 years of William's service, you will see that 8 years have been spent in the UK and 12 years have been spent in Paris so this condition is satisfied.

As **all three conditions in test 3 have been satisfied**, foreign service is "substantial" which means that the **whole** of the termination payment of £150,000 is tax free.

The important thing here is the approach to the question. If you are asked to deal with this in practice, then draw a time line breaking service up into UK and overseas service, then apply each of the 3 tests in order. If **any** of the 3 tests are satisfied, the termination payment is **fully** exempt.

Illustration 2

If we were to change the example of William very slightly, it will give rise to a significantly different result. Assume William still has 30 years of total service, but instead of originally going to Paris in March 1982 let us now assume that he originally went in March 1984.

		Years
March 1976 to March 1984	London	8
March 1984 to March 1998	Paris	14
March 1998 to March 2006	London	8
Total		30

This will reduce his foreign service from 16 years down to 14 years. We now need to apply the 3 foreign service tests again. The first two tests clearly are still not satisfied. Foreign service is clearly not more than three quarters of total service, and William has not spent the last 10 years outside the UK.

So let us reconsider condition number 3. Total service has exceeded 20 years, however for test 3 to be satisfied, at least 50% of total service must be foreign service. This is not the case here because foreign service is 14 years and total service is 30 years. This is less than 50%. As such, none of the three tests are satisfied which means that the termination payment of £150,000 is not fully exempt.

If the termination payment is not wholly exempt, it must be partly taxable. When dealing with an ex-gratia termination payment, the first £30,000 is always tax free. This leaves a chargeable amount of £120,000. Because part of William's service includes foreign service, we can take a foreign service deduction for the time spent abroad. s.414(3)

	£
Termination payment	150,000
Less: exemption	(30,000)
	120,000
Less: foreign service deduction:	
$£120{,}000 \times \frac{14}{30}$	(56,000)
Taxable	**£64,000**

This is chargeable to tax as specific employment income for 2005/06.

D13.6 Statutory redundancy pay

Redundancy payments fall into two categories, being statutory and non-statutory. Statutory redundancy is an amount which must be paid by the employer to the employee under employment law and will be a fixed amount for each year of service. **Statutory redundancy pay is exempt from tax** irrespective of the amount paid. s. 309

However, if an employee receives statutory redundancy as part of an overall termination package, the amount of the **statutory redundancy pay uses up part of the £30,000 exemption.** For example, assume an employee is made redundant and receives statutory redundancy of £2,000 plus an ex gratia payment of £100,000. The statutory redundancy is exempt from tax but instead of having an exemption of £30,000 to set against the ex-gratia award, this exemption is reduced by £2,000 down to £28,000.

The tax treatment of non-statutory redundancy is set out by the Revenue in **SP 1/94**. Non-statutory redundancy is essentially an ex gratia award and is therefore taxed in the normal way under Section 401. This means that the redundancy pay is taxable but only to the extent that it exceeds £30,000. SP1/94

D13.7 Employees approaching retirement age

Termination payments will typically be made to employees who are at or approaching retirement age. If an employee is retiring due to injury or disability and receives a termination payment, that payment is fully exempt. However, **payments made to retiring employees** under normal circumstances are taxable. The tax treatment is dealt with under SP 13/91. s.394 & SP13/91

SP 13/91 tells us that payments made to employees "on or in connection with retirement" are taxable in full. This means that the £30,000 exemption will **not** be available. This will be the case even where an employee receives a genuine ex gratia payment that is not within his employment contract and is not expected.

This rule only applies to employees "**on or in connection with retirement**". There has been much speculation as to what the Revenue mean by the term "on or in connection with retirement". The Revenue have said that they will give no "hard and fast" rules as to whether an employee is retiring and the Statement of Practice makes no reference to a specific retirement age.

The Revenue has accepted that a middle aged employee who moves on to another full time employment is not retiring. As such, if that middle aged employee receives a termination payment, the first £30,000 will be exempt because the provisions of SP 13/91 will not apply.

However, when a payment is made to an older employee, who is not moving on to full time employment, that employee will be treated as retiring. The payment will therefore be caught by the Statement of Practice, so the £30,000 exemption will not be available and the payment will be taxable in full.

As a rule of thumb, if you are dealing with any sort of termination payment being made to an employee over the age of, say, 45 years, the provisions of Statement of Practice 13/91 must be considered. Again, the Revenue can be approached in advance for clearance as to whether the £30,000 exemption applies or not.

D13.8 PILONS

Payments in lieu of notice (PILONs) have been the subject of much discussion over recent years. The **Revenue's position on PILONs** is summarised in their **Tax Bulletin number 24** issued in **August 1996** and amplified in **Tax Bulletin Number 63** issued in **February 2003.** Tax Bulletins Nos. 24, 63

If a payment in lieu of notice is **referred to in the employment contract**, the Revenue will regard it as a reward for services and will **tax it in full without the £30,000 exemption.** This principle was established in the tax case of *EMI v Coldicott.* In this case, the employment contract reserved a right for the employer to make a PILON on the termination of the employment and this provision was enough to make the payment fully taxable.

The Inland Revenue has always regarded payments to employees on "garden leave" as being taxable in full and this was confirmed in Tax Bulletin 24. Garden leave covers situations when the employee is not required to work during his notice period but is instead sent home "to do the garden" whilst still being paid. These payments are taxable in full.

However, where the employer makes a PILON **without** having any **contractual right or obligation** to do so, the **payment is likely to be treated as damages** for breach of contract and is **taxed under Section 401** in the normal way.

In Tax Bulletin Number 63, the Revenue has said that even if the employment contract is silent and makes no provision (discretionary or otherwise) for the employer to make a PILON, a subsequent payment to an employee in place of he/she working during their notice period could still be held to be taxable in full as an emolument of the employment. For example, if the making of a PILON is an automatic response by the employer to a termination of the employment, the Revenue are likely to regard the payment as an "integral part of the employer-employee relationship" and will argue that the source of the PILON is the **employment**, thereby making the payment fully taxable. In their view, the fact that the contract may be silent on the point is immaterial.

This is an aggressive view and in practice the facts and circumstances of each case should be reviewed separately on their merits.

If an employer terminates an employment contract without regard to any contractual notice period, he is treated as breaching the contract. If in return for that breach of contract, he makes a payment in lieu of notice to the employee, that payment is treated as a non-contractual payment of damages and is not taxed in full. In these circumstances, the first £30,000 of the PILON will be free of tax.

The taxation of PILONs is a very hazardous area for employers and if they have any doubts they should **seek clearance** before making any payments to their employees. Indeed many employers take the very prudent step of taxing the whole of the payment - i.e. ignoring the £30,000 exemption - and leave it to the employee to argue with the Tax Office as to whether the exemption applies.

D13.9 NIC implications

Class 1 National Insurance Contributions are paid on earnings from the employment. As far as termination payments are concerned, the National Insurance Contributions Office have said that where a termination payment is made to an employee **under a contractual obligation, this payment will be regarded as earnings for NIC.**

However, where an ex gratia payment is made - i.e. where there is **no contractual obligation** - the **payment will not be regarded as earnings** and will not therefore be charged to NIC. Therefore as a broad rule, where a termination payment is made such that the £30,000 exemption rule applies for income tax, there will be no National Insurance Contributions due.

The £30,000 rule itself does not apply to NIC. NIC is an "all or nothing" charge – i.e. the payment is either fully charged to National Insurance or fully exempt. Therefore where a termination payment is taxed in full, NIC will be levied on the full amount.

Class 1 NIC is levied on both employees and on employers. Employees have an upper earnings limit for Class 1 primary contributions which is currently £32,760 per annum. This means that if a termination payment is made to an employee who earns above this upper earnings limit, if the termination payment is chargeable to NIC, there will only be a 1% additional charge on the employee. However, secondary NICs will be levied on employers in full.

D13.10 Miscellaneous points

Many termination agreements often incorporate some sort of restrictive covenant. A typical restrictive covenant clause is where the employee promises not to work for a competitor firm for a certain period of time after the termination of his own employment. s.225

Any such restrictive covenant payments made to the employee are taxed in full and there is no £30,000 exemption. S.225 ITEPA 2003 specifically **deals with restrictive covenants.**

A termination payment need not necessarily be in cash. From time to time, assets are transferred to employees as part of the termination agreement – these are most commonly company cars. Many employers allow employees to keep their company car as part of the termination package. For tax purposes we value the company car at the date of the gift and to treat this as a cash payment.

It is possible for the ex-employee to continue to receive certain benefits from the employment even after the employment has terminated. If this is the case, these continuing benefits are simply taxed in the year of receipt and the cash equivalent of those benefits is reported to the Revenue on form P11D.

Certain minor benefits are now excluded from the s.401 charge – they are listed in the legislation. These are mostly benefits which would normally be tax free such as mobile phones, staff canteen, de minimis computer equipment etc.

The employer may have certain obligations to report termination payments. A one off report needs to be filed by the employer no later than 6 July following the end of the tax year if the termination package exceeds £30,000 and includes non-cash benefits.

Finally if a termination payment is taxable under S.401 (ie, if it exceeds the £30,000 threshold), it is taxed on the "top slice" of a taxpayer's income. This means that it will be taxed **after** dividend income. You may therefore need a 4th column in your tax computation.

Q	Now test your understanding by attempting the example which follows.

Example 1

Charles is made redundant on 30 November 2005 and receives the following:

	£
Ex-gratia cash payment	50,000
Company car (MV)	8,000
Statutory redundancy pay	5,000
Employer contribution to pension fund	17,000
Total package	£80,000

Calculate the amount chargeable to tax under s.401.

Answer 1

	£
Ex gratia payment	50,000
Car @ MV	8,000
Statutory redundancy pay	Exempt
Pension contribution	Exempt
	58,000
Less: exemption (net of statutory redundancy pay)	
£(30,000 - 5,000)	(25,000)
Taxable 2005/06	**£33,000**

SUMMARY - TERMINATION PAYMENTS

A termination payment is fully taxable if it is:
- A reward for services performed
- Contractual
- Expected

A termination payment is fully exempt if it is:
- On death/injury/disability
- A payment into an approved pension scheme
- Where foreign service is substantial

"Ex-gratia" termination payments such as redundancy or compensation for loss of office are only taxable to the extent they exceed £30,000.

PAYE will be deducted using the tax code if the payment is before the P45, but PAYE at 22% only is deducted if the payment is after the P45.

The three substantial foreign service tests are given in s.413 ITEPA 2003. If the foreign service is substantial the whole payment is exempt. If it is not substantial then only the proportion relating to foreign service is tax free.

Statutory redundancy pay is tax free but uses up part of the £30,000 exemption.

Payments made to employees on or in connection with retirement age are likely to be treated as fully taxable with no £30,000 exemption (SP 13/91).

Contractual PILONS and payments for garden leave are fully taxable. PILONS made in return for breaching a contract will be taxable to the extent they exceed £30,000.

NIC only applies to contractual termination payments.

D14a: OCCUPATIONAL PENSIONS & FURBS

In this chapter you will learn about the types of company pension schemes operated by employers, covering in particular:

- the tax advantages of occupational pension schemes;
- money purchase and final salary schemes;
- the earnings cap;
- how the employee receives tax relief for contributions;
- additional voluntary contributions;
- how the employer receives tax relief for contributions.

Statutory references are to ICTA 1988 unless stated otherwise.

D14a.1 Occupational schemes - Introduction

An occupational pension scheme is one set up and operated by the employer for the benefit of the employees.

Assuming the scheme has Revenue approval, the scheme will obtain tax advantages, primarily:

(i) **tax relief for employees** on contributions to the scheme;

(ii) **tax free benefits in kind** if the employer makes contributions on behalf of employees;

(iii) a **deduction for computing trading profits for employer contributions**; and

(iv) **tax free growth** on investments within the pension fund.

Employees cannot be compelled to join an occupational scheme and may instead prefer to make retirement provision via a personal or stakeholder pension (or a retirement annuity plan). However some employee schemes (often those run public bodies or government departments) are "non contributory" which means that the pension is funded entirely by the employer without the need for the employee to contribute. In these instances the employee is often automatically entered into the scheme (although the employee is then free to make additional pension provision outside the employer's scheme if he/she wishes).

D14a.2 Revenue approval s. 590-s. 612

There are detailed rules contained at s. 590 ICTA 1988 (and subsequent sections) outlining the conditions to be satisfied for a scheme to obtain Revenue approval. Applications are made by the employer to the Pension Schemes Office (PSO) who have scope to give discretionary approval to s. 591
schemes which do not precisely fit the detailed rules. The PSO has recently changed its name to Savings Pensions & Share Schemes (SPSS) which now has a wider remit than the old PSO.

The **advantage of having the scheme approved by the Revenue is to obtain the tax advantages as outlined** above. We shall look at the tax implications of unapproved pension schemes later.

D14a.3 Maximum retirement benefits

The benefits which may be conferred on employees depend on whether the scheme is a "money purchase" scheme or a "final salary" scheme.

(a) "Money purchase" arrangements

These are also called "defined contribution" schemes because the amount an employer and employee can together contribute is limited as follows:

(i) the **employer must make a contribution**; and

(ii) the **employee's contribution cannot exceed 15% of earnings**.

The percentage does not increase with age (unlike personal pensions) and there are no carry back rules.

In a money purchase scheme, the "money" contributed by the employer and employee is invested by the pension fund trustees and will "purchase" units in the fund. The value of the employee's pension on retirement is entirely dependent on:

(i) monies contributed; and

(ii) the performance of the underlying investments in the fund.

As a result, there is no restriction on the retirement benefits (for example if the fund performs well, the employee will reap the rewards and vice versa).

On retirement, the employee may "commute" a **tax free lump sum** from the pension fund. This lump sum **cannot exceed 25% of the fund**. The **rest of the fund will be used to purchase an annuity** which will provide the employee with an annual income. This pension income is taxable and tax is normally withheld at source under PAYE.

(b) "Final salary" schemes

These schemes are also called "defined benefit" schemes as the lump sum and the annual income from the pension fund on retirement are restricted by s. 590 ICTA 1988. **Maximum benefits from a final salary scheme are determined by "final remuneration"** - in essence, the higher the final remuneration, the higher the retirement benefits.

Once again, an employee's contributions may never exceed **15% of earnings**.

D14a.4 The earnings cap

s. 590C

The earnings cap which applies for personal and stakeholder schemes, similarly applies for occupational schemes. The earnings cap is:

2005/06	£105,600
2004/05	£102,000

When calculating maximum employee contributions, such annual contributions cannot exceed 15% x the earnings cap.

D14a.5 Tax relief on contributions

For computational purposes, any contributions by an employee to an approved occupational scheme are **deductible employment expenses - we do not gross them up and extend the basic rate band.**

	£
Salary	X
Bonuses	X
Benefits	X
Expenses reimbursed	X
	X
Less deductions:	
"s. 336" expenses	(X)
Travel expenses	(X)
Professional subscriptions	(X)
Donations to charity under Payroll Deduction Scheme	(X)
Occupational pension contributions	**(X)**
Net taxable earnings	X

In order to prevent tax overpayments from arising at the end of the year, tax relief on occupational pension contributions is given at source via the PAYE system. **The employer will deduct the pension contribution from gross salary before PAYE is applied.**

Employee contributions are not permitted to exceed 15% of earnings for the year.

D14a.6 Additional voluntary contributions (AVCs)

In "final salary" schemes, the level of an employee's contributions will be determined by the employer. These cannot exceed 15% of annual emoluments and tax relief is obtained via PAYE.

If employee contributions are less than 15% and the employee wishes to "top-up" his entitlement to benefits by making additional pension contributions, he may do so via AVCs.

AVCs may be made by an employee either to:

(a) his **employer's scheme**; or
(b) a separate scheme operated by an independent insurance/pension company (these are called "**freestanding " AVCs**).

Tax relief on AVCs to the employer's scheme is given via PAYE. Freestanding AVCs are treated like personal pension contributions - i.e. they are **paid net of basic rate tax and relief is given via the self assessment return by extending the basic rate band.**

Employees may not generally make contributions to both an occupational scheme and a personal pension in respect of the same earnings. Since the inception of stakeholder pensions in April 2001, it is possible for an employee to make personal pension contributions of £3,600 (gross) even if he is contributing to an occupational scheme. This exception only applies to employees earning no more than £30,000 who are not controlling directors of the company.

This exception allows certain employees to maximise pension provision and gives access to a tax free lump sum on retirement from the personal pension (no lump sum can be commuted from an AVC).

D14a.7 The employer's position

Employer contributions to approved schemes are free of income tax and NIC. Many employers encourage employees to sacrifice part of their salary into an approved scheme. This saves secondary NICs (currently at 12.8%) which many employers will then redirect into the pension scheme.

Employers may take a deduction for computing trading profits for pension scheme contributions. **Deductions are given in the period in which contributions are physically paid** - the accruals concept does not apply.

SUMMARY - OCCUPATIONAL PENSIONS & FURBS

An employer may offer an occupational pension scheme which the employee can contribute to.

If the scheme meets the Revenue's conditions for approval there will be tax relief via the PAYE system for employee contributions.

In addition the employer will get a DI deduction for amounts contributed and these will be a tax free benefit for the employee. Finally the fund will grow free of tax.

The two types of scheme are money purchase schemes and final salary schemes.

Money purchase schemes rely on growth in value of the amount contributed to provide the retirement fund whereas final salary schemes guarantee a certain level of pension.

The employee cannot contribute more than 15% of his earnings in any one tax year.

The same earnings cap as for personal pensions applies here too.

Employees will get a deduction for amounts contributed and PAYE will be applied to their salary after the deduction, giving tax relief at source.

An employee may wish to pay amounts in excess of the employer's set level of compulsory contributions - such additional voluntary contributions may be paid to the employer scheme or to a freestanding scheme.

Freestanding AVCs will attract relief by extending the basic rate band like personal pension scheme contributions.

Employers receive a deduction for computing trading profits for pension contributions paid during the year.

D14b: THE NEW PENSION REGIME

In this chapter you will cover the new pension rules in overview.

D14b.1 Background

In December 2002, the Revenue published a consultation document called "Simplifying the Taxation of Pensions: Increasing choice and flexibility for all". The driving force behind the document was the desire **to simplify the taxation system with regard to pensions by phasing out all existing pension regimes** and replacing them with **one new regime**.

Following consultation, legislation was included in Finance Act 2004. However, **implementation of the new regime has been postponed until 6 April 2006**.

SUMMARY - THE NEW PENSION REGIME

A new pension regime is being introduced to take effect from 6 April 2006. The new regime will integrate all existing pension schemes into one new system. The main features of the new regime are described below.

Individuals can obtain relief for pension contributions up to the higher of their relevant earnings or £3,600.

Therefore relief is potentially available up to 100% of relevant earnings.

Relevant earnings means employment income, self-employed trading profits (including FHLs) and patent income received by the original inventor.

The way relief is given depends on the type of pension contribution.

Schemes operated by an employer	Contributions deducted from earnings before PAYE is applied
Schemes operated by an insurance company etc	Basic rate relief given at source. Higher rate relief obtained by extending the basic rate band by the gross contribution

Individuals making contributions to old retirement annuity contracts continue to claim relief on their SA returns. Relief is given as a deduction from earned income.

The capital growth of a pension fund is not permitted to exceed an "annual allowance". This will be £215,000 for 2006/07 and will rise each year. Growth in excess of the allowance will be charged to tax at 40%.

The pension fund on retirement is not permitted to exceed a "lifetime allowance". This will be £1.5m for 2006/07 and will rise each year thereafter. If the value of the fund exceeds the lifetime allowance, a charge of 25% will be levied on retirement payments above this limit (55% for lump sum payments).

Individuals may draw pension benefits from the age of 50 (55 from 2010). Pension income will be taxed on an accruals basis. Lump sums can be drawn tax-free up to 25% of the fund or 25% of the lifetime allowance, whichever is lower.

Transitional arrangements are in place to deal with the movement to the new system.

Income and gains made by registered pension funds will generally be tax-free.

D14c: THE ENTERPRISE INVESTMENT SCHEME

In this chapter you will cover the Enterprise Investment Scheme including:
- limits on the tax reducer;
- carry back of relief;
- qualifying company;
- qualifying investor;
- clawback of relief.

Statutory references are to ICTA 1988 unless stated otherwise.

D14c.1 Introduction

An individual will receive tax relief in his Income Tax computation where he subscribes for shares in a qualifying EIS company. By **"subscribing for shares"** we mean that the **company is issuing new shares to the investor.** s. 289A

- In 2005/06 tax relief is restricted to the lower of the amount subscribed or £200,000 and is given by way of a tax reducer at a flat rate of 20%. The maximum amount of income tax relief that an individual can receive in 2005/06 is therefore: s. 290
  Maximum tax reducer = £200,000 x 20% = £40,000

The minimum amount an individual can invest in an EIS company in a tax year is £500.

The tax reducer is limited to the individual's tax liability for the year – i.e. the EIS relief cannot create a "negative" figure for the tax liability. The tax liability can be reduced to nil by EIS relief, leaving tax deducted at source either under PAYE or from bank interest, to be repaid to the taxpayer.

D14c.2 Carry back of relief

Income tax relief is usually given to the investor in the year in which the subscription is made. It is, however, **possible to carry back an EIS subscription to the preceding tax year.** If an individual **subscribes for shares** in a qualifying EIS company **before 6 October in the tax year**, the investor can make an **election to carry back the lower of 50% of the amount subscribed or £25,000 to the previous year**.

For example, if a taxpayer subscribes for £20,000 of shares on, say, 30 September 2005, the taxpayer could elect for £10,000 of the subscription to be carried back and relieved in the 2004/05 tax computation.

D14c.3 Qualifying company s. 293

Tax relief will only be given if the individual subscribes for shares in a qualifying EIS company. It is important therefore that we are comfortable with exactly what is a qualifying company under the EIS rules.

The company must be a trading company. Therefore, any company which derives its income wholly or mainly from making investments is not a qualifying company for EIS purposes.

There are **certain prohibited or excluded trades** for EIS purposes. Companies whose activities are primarily **financial** - by this we mean companies dealing in shares or securities or commodities etc. - are excluded, as are companies providing **legal and accountancy** services. **Farming and market gardening** are also excluded activities as is operating or **managing hotels**, and **property development.** s. 297(2

It is possible for the company to be registered outside the UK however, to qualify for relief, the company's trade must be wholly or mainly carried on within the UK. Most EIS companies will be resident in the UK.

The **company must be an unquoted company**. This means that its shares must not be marketed to the general public by being listed on a recognised Stock Exchange. s. 293(1A

Most companies qualifying for EIS relief are relatively small trading companies and the EIS rules place a limit on the value of the assets within the company. The assets of the company must not exceed £15 million before the share issue and must not exceed £16 million after the share issue. s. 293(6A

Having raised the share capital from its investors, the company must use the cash raised for a qualifying business activity within a certain period of time. The company must use at least 80% of the cash raised from the issue of EIS eligible shares within 12 months and the remainder within 24 months for a qualifying business activity. Qualifying business activity essentially means that the company must use it for some sort of trading purpose. s. 289(1)(

Finally, there must be no pre-arranged exits - i.e. the company must not guarantee the investor any sort of return on his investment. Only if the investor is taking a bona fide commercial risk, will the Revenue offer any form of tax relief. S. 299B

D14c.4 Qualifying investor

There is also one important qualifying condition as far as the investor is concerned. In order to obtain income tax relief, the **investor must not be connected with the company.** Broadly speaking an investor is connected with an EIS company if he breaches one of two main conditions. s. 291

The investor is connected with the company if he is an employee of the company. The investor can be a director of the company as long as he receives only reasonable remuneration for his services. s. 291A

The investor is also connected to the company if he holds more than 30% of the ordinary shares, or he can exercise more than 30% of the voting rights. In considering whether the 30% limit has been breached, the shareholdings of associates must also be considered. The associates here would include spouses, and ancestors or relatives such as parents, siblings and children. s. 291B

D14c.5 Clawback of relief s. 299

There are anti-avoidance provisions to prevent an investor from obtaining income tax relief on his EIS subscription, then selling the shares shortly afterwards. If the **investor disposes of his shares within three years of issue, there will be a clawback of the income tax relief originally given.**

The effect of this clawback is to increase the investor's tax liability in the year in which he disposes of his shares. If the investor gives away his shares within three years, all of the income tax relief originally obtained will be withdrawn. This will not apply when the gift is to the investor's spouse.

The clawback of income tax relief is slightly different where the shares are sold to an unconnected third party. If the shares are sold within three years, the income tax relief to be withdrawn is the sale proceeds multiplied by the rate at which tax relief was originally given. In the majority of instances, the rate at which tax relief was originally given will be 20%.

The clawback of income tax relief cannot exceed the original tax reducer. This means that if shares are sold at a profit within three years of issue, an amount equal to the original tax reducer is added back to the investor's tax liability in the year of sale.

Illustration 1

In December 2003 an investor subscribes for £50,000 worth of shares in an EIS company. In this instance the investor would qualify for a tax reducer of £10,000 in the tax year 2003/04.

The investor disposes of the shares in June 2005 - i.e. within three years of their issue.

If the disposal is by way of a gift, all of the tax relief originally obtained will be withdrawn. This means that £10,000 will be added to the investor's tax liability in the tax year 2005/06.

If the shares were sold for £60,000, the Income Tax relief to be withdrawn would again be £10,000. Remember that when the EIS shares are sold at a profit within three years, all of the original income tax relief given will be clawed back in the year of sale.

On the other hand, if the shares were sold at a loss within three years - here assume sale proceeds are £40,000 - the income tax relief to be withdrawn is the sale proceeds, multiplied by 20%. In this instance, £8,000 will be clawed back and added to the tax liability in the year of sale.

Q	Now test your understanding by attempting the examples which follow.

Example 1

Gary, an employee, had salary and benefits totalling £107,602 in 2005/06. He had no other income.

In March 2006 he subscribed £230,000 for shares in a qualifying EIS company.

Calculate his tax reducer for 2005/06.

Example 2

Which of the following trades is <u>not</u> an excluded trade for EIS purposes?

a) Research and development
b) Property development
c) Share dealing
d) Market gardening

Answer 1

	£
Employment income	107,602
Less: personal allowance	(4,895)
Taxable income	102,707
Tax	£
2,090 @ 10%	209
30,310 @ 22%	6,668
70,307 @ 40%	28,123
	35,000
Less: tax reducer (cannot exceed liability)	(35,000)
Tax liability	**Nil**

Gary subscribed £230,000 for shares in a qualifying EIS company.

The maximum tax reducer cannot exceed £200,000 x 20% = £40,000. However the tax reducer cannot exceed the tax liability for the year. This means that the tax reducer for 2005/06 will be £35,000.

Remember that a tax reducer can reduce a liability down to nil but cannot itself create a tax repayment.

Note that in this question no carry back is possible as the shares were not subscribed for before 6 October in the year.

Answer 2

The answer is A

Research and development is permitted. The others are prohibited (s.297(2) ICTA 1988)

SUMMARY - THE ENTERPRISE INVESTMENT SCHEME

When an individual subscribes for qualifying EIS shares, a 20% tax reducer is given on the lower of the amount subscribed or £200,000. The tax reducer is limited to the individual's tax liability.

A subscription made before 6 October can be carried back to obtain a tax reducer in the previous year but this is limited to the lower of 50% of the amount subscribed or £25,000.

A qualifying EIS company is an unquoted trading company carrying on its activities wholly or mainly in the UK.

Prohibited trades include financial trades, farming, market gardening, hotel and property development.

The company's assets must be less than £15m before and less than £16m after the share issue. 80% of the cash raised by the issue of EIS shares must be used for the trade within 12 months, the rest within 24 months.

The investor cannot be connected with the company, ie cannot be an employee nor hold >30% of the shares, together with his associates.

The tax reducer is withdrawn if the shares are disposed of within 3 years. If the shares are given away or sold at a profit, the whole tax reducer is clawed back. If the shares are sold at a loss the claw back is restricted to the proceeds x 20%.

E: Value Added Tax

E1: OVERVIEW OF THE VAT SYSTEM

This chapter aims to give you an overview of what VAT actually is and how it works. It will cover the way that VAT is added at each transaction in a chain of transactions ending with an ultimate sale to a final consumer.

All statutory reference are to the Value Added Tax Act (VATA) 1994 unless otherwise stated.

E1.1 Introduction

Let us begin by looking at what Value Added Tax (VAT) actually is and how it works. VAT is a tax on consumer spending. The Government have empowered Her Majesty's Revenue and Customs (HMRC) previously known as **Customs & Excise** (but hereafter called "Customs" in this text) to manage this tax and they have very wide powers to ensure that it is properly accounted for.

VAT registered businesses charge VAT on their sales at 17.5%. There are **different rates** of VAT but, for now, let us just assume that VAT is charged at 17.5%. The customer will pay the business the full sales price, including VAT. The business will then send the VAT collected to HMRC (Customs).

Illustration 1

A Solicitor performs some conveyancing work for Joe and the fee for his services is £400. Let us assume VAT does not apply. The Solicitor would send Joe a bill for £400 and Joe would then make prompt settlement, so £400 would go to the Solicitor. The Solicitor will then bank the £400 which, as far as he is concerned, is the fee that he wanted for his conveyancing service.

Illustration 2

Now we shall look at Illustration 1 again but this time adding VAT to the situation. A Solicitor will send a bill to Joe for £400 plus VAT at 17.5%, thus totalling £470. Joe will pay the Solicitor £470 and the Solicitor will bank the £470.

But the Solicitor has effectively acted as collection agent for Customs in respect of £70. Thus £70 of the money sitting in the Solicitors bank account belongs to Customs, therefore the Solicitor will remit £70 to Customs.

The Solicitor is left with £400 in his bank account. That is the fee that he wanted for his conveyancing work, so he is no worse off. The person who is worse off is Joe. Joe has now paid £470 instead of £400.

That is what VAT is all about, it is the **final consumer**, the customer or the public, that **bear the cost of VAT**. Businesses such as the Solicitor simply act as collection agents for Customs.

In summary, it is always the final consumer who bears the cost of VAT, but it is collected by businesses making supplies along the way.

E1.2 Overview of the VAT system

Businesses will pay the VAT they have collected over to Customs on a regular basis. This is normally quarterly but may vary and we will see more on this later in the text. The VAT that businesses charge and then collect from their customers, is called **output VAT** (or output tax). Any VAT paid by the business on its costs (i.e. when the business purchases goods and services for use in the business) is referred to as **input VAT** (or input tax).

Two important terms, are output VAT and input VAT. A VAT registered business will only pay the difference between output tax and input tax to Customs. Consequently, the tax payable by a business in a quarter will be output tax minus input tax; that is the output tax charged on its sales, minus the input tax it pays on its costs.

Illustration 3

Let us assume we have a shop and a customer. The shop is going to sell goods to the customer for £1,000 plus VAT. The customer, to secure the goods, will pay £1,175 to the shop.

Now from what we have seen so far, it will be quite reasonable to assume that the shop retains the £1,000, and the shop would remit £175 to Customs. Thus Customs need to end up with £175. Well, Customs do end up with £175 but not in this way.

Let us look at the supplier of the goods to the shop. The supplier has manufactured goods and sold them to the shop for £600 plus VAT. The shop to secure those goods will have to pay £705 in cash, that is £600 plus VAT, to the supplier. The supplier has acted as collection agent for Customs; the supplier only wanted £600 but got £705. The supplier will then retain £600 and will remit £105 to Customs.

Now let's move on to the shop. The shop has bought goods costing £600 plus VAT. It is then going to sell these goods to the customer for £1,000 plus VAT. The customer will then pay cash of £1,175 to the shop. The shop has incurred costs on which it has been charged VAT. So, therefore, it must calculate the output VAT minus input VAT. The output VAT charged by the shop was £175.

The input VAT it incurred was £105. The difference of £70 is the amount due which should be remitted by the shop to Customs.

Customs now have the required £175 but they got it from two sources; the supplier of the goods to the shop gave them £105 and the shop gave them £70.

This is effectively how VAT works. Customs will get the full amount of the £175 in their bank account, and that £175 will be borne by the customer. Customs will, however, receive the £175 in stages. In Illustration 3 there are only two parties involved before the actual sale to the customer. Sometimes there may be four, five or six more stages involved and Customs will get their bit at each stage; output VAT minus input VAT. Eventually they will find that they have in their bank account, the same amount of VAT that the customer suffered.

Illustration 4

A forester sells timber to a sawmill for £100 plus VAT. How much VAT will the forester pay over to Customs?

	£
Output tax £100 X 17.5%	17.50
Input tax	-
Due to Customs	£17.50

Illustration 5

The sawmill sells the wood purchased from the forester (but sawed into planks) to a manufacturer for £250 plus VAT. How much VAT will the sawmill pay over to Customs?

	£
Output tax £250 x 17.5%	43.75
Input tax paid to forester	(17.50)
Due to Customs	£26.25

Illustration 6

The manufacturer then sells a table to the retailer for £500 plus VAT. How much VAT will the manufacturer pay over to Customs?

	£
Output tax £500 x 17.5%	87.50
Input tax paid to sawmill	(43.75)
Due to Customs	£43.75

Illustration 7

The retailer now sells the table to Mrs Hall, for £700 plus VAT. How much VAT will the retailer pay over to Customs?

	£
Output tax £700 x 17.5%	122.50
Input tax paid to manufacturer	(87.50)
Due to Customs	£35.00

E1.3 Summary of the illustrations

In summary, the forester paid £17.50, the sawmill business paid £26.25, the manufacturer £43.75 and the retailer £35. In total that means that Customs have got £122.50 and this was the amount charged by the retailer to Mrs Hall. So, effectively, Mrs Hall has borne the whole of the £122.50, which is the VAT amount that she paid to the retailer, and Customs will have that amount in their bank account, but it would have been received in four parts from four separate registered businesses.

One thing the four illustrations effectively demonstrate is how VAT balances the books. Somebody's outputs, if they are selling to a registered business, will be somebody else's inputs. For example, the forester's outputs are the sawmiller's inputs. The sawmiller's outputs are the manufacturer's inputs. The manufacturer's outputs are the retailer's inputs.

This effectively acts as a payment on account system. At the forester's stage, £17.50 of VAT has been charged as output VAT and £17.50 will have been paid over to Customs. At the next stage, the total output tax charged on is £43.75 and this is effectively how much Customs will have at this point. They will have £17.50 from the forester, plus another £26.25 giving £43.75. At the next stage, the output tax charged on by the manufacturer, is £87.50 and again, this is how much Customs will then have, they will have the £43.75 from the forester and the miller, plus another £43.75 from the manufacturer. The retailer charged £122.50 in output VAT which, again is what Customs now have. They have the £87.50 plus the £35 from the retailer.

Customs ensure VAT works in this way so that as soon as the chain stops, normally with the ultimate customer, the public, they have the correct amount of VAT.

SUMMARY - OVERVIEW OF THE VAT SYSTEM

Although VAT is ultimately suffered by the final consumer in a chain of transactions the way that the VAT system works is that VAT is collected piecemeal at every stage in that long chain. So, effectively, there is a payment on account system.

At each point in the chain the supplier charges the appropriate output tax to the next person in the chain and recovers any input tax he paid to the previous person in the chain.

This series of output tax less input tax accounting of VAT will occur right up until the final sale to the member of the public or the ultimate consumer.

However, although VAT is collected piece by piece along the chain of transactions ultimately it is the final consumer who bears the full cost of the VAT being collected. In other words, the output tax charged to that final consumer will equal all the net VAT accounted for during the journey which took those goods or services to that ultimate consumer.

E2: REGISTRATION

This chapter looks at registration of a business for VAT and includes:
- compulsory registration;
- voluntary registration;
- de-registration.

E2.1 Introduction

In this chapter we will look at registration for VAT. Not all businesses must be registered for VAT but, if you are in business making taxable supplies, you will be required to be registered by Customs if, at the end of any calendar month, the value of **taxable supplies made in the previous 12 months exceeds the** Sch 1
annual registration threshold. Alternatively, you must register for VAT if at Para 1
any time there are **reasonable grounds** for believing that the value of taxable supplies to be made in the **next 30 days on their own, will exceed the annual registration threshold**.

There are two tests and Customs will use the test which gives the earlier registration date.

There are a few terms to get to grips with here; the first one will be **'taxable supplies'** as defined by Customs. Certain transactions are taxable i.e. VAT is chargeable at a certain rate. However it is only when you exceed a certain level of taxable supplies that you have to register and actually account for VAT on those taxable supplies.

Another term used is the **'annual registration threshold'**. This changes every year with the Budget and the current rate is £60,000. So if, for example, my taxable supplies for the 12 months to 30 April 2005 were £61,000 I would have an obligation to register.

Whilst the above are **compulsory registration** tests, it is possible to **voluntarily register** for VAT. Any bona fide business whose taxable turnover is below the annual threshold can apply to register voluntarily. So, for example, I might have taxable supplies of say £30,000 a year, which is below the compulsory limits, but I may choose to register. I might do this for a number of reasons, one of which is **credibility**. For example, if I did not charge VAT on my invoices, then my customers would know that my turnover is quite small. So many businesses just register to add credibility or conceal turnover.

Another reason to register would be to **recover your input VAT**. As we saw in Chapter 1, when you charge output VAT on your supplies or your sales, you are entitled to reclaim your input VAT, that is VAT which has been charged to you on your costs. So this might be quite an important reason for registering for VAT.

If your customers are registered businesses themselves, there would be a very strong incentive to register because your customers would not mind you charging VAT, since they **will claim it back as their input tax**. It is only really when your customers are the public, the final consumer, that a small business must think quite seriously about whether it should register voluntarily or not.

E2.2 Types of Registration

In summary, registration can be broken down into a compulsory registration or a voluntary registration. The compulsory registration test can be broken down into an historic test and a future test. For the historic test at the end of Sch 1
every calendar month, you look back through the previous months of a business Para 1
(but you never look back more than 12 months) and if you have exceeded the annual threshold, currently £60,000, then you have an obligation to register.

In the future test you look forward 30 days and if the business is expected to exceed £60,000 of taxable supplies in the next 30 days on their own, then you would have an obligation to register. It is important to recognise that the future test is a daily test, so every single day you must look forward 30 days and see if in the next 30 days you will exceed £60,000. It makes no reference to what went on before today. It is the next 30 days on their own that matters.

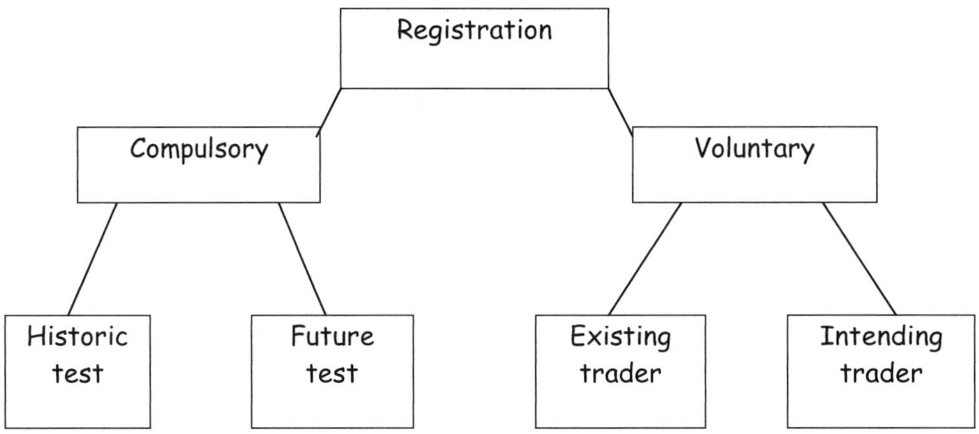

For voluntary registration existing traders can register even if their taxable supplies fall below the limits. Another form of voluntary registration is for **intending traders**. These are traders who have not actually commenced trading, but who intend to within the foreseeable future. These traders would apply to Customs for a VAT number well before they commence trading. This Sch 1
might be for a number of factors but the most common is to enable **recovery** Para 9
of VAT from Customs **whilst the business is being set up**. For example, it might take you 6 months to refit a shop but in those 6 months, if you are registered for VAT, you can reclaim input tax from Customs. These would obviously be provisional reclaims and will be dependent on the fact that you do actually commence trading.

E2.3 Historic test

Let us have a look at the historic test in more detail. As we have seen, you will be required to register for VAT if at the end of any calendar month, the value of your **taxable supplies in the last 12 months exceeds £60,000**, the current annual threshold. With a new business the £60,000 threshold might be exceeded within 2, 3 or 4 months. For ongoing businesses the rule is that you only include taxable supplies of the last 12 months - no more. Sch 1 Para 1

If you have exceeded the limit then you must **notify** Customs of your requirement to be registered by completing form **VAT 1** and submitting it to Customs **within 30 days of the month that you exceeded the limit**. The registration will be effective i.e. you will be **registered from, the first day of the second month** following the end of the month the £60,000 was exceeded. Sch 1 Para 11 to 17 SI 1995/2518 Reg 5

For example, at the end of June a business exceeds the limits then it must be registered from the 1st day of the second month following June. As July is not the second month, it must be August. So the business must be registered from the 1st day of August. It exceeded the limit in June, it will have July effectively free of VAT and from 1 August it is registered.

Illustration 1

Let us assume we are a trader in business and we are checking at the end of every calendar month the taxable supplies in the previous 12 months. At the end of April 2005 my taxable supplies amounted to £55,000 for the previous 12 months, so there is no requirement for the business to be registered.

We then go to the end of May 2005 and, for the previous 12 months to May, the taxable supplies amounted to £58,000; again below the limits. We then go to the end of June and, if we look back 12 months, the taxable supplies amount to £54,000. A fall in the value of taxable supplies like this is simply as a result of the June 2005 taxable supplies being lower than the June 2004 taxable supplies. But, in any event, we are below the £60,000 limit and there is no requirement to register.

We then go on to the end of July 2005 and for the previous 12 months our taxable supplies amount to £61,000. The business has exceeded the limits; it has a requirement to register.

Example 1

The business mentioned in Illustration 1 must notify Customs of its requirement to register for VAT on form VAT 1.

By which date must Customs be notified?

From which date will this business be VAT registered?

Illustration 2

New Business Limited commenced trading on 1 July 2004. The taxable sales were as follows:

		£			£
2004	July	4,000	2005	March	5,000
	August	4,000		April	5,000
	September	4,000		May	5,000
	October	4,000		June	6,000
	November	4,000		July	7,500
	December	4,000		August	8,000
2005	January	4,000		September	7,000
	February	4,000		October	8,500

I shall assume that this business does not want to voluntarily register. I need to find out when the compulsory registration limit of £60,000 is exceeded.

At the end of every calendar month I look back 12 months. If I have not got 12 months to look back to, for example, on a start-up, I can only look back to the start of trade. So at the end of July 2004 I look to see how much I have sold in the previous 12 months. I have sold £4,000; so no requirement to register. I then move on to August 2004; taxable supplies in the previous 12 months, well I have only be trading for 2 months so the cumulative will be £8,000. This process will continue until I exceed the £60,000 limit.

We can see from this example that when I get to June 2005, taxable supplies to June 2005 total £53,000. Thus, registration is not required. The 12 months to July 2005 amount to £56,500; again not exceeding the limit.

At the end of August 2005, in the previous 12 months, my cumulative taxable supplies amount to £60,500; that exceeds the limit of £60,000 so August 2005 is the month the limit has been exceeded and the date the business must notify Customs of its requirement to be registered is 30 September 2005, that is 30 days after the month the limit was exceeded.

And when must the business be registered from? The compulsory registration date will be 1 October 2005, that is the first day of the second month following the month the limit was exceeded. So September has been free of VAT and the first time the business will have to charge VAT is from 1 October 2005.

E2.4 Future Test

Let us move on to the future test. This is a test which applies at any time. So every single day, the trader must ask himself whether there are reasonable grounds for believing that the value of **taxable supplies in the next 30 days will exceed the registration limit**. Notification must again be made on form VAT 1 and again **within 30 days**. Sch 1 Paras 1 and 6

The **registration** on the future test does, however, have an **immediate effect.** So straightaway you must charge VAT even though you will have no VAT number at that point. On the invoices you issue you need to put something like "VAT number to be advised".

This future test is really to catch substantial orders. So, for example, if you are always below the historic test but today you went into the office and received an order for £100,000 which you were going to turn around pretty quickly, then today you know that in the next 30 days on their own, you would exceed £60,000. You have got an order for £100,000 so therefore you must exceed the limit in the next 30 days. Consequently you must notify Customs within 30 days from today and you must be registered for VAT from today, so "VAT number to be advised" must be stamped on your invoices.

Illustration 3

Let us look at an illustration where we have a business that has always traded just below the historic threshold. In the 12 months to 30 April, the taxable supplies were £58,000; the 12 months to 31 May the taxable supplies were £59,000; the 12 months to 30 June, they were £57,000. In other words the business is always just below the limits.

Let us assume that this business received an order on 10 July for £70,000. They have got the goods in stock so they are going to turn the order around pretty quickly, within say 10 days. So on 10 July if you look forward 30 days on their own, you will exceed the limit of £60,000. You have got an order for £70,000 plus whatever sales you would ordinarily do in those 30 days. So the business breaches the future test.

When must this business notify Customs of its requirements to register? The notification date is 30 days from 10 July. That was the point when you could say that there were reasonable grounds for believing that taxable supplies in the next 30 days would exceed the limits. So 9 August 2005 is 30 days.

This business must be registered from what date? As we saw earlier, the date of registration for the future test is immediate so on 10 July this business must be registered for VAT, i.e. it must charge VAT from 10 July.

Now let us just continue this illustration for just one more month to the end of July. When you do get to the end of July, you have obviously exceeded the limit because in the 12 months to the end of July, you would have breached £60,000. You have got an order for £70,000 in there so you are bound to. Following the historic test, you would have had a registration date of 1 September. However under the future test you have a registration date of 10 July. This is obviously much earlier than the 1 September date under the historic test, so Customs will take the earlier date of 10 July.

E2.5 Common Misconception

Just one point to make about a common misconception on the historic and the future tests. This is best illustrated using an example. Let us say taxable sales in the 11 months to September 2005 were £55,000. In October 2005 you have budgeted sales of £7,000. In this situation the future test does not apply because there is no point at which you can say in the next 30 days **on their own**, the business will exceed the limits. On 1 October 2005 we anticipate taxable supplies for October of £7,000 and £7,000 alone does not exceed £60,000 so therefore the future test does not apply.

The historic test will however apply when I get to the end of October. The taxable supplies made in the 12 months to 31 October amount to £62,000. The business has exceeded the limits. It must notify Customs by 30 days from the month of excess, so 30 November 2005. The registration date will be 1 December 2005 so no VAT is charged for the whole of November, and the business is registered from the first day of the second month, so 1 December.

E2.6 Deregistration

Once a business is registered for VAT, it is not always the case that it will remain registered for VAT. In certain situations a business may be required to deregister or may voluntarily deregister. Examples of **compulsory deregistration** would be:- Sch 1 Para 11

- **Sale of business** - if you sold your business you are no longer in a position to charge VAT so you are compulsorily deregistered;

- **Changing status** – a business might change from a sole trader to a limited company for example.

- **Ceasing to make taxable supplies** - a business may cease trading for example.

Voluntary deregistration is available where a business is expected to make **taxable supplies in the next 12 months of less than £58,000**. If that is the case, and the business no longer wishes to remain registered, it can inform Customs and providing they are satisfied that the business will fall below the deregistration limit of £58,000 it will be permitted to deregister. Sch 1 Para 1(3)

If a business decides to voluntarily de-register it may be for a number of reasons; administration will be easier if they did not have to account for VAT, their prices to the public would become lower if they did not have to charge VAT and so on.

Answer 1

The correct notification date is 30 August 2005. This is 30 days from the month in which the limits were exceeded.

As the business exceeds the limits at the end of July 2005, the correct registration date is 1 September 2005; this is the first day of the second month. Thus August was free of VAT and no VAT needs to be charged in August. However from 1 September the business will be registered and then must charge VAT.

SUMMARY - REGISTRATION

There are two types of registration - compulsory and voluntary registration.

For compulsory registration there are two tests which must be considered - the historic test and the future test.

The historic test looks at past cumulative turnover but we never look back more than the preceding 12 months. This turnover test is carried out at the end of every calendar month. If the cumulative turnover exceeds the VAT registration limit then Customs must be notified within the next 30 days and we register the business from the start of the second month that follows the month end.

The future test looks only at turnover in the next 30 days alone. If the registration limit is exceeded then Customs must be notified before that 30 day period expires. The business will then be registered from the start of the 30 day period.

Voluntary registration allows a business to register for VAT even if its turnover does not exceed the VAT registration threshold. Voluntary registration is also available for intending traders who have not yet commenced to trade but are intending to do so in the near future.

De-registration allows a business to de-register for VAT. De-registration may be compulsory or voluntary. Compulsory de-registration would occur where a business is sold or ceases to make taxable supplies. Voluntary de-registration is available where a business is expected to make taxable supplies in the next 12 months of less than £58,000.

E3: DEFINITION OF SUPPLIES

This chapter will look at the following:

- when a supply arises for VAT purposes;
- the definition of consideration;
- the five basic conditions required to determine whether a supply should be charged to VAT.

E3.1 Introduction

A supply for VAT purposes would generally arise where consideration is present. **Consideration** is any form of payment, be it cash or in kind. Suppose we have a registered trader that sells goods to a customer. In return, the customer pays s.5(2)
cash to the registered trader. This is the basic form of consideration. Cash has passed from the customer to the registered trader.

It is not however necessary for cash to pass; the definition of consideration says **payment in money or in kind**, so it need not be money. For example, in return for the goods the customer may offer his time i.e. he may have an arrangement where he works one morning a week in the registered trader's business. He would not get paid for that morning instead he receives goods. So the consideration in this example would be the time the customer is giving the registered trader, hence there will be a supply for VAT and the registered trader must determine whether he should charge VAT on the goods supplied. This will depend on whether the goods supplied are taxable or not. Consequently once consideration is present and we therefore have a supply, we then need to determine whether it is a taxable supply.

E3.2 Five Conditions

There are five basic conditions to determine whether a supply merits a charge s.4
to VAT.

a) The supply must amount to a supply of **goods or services**.

b) The supply must be made by a **taxable person**.

c) The supply must have been made in the **United Kingdom**.

d) The supply must have been made **in the course or furtherance of business**.

e) It must be a **taxable supply** by definition.

E3.3 Taxable Supply

Once it has been established that there is a supply we then need to determine whether the supply is **taxable, exempt or outside the scope** of VAT completely. s.4(2)

Taxable will be at one of three rates of VAT; the **standard rate, a lower rate and a zero rate.** The standard rate is currently 17.5%, the lower rate is currently 5% and the zero rate, as you would expect, is 0%. The legislation details supplies which are at the lower rate of 5%, and the zero rate of 0%. The legislation also outlines which supplies are exempt supplies and, to a certain extent, which supplies are outside the scope of VAT. If your supply is not within one of those specific definitions, which we will cover in the next chapter, then the supply is taxable at 17.5%.

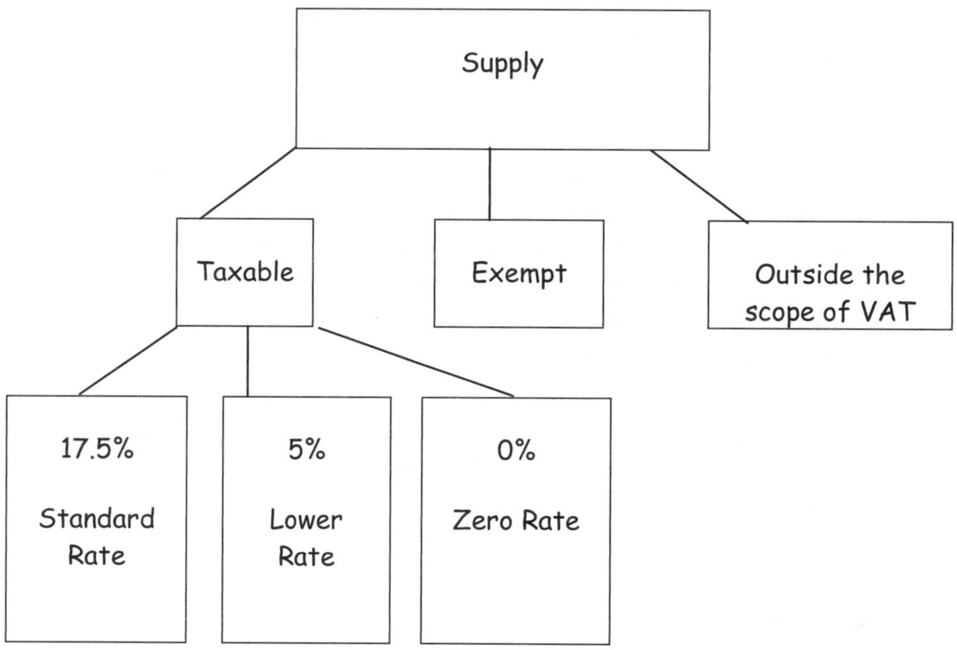

So there we have it, the five conditions. For there to be a taxable supply you must meet all five.

SUMMARY - DEFINITION OF SUPPLIES

For a supply to be charged to VAT that supply must be a supply of goods or services, made by a taxable person, in the UK, in the course or furtherance of a business. In addition, the supply must be a taxable supply and generally consideration must be present. Consideration is not necessarily cash. The definition of a consideration is payment in money or in kind.

A taxable supply is a standard rated or zero rated supply as defined by the VAT legislation.

E4: LIABILITY OF THE SUPPLY

This chapter is going to look at the following:
- how we work out whether a supply is chargeable to VAT;
- if it is, how much VAT we actually charge on that supply;
- the three types of supply;
- the way to categorise a supply in order to work out the correct VAT treatment.

E4.1 Introduction

This chapter looks at how to work out whether a supply is chargeable to VAT and, if it is, how much VAT to charge on that supply. Effectively, it could be said that there are three types of supply. The first type of supply is a **taxable supply** which is the sort of supply that VAT will apply to. The second type of supply is an **exempt supply** - there is no VAT on an exempt supply. The final type of supply is called outside the scope, these supplies are completely ignored when looking at the VAT legislation although we may have to be careful if input VAT has been paid which the business would like to recover in relation to a supply that was outside the scope because such input VAT cannot normally be recovered. This will be dealt with in a later chapter.

E4.2 Taxable supplies

Basically there are three types of taxable supply. The first type of taxable supply is called standard rated because the standard rate of VAT would apply to this supply - so **17.5% VAT will be charged on standard rated taxable supplies.**

The second type of taxable supply is a supply taxable at the **lower rate of VAT, which is currently standing at 5%.**

The final type of supply that is taxable is the zero-rated taxable supply which, of course, is taxable at the **zero rate of VAT - 0% VAT**.

In the VAT legislation there is a list of zero-rated supplies in Schedule 8 of the Value Added Tax Act (VATA) 1994. There is a list of lower rated supplies in Schedule 7A of VATA 1994. There is a list of exempt supplies in Schedule 9 of Sch 8
VATA 1994. There is some information in VAT Notice 701/39 on VAT liability Sch 9
law, but nowhere in the legislation is there a definitive list of standard rated taxable supplies.

E4.3 Method of determining liability

A business supplies widgets. How should it treat that supply of a good for VAT purposes? Firstly one looks at Schedule 8 of VATA 1994. **Schedule 8** outlines all the **zero rated** supplies made for VAT legislation purposes.

If the business cannot find the supply listed in Schedule 8 the next step is to look at Schedule 9. **Schedule 9** lists all the **exempt** supplies.

If the widget is neither zero rated nor exempt, then step three is to see if the supply is subject to VAT a the **lower rate** under **Schedule 7A.** There are specific items which are charged to VAT at the lower rate (see below). Sch 7A

The next step would be to decide if the widget was **outside the scope of VAT**. Again there are specific supplies that are outside the scope of VAT, for example, transferring a business as a going concern.

Thus if the item is not zero rated, not exempt, not charged at the lower rate and not outside the scope of VAT then what is left is a standard rated taxable supply and that is what the widget must be. This is the final step. There is no list of standard rated taxable supplies in the legislation - basically one gets there by default.

Step	
1	Schedule 8 (zero rated)
↓	↓
2	Schedule 9 (exempt)
↓	↓
3	Lower Rate (specific supplies)
↓	↓
4	Outside the scope (specific supplies)
↓	↓
5	Standard Rated

Zero rating will always take priority over exemption. If an item could fall into both Schedule 8 and Schedule 9 it will always be zero rated since this takes priority.

E4.4 Lower Rate (5%)

The lower rate of VAT is currently 5% and the supplies that are subject to the lower rate are outlined in **Schedule 7A** of VATA 1994. The main supply that is associated with the lower rate of VAT is supplies of fuel for domestic use for example, gas and electricity supplied to people's homes. Also covered by the lower rate is the supply of ladies sanitary products, the supply of children's car seats and ground source heat pumps. Sch 7A Groups 1, 4

Where dwellings are being renovated, having been empty for at least three years or more and those dwellings are basically a single household, then the lower rate of VAT also applies to the renovation. Sch 7A Group 7

Also on the list for lower rate VAT is the conversion of a residential property into a different number of dwellings. This would cover, for example, the conversion of a house into flats. By a similar token converting a non-residential property into a dwelling or a number of dwellings is also a recent addition to the list and an example of this would be converting a barn into a house. Sch 7A Group 6

The conversion of a dwelling into a care home or into a house in multiple occupation is also at the lower rate and converting a care home into a single household dwelling or dwellings is also at the 5% rate.

These are the main items which are charged to VAT at the lower rate - there are a few others covered in the Schedule, for example, the services of installing energy saving materials into homes and supplies of installing central heating or security equipment into homes of the elderly are also covered by the lower rate. Sch 7A Groups 2 & 3

E4.5 Outside the Scope of VAT

The sorts of items that are completely outside the scope of VAT are things like;

VAT Notice 700 para 8.14

- statutory charges;
- salaries and wages;
- tips and gratuities given to staff; C&E Manual V1-3 Chapter 2B Para .6
- fees and honoraria paid to clergymen;
- inter-group transactions if there is a VAT group registration in force; and s.43
- the sale or purchase of a business as a going concern. SI 1995/1268

SUMMARY - LIABILITY OF THE SUPPLY

There are three types of supply:
- taxable
- exempt
- outside of the scope

There are three types of taxable supply:
- standard rated
- lower rate
- zero rated

Schedule 8 of VATA 1994 lists the zero rated supplies.

Schedule 9 of VATA 1994 lists the exempt supplies.

Supplies subject to the lower rate of VAT are outlined in Schedule 7A of VATA 1994.

Certain supplies are outside the scope of VAT, these include:
- the sale or purchase of a business of a going concern
- inter group transactions within a VAT group
- tips and gratuities
- salaries and wages paid to staff
- statutory charges.

There is no definition in the legislation of standard rated supplies. Effectively if a supply is not zero rated, is not exempt, is not taxable at the lower rate, and is not outside the scope of VAT, then it is by exception a standard rated supply.

E5: SCHEDULE 8 VATA 1994 – ZERO RATING

This chapter will look at the types of supply listed as zero rated supplies. There are sixteen categories of zero rated supplies which are listed in Schedule 8 of VATA 1994.

E5.1 Introduction

Schedule 8 to the VAT Act 1994 is simply a list of zero rated items. These items have been collated into sixteen groups. Sch 8

- Group 1 is food
- Group 2 is sewerage and water
- Group 3 is books
- Group 4 is talking books for the blind and handicapped and wireless sets for the blind
- Group 5 is the construction of buildings
- Group 6 is protected buildings
- Group 7 is international services
- Group 8 is transport
- Group 9 is caravans and houseboats
- Group 10 is gold
- Group 11 is bank notes
- Group 12 is drugs, medicines and aids for the handicapped
- Group 13 is imports and exports
- Group 14 is tax free shops
- Group 15 is charities
- Group 16 is clothing and footwear.

If any particular supply falls within one of these Groups, then that supply will be zero rated.

This chapter will look at the more common Groups.

E5.2 Group 1 - Food

Food for human consumption is generally zero rated. There are some exceptions.

Food supplied in the course of catering would not fall within the zero rated provisions. Therefore, any food supplied by a café to be eaten in the café would be deemed to be catering. Catering is also deemed to include hot take-away food. Cold food consumed on the premises will be standard rated, cold food taken away will be zero-rated. As far as hot food is concerned, it does not matter where it is consumed, if it is on the premises it will be catering, if it is taken away it will be catering.

Another exception is that zero rating does not apply to non-essential items, such as chocolate or alcohol or crisps.

Catering has been a problematical area in practice with a lot of Case Law arising to try and establish whether a particular supply falls within food or whether it is classified as catering.

The first issue tends to be **what constitutes premises**.

Case Law has held that a caterer in a sports ground is deemed to have a licence to occupy the land on which his stall stands and the stall and the stadium are then regarded as the same premises, consequently any supplies he makes will be in the course of catering and will therefore be standard rated. The reverse of that though, is cold food supplied by mobile vans parked on a public road. These would be zero rated because they are consumed off the premises.

In cases of doubt Case Law will prove very useful in determining the nature of the supply.

Another problem with catering is why has the food been served hot? If the food has been heated for the purpose of enabling it to be consumed at a temperature above the ambient air temperature, then that will be deemed to be hot food and it will be standard rated. It therefore becomes very important as to why the food has been heated. What is the intention of the trader? If he or she heated the food for the purpose of enabling its customers to consume the food whilst still warm, the supply is standard rated.

There have been many cases on this issue and some have fallen in the taxpayers favour. If you can prove that the reason for heating the food was not for it to be consumed hot, then there is a good chance that the trader can apply zero rating. If the food has been heated to create a general ambience within the shop but the food could actually be eaten cold or hot, then zero rating may prevail.

In summary, **food is generally zero rated unless provided in the course of catering or it is a non-essential item**. The definition of catering is however problematical.

E5.3 Group 3 - Books

Under this grouping zero rating covers books, brochures, pamphlets, leaflets, newspapers, journals and periodicals, children's picture books and painting books, any printed music matter and maps.

Whilst zero rating covers the hard copies of the above, any electronic transmission of such books would not fall within the zero rating provisions. This was proven to be the case in Forexia UK Limited and Customs have announced that they see no reason for the VAT legislation to be updated to include electronic books.

Talking books for the blind and handicapped and wireless sets for the blind will also be zero rated.

E5.4 Group 5 - Construction of Buildings

The zero rating of property is a major area to look at and there is a separate session on this particular grouping later in the text. For now, we will just introduce the zero rating provision. When the legislation says construction, it is quite likely that we are dealing with a builder. When considering the construction of a building and the zero rating thereon you need two things; the right type of supply and the right type of building. You must have both. If both are present then the supply will be zero rated.

As regards the right type of supply, it must be the first grant of a major interest in that building. A **major interest** for these purposes will be a **freehold** s.96(1)
or a lease exceeding 21 years. So, for example, the builder would have to sell the freehold in a property or grant a 25 year lease.

As regards the right type of building, there are only three types of buildings which fall within the zero rating provisions;

- a dwelling would fall within this category;
- a relevant residential building would also fall within the category; and,
- a relevant charitable building.

Relevant residential buildings are defined in the legislation and would include drug rehabilitation centres, school dormitories, monasteries, nunneries - there is a defined list of relevant residential buildings in Note 4 of Group 5. However, a charitable building is a building used by a charity for a **charitable purpose.**

To summarise this grouping then, if a builder built a house and sold the freehold of the house he has the right type of supply, the freehold, he also has the right type of building; he would therefore zero rate the freehold sale.

At this point just note that this grouping also includes the supply of services and related materials in the construction of dwellings – but more on this in the later chapter.

Group 6 provides zero rating to certain aspects of listed buildings or **protected buildings**.

E5.5 Group 8 - Transport

Transport has some zero-rating provisions. Zero rating will apply to a wide range of services relating to ships and aircraft and the transport of goods and passengers. As far as transporting passengers is concerned, **vehicles must be capable of carrying 10 or more people.** This would imply that taxi fares are not zero rated. It should however be noted that not all taxi drivers decide to register for VAT; their fares are taxable at 17.5% but if they are below the annual registration limit of £60,000, then they may decide not to register for VAT.

There are some general exceptions to zero rating of transport. Fairground rides, rides at museums, rides to or from airport car parks, and recreational flights such as hot air balloon rides are excepted from zero rating.

E5.6 Group 9 - Caravans and Houseboats

Caravans and houseboats will attract zero rating but only those caravans above the size permitted on the roads and houseboats used for permanent residential occupation.

E5.7 Group 10 - Gold

The Gold Group will only apply to dealings in Gold and Gold coins by a central Bank or a member of the London Gold Market.

E5.8 Group 15 - Charities

Zero-rated under this group are:

- Goods donated or hired to a charity for sale or hire by the charity.
- Sale or hire by a charity of goods which have been donated or hired to the charity. This includes supplies into the charity and then supplies from the charity.
- Any advertising supplied to a charity.

- Repair and maintenance of relevant goods owned by an eligible body (Note 4)

Relevant goods are listed in the VAT legislation (Note 3) and are mainly connected with the medical industry. Eligible bodies are also primarily health based.

E5.9 Group 16 - Clothing and Footwear

Articles designed as clothing or footwear for children and not suitable for older persons, will attract zero rating. Articles of clothing will include hats, and other forms of headgear.

Protective boots and helmets for industrial use unless the supply is made to an employer for his employee's use can be zero rated. These boots and helmets must be BSI standard.

Protective helmets for motor cyclists and pedal cyclists again to BSI standard can be zero rated.

E5.10 A word of warning

When considering the items within these Groups, it is important that you fully read all the notes attached to the Groups (including the small print at the end of each Group) within the legislation or the VAT Notice.

Q	Now test your understanding by attempting the example which follows.

Example 1

Using the legislation, or the VAT Notice, decide which of the following are zero rated.

- A child's painting book
- Sandwiches sold and consumed in a café
- Baby's nappies
- A packet of herbal tea sold by a grocer
- Chocolate biscuits sold by a grocer
- Coach journey from London to Edinburgh
- Child's sheepskin gloves

Answer 1

- A child's painting book will be zero rated by means of Schedule 8 Group 3 Item 3.
- Sandwiches sold in the café will be standard rated; they do not fall within the zero rating provision of Schedule 8 Group 1 because they are supplied in the course of catering.
- Babies' nappies will be zero rated under Schedule 8 Group 16 Item 1.
- The packet of herbal tea sold by a grocer will be zero rated by means of Schedule 8 Group 1. Tea is food fit for human consumption; it is within the excepted items under other beverages but the items overriding the exceptions, in this case Item 4, further down in the legislation, specifically state that herbal tea overrides any exceptions to this Schedule, therefore the herbal tea sold by a grocer is zero rated. This is a good example of why it is so important to read all of the notes in each Group.
- Chocolate biscuits sold by a grocer will not be zero rated; they are deemed to be a luxury good i.e. not an essential good and are excluded from zero rating by way of Schedule 8 Group 1 excepted Item 2.
- A coach journey from London to Edinburgh will be zero rated by means of the transport zero rated group at Schedule 8 Group 8.
- A child's sheepskin gloves will be zero rated by means of Schedule 8 Group 16 Item 1. Note that articles designed as clothing or footwear for young children will be zero rated and although there is an exception whereby articles are made of fur skin, this would not apply in this instance, as sheepskin is not deemed to be fur skin under Note 3 of Group 16.

SUMMARY - SCHEDULE 8 VATA 1994 - ZERO RATING

Schedule 8 of VATA 1994 lists the type of supplies which fall into zero rating for VAT purposes. There are effectively sixteen groups of such supplies which include:

- food
- books
- construction of buildings
- transport
- clothing and footwear for children

It is important when looking at items listed within the groups in Schedule 8 that you read all the notes attached to those groups because many exceptions to the general rule lie within those notes.

E6: SCHEDULE 9 VATA 1994 - EXEMPTIONS

In this chapter the supplies which are exempt for VAT will be looked at in some detail.

E6.1 Introduction

In this chapter we are just going to have a brief look at Schedule 9 - Exemption. **Schedule 9** to the VAT Act of 1994 provides a list of exempt items. Essentially these are **15 groups** and each group is a specific exemption. Sch 9

Group			
Group	1	-	Land
	2	-	Insurance
	3	-	Postal Services
	4	-	Betting, Gaming and Lotteries
	5	-	Finance
	6	-	Education
	7	-	Health and Welfare
	8	-	Burial and Cremation
	9	-	Trade Unions and Professional Bodies
	10	-	Sport, Sports Competitions and Physical Education
	11	-	Works of Art, etc
	12	-	Fund raising events by Charities and other qualifying bodies
	13	-	Cultural Services etc
	14	-	Supplies of goods where input tax cannot be deducted
	15	-	Investment Gold

E6.2 Group 1 - Land

The exemption for land will be covered in detail later in the text. For now, we are going to provide an overview of the exemption for land. It should be appreciated that once a business has looked in Schedule 8, the zero rated Schedule and has not been able to find land within the zero rated Schedule, it must then move on to Schedule 9. Schedule 9 states that any land transaction is exempt **other than** the items actually listed in the legislation. So the legislation effectively says that any land transaction (e.g. lease, rent, sale, assignment, surrender, reverse surrender, reverse premium) is exempt other than the items it lists which is a list of standard rated items (Schedule 9 item 1 (a) to (m)).

In the list of standard rated items the most important will be item 1(a) which covers the supply of a new, freehold commercial building. So a sale of a new freehold commercial property is standard rated. New is deemed to be under 3 years old (Schedule 9, Group 1, Note 4).

Also in this long list are things like hotel accommodation, theatre and concert tickets, camping and caravan sites and car park charges.

Finally for completeness, an option to tax is available which will change an exempt supply of land into a taxable supply. The option to tax can only apply to land or commercial property. Remember this is an overview of the land exemptions and these, plus the option to tax, will be covered in much more detail in a later chapter. Sch 10

E6.3 Other exempt items

Let's look at other exemptions briefly.

Group 2 – insurance. Most insurance premiums are exempt from VAT, many large insurance companies also make taxable supplies so they will be registered for VAT, but the predominant supply within their business will be exempt.

Group 3 – postal services. Currently only the postal services provided by the Post Office are exempt. Businesses which charge customers postage must add on this charge before calculating the VAT due on their invoices. Consequently VAT is charged on postage and carriage charges levied by ordinary businesses.

Group 4 – betting, gaming and lotteries. Although betting duty has been abolished the revenue from those sources will continue to be exempt for VAT purposes.

Group 5 – finance. A wide range of financial transactions and generally charges for credit and interest on loans etc. are exempt from VAT.

Group 6 – education. Education, research and vocational training supplied by recognised bodies such as schools, colleges and universities will be exempt from VAT.

Group 7 – health and welfare. Generally speaking the services provided by health professionals are exempt from VAT, as are the fees charged to residents in nursing and rest homes.

Group 8 – burial and cremation. Services provided in connection with burial and cremation, such as undertakers' services are exempt from VAT.

Group 9 – trade unions and professional bodies. Membership subscriptions to trade unions and other professional bodies are exempt.

Group 10 - sport, sports competitions and physical education. The charge for entering competitions and playing members subscriptions are exempt from VAT. Consequently subscriptions of non-playing members of sports clubs, such as social members are subject to VAT at the standard rate.

Group 11 - works of art etc. The sale of works of art, antiques and collectors items, which are not subject to a state duty or inheritance tax, are exempt.

Group 12 - fund raising events by charities and other qualifying bodies. The entrance fees to events such as annual (or more frequent) fund raising events organised by charities for the benefit of the charity are exempt.

Group 13 - cultural services. Entrance fees to museums, art galleries, art exhibitions and zoos are exempt. The main criteria here is that the service must be both cultural and supplied by a public body.

Group 14 - supplies of goods where input tax cannot be recovered. This group prevents double taxation on goods where input tax cannot be recovered, such as the purchase of a car used for both business and private purposes. Any subsequent sale in these circumstances will be exempt.

Group 15 - investment gold. This exemption provides a route for the creation of a stock of investment gold to be traded within an exempt market.

E6.4 A word of warning

It should be appreciated that if a transaction falls specifically within one of the groups listed in Schedule 9 then it will be exempt. There is however, a lot of detail in these groups within the legislation, and you must read fully the legislation and the notes to the legislation to determine whether or not your particular transaction is actually exempt. If it does not fall within the zero-rated Schedule 8 or the exempt Schedule 9 then the transaction will normally be standard rated.

SUMMARY - SCHEDULE 9 VATA 1994 - EXEMPTIONS

There are fifteen groups of supplies which are listed in Schedule 9 of VATA 1994 as exempt supplies. Exempt supplies include:

- land
- insurance
- finance
- house and welfare
- burial and cremation
- fundraising events by charities

It is crucial that the legislation is looked at closely when determining if a supply is exempt or not as many exceptions to the general rule are outlined in the notes to each of the groups.

E7: VALUE OF THE SUPPLY

In this chapter we shall look at how you value a supply. The chapter will cover:
- special rules for valuing supplies in certain situations;
- prompt payment discount;
- the treatment of vouchers;
- mixed and composite supplies.

E7.1 Introduction

The chargeable value for VAT is outlined in **Section 19 of VATA 1994**. The gross value of a supply is the price paid for the item plus the VAT. As a basic rule, the gross value of the supply equals something known as the consideration. s.19 (2) Thus the gross value of the supply is the value of the consideration that is given for it. Therefore the starting point for VAT is what a trader receives for a supply rather than what the trader actually supplies.

Consideration = Price of the item + the VAT

Therefore the normal calculation is that **40/47ths** of the consideration is **the actual output** and **7/47ths is the VAT**. Trade prices and contracts usually state that the price is VAT exclusive so this would mean that the price being quoted is the value of the supply and that VAT will be added on top of this price at 17.5%. However, in practice, this procedure is actually the opposite of the VAT rules because the VAT rules say that where a contract says nothing about VAT then the starting point is the consideration so, in other words, if you are quoted a certain price and VAT is not mentioned, that price is VAT inclusive and hence is the consideration. This is what happens when people go shopping in supermarkets and shops, the price they see, which never mentions VAT, is the price including VAT.

Example 1

Outlined below are three items or services being sold; you have to calculate the tax to the nearest penny.

a) Marks & Spencer sell a ladies coat at £99.00
VAT due is £

b) A plumber charges £250 plus VAT to repair a leaky tap
VAT due is £

c) A book costs £12.00 in Waterstone's Book Shop
VAT due is £

E7.2 Special Rules

Schedule 6 of VATA 1994 contains special rules for valuing supplies in certain situations. Customs can direct that an **open market value is used for supplies between certain connected persons**. This will apply where the purchaser cannot recover all of the input tax being charged (for example, an exempt or a partially exempt trader) and there is some consideration in money being paid but it is less than the open market value. There must be some consideration for the open market value to be applied between connected persons. If there is no consideration, for example, it is some sort of barter transaction, then this rule cannot be applied. Sch 6 Para 1

If a mail order company sells goods using unregistered agents, then that **mail order company can be forced by Customs to account for VAT on the full retail price of those goods.** If this was not the case, then the margin of profit given to the agent would escape a charge of VAT and, the VAT being paid would not be 7/47ths of the actual amount paid by the customer. Sch 6 Para 2

If a trader takes goods for his own use then there is a **deemed supply** of goods. Sch 6 Para 6

This is also the situation which occurs at deregistration. The value of those goods is the replacement cost of those goods. If a business deregisters for VAT whilst still owning goods it could, post-deregistration sell those goods and it will not have to charge VAT on their sale. Hence the special rule that when a business deregisters for VAT there is a **deemed supply at the date of deregistration of all the assets that were held** on the date the business deregistered. The output tax is charged on replacement cost of the assets, replacement cost being the cost of an asset in exactly the same condition. Sch 64 Para (8) Sch 6 Para 6

The other thing to bear in mind is that this only applies to assets on which input tax is claimed originally. So if there is a car in the business when it de-registers, and there was **no initial input tax recovery** on that car, you **do not charge output tax under this rule**. There is also no charge but when you work out the output tax that is due it comes to **£1,000 or less.**

Accommodation in a hotel or similar establishment is generally a standard rated supply but if somebody was just renting property that would be an exempt supply. The special rule, which exists in this situation, states that if **someone stays in an hotel for more than four weeks** then, after that point in time, the hotel is permitted to start to **treat some of the amount they are charging that individual as if it was effectively rent**. Hence, this is exempt from VAT. Sch 6 Para 9

Any **other things** that are being paid for, i.e. cleaning the room, other services, the provision of restaurant facilities etc., of course are **still VATable**. These items must **not be less than 20%** of the total amount being charged (Schedule 6 Para 9).

If accommodation and food are provided to staff at a subsidised cost, or maybe no cost at all, then the supply is valued at the actual consideration paid by the staff. Sch 6 Para 10

If a supply is invoiced in a foreign currency, then that supply is valued at the appropriate exchange rate in force on the day the supply is made. Sch 6 Para 11

E7.3 Prompt Payment Discount

Some traders offer a prompt payment discount to encourage customers to pay on a timely basis. When valuing goods for VAT always **assume** that if a prompt payment discount is offered, the **discount will be taken up** by the customer. Thus the VAT is always charged on the discounted price whether or not the discount was actually taken. Sch 6 Para 4

Illustration 1

Let us say that a trader sells goods for £500 exclusive of VAT. This trader offers a 10% discount if payment is made within 7 days. The goods are £500 if you pay late, or £500 less a 10% discount, so £450, if you pay early.

Because a prompt payment discount is offered, whether it is taken or not, VAT is calculated on the discounted amount. Thus the VAT is calculated on the £450 value of goods, which at 17.5% gives £78.75 of VAT. This is added on to £500 worth of goods if the goods are paid for after 7 days, (£578.75) or it is added on to the £450 worth of goods if the goods are paid for within 7 days (£528.75).

Example 2

Joe sells goods for £1,000 exclusive of VAT to ABC Limited. Joe offers a 2% discount for payment within 10 days. Calculate the VAT due if ABC Limited pays 30 days later.

E7.4 Further points

The next item to consider is a gift. A gift is where goods are given over to one person but **no consideration** is given back for the goods. For VAT you must value the goods and you value them at their replacement cost. **VAT is then charged on a consideration which equals the replacement cost** of those goods. Sch 6 Para 6(1)

For a barter transaction, (i.e. I give you goods and in return you give me something back, but not money), we are effectively looking at non-monetary consideration. The legislation states that this **non-monetary consideration must be valued** and this value is what the output tax is calculated in respect of. s.19(3)

E7.5 Vouchers

No VAT is payable when a face value voucher is sold where the seller both issues the voucher and undertakes to redeem it for goods or services except to the extent that the consideration exceeds the face value. VAT only becomes due when the vouchers were redeemed for goods or services. Sch 6 Para 5

The person who issued the voucher accounts for VAT on the amount for which the voucher was initially sold regardless of redemption value.

However, this is not the treatment applied to sales of vouchers between intermediate suppliers. Intermediate suppliers are liable to VAT on the full amount for which they sell a voucher. The VAT is due when the voucher is sold. Adjustments are allowed when it is known that the voucher has been redeemed for zero-rated goods or services.

Illustration 2

The M&S store in Brighton sells a gift voucher for £10 to Peter. Peter then gives that voucher as a present to Bridget. Bridget goes into the M&S store in Norwich and buys a jumper for £15 and gives the shop £5 in cash plus the £10 voucher. How would VAT be accounted for on these transactions?

We will begin with what happens when the store sells the voucher for £10 to Peter. This is a voucher where M&S will both issue the voucher and undertake to redeem it for goods. The voucher can only be redeemed at M&S stores. Thus the store charges no VAT on that sale. If they had perhaps charged Peter an extra £1 for a fancy card Peter would have paid £11 - the extra £1 being for the card. VAT would thus have been included within the £11 as 7/47ths of £1 paid for the card. But the voucher itself has no VAT.

Bridget goes into the shop and she buys a jumper. She pays £15 as £5 in cash plus the £10 voucher. For the store the VAT on this is 7/47ths of the full amount of £15.

So effectively in a case like this the voucher is like cash and it is when the store has that final £15 sale that the full amount of VAT is accounted for.

Unfortunately though, voucher schemes have many, many variations which can cause considerable problems for VAT. A classic example is where you get a free bottle of wine with your meal or you can have two meals for the price of one. These are quite popular schemes but are not regarded by Customs as falling into the normal voucher rules even if the customer holds a piece of paper which outlines the offer stating that there was some sort of **face value** given - for example a free meal to a maximum of £20. For such vouchers there is VAT on the amount you pay (if anything) for the voucher when the voucher is acquired by the customer, rather than it being treated as VATable on the face value when the voucher is cashed in.

If the restaurant or the shop take vouchers then they do not account for VAT on any more than the discounted price paid by the customers who holds the voucher. Effectively the voucher is a discount on prices rather than valuable consideration.

E7.6 Mixed and Composite Supplies

There are two different types of supply. The **mixed** (or multiple) supply and the **composite** (or compound) supply.

A **mixed** supply is where there are **individual elements** within the supply that are **treated separately for VAT**. An example of this would be where a student goes on a course and has to purchase some books as part of the course. A course is standard rated and books are zero-rated. They are effectively treated as separate supplies, even though the student might purchase them together. The individual elements are being treated separately for VAT.

This is contrasted to the **composite** supply where there is just a **single supply** although it might be made up of lots of different things. A compound supply is a single supply with a **single VAT liability**. An example of this is a plane ticket to fly to New York. The traveller will also probably be provided with a meal on the flight. Air transport is zero-rated and catering is standard rated. However the traveller is buying a complete package and it is difficult to separate the two elements plus, of course, the meal is just a small insignificant piece of the overall flight to New York. In such a case, this composite supply would just be treated as a single zero-rated supply of a plane ticket to New York.

With a mixed supply, there is the need to perform some sort of apportionment s.19(4) to split the individual elements of the supply in order to calculate the VAT due. With a compound supply only a single rate of VAT applies to the whole supply.

The purchaser's perception of what they are buying will often determine whether a supply is a mixed or composite supply. When you buy a plane ticket, the in flight meal is ancillary to the plane ticket and therefore the supply is a composite supply. If the purchaser believes the two elements of a supply are of equal importance the supply will generally be mixed.

Illustration 3

A training company offers a lecture course and study materials for £2,000 plus VAT. The cost to the training company for the manuals is £100 and the cost of the course is £500.

The manuals are a zero-rated supply of printed matter and the course a standard -rated supply. This is a mixed supply.

Notice 700 published by HMRC suggests using either the cost of each element or the selling price of each element to apportion total consideration. In our illustration we shall use cost to apportion this mixed supply. The total cost of £500 and £100 is £600. Notice 70

100/600	X £2,000	= zero rated output =	£333
500/600	X £2,000	= standard rated output =	£1,667
			£2,000

VAT due:

£333 @ 0%	£nil
£1,667 @ 17.5%	291.73
Total VAT Due:	£291.73

E7.7 Mixed / Composite Supply Cases

There is an absolute wealth of case law on the topic of mixed and compound supplies.

Card Protection Plan Limited (1996) v CCE

Card Protection Plan Limited provided **services** relating to lost credit cards. It also offered some insurance benefits. Customs argued that the whole supply was standard rated with the insurance benefit being just incidental to the main service i.e. a compound supply. The taxpayer argued either that the whole amount should be exempt or that the charges should be apportioned as a mixed supply. This case bounced back and forth, going to the ECJ and finally the House of Lords and in 2001 the House of Lords decided that the principle feature of the supply being made was actually the insurance element. The card registration services were incidental to the main supply. Hence, the whole supply was a **compound supply** and it was an **exempt** supply.

CCE v United Biscuits (UK) Limited (t/a Simmers) (1992)

United Biscuits sold **biscuits in a tin**. The tin actually cost the company more than the biscuits themselves and was a nice tin that the customer would probably keep after he had eaten all the biscuits to store something else in.

Customs argued that there was a mixed supply here with zero-rated biscuits and a standard rated tin. However, United Biscuits argued, and the Court actually upheld, that there was just a **zero-rated compound supply** of biscuits in a tin.

British Sky Broadcasting Limited (1994)

Sky would sell television **subscription services** to customers. Once they had subscribed the customers would also receive a Sky magazine which contained a listing of all the programmes.

The company argued that there was a mixed supply here because there was the supply of a zero-rated publication, the magazine, and then there was the supply of the subscription for television services.

The Tribunal held that the magazine was just an incidental part of the main supply. The supply of the magazine was not an aim in itself but rather it just allowed subscribers to get more enjoyment from the main television services supply.

It was held that there was a compound supply here; a **single supply** of television services with the whole subscription being subject to **VAT at the standard rate**. The *British Sky Broadcasting* case contrasts quite nicely with the next case which is *The Automobile Association.*

CCE v The Automobile Association

In this case it was held that the **membership subscription** to the AA could be apportioned between the **standard rated breakdown service** and a **zero-rated handbook and magazine** so hence was an example of a **mixed** or multiple supply.

Sea Containers Services Limited and CCE

Sea Containers Services Limited owns the Orient Express which can be hired from the company for excursions. As part of an excursion to a place, meals will be provided. The company argued that there was a single supply of zero-rated transport i.e. a compound supply.

The High Court agreed with Customs that catering was an important part of the excursion for the customers. They were probably really looking forward to a very nice meal as well as the actual journey to the place of interest and thus it was held that there was a **mixed** supply of **zero-rated transport** and **standard rated catering**.

Leightons Ltd; Eye-Tech Opticians

In 2001, Customs announced that many supplies on the compound/multiple borderline should be reviewed in the light of the Card Protection Plan decision, and gave a list of some which they considered should be regarded differently from how they had been treated before.

Most controversial among these was the assertion that opticians should go back to the position before the Leightons Ltd decision in the High Court in 1995, and regard the sale of spectacles as a single compound taxable supply of goods, rather than a mixed supply of goods and exempt dispensing services. Customs eventually lost this argument comprehensively in the Tribunal.

Customs argued that Card Protection Plan required a two-stage approach:

- ascertain the essential features of the transaction;
- identify if any of the supplies was incidental to any of the others.

In this case, according to Customs, the purchase of spectacles was the essential feature; the dispensing services could not be an aim in themselves for the purchaser, but were merely a means of better enjoying the principal supply. Any attempt to split the supplies would, in Customs' view, be artificial.

The taxpayer argued that both elements of the supply were significant to the purchaser. It was possible to buy spectacles without dispensing ("Ready Spex" can be purchased at newsagents); the purchaser who went to an optician did so because the dispensing was significant. It was also, in some cases, possible to buy dispensing services without buying the spectacles (in the case of safety spectacles).

The Tribunal found for the appellants. This is a significant set-back for Customs' views on mixed and compound supplies, because they had been insistent that the situation had changed following CPP. In fact, nothing changed.

As you can see from this very small selection of cases the area of mixed or compound supplies provides lots of controversy in the world of VAT!

Example 3

For each of these supplies decide whether there is a mixed / multiple supply or a compound / composite supply.

		Mixed Supply	Compound Supply
a)	A box of Earl Grey Tea comes with a china teapot as a special Christmas promotion	☐	☐
b)	A language school sells courses and books for a total fee of £500.	☐	☐
c)	Ticket to fly to Rome includes a standard lunch	☐	☐

Answer 1

a) £14.74
The first item is for sale in Marks & Spencer and the price shown will be the consideration, i.e. the VAT inclusive price. Thus 7/47 of £99 gives us £14.74.

b) £43.75
The second item is a plumber charging £250 plus VAT for services, so the price being shown is not the consideration because the VAT is not included and has to be added on top to get to consideration. To work out the VAT we charge 17.5% of £250 and get £43.75.

c) Nil
The third item is a book being sold for £12. It is a shop, just like the Marks & Spencer example, so the price being shown is the consideration. Normally we would take 7/47 for the VAT except books are zero-rated supplies so it is actually 0% VAT added on to this price paid to give us both a price paid and a consideration of £12 and zero VAT.

Answer 2

The correct answer calculates VAT on the discounted amount even though the discount was not taken because the company paid late. £1,000 less 2% discount is £980, which at 17.5%, gives us £171.50 of VAT. The company will pay £1,000 plus £171.50 of VAT (i.e. £1,171.50).

Answer 3

A box of Earl Grey tea is the main supply here. The china teapot, which probably costs a lot more than the tea, is just a promotional incidental supply. This is very similar to the case with the biscuit tin in United Biscuits Limited. This is a single supply, a compound / composite supply, of Earl Grey tea which will be zero-rated.

A language school selling a course and books will probably be making a mixed / multiple supply because you will be able to apportion VAT between the two elements provided, i.e. the course and the books.

If you buy a ticket to fly somewhere and they provide a meal, the meal is generally just an incidental part of the main supply. So this would be a zero-rated single compound supply of air transport services, with the standard rated catering meal being incidental the main supply, and hence ignored.

SUMMARY - VALUE OF THE SUPPLY

VAT is 7/47ths of the consideration.

Consideration is valued from the point of view of the person receiving the consideration.

If there was a prompt payment discount offered always deduct it when calculating VAT even if the discount is not actually taken up by the customer.

A gift needs to have a value for consideration in order to work out VAT and we would use replacement value in such a case.

If we are looking at a barter transaction then the value of consideration is the value of the non-monetary consideration we are receiving.

A mixed/multiple supply is a supply that you can apportion into its individual elements and then charge VAT upon each element accordingly.

A composite/compound supply is really just a single supply with a single VAT liability. If there are separate elements then there must be a main supply with the other element or elements just being incidental to that main supply.

E8: DEEMED SUPPLIES AND SELF-SUPPLIES

This chapter looks at deemed supplies and self-supplies. By the end of the chapter you should be able to:

- account for VAT on deemed and self-supplies;
- be aware of how to treat a gift of goods;
- understand the treatment where there is private use of assets or motor fuel is provided for private use;
- outline the treatment of goods held on de-registration of a business;
- understand the treatment of stationery and construction services provided for own use by a business;
- outline the VAT treatment of motor cars used in a business.

E8.1 Introduction

Deemed supplies and self-supplies are in existence basically as an anti-avoidance strategy. This anti-avoidance legislation requires a trader to **account for output tax even though there is no regular supply**; in other words, even though there is no supply for consideration to a third party. The anti-avoidance legislation effectively covers two types of avoidance. The first type is where a taxable business buys something, recovers the input tax, and then puts those items to a non-business use. If those items had been bought for a non-business use in the first place, input tax would not have been recoverable. This is the **deemed supply legislation**.

The second scenario is to do with partially exempt and exempt businesses, so businesses that make exempt supplies and cannot recover input tax in full. It is to prevent such businesses from getting a full input tax recovery that they would not normally achieve. This is the **self-supply legislation**.

E8.2 Deemed supplies

Examples of deemed supplies include **goods and services bought for business purposes but then supplied free for private consumption**. The input tax originally claimed on the purchase is clawed back using an output tax charge. Sch 4 Para 5

Where petrol or diesel for motor cars is purchased by a business but then supplied to the employee of that business at a price that is below cost there is a deemed supply and output tax is charged on the supply using a fixed standard scale. We will look at this in more detail later. s.56

Another example is where a business is registered for VAT but is now going to deregister. Any goods held by the business on deregistration are treated as deemed supplies if those goods had input tax recovered on their purchase. Sch 4 Para 8

E8.3 Self-supplies

Self-supplies operate in a very similar way to deemed supplies. The self-supply legislation basically ensures that there is no VAT saving in a situation where input tax should have been irrecoverable.

If **construction services** are carried out in-house, this is another example of a self-supply with **output tax charged on open market value**. SI 1989/472

Another scenario where we have a self-supply is when cars are purchased for 100% business use, but used privately. Let us say a car dealer buys brand new cars which he plans to sell to the public, but later puts one of those cars to private use. One of those **cars** is thus taken out of stock and **used by an employee**. This would be a self-supply and there is an **output tax charge on the cost of the car**. SI 1992/3122 Art 5

E8.4 How to account for deemed/self-supplies

A business that makes a deemed or a self-supply will have to account for output tax on the supply, so there will be output tax to put in box 1 of the VAT Return. This amount will have to be paid to Customs when the VAT Return is submitted.

This **self-supply or deemed supply counts towards the registration limit** when looking at whether a business should register for VAT or not.

In addition to accounting for output tax, input tax has to be accounted for. This input tax can only be recovered to the extent that the item is to be used for making taxable supplies.

The deemed and self-supply rules apply to all businesses, whether taxable or exempt. It is quite possible to have a fully taxable business provide some in-house construction services. The impact of this would be two entries, equal and opposite, on the VAT return - output tax in the output tax box equalling the amount of input tax in the input tax box. Overall there is a nil impact on the business. Having said that, the business cannot omit the entries from the VAT return because otherwise it will have made an incorrect VAT return and of course could open the business up to misdeclaration penalties.

E8.5 Gift of goods

Input tax is clawed back on goods that are gifted for private use by making an output tax charge on the replacement cost of such goods. The legislation says that output tax should be charged where goods forming part of the assets of a business are transferred or disposed of by or under the directions of the person carrying on the business so as no longer to form part of those assets whether or not for a consideration. Sch 4 Para 5

The motive for making the gift is actually irrelevant and so this output tax charge applies in exactly the same way to gifts given to the proprietor for his own use as to a promotional gift, and to a gift to an employee - all are treated in exactly the same way.

However, **two types of gift are exempt** from this legislation. The first exemption is where there is a gift of goods made in the course or furtherance of the business where the **cost to the donor is not more than £50.** The exemption applies to one-off gifts and the cost to the donor could also include the cost of producing the goods if they are produced internally.

No output tax will be due on a series of gifts provided the total cost of gifts made to the same person does not exceed £50 in any 12 month period. If the £50 is exceeded VAT will be due on all the gifts made in the previous 12 months. Those gifts are then disregarded for the purpose of any future application of the rules.

The other situation where the rules do not apply is where there is a **gift to any person of a sample of any goods.** This applies only to the first gift where a succession of identical samples is given to the same person. There is no monetary value on these sample gifts either.

So to summarise, with a gift of goods which cost £50 or less, then one needs to look at what the motive for the gift was. If the motive was a business purpose then the gift is ignored and does not trigger an output tax charge and any input tax reclaimed by the business is allowed. If the gift of goods costs over £50 (can be cumulative) then input tax will effectively be clawed back as an output tax charge unless it is the gift of a business sample.

E8.6 Private use of business assets

Consider the scenario of instead giving someone an asset for their private use, the asset was just made available for them to use privately but the ownership remained with the VAT registered business. The rules on gifts of goods do not apply where an asset is only made available for private use without charge but remains part of the assets of the business. A special piece of the legislation therefore exists for a case where a business asset is used **privately**. It ensures that there is an output tax charge in every VAT quarter in which private use takes place with that output tax charge reflecting the cost of providing that asset for private use. Sch 4 Para 5(4)

This rule does not apply if input tax recovery did not occur on the acquisition of the goods.

Thus the **Lennartz** rule allows purchasers of goods which are to be used both for business and private or non business purposes to recover the VAT in full on the purchase of the item and then charge output tax on the market value of the non business and private use as it arises. For buildings, traders buying a dual purpose building from new will obtain full VAT recovery, and subsequent use of the asset over a period of years will produce only a small amount of output tax in relation to the purchase; the building may also be sold as exempt and the original over-recovery never be fully clawed back. Customs are therefore to introduce a statutory over ride to the Lennartz principle in the case of land and buildings so that all private or non business use is recognised in an apportionment of the input tax at the point of purchase.

If a car is provided for the private use of an employee, no supply actually arises whether or not the employee makes an actual payment for the private use. This seems a very odd rule but this rule has come about because some or all of the input tax on the car has been blocked in the employer's hands. However, do take care with fuel, which we are going to look at later in the chapter.

If a mobile phone is provided there are some very complex rules that go with this which are outlined in Business Brief **14/99**. Effectively a business can deduct all the input tax on the initial provision of the mobile phone providing the payments contain no element for calls which might be used for private purposes and obviously as long as there is some business use. If the business prohibits private use of the phone then all the input tax will be deductible. If the business charges employees for private calls made then again all input tax is deductible but the business must account for output tax on the charges. If the business allows employees to make private calls without charge, then the business has got to apportion the input tax on the call charges and only claim the business proportion.

Illustration 1

ABC Limited own a horse used for business purposes 40 days per quarter and for private purposes by the company employees 30 days per quarter.

Costs associated with keeping the horse are:

Stable fees per annum	£5,000
Vets bills, livery fees etc per annum	£1,000
Use of trekking facilities in quarter:	
- business days	£400
- private days	£300

We have to work out the private cost of keeping the horse. That will be our deemed supply for one quarter.

Deemed supply for one quarter:	£
Stable fees	
£5,000 x ¼ x 30/70	536.00
Vet etc fees	
£1,000 x ¼ x 30/70	107.00
Trekking fees – private days	300.00
Cost of private use	943.00
VAT = 17.5% x £943.00	£165.03

E8.7 Motor fuel provided for private use

If a business buys petrol or diesel and allows private use of it by an employee or the owner of the business, the partner or sole trader, then effectively the business has three choices as to what it will do from a VAT point of view. The first choice is that it could **claim all input tax** incurred on all fuel purchased and then, using the **scale charges** set by Customs, calculate the appropriate output tax. The fuel scale rates are dependent on engine size and whether the fuel is petrol or diesel. The scale rates are VAT inclusive so you multiply them by 7 over 47 to find the output tax due.

s.56

s.57

The second choice is to **claim absolutely no input tax** on all fuel purchased even the fuel purchased for business use but instead to not account for output tax. This is probably the simplest option.

VAT Notice 748
ESC 3.1

The final choice is for a business to **keep very detailed mileage records** so that they can prove that the fuel that they have bought is only used for business purposes and effectively the business therefore does not pay anything towards the cost of fuel used for private purposes. In such a case input tax can be recovered and there is no output tax charge.

Example 1

Jonas Limited purchases petrol in the quarter ended 30 September for £302.50. The petrol was for Jonas's car in which he travels 1,000 business miles and 1,000 private miles.

The appropriate quarterly fuel scale charge is, say, £500.

What is the net VAT payable or (recoverable) for the business for this quarter if it wishes to recover the input tax on the fuel?

E8.8 Goods held on deregistration

When a business deregisters for VAT this will mean that the assets contained in the business, when eventually sold, will not have VAT charged on their sale. Therefore, Customs and Excise can see a potential for losing a VAT charge. Therefore we have a special rule which says that when a business deregisters for VAT there is a deemed supply at the date of deregistration on all the assets that were held on the date the business deregistered. The output tax is charged on replacement cost of the assets. Replacement cost is the cost of an asset in exactly the same condition. This rule only applies to assets on which input tax was claimed originally. For example if there is a car in the business when it deregisters, and there was no initial input tax recovery on that car, output tax is not charged.

Sch 6 Para 6

There is also **no charge** if the **output tax** that is due comes to **£1,000 or less.**

E8.9 Construction services

The self supply of construction services rule applies to prevent exempt or partially exempt businesses from employing their own people to carry out construction services rather than using a third party contractor to carry out the construction services for them who, of course, will charge them VAT, which they probably could not recover in full.

SI 1989/472

The self-supply rule applies where there is a **construction of a building or an extension to an existing building** – the extension **increasing floor space by at least 10%.**

The value of the construction services must be **over £100,000 in a year** for this self-supply rule to apply.

The self-supply rule basically calculates output tax on the open market value of the construction services and so this output tax has to be accounted for by the business on the VAT Return.

By the same token, this output tax forms input tax which the business can recover in the normal way so, if it uses the building to make taxable supplies in any way, then that proportion of input tax can be recovered. However, there is also some other input tax that might have been incurred by the business and this is input tax incurred in actually carrying out the work – perhaps purchasing materials that sort of thing - can be deducted in full.

E8.10 Motor cars

The self-supply charge on motor cars applies where a car dealer purchases a car from a manufacturer to put into stock. Because the car is part of his stock, he is allowed to recover input tax in full on that car. Then the car dealer takes the car out of stock for private use. Normally the purchase of a car for private use is subject to a blocking order on the input VAT which basically means input VAT on a motor car cannot be recovered. The self supply legislation **aims to stop a car dealer being able to get a car into private use and yet still recover input tax** by using this torturous route. SI 1992/3122 Art 5

The self-supply charge claws back the VAT that was recovered when the motor car was purchased as stock. It is calculated on the cost of the car and not on the selling price of the car.

VAT on the purchase of demonstrator cars provided by motor dealers and manufacturers is excluded from the blocking order which generally prevents VAT recovery on the purchase of motor cars. Instead, VAT is due on the private use of such cars. Certain businesses have sought to minimise the VAT due on private usage by charging employees a nominal sum for the use of the car.

Following FA2004, from a date to be announced, the Commissioners will be able to direct that VAT is to be accounted for on the open market value of demonstrator cars supplied to employees. This measure requires a derogation from European Community legislation; such a derogation has been applied for.

There are some other self-supply rules in the VAT legislation but this chapter has covered the main ones that you are likely to see in practice. Most self-supply rules deal with tax avoidance schemes that, because there now is a self-supply rule, no-one bothers to try any more!

Example 2

Draw a line between the supply and the correct title box.

Goods and services bought for business use and supplied free for private use	Cars bought for business use and transferred to private use	Motor fuel purchased by business for private use
In-house construction services	Goods held on deregistration	

DEEMED SUPPLY	SELF-SUPPLY

Answer 1

The business bears the cost of private fuel and so the choice it has made is to recover input tax in full but then to charge output tax using the scale charge. The business mileage actually travelled by the car is irrelevant except that we need to know that it does actually do some private mileage. We take our scale charge of £500 which is VAT inclusive, multiply it by 7 over 47 to get our output tax. We then take the cost of the petrol £302.50, which again is VAT inclusive, multiply it by 7 over 47 to get our input tax and this leaves us with net VAT payable of £29.42 by the company.

The business bears the cost of private fuel.

	£
Output tax	
£500 x 7/47	74.47
Input tax	
£302.50 x 7/47	(45.05)
Net VAT payable	29.42

In this example Jonas Limited should be advised to claim no input tax on fuel. If this were the case, the fuel scale charge need not be accounted for and the business would save £29.42 this quarter.

Answer 2

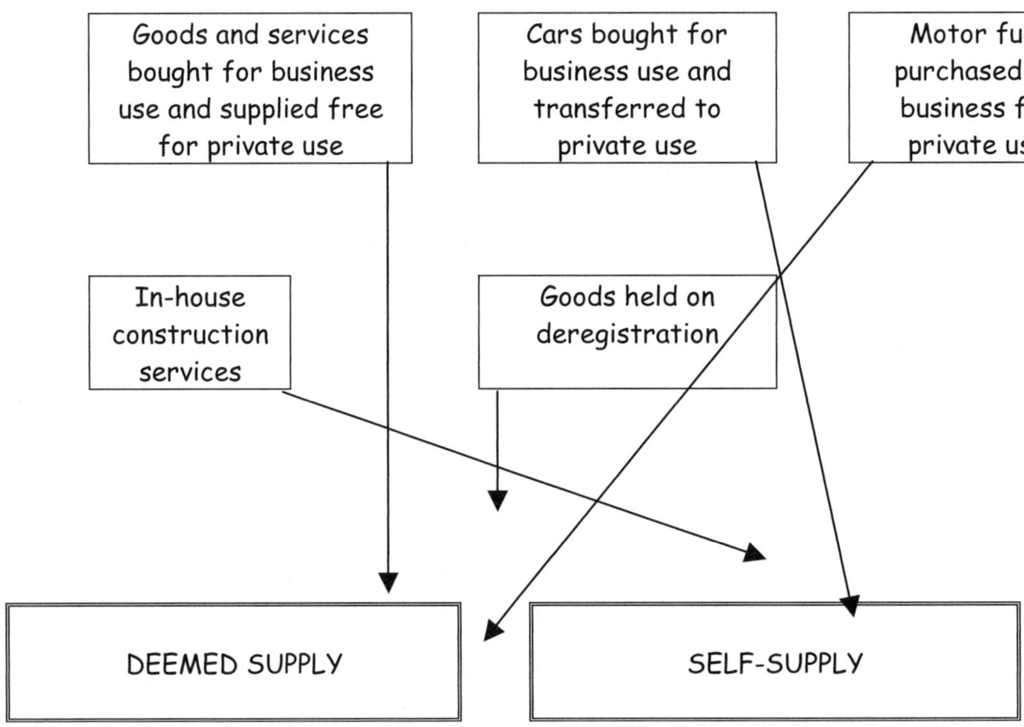

SUMMARY - DEEMED SUPPLIES AND SELF-SUPPLIES

This chapter has looked at two types of supply - deemed supplies and self supplies. The rules that apply to both of these supplies are very similar and they are mainly to prevent a loss of VAT and a distortion of competition.

However, it is important to categorise the supplies separately because a self supply is the sort of supply where we charge VAT on an item to ourselves. Thus there is an output tax and an equal and opposite input tax charge on a self supply.

The treatment of a deemed supply is not the same as a self supply.

On a gift of goods input tax is clawed back on those goods where they are gifted for private use. The way to do this is to make an output tax charge on the replacement cost of such goods.

Where a business asset is used privately then there is an output tax charge in every VAT quarter in which private use takes place. The output tax charge reflects the cost of providing the asset for private use.

Where a business purchases fuel for private use by an employee or the owner of a business then where input tax is recovered on that purchase, output tax must be accounted for using the scale charges set by Customs.

Any assets held by a business when it de-registers for VAT must have output tax accounted for based on their replacement cost. However, if the output tax due comes to £1,000 or less Customs waive their requirement to pay over the output tax.

The self supply rule applies where construction services are provided by an exempt or partially exempt business to itself.

A self supply charge occurs where motor cars are taken out of stock for use by an employee or owner of a business - so this applies to car dealers.

E9: TIME OF SUPPLY

In this chapter we will have a look at the following:

- how the time of a supply is calculated;
- the situations when a basic time of supply (tax point) can be overridden and changed to a different date;
- the time of supply where deposits are paid for a supply;
- special rules which fix tax points for unusual situations that the trader may incur.

E9.1 Introduction

The time of supply is a very important piece of the VAT legislation because the time of supply basically gives you a date on which an item is purchased or an item is sold. That date is crucial because it will determine which VAT Return you account for the output tax on a sale or you recover the input tax on a purchase. s.1(2) The date is also crucial in case there was a change in the rate of VAT because the date will determine which rate of VAT to charge – the old or the new rate. It is also crucial if there was a change in the law because the date will fix when the supply occurs and whether it happens under the old law or the new law. The time of supply is very important especially when preparing your VAT Return since it determines which items to put on a particular VAT Return. If a business puts a transaction in the wrong VAT Return the business opens itself up to penalties.

The main rule is that there is a **basic tax point** for all goods and all services supplied.

E9.2 Basic tax point

For goods the basic tax point is the date the **goods are removed** from the supplier to the purchaser so, for example, if a customer goes into a shop and purchases a sandwich, he is removing the sandwich from the supplier on the date that he buys that sandwich. If, as another example, he orders some widgets – it is the date those widgets leave the factory where they are being manufactured in order to come to the customer that determines the basic tax point – the date of supply. s.6(2)

For services, the date of supply is **when the services are performed**. For 'performed' think of 'completed'. If a plumber comes to your house to install central heating, then it is the date he finishes the installation – the date the services are really performed and finished – that is the basic tax point. s.6(3)

E9.3 Basic tax point overridden

The basic tax point can actually be overridden by a different date in two situations. One situation actually makes the actual tax point we use earlier than the basic tax point date. This will occur where there is a **receipt of a payment** on a date before the basic tax point date or when the **tax invoice is issued** on a date before the basic tax point date. In these cases, the **earlier date becomes the actual tax point date** that we will use. s.6(4)

The second scenario gives us a later tax point date than our basic tax point. The later tax point will only apply if we have not had an earlier tax point imposed on us. So our starting point is our basic tax point date. If a **tax invoice is issued in the 14 day period after the basic tax point date** the tax invoice issue date, i.e. the later date, becomes the actual tax point that we will use. The trader can waive this 14 day rule if he does not want to have this later date as his tax point. He can chose to stick with the basic tax point date. Customs have the power to extend the 14 day period and, in many cases, they will extend it up to 30 days. A 30 day extension would help businesses that only have one invoice run - usually at the end of every month. This allows those businesses to use the invoice date as their actual tax point for all supplies made in that month. s.6(5)

Illustration 1

Anne orders a wedding dress from Dresses Limited on 1 November 2005. The company makes the dress in November and Anne collects the dress on 1 December 2005. The company issues an invoice on 9 December 2005, which Anne pays on 20 December 2005.

Basic tax point	-	1.12.2005
Earlier tax point	-	Not applicable
Later tax point	-	9.12.2005
Actual tax point used	=	9.12.2005

The basic tax point is the date that the goods, the wedding dress, is removed from the supplier to the purchaser - so this will be the date that Ann collects the dress and hence will be 1 December 2005. If there was a payment made before this date or the tax invoice was issued before this date then an earlier tax point would apply. That is not what happens in this example.

If the tax invoice is issued within 14 days of the basic tax point, then the later date becomes the actual tax point we use. The invoice was issued on 9 December 2005 - this is within 14 days of our basic tax point on 1 December 2005 hence the later tax point is the actual tax point that we will use for this supply, unless the company waives the right to use the later date which is not very often the case in practice.

Example 1

Same as Illustration 1 except Anne orders the dress on 1.11.2005, pays for the dress on 1.12.2005, collects the dress 5.12.2005 and the invoice is issued on 9.12.2005.

Which of the following is the tax point for the supply?

a) 1.11.2005

b) 1.12.2005

c) 5.12.2005

d) 9.12.2005

E9.4 Deposits

It is possible to have more than one tax point for the same supply - an example of this would be where a deposit is paid upfront and then, when the goods are delivered at a later date, the balance is paid.

Illustration 2

Let us have a look at how a deposit would affect the example with Anne. Anne orders a dress on 1 November and pays her £500 deposit when she orders the dress on 1 November. She then collects the dress on 1 December. The company then invoices Anne for the balance due on 9 December and Anne pays the balance on 20 December.

Starting with the deposit. The basic tax point for this supply is the date that the dress is collected on 1 December 2005. The deposit was paid earlier than the basic tax point - it was paid on 1 November and the normal tax point rules would say that the earlier date is the date used as the tax point.

Thus 1 November becomes the actual tax point for the deposit because it was earlier than the basic tax point for the supply.

When considering the balance of the payment, once again the basic tax point is the date the dress is collected on 1 December. The company then issue an invoice for the balance that is due on 9 December. This is within 14 days of the basic tax point for that balance and hence the later date is the tax point for the balance. So 9 December is the tax point for the balance.

There are two tax points for this supply - 1 November is the tax point for the deposit, 9 December is the tax point for the balance.

Anne:

Orders dress	1.11.2005		
Pays £500 deposit	1.11.2005	◄────	Tax point for deposit
Collects dress	1.12.2005	◄────	Basic tax point
Invoice for balance	9.12.2005	◄────	Tax point for balance
Pays balance	20.12.2005		

E9.5 Special rules

It is only possible to issue a tax invoice showing VAT payable for a standard rated taxable supply by a registered person. When you are looking at the **tax point of an exempt supply or a zero-rated supply, or a supply by an unregistered person** (which could be important for registration liability calculations), then one does **not consider the issue of a tax invoice**. Thus when looking at the tax point rules, one only looks at payment or basic tax points for supplies that are not standard rated supplies.

Sometimes with services the service can be supplied continuously and never actually finish or, as the legislation puts it 'performed'. An example of this would be rent - a business is constantly being provided with the property for SI 1995/
which it pays rent. Another example is consultancy work, which can constantly be 2518
on going but never really completed. For a **continuous supply of services** one reg 90
does not consider basic tax point because there is not one - the service is never performed so it is never completed. With a continuous supply of services there is only payment and invoice - so the earlier of the two will determine the tax point.

Thus supplies which are subject to the continuous supply rule generate a tax SI 1997/
point only by the issue of a tax invoice, or payment passing. When these supplies 2887
are between connected parties, for example group companies, the charges are reg 2
frequently passed between companies for accounting purposes, but no invoices are issued. In such a case, output tax is not declared nor is input tax recoverable.

However, where the input tax would not be recoverable, for example because the recipient is wholly or partially exempt, this causes a loss of revenue to Customs. A new rule introduced by FA2003 imposes a periodic tax point on continuous supplies between connected parties, generally leading to an annual VAT output tax charge. The type of supplies affected by this new rule are those for management charges, telephone, electricity, piped gas and water and leasing of property and equipment.

When supplies are deemed to be made under the reverse charge rules, then the tax point is only determined by payment. In other words, it is only determined by the date the services are paid for. When the services are actually performed, or when an invoice is issued is irrelevant under the **reverse charge** rules. SI 1995/ 2518 reg 82

Example 2

Karen orders a toy over the telephone from a mail order supplier quoting her debit card number on 12 November 2005. On 14 November 2005 the supplier sends the toy to Karen. On 16 November 2005 an invoice is issued showing full payment has been made:

Which of the following is the tax point for the supply?

a) 12.11.2005

b) 14.11.2005

c) 16.11.2005

d) 1.12.2005

Answer 1

The correct answer is B

The basic tax point is the date the dress was collected which is 5 December.

However if a payment was made before this basic tax point or if an invoice was issued before this tax point, then we use the earlier date.

In this example a payment was made on 1 December and so that date becomes the actual tax point that we would use for this supply.

Answer 2

The correct answer is A

The basic tax point is the date the goods were supplied or left the premises of the supplier; so that would be 14 November.

Because a payment was made earlier than this basic tax point date, on 12 November 2005, we use the earlier date as the tax point date for these supplies. The actual tax point used is therefore 12 November 2005.

SUMMARY - TIME OF SUPPLY

The basic tax point for goods is the date the goods are removed from the supplier. The basic tax point for services is the date the service is performed.

The basic tax point is overridden in two situations. If there is receipt of a payment or a tax invoice is issued on a date before the basic tax point date then the earlier date becomes the actual tax point date used.

If an earlier tax point does not apply and an invoice is issued within 14 days after the basic tax point then the invoice issue date becomes the tax point date used ,i.e. the later date is the tax point used by the business.

When considering deposits, the deposit and the balance paid are considered separately; each will have their own tax points calculated in the normal way which more often or not are completely different dates from each other.

If services are supplied continuously, then the tax point becomes the date money is paid or an invoice is issued. A special rule exists for continuous supplies between connected parties.

Supplies deemed to be made under the reverse charge rules have a tax point determined by the date of payment.

E10a: INPUT TAX: WHEN TO RECOVER

In this chapter we will look at when to recover input tax including:

- the numerous conditions which must be satisfied before input tax can be reclaimed by a business;
- how we determine a direct and immediate link with a taxable transaction;
- the situations when input tax recovery is not available.

E10a.1 Introduction

As a general rule, when input VAT is incurred by a taxable person it is available for credit (which basically means it is included as input VAT on the VAT Return) for the period in which it arises. It is deducted from output tax and hence recovered from Customs. If the input tax on a VAT Return exceeds the output tax, then Customs actually make a repayment of the net amount. This chapter is going to look at the **conditions** which have to be met before input tax is available for credit.

s.24 & s.26
SI 1995/2518
Reg 29

The conditions are numerous and can be summarised as follows:

- A **supply of goods or services** is being made;
- This supply must be **made to the taxable person** and the trader is a taxable person at the time the supply was made;
- The supply of goods or services must have been made for a **business purpose;**
- The claimant must hold the required **evidence** of their purchase;
- Input tax on the supply must have been **correctly charged**; and
- The goods or services being supplied must have a **direct and immediate link** with a taxable transaction.

E10a.2 No Input VAT recovery

The most common reason why input tax cannot be recovered by a business is because the **proper evidence**, which in most cases is a valid VAT invoice, is **not held** by the business.

If the **supply was made to somebody else**, for example, if a businessman pays someone else's bill, then input tax cannot be recovered – a trader can only recover his own input tax not someone else's.

Maybe the supplier did not charge VAT at the correct rate, or should not have charged VAT in the first place – so the **tax** being shown as charged was **not charged correctly**. That input tax cannot be recovered.

Input tax cannot be recovered **if the supply did not go ahead**. Let us say that the trader paid a deposit for "something" but that "something" was never actually made and delivered. There might be a VAT invoice showing what the trader paid but because the supply never took place the trader has not paid valid input tax and cannot recover that input tax from Customs. His only recourse is to try and get it back from the supplier whom he paid in the first place.

Items purchased for private use result in irrecoverable input tax on that item. Only business use is allowed.

In addition to the above there is irrecoverable input tax on items that are blocked such as **motor cars** and **business entertaining** - input tax can never be recovered on these items even if the trader meets all the conditions outlined in the chapter. Thus even if a business holds the proper evidence and has used the item for business purposes etc- it still cannot recover input tax as it is specifically blocked. SI 1992/3222

Finally, one can only recover input tax if the thing purchased (i.e. the input) is used in making a taxable supply. If a business purchases an input which is used **to make an exempt supply, input tax** incurred on its purchase is **irrecoverable**.

SUMMARY - INPUT TAX: WHEN TO RECOVER

There are numerous conditions which have to be satisfied before input tax is available for credit.

Firstly a supply of goods or services must have actually taken place.

Secondly that supply must have been made to a taxable person. That taxable person must have been a taxable person at the time of the supply. There are however some exceptions to this rule including pre-registration input tax and pre-incorporation input tax.

The goods and services must be used for a business purposes if input tax credit is to be allowed.

The claimant must hold the required evidence that input tax has been incurred. The most common evidence a business will hold is a VAT invoice provided by the supplier of the goods or services.

Credit for input tax is restricted to the amount properly chargeable on a supply. If VAT was incorrectly charged on the supply then that VAT cannot be recovered as input tax.

The final condition required to be satisfied is that the goods or the services purchased must have a direct and immediate link with a taxable transaction.

E10b: PARTIAL EXEMPTION

In this chapter you will look at:
partial exemption, where a business makes both taxable and exempt supplies;
determining the amount of input tax that the business can recover;
- the apportionment of input VAT;
- the de minimis input VAT limits;
- the annual adjustment required by partially exempt businesses;
- the special methods of apportionment available to businesses.

E10b.1 Introduction

A partially exempt business is simply a business which supplies taxable and exempt sales, i.e. part of its business is taxable and part of it is exempt. This could be a firm of business advisers. Part of what they do is consultancy services and they may also provide insurance services. The consultancy services will be taxable, the insurance services exempt. The issue with partially exempt businesses is how much input tax they can reclaim.

Illustration 1

ABC Limited is partially exempt, i.e. some of the company's turnover is standard rated and some is exempt.

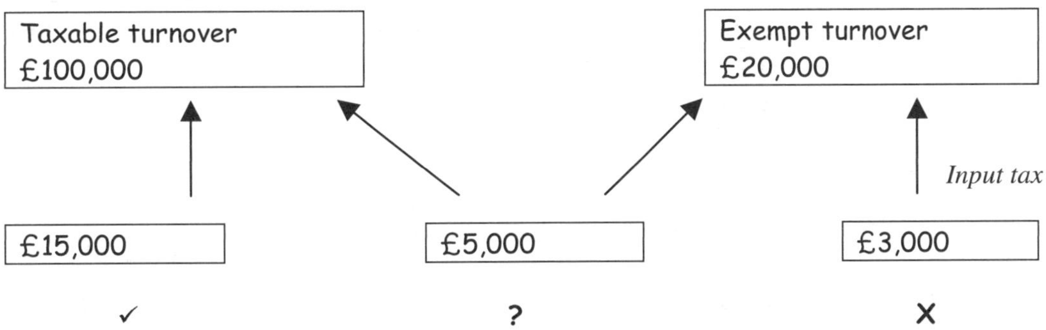

The input tax relating to the taxable business of £15,000 is fully recoverable. £3,000 of input tax relating to the exempt business would not be recoverable. This could be input tax incurred on telephone bills, accountancy fees, legal fees, and repairs to that part of the property for example. There is also input tax which relates to both the taxable and exempt business. This £5,000 is effectively attributable to both. The business will need to apportion the £5,000 between the taxable and exempt supplies to determine recoverability of the £5,000.

To summarise, input tax is recoverable to the extent that it relates to taxable supplies or sales. The £15,000 is recoverable, the £3,000 is not recoverable, the £5,000, which relates to both, is partly recoverable. This £5,000 is often referred to as residual or indirect or non-attributable or overhead input tax. All of these descriptions are simply saying it is not directly attributable to one particular part of the business and consequently an apportionment must be made.

E10b.2 Apportionment

The standard method of apportionment is as follows.

SI 1995/2518 Reg 101 (2

$$\frac{\text{Taxable supplies (excluding VAT)}}{\text{Total supplies (excluding VAT)}}$$

This fraction is then **expressed as a percentage.** For certain businesses this fraction is **rounded up** to the next whole number. If it came out to 83.0001 it would become 84%. The benefit of rounding up in the standard method will only be available to businesses whose residual input tax is less than £400,000 a month. This new rule was introduced with effect from 1 April 2005. Prior to this date rounding was available to all businesses regardless of size. SI 1995/2518 Reg 101 (4

This percentage is applied to the residual input tax, i.e. to the £5,000 in the previous illustration. SI 1995/2518 Reg 101 (3

Please note at this stage that when calculating this fraction a business should always **exclude supplies of land, capital goods or self-supplies**. Effectively the fraction should reflect the normal trading activity. Anything unusual should be excluded, since this would distort the fraction.

Illustration 2

Taxable turnover £100,000		Exempt turnover £20,000
Input tax £15,000 Taxable supplies	£5,000 Residual	£3,000 Exempt supplies
		Round up from 83.33%

$$\frac{100{,}000}{100{,}000 + 20{,}000} \times 100 = 84\%$$

Applying the formula to the illustration, £100,000 over £120,000 x 100 which equals 84%. 84% has been rounded up from 83.33%.

Consequently 84% of the £5,000 relates to the taxable business or taxable sales and 16% relates to the exempt business. This equates to £4,200 on the taxable side and £800 on the exempt side. The input tax that relates to the taxable supplies, (£4,200) is recoverable, and the input tax relating to the exempt business is irrecoverable.

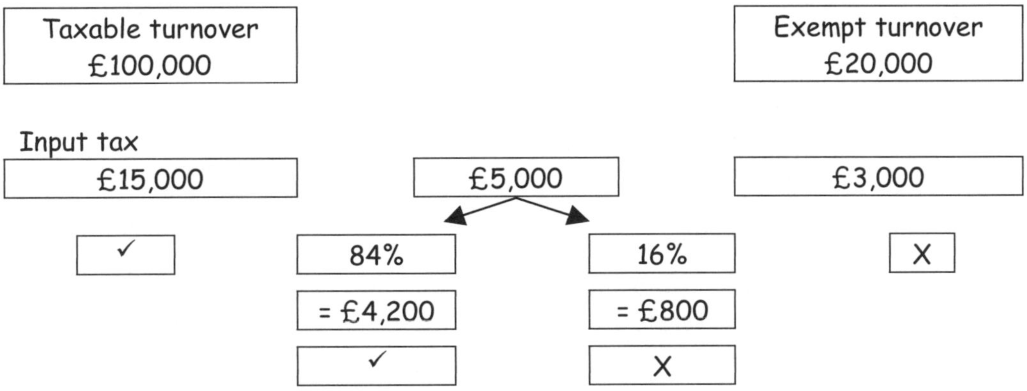

Consequently in this quarter the business will recover £19,200 (£15,000 + £4,200) of input tax.

Example 1

In the quarter to 31 March, Zap Limited had the following:

	£
Taxable supplies (excluding VAT)	292,000
Exempt supplies	40,000
Input tax:	
Directly attributable to taxable supplies	7,000
Directly attributable to exempt supplies	4,000
Residual	14,000

Taxable supplies include £12,000 (excluding VAT) for the sale of equipment during the quarter.

You are required to calculate the recoverable input tax.

E10b.3 De Minimis Input VAT

One of the more important points is the de minimis input tax limits. It is possible to reclaim the input VAT relating to exempt supplies if the amounts involved are below a certain limit. Such input tax is normally irrecoverable, but Customs state that if the amounts are low enough they will allow the trader to reclaim the input tax even though it relates to making exempt supplies. SI 1995/2518 Reg 106(1)

To be de minimis the **total exempt input tax** must be **less than or equal to £625 per month on average** <u>and</u> **less than 50% of total input tax**. This is a very important test and the trader must satisfy both conditions.

Total exempt input tax is the input tax directly attributable to exempt supplies plus the exempt proportion of the residual input tax.

The £625 per month on average equates to £1,875 per quarter, or £7,500 per annum.

Illustration 3

Quarter to 31 December	
Taxable supplies	£60,000
Exempt supplies	£9,000
Input tax:	
Directly attributable to taxable supplies	£5,000
Directly attributable to exempt supplies	£1,600
Residual input tax	£1,200

The recoverable input tax for the quarter is calculated as follows:

Quarter to 31 December	
Taxable supplies	£60,000
Exempt	£9,000
60/69 x 100 = 87%	

Input tax	Total	Taxable	Exempt
Directly attributable to taxable supplies	£5,000	£5,000	
Directly attributable to exempt supplies	£1,600		£1,600
Residual input tax	£1,200	£1,044	£156
	£7,800	£6,044	£1,756
			De-minimis

The recoverable input tax is £7,800.

The direct taxable input tax of £5,000 would go into the taxable column. The direct exempt input tax of £1,600 would go into the exempt column. The residual (or indirect) input tax would have to be apportioned.

The fraction to use is 87% - £1,200 times 87% = £1,044 into the taxable column. This leaves £156 in the exempt column. Therefore the total figures are £7,800 for total input tax, £6,044 for taxable input tax and £1,756 for input tax which relates to exempt supplies.

The total exempt input tax of £1,756 is below the de minimis limits of £625 per month on average or £1,875 per quarter; and is less than half of the total input tax. Half the total input tax is £3,900, so £1,756 is below this limit. Thus in this particular quarter the trader can claim all of his input tax back, i.e. £7,800.

Example 2

In the quarter to 30 June, Zap Limited had the following:

	£
Taxable supplies (excluding VAT)	300,000
Exempt supplies	50,000
Input tax:	
Directly attributable to taxable supplies	9,000
Directly attributable to exempt supplies	1,000
Residual	4,000

Taxable supplies include £5,000 (excluding VAT) for the sale of equipment during the quarter.

You are required to calculate the recoverable input tax.

E10b.4 Annual Adjustment

The calculations are made on a quarterly basis and input tax is recovered every quarter. These calculations are however not final. At the end of the trader's VAT year he must perform an annual calculation. Effectively it is the same calculation again, but this time using annual supplies and annual input tax figures. When considering the de minimis limits the **annual** de minimis limit is applied which is less than £7,500 (that is £625 times 12 months) and 50% of total input tax.

The trader should calculate the correct reclaim for the year based on these annual figures. The trader then compares the quarterly reclaims to the correct annual claim. The difference is known as the annual adjustment.

The annual adjustment is **accounted for on the first VAT return of the new VAT year.** A VAT year will depend on the traders VAT Stagger Group. It will either be the year ended 31 March (Stagger 1), 30 April (Stagger 2) or 31 May (Stagger 3). Consequently a trader's annual adjustment for the VAT year to 31 March, if that is their stagger, will be made in the quarter to 30 June, i.e. the quarter following the VAT year end.

Illustration 4

A trader with four quarters results. The taxable supplies are stated exclusive of VAT.

	Qtr to 31.7.05	*Qtr to 31.10.05*	*Qtr to 31.1.06*	*Qtr to 30.4.06*	*Year to 30.4.06*
Supplies:	£	£	£	£	£
Taxable	80,000	71,000	77,000	81,000	309,000
Exempt	10,000	14,000	8,000	15,000	47,000
Total	90,000	85,000	85,000	96,000	356,000
%	89	84	91	85	87

The correct percentages are calculated as follows;

- 89% for quarter 1 i.e. £80,000 over £90,000 times 100 rounded up to 89%.
- Quarter 2 is 84%, i.e. £71,000 divided by £85,000 times 100 and that is then rounded up to 84%.
- Quarter 3 is £77,000 divided by £85,000 times 100 which equals 91%.
- Quarter 4 is £81,000 divided by £96,000 times 100 which rounds up to 85%.
- To calculate the annual percentage apply the same method. £309,000 divided by £356,000 times 100, rounded up equals 87%.

Now we have our percentages we can move on to the input tax reclaims.

	Qtr to 31.7.05	*Qtr to 31.10.05*	*Qtr to 31.1.06*	*Qtr to 30.4.06*	*Year to 30.4.06*
Input tax:	£	£	£	£	£
Direct Taxable	6,000	7,500	7,000	6,750	27,250
Direct Exempt	2,000	1,500	1,700	1,800	7,000
Residual	1,500	1,800	1,650	700	5,650
Taxable	1,335	1,512	1,502	595	4,916
Exempt	165	288	148	105	734
Total taxable	7,335	9,012	8,502	7,345	32,166
Total exempt	2,165	1,788	1,848	1,905	7,734
Claim	7,335	10,800	10,350	7,345	32,166

In the first quarter multiply the residual of £1,500 by the percentage for that quarter. £1,500 times 89% equals £1,335. The remainder of the residual is exempt, i.e. £165.

Similar calculations are performed to calculate the amounts for quarters 2, 3 and 4.

In quarter 2 the £1,800 residual gets apportioned 84% to taxable supplies (£1,512), the balance to exempt (£288).

In quarter 3, £1,650 times 91% is £1,502, the balance is exempt tax of £148.

In quarter 4 £700 times 85% which gives £595 with the balance going to exempt tax of £105.

At this point there is a great temptation to add right the way across to find the annual figures, but that would be incorrect.

For the annual calculation use the annual percentage of 87% and apply that to the annual residual, £5,650. That gives annual taxable within the residual box of £4,916 with the balance of £734 being allocated to exempt input tax.

Re: the total figures. In quarter 1 £7,335 is the £6,000 direct taxable plus the residual allocated taxable of £1,335. The total exempt for quarter 1 is **the** direct exempt of £2,000 plus the allocated residual exempt of £165, £2,165. The same method is used for the next three quarters.

On the annual calculation adopt the same method - do not add across. To get £32,166 as the total taxable for the year add the £27,250 to the allocated residual for the year of £4,916. The £7,734 is the £7,000 for the year of direct exempt plus the residual allocation of £734.

The final line is the claim figure. In quarter 1 the total exempt is £2,165. This is not de minimis since exceeds £1,875. Consequently the claim is only the taxable amount, the £7,335.

In quarter 2 the £1,788 is de minimis. It is less than £1,875 and it is less than 50% of total input tax - in this case 50% of £10,800. Consequently the claim is for the total input tax, that is £10,800.

In quarter 3 the £1,848 is de minimis. It is less than £1,875 and it is less than 50% of the total input tax - in this particular quarter that is 50% of £10,350. Consequently the claim is the total input tax, i.e. £10,350.

In quarter 4 the exempt input tax of £1,905 is not de minimis. It is greater than £1,875. Therefore the claim for quarter 4 is the £7,345 total taxable input tax.

Finally, on the annual adjustment consider whether the £7,734 is recoverable. The annual limit is £7,500. Therefore £7,734 is not de minimis, since it is greater than the annual amount. Consequently the claim amount is only £32,166. The total claimed in the year is simply the 4 quarter's amounts which total £35,830. These would have been claims made each quarter. The annual claim is, however, restricted to £32,166. This leaves an annual adjustment of £3,664. That will be a negative input tax in the quarter to 31 July 2006. Effectively the trader owes another £3,664 to Customs in the first quarter after the VAT year. That is called the annual adjustment.

Example 3

	Qtr to 31.8.05	*Qtr to 30.11.05*	*Qtr to 28.2.06*	*Qtr to 31.5.06*	*Year to 31.5.06*
Supplies:	£	£	£	£	£
Taxable	60,000	63,000	61,000	70,000	254,000
Exempt	9,000	7,000	14,000	10,000	40,000
Total	69,000	70,000	75,000	80,000	294,000
%					
Input tax:					
Direct Taxable	4,000	3,000	500	3,500	11,000
Direct Exempt	1,500	1,200	1,500	2,000	6,200
Residual	2,700	2,500	1,000	1,900	8,100
Taxable					
Exempt					
Total taxable					
Total exempt					
Claim					

Note: The taxable supplies are exclusive of VAT.

You are required to fill in the missing figures in the above example.

E10b.5 Special Methods

Generally the standard method applies by default. If a trader is partially exempt they should apply the standard method, unless a special method is agreed with Customs. A special method is usually opted for where it produces a fairer apportionment of the residual input VAT. It may be that the standard method of apportionment does not give a fair fraction, so therefore a special method is agreed. It is fair to say that the majority of partially exempt traders in practice will be using a special method - a method which is very distinct to their business.

SI 1995/2518 Reg 102

Special methods **can be based on the number of transactions**, for example, the number of taxable transactions in a quarter over total number of transactions in the quarter. It could be based on **floor area,** that is the floor area used to make taxable supplies and the floor area used to make exempt supplies. It could even be on **staff numbers**, that is the total staff employed on the taxable business compared to the staff numbers used in the exempt business.

These are obviously very simplistic examples, but they just give you an idea of what can be agreed with Customs. In practice special methods can be quite complicated; every business is different and they have their own idiosyncrasies.

Once a special method has been **agreed with Customs** the trader must apply the method until both parties agree it is no longer appropriate.

Since 1 January 2004 Customs have also had the power to issue a special method override notice under Reg 102A where they feel it appropriate.

Furthermore a package of three measures were introduced with effect from 1 April 2005, which impact further on special methods:

1. Customs will serve a special method override notice where they have clear evidence that the current special method is not fair and there is significant loss of revenue. They will only do this where they decide that the direction of another special method is not appropriate.

2. Approval or direction of special method must be in writing.

3. Where a special method makes no provision for certain types of input tax, it will be recovered to the extent that supplies on which it was charged are used in making taxable supplies.

E10b.6 The standard method override adjustment

An anti-avoidance measure came into effect from 18 April 2002 which requires partly exempt businesses to override the standard method of apportioning residual input tax where *'the result does not reflect the use made of the*

SI 1995/2518 Reg 107A-E

purchases, including cases of deliberate abuse'. The rule does not apply to businesses using a 'special method' to apportion their input tax.

The 'standard method' is where non-attributable (residual) input tax is apportioned to taxable supplies using the formula;

$$\frac{\text{Taxable Turnover in period}}{\text{Total turnover in period}}$$ (rounded up to next whole percentage)

Under the new rule, businesses are required to adjust the input tax deductible under the standard method at the end of their VAT year if that amount is *substantially* different from an attribution based on the use of purchases.

'Substantially' is defined as: SI 1995/2518 Reg 107C

- £50,000 or more; or
- 50% or more of the value of the residual input tax, but not less than £25,000.

Where the amount of residual input tax is less than £50,000 businesses can rely purely on the standard method with one exception: businesses that are defined as group undertakings by the Companies Act 1985 must follow the new rule where the residual input tax is greater than £25,000.

No adjustment was required in respect of input tax incurred up to and including 17 April 2002.

A business that has to apply the adjustment must, at the VAT year-end, calculate the difference between the input tax deductible under the standard method and that deductible according to use. This difference is the adjustment required to be made on the VAT return that follows the year-end (i.e. the same VAT return as that for the annual adjustment).

Illustration 5

XYZ Ltd uses the standard method to apportion residual input tax. Using this method deductible input tax for the four VAT quarters to 30 April 2006 was calculated as:

	£
31 July 2005	58,500
31 October 2005	62,150
31 January 2006	74,224
30 April 2006	49,367
Total	244,241

At the VAT year end a calculation of deductible input tax based on the results of the whole year is performed. The company's results for the year ended 30 April 2006 are as follows:

	£
Total input VAT	350,000
Analysed as relating to:	
Taxable supplies only	125,000
Exempt supplies only	75,000
Residual	150,000
Taxable supplies made in the year (excluding VAT)	1,150,000
Exempt supplies made in year	550,000
Value of taxable transaction included in turnover consuming little or no inputs	1,000,000
Deductible input tax:	
Wholly attributable to taxable supplies	125,000
Residual	
$\frac{1150000}{1150000 + 550000} = 68\%$	
68% x £150,000	102,000
Deductible input tax	227,000

The normal annual adjustment calculation performed at the year-end states that £227,000 of input tax for the year is deductible. This is compared to the provisional claim in the four quarters (£244,241). The difference of £17,241 is the annual adjustment figure which is effectively repaid to Customs on the VAT return to 31 July 2006.

However the business incurred £150,000 of residual input tax which exceeds the £50,000 threshold in respect of the standard method over-ride adjustment. In addition we are told that in the year there was a taxable transaction included in turnover valued at £1,000,000 which consumed little or no inputs.

Thus the input tax deducted using the standard method may not be fair and reasonable reflecting the extent to which purchases are used in making taxable supplies because few, if any, purchases were used in making the high value taxable transaction.

The business must determine the amount of input tax deductible on the basis of use and check whether the difference is substantial.

In this example all supplies other than the high value taxable transaction consume purchases in proportion to their values. Accordingly a fair and reasonable attribution can be achieved by excluding the high value transaction from a calculation based on the standard method.

Deductible input tax:	£
Wholly attributable to taxable supplies	125,000
Residual	
$\frac{1150000 - 1000000}{1350000 + 550000 - 1000000} = 22\%$	
22% x £150,000	33,000
	158,000

Thus the total input tax deductible on a basis of use is £158,000 whereas using the normal standard method it is £227,000.

The difference of £69,000 is 'substantial' if it exceeds £50,000 or 50% of the residual input tax and £25,000. In this illustration £69,000 exceeds £50,000 so an over-ride adjustment must be made. This adjustment of £69,000 is an over claim of VAT so must be accounted for (i.e. repaid) on the same VAT return as the annual adjustment (i.e. the VAT return to 31 July 2006).

When the override applies

The override will only apply where the standard method fails to provide a fair and reasonable deduction of input tax, when compared to the extent to which purchases are used to make taxable supplies.

Examples of when the standard method may not provide a fair and reasonable result are:

1. Where purchases are incurred in one tax year, but used in a different tax year in which the proportion of deductible VAT is very different; or
2. Where purchases are not used in proportion to the values of taxable and exempt supplies made;
3. Purchases are made in one period or tax year in setting up a new area of business which will significantly affect the relative values of taxable and exempt supplies in future tax years when the purchases are to be used.
4. Exceptionally high value transactions are undertaken which do not consume inputs to an extent significantly greater than transactions of lower value; and
5. The pattern of business is such that the inputs are simply not consumed in proportion to the values of outputs.

All tax avoidance schemes which exploit the standard method to deduct more input tax than relates to taxable supplies are most likely to trigger the partial exemption override.

How is the extent of use calculated?
Any calculation will be allowed if it provides a fair and reasonable attribution of input tax according to use or intended use of the purchases.

If the proportions for taxable and exempt supplies in the period in which the inputs are to be used and those in which they are incurred are different, then it should be sufficient to apply the projected proportions in the period of use.

If exceptionally high value supplies are distorting the standard method calculation then it should be sufficient to exclude these supplies from the calculation. (See Illustration 1).

If purchases are not used in proportion to the value of supplies made, it will be necessary to apply another suitable measure.

Answer 1

	Total £	*Taxable* £	*Exempt* £
Inputs:			
Direct taxable	7,000	7,000	
Direct exempt	4,000		4,000
Residual	14,000	12,320	1,680
	25,000	19,320	5,680

Taxable supplies - exclude Capital Items i.e. equipment

£292,000 - £12,000 = £280,000

Fraction

$$\frac{\text{Taxable supplies}}{\text{Total supplies}} \times 100 = ?$$

$$\frac{£280{,}000}{£280{,}000 + £40{,}000} \times 100 = 88\% \text{ (rounded up from 87.5)}$$

88% x 14,000 = £12,320

The direct taxable input tax, i.e. the input tax relating directly to the taxable sales were £7,000 - £7,000 goes into the taxable column. The direct exempt input tax was £4,000 - £4,000 goes into the exempt column. The residual is £14,000. This is the amount which must be apportioned between taxable and exempt supplies. This is done using the standard method. The starting point is taxable supplies, remembering to exclude capital items, which in this case would be the sale of the equipment. Thus £292,000 minus the capital equipment of £12,000 which gives £280,000.

The fraction is taxable supplies over total supplies times 100, which equals 88%. This is rounded up from £87.5%. This percentage is then applied to the residual input tax. The residual input tax which relates to taxable sales thus amounts to £12,320. (i.e. 88% times the £14,000) The balance of residual input tax is exempt, i.e. £1,680.

The total figures for the quarter are therefore £25,000 worth of total input tax, £19,320 of taxable input tax and £5,680 of exempt input tax. The trader will be able to claim £19,320 of input tax. The £5,680 is irrecoverable as it relates to exempt sales.

Answer 2

	Total £	*Taxable* £	*Exempt* £
Inputs:			
Direct taxable	9,000	9,000	
Direct exempt	1,000		1,000
Residual	4,000	3,440	560
	14,000	12,440	1,560

Taxable supplies exclude £5,000 capital items

£300,000 - £5,000 = £295,000

Fraction

$$\frac{£295,000}{£295,000 + £50,000} \times 100 = 85.5\% \text{ (i.e. } 86\%)$$

£4,000 x 86% = £3,440.

The input tax directly attributable is £9,000 to taxable and £1,000 to exempt supplies. The residual of £4,000 needs to be apportioned. To apportion use taxable supplies, which exclude capital items, i.e. exclude the sale of equipment. Consequently the taxable supplies for the fraction are £300,000 minus £5,000 which equals £295,000.

The fraction is taxable supplies over total supplies times 100 rounded up which equals 86%. This is rounded up from 85.5%.

Applying the 86% to the £4,000 = £3,440 in relation to taxable supplies. The balance of residual input tax of £560 relates to the exempt sales. This gives totals of £14,000 for the total input tax in the quarter, £12,440 of input tax relating to taxable supplies, £1,560 of input tax relating to exempt supplies.

The question is whether the exempt input amount is de minimis? It is less than £1,875 and it is also less than 50% of £14,000 the total input tax.

Consequently in the quarter the trader can reclaim the whole of the input tax, the £14,000.

Answer 3

	Qtr to 31.8.05	*Qtr to 30.11.05*	*Qtr to 28.2.06*	*Qtr to 31.5.06*	*Year to 31.5.06*
Supplies:	£	£	£	£	£
Taxable	60,000	63,000	61,000	70,000	254,000
Exempt	9,000	7,000	14,000	10,000	40,000
Total	69,000	70,000	75,000	80,000	294,000
%	87	90	82	88	87
Input tax:					
Direct Taxable	4,000	3,000	500	3,500	11,000
Direct Exempt	1,500	1,200	1,500	2,000	6,200
Residual	2,700	2,500	1,000	1,900	8,100
Taxable	2,349	2,250	820	1,672	7,047
Exempt	351	250	180	228	1,053
Total taxable	6,349	5,250	1,320	5,172	18,047
Total exempt	1,851	1,450	1,680	2,228	7,253
Claim	8,200	6,700	1,320	5,172	25,300

Claimed in year £21,392
Annual Adjustment £3,908 – Qtr to 31.8.06

The correct percentages are 87, 90, 82, 88 and 87. The calculation each quarter is taxable over total times 100 rounded up. For example, in quarter 1, 60,000 over 69,000 times 100 rounded up to 87%.

In quarter 1, the taxable apportionment of residual is £2,349, i.e. £2,700 times 87%. The balance of residual of £351 is treated as the exempt proportion. This gives a total taxable for the quarter of £6,349, i.e. £4,000 plus £2,349. The total exempt is £1,500 for the quarter plus the £351. When considering the claim for the quarter consider whether the £1,851 is de minimis. In this case it is de minimis as it is less than £1,875. The total claim for quarter 1 is £8,200.

Similar calculations have been performed for quarters 2, 3 and 4.

The claim in quarter 2 is simply the whole input tax for the quarter. The £1,450 of inputs relating to the exempt supplies is de minimis, therefore full reclaim.

In quarter 3 there is £1,680 of input tax relating to exempt supplies. This does pass the first de minimis test. It is less than £1,875, but it is not less than 50% of total input tax, that is 50% of £3,000. Consequently it is not de minimis. The reclaim is restricted to the input tax relating to taxable supplies in that quarter, that is £1,320.

In quarter 4 the input tax relating to exempt supplies of £2,228 is not de minimis as it exceeds £1,875.

Finally, the annual figures: Calculate the annual apportionment of £7,047 by multiplying the residual for the year of £8,100 by 87%. Next consider the total figures for the year. The £18,047 is £11,000 plus the apportioned residual of £7,047. This same principle applies for the total exempt - £6,200 plus the £1,053, giving £7,253.

Consider whether the £7,253 is de minimis. It is less than £7,500, (£625 x 12) and it is less than 50% of total input tax. Consequently the claim for the year should be £25,300. The business actually claimed in the year £21,392. This leaves an annual adjustment of £3,908 of additional input tax to reclaim on the quarter to 31 August 2006. That is the first quarter after the VAT year-end.

SUMMARY - PARTIAL EXEMPTION

Partial exemption is all about recovering input tax.

Generally, input tax is recoverable if it relates to a taxable supply.

If a trader is not sure what the input tax relates to then he must apportion it.

There is a standard method of apportionment and a special method of apportionment, a trader can use either, but special methods must be by explicit agreement.

The trader claims input tax through the quarters, but these are only interim calculations. The correct calculation is done at the end of the VAT year. This may result in annual adjustment, which is accounted for on the first return of the next VAT year.

E11: VAT RECORDS AND RETURNS

In this chapter we will look at the records which must be kept by a VAT registered trader including:

- the VAT account and the time limit for retention
- special record-keeping requirements for special schemes
- the tax invoice
- when a less detailed tax invoice may be used
- VAT returns themselves.

E11.1 Introduction

This chapter looks at how important records and returns are in the VAT system. Because VAT is collected at every level along a chain of a supply, it is important that records should exist of all transactions made and received by a business. The importance of records is paramount when the business wants to claim a refund of input tax because they will need to be able to prove that the tax they are reclaiming was, in the first place, paid by the business. The best proof of this is the records that the business keeps.

E11.2 Records

Customs have a general power to require traders to keep such records as they require and these general requirements are set out in the VAT Regulations 1995 in Regulation 31. Each taxable person has an obligation to keep and to preserve; Sch 11 Para 6(1)

- his business **accounting records**; SI 1995/2518 Reg 31
- copies of all **tax invoices** which have been **issued** by the business;
- all **tax invoices** which have been **received** by the business;
- **documentation** relating to all **imports and exports**, and documentation relating to all **EC acquisitions** of goods and **dispatches** of goods;
- **credit notes, debit notes** and similar documents which evidence changes in the consideration for supplies made or received and that includes documentation both issued by the business and received by the business; and
- a **VAT account**.

Business records must be kept for a **minimum of 6 years** unless an agreement is reached with Customs for a shorter retention period. Sch 11 Para 6(3)

It is possible for a trader, instead of keeping original paper records, to keep copies on microfilm or microfiche. This will be allowed if the copies can be produced for Customs to view and that there are adequate facilities for Customs Officers to view them. The trader must seek the permission of Customs if he wishes to retain records on microfilm or microfiche.

In a similar way, if a trader wishes to keep records on computer then he must get approval of the system he is going to use from Customs. Approval will not be needed if the records are going to be produced by computer but then stored on paper.

Notice 700 Para 19.2

E11.3 The VAT Account

The required contents of the VAT account are specified in the VAT Regulations 1995 in Regulation 32. The VAT account must be divided into separate parts for the different prescribed accounting periods for which the business makes VAT returns. Then each part must be sub-divided into a VAT payable portion and a VAT allowable portion.

SI 1995/2518 Reg 32

In the VAT payable portion, for each VAT return period, it should show:

- The output tax due on all the sales made in that period;
- The output tax due on all the acquisition of goods from other EU member states in the period;
- Any earlier output tax errors that have been discovered during this period where adjustment is allowed in the current period;
- Any increases or decreases in output tax which have arisen during the period from changes in the consideration for supplies. An example of this would be a price adjustment or some sort of dispute that has resulted in a change in output tax; and
- Finally, any other adjustments to output tax which are required or allowed under the VAT legislation.

In the VAT allowable portion for each return period, you have to show:

- The input tax allowable for the period on all supplies made to the business in the VAT period;
- The input tax allowable for the period on intra-EU acquisitions;
- If any earlier input tax errors were discovered during the period, then any adjustments being made in the current period must also be shown;
- Any increases or decreases in input tax arising during the period from changes in the consideration for supplies received. So once again price adjustments, disputes and so on; and
- Finally, any other adjustments to input tax which are required or allowed under the VAT legislation.

Examples of adjustments required or allowed under the VAT legislation include a partial exemption annual adjustment, a capital goods scheme adjustment or a bad debt relief claim. Such adjustments could be seen in both the VAT payable and the VAT allowable portion of the VAT account.

E11.4 Special Record Keeping Requirements

Apart from the records needed by all traders, if a trader operates a special scheme then he is usually subject to additional record keeping requirements on top. These requirements will be specified by Customs usually in notices which have the force of law for this purpose. Special record keeping requirements arise for retail schemes, margin schemes (for example the second-hand good schemes), for bad debt relief claims and for traders using the cash accounting scheme.

E11.5 Tax Invoices

The tax invoice is probably the most important document for VAT purposes. The requirements were amended from 1 January 2004 (see Business Brief 23/2003), in order to implement the EC Invoicing Directive (2001/115/EC). In order to be a valid tax invoice it must show all of the following information as listed in SI 1995/2518 reg 14: SI 1995/2518 Reg 14

- An identifying **invoice number**;
- The **date** of the supply;
- The date when this tax invoice is being issued;
- The **supplier's name and address** and the supplier's VAT **registration number**. If a supply has been made to a customer in another EU member state then the VAT registration number must be prefixed by the letters GB;
- It must show the **recipient's name and address** and if the recipient is in another EU member state, then it must show the recipient's **VAT registration number** in that member state;
- There is a requirement to include unit price on an invoice as it applies to countable goods or services. For services the countable element might be, for example, an hourly rate or a price for standard services.

  If the supply cannot be broken down into countable elements, then the total tax exclusive price will be the unit price. Additionally, the 'unit price' may not need to be shown at all if it is not normally provided in a particular business sector and is not required by the customer. It is no longer a requirement to show the **type of supply** (whether the supply is a supply by sale, by hire purchase, by loan, by exchange, by hire, lease or rental, a supply of producing goods from the customer's materials, a supply by sale on commission or a supply on sale or return or similar terms) although businesses may continue to give this information on invoices;

- There must also be a **description** sufficient to identify the goods or services being supplied;
- The invoice must also for each description on that invoice show the **quantity** of goods or the extent of services supplied, show the **rate of VAT** applicable and the **amount** that is being **charged,** which is net of VAT. Prior to 1 January 2004 the VAT exclusive amounts had to be shown in sterling. Now they an be shown in any currency;
- The invoice must also show the **total amount being charged**, again net of VAT;
- If a cash discount is offered the invoice must show the **rate of discount**;
- From 1 January 2004 it is no longer a requirement for the invoice to show the amount of tax that is chargeable at each rate, and
- Finally the invoice must show the total amount of tax chargeable expressed in sterling.

Where a tax invoice is required the trader has an obligation to issue the tax invoice within 30 days after the tax point.

Effectively the EC Invoicing Directive requires one extra item to be added to VAT invoices (the 'unit price') and businesses can still choose to show those items that are no longer mandatory if they wish to. There should therefore be no need for pre-printed VAT invoice forms to be wasted. A 12 month transitional period will enable businesses to use up old stocks and build in any changes to their new invoices.

The UK has not taken up the option available in the Directive for Member States to require invoices for supplies in their territory to show the customer's VAT registration number.

The customer's VAT registration number will only be required on invoices provided to persons in other Member States as per Regulations 14(2)(c). SI 1995/2518.

Invoices do not currently have to be issued for zero-rate and exempt transactions when supplied in the UK and this will not change. If such supplies are included on invoices with taxable supplies, those items must show clearly that there is no VAT payable and their values must be totalled separately (paragraph 16.5, of Notice 700 *The VAT Guide).*

However, UK businesses may still have to issue VAT invoices for zero rate or exempt supplies made to customers in other Member States if those other Member States require them. These invoices should either:

- Indicate that the supply is exempt; or
- Refer to the relevant provision in EU or UK law.

This means that information such as the description of the goods (e.g. medical supplies) or the customer (e.g. health service) will be enough to indicate that a supply is exempt for invoicing purposes

E11.6 Less Detailed Tax Invoices

Customs allow the issue of a less detailed invoice in certain circumstances. Effectively two conditions must be satisfied for a less detailed invoice to be allowable. First of all, the supplier must be a retailer, so must be selling directly to the public, and secondly, the value of the **supply,** and this is **including VAT**, must be **less than £250.** SI 1995./2518 Reg 16

If both conditions are satisfied a less detailed invoice can be issued which will comprise of the following:

- The name, address and VAT registration number of the supplier;
- The date of the supply;
- A description sufficient to identify the goods or the services supplied;
- The total payable which is including VAT; and
- The rate of tax applicable.

A credit card voucher can be used as a less detailed tax invoice provided that the retailer adapts it to show the information required. A retailer can also issue a tax invoice in a modified form if the customer agrees. The modification would be to show separate supplies and tax inclusive values and the total VAT, as well as the total of the VAT inclusive and exclusive values of supplies at different rates.

A tax invoice for petrol may be issued as a less detailed invoice if the value of the supply is below £250. If the value, however, is £250 or more, then the trader is allowed to show the vehicle registration number instead of the customer's name and address and omit details of the quantity of supplies.

A cash and carry wholesaler is also allowed to use till slips as tax invoices provided that he maintains product code lists and can provide up-to-date copies of these code lists to all VAT registered customers.

Example 1

Look at this tax invoice carefully and decide if there is anything wrong with it.

The Little Card Shop
22 High Street, Didsbury, Cheshire M2 OBD
tel: 0161 445 2222 / email: t1cs.com

INVOICE
Vat Reg.No: 232 4572 81

Dated: 24.12.2005

	£
Glorious Santa Christmas Cards x 1	15.18
Gift wrapping x 1	4.46
	19.64
Total including VAT	23.08

E11.7 Electronic Invoices

The Invoicing Directive allows for electronic invoicing using an advanced electronic signature, or Electronic Data Interchange (EDI). All Member States must accept these two methods. Member States can also accept other means of e-invoicing for supplies on their territory.

Electronic signatures are linked to the data to which they relate in such a way as to allow someone receiving the data over an electronic network to determine the authenticity of the origin of the data, and to check that the data has not been altered or corrupted during transmission.

EDI is a computer-to-computer exchange of structured data that permits automatic processing by the recipient. It is more commonly used for high volume data transfers between businesses, using agreed standards (for example, UN/EDIFACT) to structure the data.

Customs do not publish a definitive list of acceptable systems since new technologies are constantly emerging. Customs are keen to facilitate the development of electronic invoicing systems and criteria for e-invoicing will be set out in new Notice - 700/63 *Electronic invoicing*. Providing that a particular invoicing system meets these criteria it can be used to transmit VAT invoices.

A trader will have to notify Customs within 30 days from the date that he starts to invoice electronically.

However, if Customs have already given approval for the trader to invoice electronically, he does not need to notify Customs again.

It will be for businesses to decide whether to invoice by traditional paper methods or electronically. Indeed some businesses may use both methods for separate supplies/suppliers.

If a business is not e-enabled it may not be able to receive e-invoices. Whether E-invoicing is appropriate is a commercial matter and customs cannot oblige a business to e-invoice or make customers accept it if they don't want to.

Rules on e-storage are in keeping with existing rules on record keeping and production i.e. records must be produced within a reasonable period of time either at the principal place of business or another reasonable place. Compression of data will be permitted, to allow far more efficient storage, providing that integrity and authenticity of the data can be maintained.

The retention period for invoices remains at 6 years unless Customs agree a shorter retention period. (paragraph 19.2.3 of Notice 700 *The VAT Guide)*

E11.8 VAT returns

A taxable person must furnish a VAT return, (form **VAT 100)** in respect of each prescribed accounting period. A prescribed accounting period is usually a three-month period although traders can request to have monthly prescribed accounting periods. Prescribed accounting periods are staggered for administrative convenience and can be the quarters ended 31 March, 30 June, 30 September, and 31 December for stagger group 1. 30 April, 31 July, 31 October and 31 January for stagger group 2. 31 May, 31 August, 30 November and the end of February for stagger group 3. SI 1995/2518 Reg 25

For each of those three stagger groups, the **VAT year end** will end on **31 March, 30 April or 31 May** as appropriate. VAT Notice 700 para 20.5

The stagger groups are allocated to traders when they register for VAT. Traders can request certain accounting dates for their convenience (for example to coincide with their financial year end) but the allocation is entirely at Customs discretion.

The VAT return deals with all UK transactions that fall within VAT and also will include entries for intra-EU trade as well as tax on imported goods which have to be dealt with on the VAT return.

HM Customs and Excise

Value Added Tax Return

For the period
01 06 04 to 31 08 04

For Official Use

Registration Number | **Period** 08 04

You could be liable to a financial penalty if your completed return and all the VAT payable are not received by the due date.

Due date: 30 09 04

For Official Use

If you have a general enquiry or need advice please call our National Advice Service on 0845 010 9000

Before you fill in this form please read the notes on the back and the VAT leaflet *"Filling in your VAT return"*. Fill in all boxes clearly in ink, and write 'none' where necessary. Don't put a dash or leave any box blank. If there are no pence write **"00"** in the pence column. **Do not** enter more than one amount in any box.

For official use

	Box	£	p
VAT due in this period on **sales** and other outputs	1		
VAT due in this period on **acquisitions** from other **EC Member States**	2		
Total VAT due **(the sum of boxes 1 and 2)**	3		
VAT reclaimed in this period on **purchases** and other inputs (including acquisitions from the EC)	4		
Net VAT to be paid to Customs or reclaimed by you **(Difference between boxes 3 and 4)**	5		
Total value of **sales** and all other outputs excluding any VAT. **Include your box 8 figure**	6		00
Total value of **purchases** and all other inputs excluding any VAT. **Include your box 9 figure**	7		00
Total value of all **supplies** of goods and related services, excluding any VAT, to other **EC Member States**	8		00
Total value of all **acquisitions** of goods and related services, excluding any VAT, from other **EC Member States**	9		00

If you are enclosing a payment please tick this box. ☐

DECLARATION: You, or someone on your behalf, must sign below.

I, ... declare that the
(Full name of signatory in BLOCK LETTERS)
information given above is true and complete.

Signature .... Date..

A false declaration can result in prosecution.

L

VAT 100 (half) **Page 1** PT1 (April 2004)

The VAT return is completed as follows:

Box 1 shows the **output tax** due on supplies and deemed supplies made by the taxable person.

Box 2 shows the **VAT due** on acquisitions from other EU countries.

Box 3 shows the total of **Boxes 1 and 2, i.e.** the total VAT due on sales and on EU acquisitions.

Box 4 shows the **input tax** available for credit on all purchases. So that will include imports and EU acquisitions.

Box 5 is effectively the **net figure**, so Box 3 minus Box 4 and thus will show the VAT payable to or by the Commissioners.

The remainder of the VAT return is effectively to collect statistical information partly for checking the reasonableness of the input and output tax figures but also in respect of information on trade with other EU member states.

Box 6 shows the **total value of sales and all other outputs** (but this excludes VAT) made during the period and will include the amount shown in Box 8.

Box 7 shows the **total value of purchases and all other inputs**, again excluding VAT, received during the period and this includes the amount shown in Box 9.

Box 8 shows the **total value of all supplies** of goods and related services excluding VAT **to other EU member states**.

Box 9 shows the **value of all acquisitions** of goods and related services, excluding any VAT, **from all other EU member states**.

Although all nine boxes should be completed, if a business has nothing to put in a box it should write "None". Most traders who do not have any transactions with other EU countries will only actually be entering figures in Boxes 1, 3, 4, 5, 6 and 7.

The VAT return has to be **signed by a relevant person** and submitted with a cheque for payment of any VAT due **within one month** of the end of the prescribed accounting period for which the return is made. SI 1995/2518 Reg. 25(1)

Example 2

JJ Limited has an accounting year-end of 31 January 2006. The company is in VAT stagger group 2.

VAT returns to which quarters were made based on the year's results?

a)	30.4.2005	31.7.2005	31.10.2005	31.1.2006
b)	31.3.2005	30.6.2005	30.9.2005	31.12.2005
c)	31.3.2005	30.6.2005	30.9.2005	31.1.2006

Answer 1

I hope you realised that the invoice shown was a less detailed tax invoice. The Little Card Shop is a retailer and the value of the supply, including VAT, is less than £250, so this trader may issue a less detailed tax invoice.

Name of supplier	✓
Address of supplier	✓
VAT Reg Number of supplier	✓
Date of supply	✓
Description	✓
Total payable including VAT	✓
Rate of tax applicable	X

A less detailed tax invoice shows the name, address and VAT registration number of the supplier.

Also needed: the date of the supply.

Also needed: a description sufficient to identify the goods or services supplied. The question states that there are various Glorious Santa Christmas Cards and some gift wrapping, which is a sufficient description for VAT.

A less detailed invoice needs to show the total including VAT.

And finally a less detailed invoice has to show the rate of tax applicable and that is where this tax invoice falls down. Nowhere is the rate of VAT applicable to the item shown. Hence it is not a valid tax invoice.

To conclude there is just one item that is incorrect in respect of this less detailed tax invoice.

Answer 2

The correct answer is A

These are the quarterly VAT returns a trader would have to make if you were allocated into stagger group 2.

SUMMARY - VAT RECORDS AND RETURN

Customs have a general power to require traders to keep such records as they require. As well as the business's accounting records copies of all tax invoices issued and received must be retained by the business in addition to credit and debit notes.

Finally each business must maintain a VAT account which shows all output tax and input tax movements during the VAT period.

Records must be kept for a minimum of six years.

If a VAT registered trader operates a special scheme then he will be subject to additional record-keeping requirements.

The tax invoice is a crucial document and must meet all the conditions specified by Customs if input tax is to be recovered by a purchaser.

Customs allow the issue of less detailed tax invoices in certain circumstances - basically where the supplier is a retailer and the value of the supply including VAT is less than £250.

A VAT Return is submitted periodically (usually quarterly) by VAT registered businesses outlining output VAT, input VAT and net VAT payable or repayable for the period.

E12: ACCOUNTING FOR VAT

This chapter looks at the payment and repayment of VAT dealing with the following:
- when VAT should be paid;
- in which circumstances VAT will be repaid.;
- the annual accounting scheme which allows businesses to submit VAT returns on an annual basis;
- the cash accounting scheme which allows businesses to account for VAT ignoring the normal tax point rules but instead looking at transactions passing through the cash book.

E12.1 Introduction

This chapter looks at four different but related topics which would all come under the umbrella of accounting for VAT. First the payment or repayment of VAT; then monthly payments on account of the VAT liability; and finally two different schemes which have the aim of simplifying accounting for VAT for the smaller trader - the annual accounting scheme and the cash accounting scheme.

E12.2 Payment and Repayment of VAT

VAT returns must be **submitted** to Customs not later than **one calendar month after the end of the VAT return period** in question. When a return is sent to Customs any VAT that is due for payment, as shown on the VAT return, should be sent to Customs at the same time. So every VAT return going to Customs showing VAT payable will also have a cheque being sent to Customs at the same time and within the same time limit. **Late returns and late payments of VAT due can result in penalties.**

SI 1995/2518
Reg 25 & 40

If the VAT return shows input tax exceeding output tax for the return period then Customs will owe the business some money. In this case when Customs receive the VAT return they will send money back to the business. Where possible Customs like to make repayments of VAT though the Bankers Automated Clearing System (BACS).

Normally a VAT return will only show the VAT due from that trader. Thus a trader is only liable for his own VAT due to Customs shown on his VAT return.

However FA2003 introduced joint and several liability for certain traders. This measure is industry specific, and is intended to apply to the following sectors only:

- Telephones, telephone parts and accessories, and
- Computer equipment, including parts, accessories and software.

Joint and several liability is specifically targeted at missing trader fraud. Where a business receives a supply of specified goods or services in circumstances where they knew or had reasonable grounds to suspect that VAT on those goods and services would go unpaid, the trader will be held jointly and severally liable for the tax due in the event of default by the supplier. This introduces the concept of joint and several liability throughout the supply chain for fraudulent transactions in these goods.

E12.3 Payment of VAT

Businesses which **pay VAT electronically** will automatically receive a **7 day extension** to the deadline for the submission of the VAT return and the VAT due. The 7-day extension is 7 calendar days.

An electronic payment, or an e-payment, is one of the following:

- BACS - Bankers Automated Clearing System; VAT Notice Para 21.3
- CHAPS - Clearing House Automated Payment System; or
- Bank Giro Credit transfer.

However this 7-day extension is not available to traders making payments on account or using the annual accounting scheme.

Customs have stated that businesses may pay their VAT in Euros if they wish but the declarations of their liability must be made in sterling and VAT repayments will also be made in sterling.

E12.4 Monthly Payments on Account

Very **large traders** are required to **pay their VAT monthly in advance** on account of their actual VAT liability for a return quarter. Returns are still only submitted quarterly but payments are made monthly. For two months a payment on account is made and for the third month of a VAT return the true payment is made. So the true payment due, as shown on the VAT return, is made when the VAT return is submitted. Monthly payments on account are not required if the trader makes monthly VAT returns.

VAT Noti[illegible] 700/60/9[illegible]

SI 1993/2[illegible]

Businesses meeting the definition of a very large trader make these monthly payments on account. There are two tests. **Test 1** states that the trader's total **VAT liability** for the previous year ended 30 September, 31 October, or 30 November **exceeded £2 million**.

The September, October or November dates apply according to whether the trader is a group 1, group 2 or group 3 trader. For example if a trader was in stagger group 2 it would be the total VAT liability for the year ended 31 October. If it has exceeded £2million, then the business would be a very large trader.

It is the total VAT liability for the previous year to either September, October or November, depending on whether it is stagger group 1, 2 or 3 types of business, that determines if a trader is large or not.

Test 2 considers the businesses' total VAT liability in any subsequent period of one year tested at the end of each prescribed accounting period i.e. each VAT return period. If it exceeds £2 million then the business is a very large trader. At the end of every VAT return period if one year's total of VAT exceeds £2 million, the business' is a very large trader.

Whether a trader is defined as large under test 1 or test 2 is important because it effects the periods in respect of which the payments on account are required. If test 1 is satisfied then payments on account will be required for the whole of the **following** VAT year. VAT years commence on 1 April, 1 May or 1 June, depending on whether it is a group 1, 2 or 3 trader. In the earlier example, look at the VAT liability to the year ended 31 October and if it exceeded £2 million, then from the next 1 May the trader would be making payments on account.

If the business satisfies test 2 then the liability to make payments on account commences from the very next prescribed accounting period, i.e. VAT return period. So the next VAT return period after the VAT return period in which the £2 million threshold was exceeded, becomes the first time the trader will start to make payments on account.

Illustration 1

Giant Limited has a VAT year-end of 31 May. In the year to 30 November 2005 its VAT liability totalled £2.1 million.

Giant Limited has a VAT year-end of 31 May so it is a group 3 trader. The company exceeds the £2 million threshold in the 30 November year-end period considered in test 1.

Hence, Giant Limited is a very large trader and is now liable to make payments on account. These payments on account, because it satisfies test 1, will commence with the VAT year beginning 1 June 2006.

If the year to 30 November 2005 was the very first time that Giant Limited had exceeded the £2 million threshold then look at test 2 as well. At the end of a VAT return period, if for the year then ending the VAT liability exceeds the £2 million threshold, the trader is due to make payments on account from the next prescribed accounting period. So payments on account will be due from Giant Limited for the 28 February 2006 return period as well.

Example 1

Enormous Limited has a 31 March VAT year-end. The company's VAT liability over recent return periods has been:

	Liability	Annual Total
	£	£
31.12.04	300,000	
31.3.05	400,000	
30.6.05	500,000	
30.9.05	600,000	1,800,000
31.12.05	400,000	1,900,000
31.3.06	450,000	1,950,000
30.6.06	750,000	2,200,000

Which is the first VAT return period affected by POA?

E12.5 Due Date for Payments on Account

Payments on account are due at the **end of the second month and the third month** in the prescribed accounting period i.e. the VAT return period. The balance is then due when the VAT return is submitted so, in other words, one month after the prescribed accounting period ends.

If the payments on account exceed the total amount due for the VAT return period then Customs will repay the excess when the VAT return is submitted.

How much is the payment on account? It is **1/24th of a total VAT liability for a year** but which total VAT liability for the year depends on whether test 1 or test 2 was satisfied.

If test 1 was satisfied then it is the total VAT liability to that 30 September, 31 October, 30 November year end date as appropriate to the stagger group for the trader. If it was test 2 that was satisfied, then it is 1/24th of the total VAT liability for that year in which the £2 million threshold was exceeded.

In both cases VAT due on goods imported from outside the EU is excluded.

Customs are required to notify the trader of the amount payable, how it has been calculated and when the payment is due. In certain circumstances, Customs have the power to reduce or increase the amount of the payment on account.

There is one other thing I want to mention about test 2 – where the threshold is exceeded for the very first time under test 2 then only one payment on account is required in the first return period under the scheme. The balance is then due with the return. The usual payments on account regime kicks in after that.

E12.6 More on POA

The default surcharge regime does apply to payments on account. Thus a business will still have to get everything paid on time and a return sent in on time under the scheme.

If the total VAT liability in four successive returns falls below 80% of the total that was used for the reference period (the reference period being the period on which the payments on account have been calculated), then the trader can apply for a reduction in the payment on account. The trader can apply for this reduction immediately, rather than waiting for the next annual revision which is always based on the test 1 reference period.

If a trader's VAT liability falls to less than £1.6 million for a one year period ending under tests 1 or 2, then the trader can apply to Customs to be released from his duty to make payments on account. When Customs have given their written approval the trader can leave the payments on account system.

E12.7 Annual Accounting

Annual accounting allows small and medium sized taxable persons to pay VAT on an annual basis. It allows them to only submit one VAT return and make some estimated payments on account during the year with a final VAT balance due at the year end.

SI 1995/2518 Reg 49-55

VAT Notice 732

Under the annual accounting scheme **the VAT liability** for the current year is actually **estimated** by Customs. **90% of this estimate is then paid by direct debit in nine equal instalments** on the last day of months 4, 5, 6, 7, 8, 9, 10, 11 and 12 of the VAT year. The VAT year is the year ended 31 March, 30 April, or 31 May depending on the stagger group of the trader.

The **balance** of VAT due is sent with the **single annual VAT return on the last day of the second month following the year-end**. There is only one VAT return every year which is filled in with the whole year's details and there is two months after the year end to get this return filled in and calculate the VAT that is due. The payments on account already made are then deducted and the balance is sent to Customs with the return. If a repayment is due to the trader, this will be repaid by Customs when the VAT return is submitted.

A business may apply to make only 3 interim payments instead of 9 and, if this request is approved, the business will pay 25% of the estimated tax on the last day of the 4th, 7th and 10th month with the balancing payment due on the last date of the 14th month.

Illustration 2

June pays VAT for the year to 30 April 2006 under the annual accounting scheme. Customs had estimated that she would be due to pay £25,000 for the year and she based her payments on this estimate.

On completing her VAT return for the year £29,000 of VAT is due.

Customs had estimated that June would be due to pay £25,000 for the year so her payments on account were based on this estimate. Thus 90% will be paid in nine equal instalments - so 90% of £25,000 divided by 9 is £2,500. These will be paid on the last day of months 4, 5, 6, 7, 8, 9, 10, 11, and 12. Month 4 is August, so the 31st August 2005 is the date of the first POA and thus June pays £2,500 by this date.

June will then pay £2,500 every month until the 30th April 2006. Over 9 months June will pay £22,500.

June's payments were thus:

	£
31 August 2005 (£25,000 x 90% ÷ 9)	2,500
30 September 2005	2,500
31 October 2005	2,500
30 November 2005	2,500
31 December 2005	2,500
31 January 2005	2,500
28 February 2006	2,500
31 March 2006	2,500
30 April 2006	2,500
	22,500
VAT balance due with VAT return on 30 June 2006	6,500
	29,000

When the VAT return is sent in June will pay any balance due. The return is due two months after the year-end so it will be due on the 30th June. The balance of £6,500 to make up to the £29,000 of VAT will also be due at this time.

E12.8 Annual Accounting Conditions

There are various conditions which have to be met by the trader before he can use the annual accounting scheme. Firstly if the annual value of taxable supplies is expected to be up to £150,000 then the trader may join the scheme at any time once registered for VAT. If annual turnover is more than £150,000 but is no more than £660,000 the trader may join the scheme when he has been registered for 12 months.

Secondly, the trader must believe that his **taxable supplies will not exceed £660,000**– this figure excludes VAT – in the forthcoming year.

Thirdly, the trader must not have ceased to operate the annual accounting scheme in the past 12 months.

Finally, the trader was **not a member of a VAT group** registration or a divisional registration.

In certain circumstances the trader is obliged to leave the scheme. Firstly he must **leave the scheme if his turnover exceeds £825,000**. So, if at the end of the year, the value of his taxable supplies has exceeded £825,000 in that year, he must cease to use the scheme immediately. Also if at any time he has reason to believe that the value of his taxable supplies in the current year will exceed £825,000 then he must also inform Customs and leave the scheme.

A trader must **leave the scheme if he becomes insolvent**, on his death or if he ceases to trade.

Customs have the power to withdraw authorisation from a trader to use the annual accounting scheme in certain circumstances. As a general rule, this will occur where the trader has done something wrong.

For example, Customs can withdraw their authorisation to a trader to use the annual accounting scheme;

- If a false statement was made on the application for authorisation in the first place; or
- If the trader fails to furnish his annual VAT return on time; or
- If the trader fails to make any payments under the scheme; or
- If a trader fails to pay the full amount of any tax due in respect of a return that he submitted before he joined the annual accounting scheme, he can be made to leave the scheme.

Other situations when a trader can be forced to leave the scheme include:

- if the trader breaches the £825,000 turnover test but has failed to leave the scheme; and
- finally where it is necessary for the protection of the Revenue.

There may be cash flow advantages for a trader when he uses the annual accounting scheme and it's main advantage is that a trader knows exactly what he is paying and when he is paying it which can help many traders to budget.

Another advantage of the annual accounting scheme is the fact that the default surcharge can hardly be applied because there is only one VAT return every year. However if a trader fails to submit his VAT return on time he can have authorisation to use the annual accounting scheme withdrawn.

E12.9 Cash Accounting

VAT Noti 731

Under the normal rules of VAT, we use 'tax points' to decide which VAT return period a trader accounts for items in. Smaller businesses are allowed to dispense with the normal VAT rules for accounting for VAT and instead are allowed to use the cash accounting scheme as an alternative. The idea of the cash accounting scheme is that a trader only has to account for VAT in respect of when money is received and money is paid. We therefore use the cashbook to decide when input tax can be reclaimed and output tax is accounted for. What is important is the **date cash is paid or received, not the tax point.**

SI 1995/2 Reg 56-6

VAT Noti 731 para 1.3

One of the major advantages of the cash accounting scheme is **automatic bad debt relief**. For most traders that sell on credit it is very possible that the time comes for them to pay over the output tax to Customs before it has even been collected from the customer. If the customer does not pay, then the VAT still has to be accounted for to Customs. The bad debt means that the trader has suffered and he has to wait 6 months before he can even think about claiming bad debt relief and getting back from Customs the output tax he had to pay them even though he never collected it from his customer. Under the cash accounting scheme, if the cash was never received from the customer, then the output tax is not paid to Customs hence automatic bad debt relief.

Obviously there are some conditions to satisfy before operating the cash accounting scheme.

The main condition is that there must be reasonable grounds for believing that the value of **taxable supplies will not exceed £660,000** in the next 12 months.

In addition to this all VAT **returns must have been made up to date** and any **outstanding VAT has been paid**. If the VAT has not been paid then if an arrangement has been made with the Commissioners to pay that VAT by instalments, this should not bar a trader from joining the cash accounting scheme.

In addition, in the past year, the trader has not been convicted of any offence in connection with VAT or has not been assessed to a Section 60 penalty - this is where there is tax evasion involving dishonesty - or has not been removed from the cash accounting scheme for the protection of the revenue.

If the conditions are satisfied it is not necessary to apply to Customs or even to notify them that a trader is going to use the cash accounting scheme.

The way the scheme works is that output tax is accounted for when the customer pays. Input tax is only accounted for when the trader pays the creditor or the seller.

When the scheme is first used it is necessary to identify separately receipts from debtors outstanding at the beginning of the period. The output tax on these debts will have already been accounted for under the normal rules so do not include them again. Similarly, the payment of creditors needs to be kept separate. However, once the scheme is up and running it is just receipts into the cashbook and payments out of the cashbook that determine output tax and input tax for the VAT return.

E12.10 Receipts and Payments for Cash Accounting

If a trader receives cash then the date used to decide whether an item falls into a particular VAT return is the date the cash was received.

VAT Notice 731 para 3.4

If it is a cheque that the trader receives then the date of interest is the later of the date on the cheque or the date the cheque was received. If a cheque bounces then do not treat it as a receipt until it is honoured.

If it is a credit card sale use the date on the sales voucher.

If money comes as part of a bank transfer then it is the date the bank account was credited.

Payments are effectively a mirror image of receipts. If it is cash that the trader is paying then use the date on the invoice that you are paying.

If it is a cheque then it is the later of the date the cheque was dispatched or the date on the cheque.

For a credit card payment, it is the date on the voucher.

For a bank transfer is the date the bank account was debited.

It is still necessary to meet all the other conditions for VAT and so if the trader wants an input tax deduction, he must hold a valid VAT invoice etc.

A very detailed cashbook called an analysed cash book is required, which shows how much VAT is included in receipts and payments. The VAT return is completed using the information in the analysed cashbook.

E12.11 Leaving the Cash Accounting Scheme

There will be situations when a trader will leave the cash accounting scheme. A trader is actually required to **leave the cash accounting scheme if the turnover** in the 12 months to the end of a return period **exceeds £825,000**. A trader can also leave the scheme voluntarily at the end of a return period if the trader feels it is not beneficial or if the trader feels he is unable to meet the requirements for cash accounting scheme. Customs themselves can actually expel a trader from the scheme if it appears necessary to do so for the protection of the revenue.

VAT Notice 731 paras 2.6, 5.1, 5.3

From 1 April 2004 businesses that leave the cash accounting scheme either voluntarily or because they have exceeded the turnover limit can bring outstanding VAT into account on a cash basis for six moths after they leave the scheme. This new rule only applies to supplies made and received whilst using the cash accounting scheme.

Example 2

Fill in the missing 12 months taxable turnover figures:

	Maximum Joining Limit	Leaving Limit Maximum
Cash Accounting Scheme	£..............	£.................
Annual Accounting Scheme	£..............	£.................

Answer 1

The year-end for this group 1 trader is the 30th September. The results to the 30th September 2005 are given and the annual VAT liability for the year then ending is £1.8 million. This does not exceed £2 million and so test 1 is not satisfied.

Test 2 says that at the end of every quarter, look at the year's VAT liability for the quarter then ended. By 30th June 2006, the annual VAT liability for that period then ending exceeds £2 million because it is £2.2 million. The VAT return to 30th June 2006 is the one which satisfies Test 2 and so payments on account start from the next VAT return period which will be the quarter to 30th September 2006.

Thus the quarter to 30th September 2006 is the correct answer.

Answer 2

	Maximum Joining Limit	Leaving Limit Maximum
Cash Accounting Scheme	£660,000	£825,000
Annual Accounting Scheme	£660,000	£825,000

SUMMARY - ACCOUNTING FOR VAT

Large traders with a total VAT liability for the previous year exceeding £2 million are required to pay their VAT monthly in advance. Returns are still submitted quarterly and with the balancing payment due

Thus a payment on account is made at the end of month 2 and month 3 with the balancing payment being due a month later when the VAT return is submitted.

VAT returns and any VAT due must be submitted to Customs within one calendar month after the end of the VAT return period in question.

If a VAT repayment is shown as due on the return this will be repaid to the trader as soon as Customs receive the VAT return.

Businesses which pay VAT electronically automatically receive a 7 day extension to the normal submission date for the VAT return.

Annual accounting allows small and medium sized businesses to pay VAT on an annual basis. There is one annual return to be made two months after the VAT year end.

During the year 90% of the estimated VAT liability is paid by direct debit on the last day of months 4, 5, 6, 7, 8, 9, 10, 11 and 12. As an alternative the trader may choose to make three payments of 25% in months 4, 7 and 10. When the VAT return is submitted the balance of VAT actually due is paid at the same time.

The annual accounting scheme is only available to traders with taxable supplies not exceeding £660,000 per annum. Traders must leave the scheme when turnover exceeds £825,000 per annum.

If a trader has a taxable turnover below £150,000, that trader may join the scheme at any time. Other traders must be VAT registered for at least 12 months prior to joining the scheme.

The cash accounting scheme allows traders to dispense with the normal tax point rules to decide which VAT return to account for input tax and output tax on.

Instead movements through the cash book - i.e. input tax received and output tax paid determine which VAT return items are accounted for on. The major advantage of the cash accounting scheme is the benefit of automatic bad debt relief.

The cash accounting scheme is only available to businesses with a taxable supply total per annum not exceeding £660,000. Such traders must leave the scheme when taxable supplies exceed £825,000.

E13: BAD DEBT RELIEF

In this chapter you will cover the way in which relief is given in respect of VAT where a trader has a bad debt.

E13.1 Introduction

Consider the situation with two traders, Trader A, Trader B, and Customs. Trader A sells goods to Trader B. Trader A also raises an invoice for the goods at £1,000 plus VAT. Trader B pays the invoice fairly promptly so £1,175 is paid to Trader A. s.36 and SI 1995/2518 Reg 165-172

On the VAT Return of Trader A there is output VAT of £175, and this will be paid to Customs. On Trader B's VAT Return there is input tax of £175 and this will be reclaimed from Customs on Trader B's VAT Return. Thus the output and input position is circular. No one has actually yet borne the output VAT and this is quite right because it is only the final consumer that bears the VAT. The final consumer has not yet been introduced into the chain.

Customs have balanced their books, they have received output tax from Trader A, but they have given it back to Trader B by way of an input reclaim.

E13.2 The problem

Problems arise where Trader B fails to settle the invoice promptly. Using the same example, with Customs, Trader A and Trader B. Goods are sold from Trader A to Trader B and Trader A raises an invoice for £1,000 plus VAT. Trader B in this example is a late payer, so no cash actually goes across from Trader B to Trader A. Assuming that both traders are under invoice accounting, Trader A will still have an obligation to pay output tax to Customs of £175. As far as Trader A is concerned the tax point has passed and output VAT is due.

In Trader B's books they again account for VAT on an invoice basis so therefore they are entitled to reclaim from Customs £175 by way of input tax. This is regardless of whether or not they have paid Trader A. So at the moment there is inequity. Customs are in the same position as before because they receive money from Trader A and have paid it out to Trader B.

Trader A is not entirely happy. They have accounted for output tax of £175 without receiving anything from Trader B. Trader B however, is extremely happy. Customs have given him £175 and he has not paid Trader A.

Let us assume 6 months have passed from the due date of the invoice. At this point Trader A is entitled to claim bad debt relief. A bad debt claim is where Trader A claims back £175 from Customs and this claim will be as part of the input tax on Trader A's VAT return, but this cannot be made until 6 months have passed since the original due date. Customs are now out of pocket, they have paid back £175 to Trader A. s.36(1)

In order for Customs to balance their books, there is a requirement for Trader B to repay the original input tax claim to Customs once 6 months has passed. When Trader B does eventually pay Trader A it will account for the output tax, and Trader B can then claim back the input tax again.

E13.3 Conditions

The first condition is that Trader A must have **supplied goods or services and must have accounted for and paid the output VAT on the supply.** s.36

The whole or part of the **consideration has been written off** in Trader A's accounts as a bad debt. This is simply an entry in the bad debts account within Trader A's books.

Six months must have elapsed since the date of supply and the due date of the invoice. So consequently it is very important to show terms of payment on invoices.

Q	Now test your understanding by attempting the example which follows.

Example 1

Thud Ltd raised the following invoices on Lex Ltd:

Invoices	*Net*	*VAT*	*Gross*
	£	£	£
15.3.06	1,000	-	1,000
20.4.06	200	35	235
24.4.06	600	105	705
29.5.06	2,000	350	2,350
29.5.06	500	-	500
16.6.06	800	140	940

Lex Ltd paid £235 on 15.5.06 and stated that the payment was in respect of the invoice raised on 20.4.06.

Lex Ltd paid a further £3,000 on 31.8.06

Calculate the bad debt relief claim to be made on the return to 30 November 2006.

Answer 1

Invoices	*Net*	*VAT*	*Gross*	*Cash paid*	*Outstanding*
	£	£	£	£	£
15.3.06	1,000	-	1,000	1,000	-
20.4.06	200	35	235	235	-
24.4.06	600	105	705	705	-
29.5.06	2,000	350	2,350	}	See below
29.5.06	500	-	500	} 1,295	See below
16.6.06	800	140	940	-	940

The cash paid on 15 May 2006 was specifically allocated against the invoice dated 20 April 2006. The second payment on 31 August 2006 is allocated in the normal way, that is against older invoices first. £1,000 goes against the invoice dated 15 March 2006. £705 goes against the invoice dated 24 April 2006, and finally, £1,295 goes against the invoices dated 29 May 2006. Those invoices have been raised on the same day so they are effectively treated as one invoice.

The bad debt claim is therefore on the taxable amount outstanding on the invoices dated 29 May 2006. To calculate what proportion of the £2,350 is still outstanding, apportion the cash allocation of £1,295 to these two invoices.

$$\pounds[2{,}350 - (1{,}295 \times \frac{2350}{2350 + 500}) \times \frac{7}{47}] = \pounds 190.96$$

Thus the bad debt relief claim on the return to 30 November 2006 will be £190.96.

The invoice raised 16.6.06 is not 6 months old so does not qualify for bad debt relief.

SUMMARY - BAD DEBT RELIEF

Bad debt relief is available to traders when a debtor of 6 months standing has not yet paid over the VAT which the trader has already paid to Customs. Various conditions must be met to enable a bad debt relief claim to be made.

The first condition is that Trader A must have supplied goods or services and must have accounted for and paid the output VAT on the supply.

The whole or part of the consideration has been written off in the trader's accounts as a bad debt. This is simply an entry in the Bad Debts Account.

Six months must have elapsed since the date of supply and the due date of the invoice.

E14: CONTROL VISITS, APPEALS AND ASSESSMENTS

In this chapter you will look at control visits covering in particular:
what a control visit is;
- what happens if any irregularities are discovered;
- the time limits for HMRC Officers to raise assessments;
- the formalities in respect of an appeal to the VAT Authorities.

E14.1 Introduction

This chapter looks at how HM Revenue and Customs (HMRC) enforce compliance with the VAT legislation.

Firstly it will consider the way HMRC use the control visit procedure to monitor the operation of VAT by the taxable person.

E14.2 The Control Visit

HMRC (Customs) officers will periodically visit taxable persons. These visits will be by prior appointment, although Customs obviously reserve the power to enter and search premises on a warrant granted by a magistrate. In the past, registered traders could expect their first control visit within three years of registration. Visits are now more targeted and a "low risk" trader may not have his first visit for many years. Traders who receive cash takings or work in a complicated area might be regarded as "high risk" and as such they can expect regular visits from Customs. Control visits will vary in duration depending on the perceived risk factor and the size and complexity of the business.

In addition, a trader who sends in a late VAT return or VAT returns that are incorrect, or inconsistent, can also expect to be visited more frequently than would perhaps otherwise be the case.

The control visit usually takes place on the business premises and Customs will inspect the accounting records of the trader. They will also test the accuracy of VAT returns that have been submitted so far.

A control visit **cannot be regarded as an audit**. The fact that a control officer does not discover any errors does not equate with giving the business a clean bill of health.

The purposes of a control visit are wide ranging. The primary objective of the control visit is to ensure that the full amount of VAT due has been properly accounted for, hence the check of records and the check of VAT returns previously submitted. The records of the business and also the activities carried on by the business will be scrutinised by the control officer.

The control officer will also discuss various aspects of the business with the taxable person. If a trader uses the opportunity afforded by the control visit to seek the advice of HMRC on particular issues then the trader must ensure that any advice on which he is going to rely is confirmed in writing.

The control officer will also discuss any VAT problems that the business may be experiencing and perhaps may offer advice on how to cope with these. Once again, such advice needs to be in writing.

Finally, the control officer will highlight any errors that have been found during the control visit and will explain what happens next and how the business should act to correct them.

If under-declarations of VAT do come to light during the visit, or maybe if excessive amounts of input tax have been claimed, then the control visit will be followed by the issue of an assessment and perhaps also interest and penalties may be charged.

E14.3 Examination of records

A control visit will normally take place at **the trader's main place of business**. This is so that the officer cannot only examine the business records, but can also have a look at the business activities carried on. All of the records which the trader is obliged by law to keep should be made available. If any records are not kept at the main premises Customs should be so informed at the time that the appointment is made for the control visit. Customs can then outline which of the remote records the control visit officer will need to examine.

Where records are held on computer the trader is obliged to give the officer assistance in assessing those records.

A taxable person is liable to civil penalties if he fails to provide information or documents demanded or if he fails to retain records that he is required by law to keep.

The person who is responsible for dealing with all the VAT affairs of the business should also be available whilst the control officer is conducting the control visit. The trader's accountant, or maybe another professional adviser, may also be there if the trader feels this would be helpful.

The particular procedures followed during the control visit vary according to the nature of the business, but if lots of cash transactions are carried out in the business then it is likely that the **control officer will carry out a gross profit calculation or a mark-up computation**. Control officers use a number of techniques to test the credibility of output tax figures and, especially as regards retailers selling goods, quite a popular credibility check is the mark-up computation.

A mark-up computation makes use of the known value of purchases, which can be obtained from the tax invoices which have been retained as evidence of an input tax credit. It also uses the profit margin mark-ups that are made on each of the various types of goods sold.

The control officer will use this information to effectively estimate the value of sales in a period and hence the value of output tax that should have been accounted for. This will be compared to the actual output tax accounted for and if a large difference occurs then perhaps a further investigation will be carried out.

Illustration 1

Alex sells children's toys which are all taxed at the standard rate of VAT. His average rate of mark-up is 40%. He estimates that 5% of his stock is lost due to shoplifting, theft, etc. In January he has a sale where approximately 50% of his stock is sold at an average mark-up of only 10%.

Purchases for the test period total £50,000 (excluding VAT).

Output tax declared for the test period was £7,250.

How credible is the output tax declared?

The mark-up computation for the test period will start off by taking the purchases in the test period and adjusting them for theft, shoplifting, etc. In the example, there were £50,000 worth of purchases in the test period of which about 5% would normally be pilfered. So £2,500 is deducted from £50,000 purchases to give £47,500 of purchases in the test period.

	£
Total purchases	50,000
Deduct: 5% for theft etc	(2,500)
	47,500

The next part of the calculation is to take these purchases and assume that they are all sold, thus working out hypothetical sales for the test period.

Hypothetical Sales:

	£
50% x £47,500 @ 1.40 (i.e. 40% mark-up)	33,250
50% x £47,500 @ 1.10 (i.e. 10% mark-up)	26,125
	59,375

In the test period, 50% of stock is sold with a 40% mark-up and 50% is sold in the sale period with only a 10% mark-up. So take 50% of £47,500 of purchases and multiply it by 1.4%, i.e. the 40% mark-up to give sales in that test period of £33,250.

The other 50% of purchases in the period multiply by 1.10 to give a 10% mark-up and hence sales of £26,125.

Total sales in the test period are £59,375.

Next work out the VAT that should have been accounted for on these sales.

	£
Output tax due thereon	
£59,375 x 17.5%	10,391
Output tax declared	(7,250)
Difference	3,141

£59,375 at 17.5% equals £10,391 output tax which should have been paid over to Customs, but Alex only actually declared (i.e. paid over) £7,250 of output tax. There is a £3,141 difference and that, on these figures, is fairly significant. With a result like that the control officer will probably investigate Alex further and perhaps raise an assessment on him for what he would assume to be the missing output tax figure.

E14.4 Assessments

A control officer will issue an assessment where it appears that a VAT return has not been submitted, or if it has been submitted, it is incomplete or s.73 incorrect. The underlying phrase must be made to the best of the Commissioners' (1)-(3) judgement. The underlying phrase comes from an important case, *Van Boeckel v CCE (1981).* The phrase effectively means that Customs officers must consider fairly all the material put before them by the trader and that is what they must base their decision on. That decision must also be a reasonable decision.

So long as there is some material on which the customs officer can act, however, they are not required to make any further investigation. In other words the customs officer will use the information given to him to raise his assessment but does not actually have to delve further to find out if the figures he is coming up with are precisely accurate.

The following tribunal case gives a good example of using best judgement when raising an assessment. Mr Singh, a firework wholesaler, was visited by Customs who examined his purchase records. They concluded that he had recorded all of his purchases accurately. However, they did not carry out a mark-up exercise, instead they made an assessment based on a month's till rolls.

The tribunal concluded from the evidence that Mr Singh's till had been used as an all-purpose calculator. Apart from recording actual sales, it was used:

- To calculate the value of customers' selections prior to sale;
- To calculate the value of potential sale for telephone enquiries;
- To calculate the value of faxed orders prior to sale;
- For training exercises
- For calculating the total value of purchases;
- For calculating bankings; and
- To calculate sandwich orders.

Mr Singh explained that certain entries on the till rolls could not have been sales; they were too large. His customers were local newsagents and grocers and would not have had a licence to transport the quantities of fireworks implied by the size of the figures on the till rolls.

The tribunal noted that a mark-up exercise would have produced figures very close to those on Mr Singh's VAT returns. Customs were aware that the till was used other than for recording sales and were happy with Mr Singh's purchase records. They also knew his mark-up and so had not, in the tribunal's opinion, used best judgement in making their assessment. 18480: Jhalman Singh (4.4.04)

E14.5 Assessment Time Limits

There are time limits to be observed for the raising of an assessment by Customs. An assessment must be raised by the later of; s.77

- Two years after the end of the prescribed accounting period in question; or
- One year, after evidence justifying the raising of an assessment comes to light.

So the later of these two dates is the last date on which Customs can raise an assessment, but there is also an overall time limit. This over-riding time limit for the issue of an assessment states that an assessment must be issued not later than three years after the end of the prescribed accounting period concerned, or where an individual has died, not later than three years after his death.

However, where an underpayment arises from fraud or dishonest conduct then the three-year limit is increased to twenty years.

Time limits are very important because Customs can only raise assessments within the strict defined periods of time.

Example 1

During a control visit on the 29th January 2006 the Customs Officer discovers an under-declaration of output VAT on the VAT return to the quarter 31st March 2005.

By which date must a Control Officer raise an assessment to collect this VAT that's due?

a) 31 March 2007
b) 29 January 2007
c) 31 March 2008

E14.6 Global Assessment

It is possible for Customs to make a global assessment. This is basically an assessment for two or more prescribed accounting periods, but which does not allocate the amount of tax involved into each of the individual periods. In the case of a global assessment the time limit operates from the end of the earliest period included in the assessment.

Do not confuse a global assessment with a document which is made up of a number of assessments for different prescribed accounting periods which just happen to be notified together. The question of whether a global assessment has been made, or a number of separate assessments have been made, is one of fact and will be based upon the form in which Customs notify the trader.

E14.7 Appeals

In the event of a dispute with Customs there are effectively two routes open to resolve the issue in question. In most cases the taxpayer will ask Customs to reconsider their decision. This is sometimes called a **'local review' or a 'local reconsideration'**. s.82-87

If this course of action is chosen the request should be **made in writing within 30 days of the disputed assessment** and relevant information should be provided to Customs to back up the case for a local review. It is at this point that the trader should also ask Customs to extend the usual time limit for an appeal, just so that the second option is left open to the trader if a local review fails to satisfy. Notice 7[illegible] Paras 28.2, SI 1986/[illegible]

The second route available is the **right of appeal** against certain Customs assessments or decisions. An appeal must be made in writing within 30 days of the date of the disputed Custom's assessment or Custom's letter. These time limits are very important and have to be met.

If a local review has been requested it may result in a revised decision in which case the taxpayer has 30 days to appeal against this to a tribunal provided that Customs agreed to extend the appeal time limit in the first place.

On the other hand, Customs, after a local review, may just confirm their original decision. In this case, again assuming that an extension to the appeal period time limit has been granted, the trader has 21 days from the date of the confirmation of the original decision to appeal to the tribunal.

This is summarised as follows:

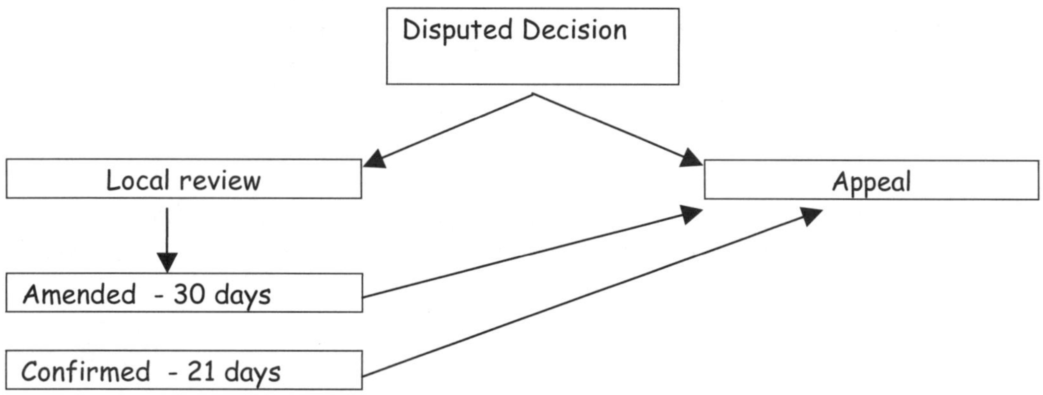

A significant disadvantage of a local review is that unlike an appeal there is no legal entitlement to the recovery of costs. However, Customs may make an ex-gratia payment of costs in cases where a decision is reversed following a local review.

E14.8 Appealable Matters

It is only possible to appeal in respect of certain matters which include the following: s.83

- Registration or cancellation of a registration;
- Refusal of a group registration application;
- Assessment for VAT and/or assessment for penalties;
- The VAT that is chargeable on a supply of any goods or any services;
- The input tax that can be reclaimable by a taxable person;
- The use of special schemes including retail schemes, cash accounting, flat rate for farmers scheme etc.

An important advantage to actually making an appeal is the legal entitlement to the recovery of costs if the appeal is successful. The major disadvantage of an appeal is that it can be quite a lengthy procedure particularly if it then becomes a case that is pursued through higher courts and, of course, it can be costly if unsuccessful. In addition to all this, pre-payment of the disputed tax is often a requirement and the appeal hearing is public which can lead to unnecessary, perhaps unwanted, publicity.

In practise it is probably the cost of an appeal that is the major deciding factor in whether a trader goes ahead or not. This is especially so if the case on which the appeal is being made is not a rock solid one.

E14.9 Before an appeal can be made.

Before an appeal can be made a trader must have made all VAT returns which he is required to have made to date and have paid all the tax due on those tax s.84
returns to date as well. The effect of this rule is that a trader is unable to appeal against any decision or any assessment if he has outstanding VAT returns or an outstanding VAT liability.

However in PW Coleman (VTD 15906,VTD 16178) (TVC 2.10) it was held that an appellant had a directly enforceable right under the EC 6th Directive to have an appeal heard and this right overrode the conditions in VATA 1994, s.84(2).

Following that case, Customs now accept that the condition that all returns and payments have to be up-to-date is contrary to the EC principle of proportionality. Pending any change in the UK legislation Customs will not apply for appeals to struck out solely because returns and payments are outstanding for VAT periods which are not under dispute. They will continue to make applications where a return has not been rendered for a VAT period subject to a disputed assessment or where the VAT in dispute has not been paid. (C&E Business Brief 23/99,17 November 1999).

In the case of an appeal against an assessment (and other certain areas):

(i) The amount which Customs have determined to be payable as VAT has been paid or deposited with them; or

(ii) On being satisfied that the appellant would otherwise suffer hardship, Customs agree, or the appeal body decides, that the appeal be entertained notwithstanding non-payment. Note that if the hardship application is granted but, subsequently, the appeal is lost, default interest on the amount of the disputed VAT may be payable. Conversely, if the hardship application is lost but, subsequently, the appeal is won, Customs are liable to pay interest on any amount of disputed VAT paid or deposited with them which is repayable.

The tribunal in PW Coleman held that the condition (i) above was acceptable and (VATA 19
did not conflict with EC 6th Directive because of the hardship provision under (ii) s.84(3)(3A)
above and because Custom's decision on that is reviewable by the appeal body. 1997,
s.45(3)(5

To summarise, where an appeal is being made in respect of the VAT chargeable on a supply, or on the assessment of a penalty, there is an additional requirement. This requirement is that the trader must have either paid or deposited the tax demanded, or if not paid, has satisfied the appeal body that he would suffer hardship if the payment was made.

To apply to the appeal body to consider waiving the requirement to pay is subject to the same time limits as the appeal. If Customs oppose the hardship application the appeal body will hold a preliminary hearing to decide whether or not to allow the application.

E14.10 Procedure

A VAT appeal body generally is comprised of a chairman and 2 other members. At least one of these is likely to have an accountancy background. However, the chairman may just sit alone, especially if it appears that the matter under dispute is a question of law only, rather than a question of fact. Sch 12 Para 9

Customs must make available to the trader any documents which they intend to provide to the tribunal and also provide a list of any cases which they are going to cite. The trader has to do likewise.

At the appeal the taxpayer can conduct his own case or any person he wishes to appoint, so for example his accountant, can represent him. Customs may likewise be represented by any person they wish to appoint and they are usually represented by a member of their own Solicitors office. SI 1986/590

At the appeal hearing each party to the appeal is allowed to address the appeal body to give evidence, to call witnesses and to cross-examine witnesses. Usually the procedure is thus; the appellant normally presents first, followed by Customs and then the appellant has a right of reply.

In a tax evasion appeal, (this is an appeal against a liability for a penalty which has been imposed for conduct involving dishonesty) the burden of proof lies with the Commissioners. This means that the Commissioner's representative and not the appellant will open the case. This changed order for the hearing will also apply where there is an appeal against both an assessment and an accompanying penalty for dishonest conduct.

At the end of the appeal hearing it is very unlikely that a decision will be made. Decisions are usually given in writing a few days later.

The appeal body may also direct the payment of costs by one party to the other. The general rule is that costs are awarded to the successful party. Costs are not awarded to an unsuccessful party unless there are exceptional circumstances. It is also a condition that the costs are incidental to and consequent upon the appeal, and no entitlement to costs arises if a dispute is settled without a formal appeal. Costs which arose before the notice of appeal was served are not generally allowable, but once the appeal has been lodged a right to costs arises even if the dispute between the parties is settled and the appeal is withdrawn.

As a general rule Customs do not seek costs against unsuccessful appellants. They do however, ask for costs in certain narrowly defined cases in order to provide protection for public funds. Therefore Customs ask for costs at appeal hearings of substantial and complex cases where large sums are involved which are comparable with High Court cases, unless the appeal involves a general point of law which requires clarification.

Customs will also seek costs where the appellant has misused the appeal procedure. Examples of this include a frivolous appeal or where the appellant has failed to appear or to be represented at a mutually arranged hearing without sufficient explanation.

A **right of appeal exists to the High Court** in a case where either party is dissatisfied on a **point of law** with the decision. The decision of the appeal body on questions of fact is final. From the High Court the appeal can proceed, if necessary, to the Court of Appeal and then to the House of Lords.

In certain circumstances it is possible to leapfrog over the Court of Appeal and for the appeal to proceed directly from the High Court to the House of Lords. It is also possible for an appeal against a decision of the appeal body to be heard by the Court of Appeal, hence leapfrogging over the High Court. This can only apply where the point of law at issue is a question of statutory interpretation and the decision of the Court of Appeal is really required.

Example 2

Tick which three of the following six statements which are correct.

	If correct	✓
1.	Control visits are effectively an "audit" of the trader's VAT records.	
2.	Control visits take place at the trader's business premises	
3.	Assessments are made to the best of the trader's judgement.	
4.	The normal time limit for an appeal against an assessment is 30 days after the assessment was issued.	
5.	Costs are always awarded to a successful appellant.	
6.	The right of appeal to the High Court can only be made on "a point of law".	

Answer 1

The correct date is 31 March 2007.

The later of:

(i) 2 years after the end of prescribed accounting period in question 31.3.05 + 2 = 31.3.07

(ii) 1 year after evidence justifying an assessment comes to light 29.1.06 + 1 = 29.1.07

Later of 2 dates = 31.3.07

3 year overall limit

3 years from end of PAP in question
31.3.05 + 3 = 31.3.08

When considering the 3 year overall limit of 31st March 2008. The 31st March 2007 date calculated earlier is well within this 3 year overall time limit and so 31st March 2007 will be the latest date by which an assessment must be raised by the control officer.

Answer 2

1.	Control visits are effectively an "audit" of the trader's VAT records.	X
2.	Control visits take place at the trader's business premises	✓
3.	Assessments are made to the best of the trader's judgement.	X
4.	The normal time limit for an appeal against an assessment is 30 days after the assessment was issued.	✓
5.	Costs are always awarded to a successful appellant.	X
6.	The right of appeal to the High Court can only be made on "a point of law".	✓

SUMMARY - CONTROL VISITS, APPEALS & ASSESSMENTS

Control visits are one way in which HMRC can enforce compliance with the VAT legislation.

The length of a control visit and the interval between control visits will depend on the size, complexity and VAT compliance of the business.

The primary objective of the control visit is to ensure that VAT has been accounted for properly. If VAT is found to be due, a control Officer will raise an assessment.

Assessments must be made to the best of the Commissioners judgement. They must also be made within specific time limits.

In the event of a dispute with Customs, there are effectively two routes available to resolve the issue. The first route is called the local review where a taxpayer will ask Customs to reconsider their decision. The second route is to raise an appeal.

An appeal must be made in writing within 30 days of the date of the disputed Customs assessment or letter. It is only possible to appeal in respect of certain matters.

Before an appeal can be made, the trader must have made all VAT returns to date and paid all tax due to date.

A VAT Appeal body generally comprises a chairman and two other members of which one is likely to have an accountancy background.

At the appeal the taxpayer may conduct his own case or choose any person he wishes to represent him. Likewise Customs may be represented by any person they wish to appoint.

At the appeal hearing each party to the appeal is allowed to address the Appeal body to give evidence, to call witnesses and to cross-examine witnesses.

The Appeal body may also direct the payment of costs by one party to the other. As a general rule Customs do not seek costs against unsuccessful appellants. However, they will ask for costs in certain cases in order to provide protection for public funds.

A right of appeal exists to the High Court and to the Court of Appeal and House of Lords.

E15a: MISDECLARATION PENALTY

The misdeclaration penalty penalises a trader who submits an incorrect VAT return or who accepts an assessment for VAT which has underestimated the VAT due. In this chapter we will look at:
when the penalty is charged;
- how the penalty can be avoided.

E15a.1 Introduction

This chapter looks at the misdeclaration penalty. A misdeclaration penalty may arise where an incorrect return is prepared or an underassessment is accepted. If the error or underassessment exceeds certain limits Customs have the power to impose a **15% penalty** i.e. 15% of the error or underassessment. Interest may also be charged on the error or underassessment.

s.63 and Notice 700/92/02

So in summary, the error or underassessment must be paid, a 15% penalty may be levied and interest may also be due.

E15a.2 Error in VAT return

A trader may have omitted certain outputs from his return or over claimed inputs. Either way there is an under declaration of the VAT due.

Illustration 1

A trader has submitted a VAT return which shows output tax of £110,000, input tax of £75,000, leaving an amount due of £35,000.

It later transpires that the correct position is output tax of £200,000, input tax of £75,000 and VAT due of £125,000.

Consequently there is an error of £90,000.

The VAT of £90,000 would obviously have to be paid and interest would also be running on the £90,000 too.

The question is, is a penalty due?

There are two tests for a misdeclaration penalty as follows:

1. Is the error **greater than or equal to £1 million**? In Illustration 1 it is obviously not greater than £1 million and ordinarily it would be unlikely to be so.

2. Is the **error greater or equal to 30% of the gross amount of tax (GAT)**? The gross amount of tax is simply the **correct output tax plus the correct input tax.** In Illustration 1 GAT would be £200,000 plus £75,000, which equals £275,000. Consequently 30% of GAT is £82,500 (£275,000 x 30%). The error of £90,000 exceeds £82,500.

Thus a misdeclaration penalty of £13,500 will apply (i.e. 15% x £90,000).

Example 1

Alpha Limited prepared it's VAT return for the quarter to 31st December 2005 as follows; Output tax £700,000, input tax £600,000, amount due £100,000.

On a subsequent control visit Customs found that input tax had been incorrectly claimed on the fleet of company cars. The error amounted to £350,000.

What is the amount of misdeclaration penalty, if any?

E15a.3 Underassessment

Where an assessment is made which understates a trader's liability to VAT, and at the end of the period of 30 days beginning on the date of assessment no action is taken to draw the underassessment to the attention of Customs, a penalty may arise. This could occur in cases where no VAT return is submitted. Customs would ordinarily raise an assessment in such circumstances. If the trader does nothing for 30 days, they are deemed to have accepted it. If the assessment is greatly different from the actual amount due, the trader may be liable to a misdeclaration penalty.

Illustration 2

No VAT return has been submitted by a trader for the quarter to 31st March 2005. Customs issue an assessment for £200,000 and the trader takes no action within 30 days. When the return is finally submitted the VAT due amounted to £375,000 per the actual return. Is a penalty due?

Again there are two separate tests.

1. Is the underassessment **greater or equal to £1 million**? Again, in the example it is not and generally it is unlikely to be so.

2. Is the underassessment **greater than or equal to 30% of the true amount of tax (TAT)**? TAT is simply the correct VAT amount, i.e. **correct output tax minus correct input tax**. In the example this is £375,000. 30% of £375,000 is £112,500. The underassessment amounts to £175,000 which exceeds 30% of TAT (£112,500).

Consequently a penalty of £26,250 will be due which is 15% of the underassessment.

Example 2

No VAT return is submitted for the quarter to 30 June 2005. Customs issue an assessment for £125,000 and the trader takes no action within 30 days. The correct position is established by Customs on a subsequent control visit. They determine that output tax should be £400,000, input tax £225,000, leaving VAT due of £175,000.

What is the amount of misdeclaration penalty, if any?

E15a.4 Avoiding the Penalty

Reasonable excuse is one way of completely avoiding the penalty. Has a trader got a reasonable excuse for the error or underassessment? A reasonable excuse is quite difficult to prove and there are very few cases which Customs will accept as a reasonable excuse. A serious illness in the family may be regarded as a reasonable excuse by Customs, but it will depend on the actual circumstances.

Voluntary disclosure of an error will avoid the possibility of a misdeclaration penalty. This voluntary disclosure however must not be prompted by a pending Customs visit. Customs must feel the reason for your voluntary disclosure is totally unconnected with any forthcoming control visit.

Discovery within the period of grace may avoid the penalty. For example a trader has an error in the quarter to 31 December 2005. Customs have a control visit in February or March 2006. At this visit Customs find the error in the quarter to 31 December 2005. The period of grace starts from the first day after the error quarter and runs to the filing date of the next return, i.e. the 30 April 2006. Consequently as the error has been discovered within the period of grace there is no misdeclaration penalty.

This effectively gives the benefit of doubt to the trader. There is a presumption that when the trader came to prepare the next quarter's return he may well have found the error himself, so no misdeclaration penalty is charged.

Tax point errors often give rise to errors on VAT returns. Simply including an output in a later quarter will not give rise to a misdeclaration penalty.

Additionally Customs have indicated that a penalty will not normally be imposed if the penalty amount would be less than £300.

Finally, **misdeclarations under £2,000** will never give rise to a misdeclaration penalty. This £2,000 figure is the net error. Thus a trader could have one error for £100,000 and another error going the opposite way for £99,000. Overall the net misdeclaration is only £1,000, therefore no misdeclaration penalty.

E15a.5 Reducing the Penalty

Customs can mitigate a penalty by any amount they feel appropriate. The **VAT tribunal can also mitigate penalties on appeal**. s.71

When considering mitigation Customs **cannot take into account** the following:

- Insufficiency of funds;
- No significant loss of tax; or
- The trader acted in good faith.

Factors which **may be taken into account** are as follows:

- Disclosure;
- Co-operation; and
- Attendance at meetings.

The mitigation can be anywhere from 0% to 100%, it just depends on the factors involved.

Ideally a misdeclaration penalty should be avoided in the first place by the timely completion of accurate VAT returns. However, if this has not been the case for whatever reason, it may be possible to avoid the penalty or reduce the penalty by way of mitigation. Obviously every case is different and individual factors must be taken account of.

Answer 1

The correct position, which is always our starting point to determine GAT, is as follows;

Output tax £700,000; and
Input tax £250,000 (input tax was originally £600,000, but £350,000 of that had been misclaimed).

This leaves an amount due of £450,000.

GAT is therefore £700,000 plus £250,000 i.e. the correct output tax plus the correct input tax. That equals £950,000.

30% of £950,000 is £285,000 and we compare this to an error of £350,000.

The error is bigger therefore a penalty of 15%, i.e. £52,500 will be levied. This is in addition to the trader having to pay £350,000 of additional VAT, i.e. the overclaimed input tax and the interest on that amount.

Answer 2

The correct answer is zero. There is no penalty due. The true amount of tax is £175,000 i.e. correct output tax minus correct input tax. 30% of this is £52,500. The underassessment was for £50,000. This is lower than the penalty-qualifying amount.

Consequently no misdeclaration penalty will be levied.

Do remember however, that the trader will still have to pay the extra VAT due i.e. the £50,000 plus interest on that amount.

SUMMARY - MISDECLARATION PENALTY

If a VAT return is submitted which is incorrect, a misdeclaration penalty will only be charged if the error exceeds certain limits.

The first limit is where the error is greater than or equal to £1 million.

The second limit is where the error is greater than or equal to 30% of the gross amount of the tax - i.e. output tax plus input tax as corrected for the error.

Where the error exceeds these limits a penalty will apply which is equal to 15% times the error.

If an assessment is issued which understates a trader's liability to VAT and within 30 days following the assessment no action is taken by the trader to draw the underestimate to the attention of Customs, then a penalty may arise.

Again the penalty arises if the amount of the error - i.e. the underassessment exceeds certain limits.

These limits are greater than or equal to £1 million or greater than or equal to 30%, this time of the true amount of tax which is the true tax that should have been assessed.

If a penalty is charged it is 15% of the error.

Reasonable excuse is one way to avoid the misdeclaration penalty. Voluntary disclosure of an error will also avoid the penalty.

If the error is charged then Customs have the power to mitigate the penalty by up to 100%.

E15b: LATE REGISTRATION PENALTY

This chapter looks at the penalty that is charged where a trader is late notifying Customs that he should have been registered for VAT.

E15b.1 Introduction

When a trader is late notifying Customs that he should be registered for VAT three things happen:

- His **registration is backdated** to the date from which he was liable to be registered. So in other words, from the date to which he should have been registered if he had notified them on time.
- He must also **account for output tax on his supplies and deemed supplies** from that date, i.e. from the date on which he should have been registered and charging VAT he will have to account for VAT on all those supplies made to the date when he finally gets around to notifying Customs. However, credit for input tax can be given, if the normal recovery rules have been satisfied on purchases made in the same period of time.
- He is **liable to a late registration penalty** for the period of default, unless he can convince Customs that there is a reasonable excuse for his delay.

E15b.2 The Penalty

The late registration penalty is a percentage of the net tax due for the period of default and that percentage depends on the delay involved. The period of delay is from when Customs should have been notified to when they finally were notified or discovered the fact that the trader should have been registered for VAT. s. 67

If registration is **no more than 9 months late**, so less than or equal to 9 months late, then a **5% penalty** is imposed.

If registration is **over 9 months, but not more than 18 months late**, then a **10% penalty**.

If registration is **over 18 months late** then a **15% penalty**.

There is a **minimum penalty of £50** for late registration and Customs have the power to **mitigate** (s.70) any penalty charged by up to 100%. Interest is **not** chargeable on any outstanding VAT which is subject to the late registration penalty.

Example 1

G Limited became liable to register for VAT from 1 April 2005, but the Company did not realise this until after the appointment of a new Finance Director in December 2005. Sales in the period from 1 April 2005 to the date Customs were notified, (which was 31 December 2005) were £150,000. Proper documentation for purchases was not kept so input tax cannot be recovered for this period.

You are required to calculate the penalty payable by G Limited.

E15b.3 Reasonable Excuse

If a taxpayer has a reasonable excuse for notifying Customs late that he should have been registered for VAT then they have the power not to impose the late registration penalty. There is no definition of reasonable excuse in the legislation. There is, however, a definition of what is not a reasonable excuse.

VAT Notic 700/41/0 para 3.1

The legislation states that an **insufficiency of funds** to pay the tax is **not** a reasonable excuse for not paying VAT and that **reliance on another person** to perform the task is **not** a reasonable excuse. Reasonable excuse applies to several different penalties.

For example, if a business had been waiting for its accountant to tell it when it should register for VAT and the business uses that as a reasonable excuse for being late, then that is reliance on another person to perform the task and that is not a reasonable excuse. Hence the penalty would still be imposed.

Customs have issued a leaflet which gives ideas as to when a reasonable excuse could be accepted for late registration. In particular, Customs identify **compassionate circumstances** and give an example of the serious illness of a sole trader, or a close member of his family.

Also given as an example of a reasonable excuse is where there is a transfer of a business as a going concern where there was little break (or perhaps no break at all) in activity, returns were made on time, tax was paid on time, but under the previous owner's registration number. This would be a reasonable excuse.

If there was any doubt about the liability of supplies, for example, if they were exempt or standard rated, and where correspondence had been ongoing with Customs then that might be a reasonable excuse.

Doubt about employment status, where correspondence has been ongoing with the Revenue on whether the individual is self-employed and hence subject to VAT, or an employee and hence not subject to VAT. This could be another example of a reasonable excuse.

Example 2

Fran uses her redundancy pay to start up a tea rooms in Didsbury village. Her takings are as follows:

	£ 2005	£ 2006
April	2,000	8,000
May	5,000	12,000
June	7,000	18,000
July	8,000	25,000
August	10,000	30,000
September	15,000	27,000
October	nil	nil
November	14,000	15,000
December	8,000	
January 2006	3,000	
February 2006	3,000	
March 2006	6,000	

Fran's only costs are food (which of course is zero rated and has no VAT input tax on it), staff wages and rent on the shop. Fran closes in October each year to go on holiday.

In November 2006 Fran realises that she should have registered for VAT and she then notifies Customs on Form VAT 1 on 30 November 2006.

You are required to calculate the penalty Fran will be liable to pay due to her late notification.

Answer 1

G Limited had sales in the default period, 1 April 2005 to 31 December 2005 which are deemed to be VAT inclusive. It did not charge VAT because it was not VAT registered, but must treat the amount charged as if it included VAT, because really it should have included VAT since the trader should have been VAT registered.

So £150,000 x 7/47 gives the output VAT due which is £22,340.

The penalty is a percentage of this output VAT due. The Company notified Customs not more than 9 months late so a 5% penalty will apply which gives an overall late registration penalty of £1,117.

Answer 2

Adding up Fran's turnover on a monthly basis one finds that by the time she gets to the end of November 2005 she has had a turnover of £61,000.

This exceeds the VAT registration limit of £60,000.

Therefore Fran should have notified Customs by the end of December 2005 and they would have registered Fran from 1 January 2006. Thus the date on which she should have been registered for VAT is 1 January 2006 and this is basically the start of her default period.

The default period will then run until the date Fran finally got around to notifying Customs which was 30 November 2006 and in this period of time her sales total £147,000. These sales are deemed to be VAT inclusive. So VAT at 7/47ths is £21,894.

Because Fran was between 9 and 18 months late notifying Customs there is going to be a 10% penalty which is a £2,189 penalty for late notification of registration.

SUMMARY – LATE REGISTRATION PENALTY

A late registration penalty is applied to the VAT which is due and payable on the first VAT return that must be submitted by the trader which covers the period from the date the trader should have been registered until the date he finally notifies Customs of his liability to registration.

The late registration penalty is a percentage of the net tax due for the period of default and the percentage depends on the delay involved.

The period of default is the period of delay from when Customs should have been notified to when Customs finally were notified that the trader was liable to register for VAT.

If registration is no more than 9 months late a 5% penalty applies.

Over 9 months but not more than 18 months late, a 10% penalty applies.

Over 18 months late results in a 15% penalty.

There is a minimum penalty of £50 and Customs have the power to mitigate any penalty charged by up to 100%.

If a taxpayer has a reasonable excuse for notifying Customs late, then Customs have the power not to impose the penalty.

E15c: DEFAULT SURCHARGE

Where a VAT return is submitted late or a payment of VAT is made late, then a default surcharge may arise. This chapter looks at when the default surcharge arises and how it can be avoided.

E15c.1 Introduction

A default is where either a VAT return is submitted late or a payment of VAT is made late. In such a case a default surcharge may be imposed on the wrongdoer. The **first time** a default occurs Customs effectively **issue a warning**. The warning is the issue of a default surcharge liability notice and such a notice will cover a period of 12 months. In other words the trader is put on warning for the next 12 months. The 12 month period is effectively the period that ends on the anniversary of the end of the accounting period of the default. This **12 month period is called the Surcharge Period.** s.59

A default during this 12 month surcharge period has 2 consequences. Firstly a surcharge is calculated. The surcharge is a percentage of the unpaid tax due. The second consequence is that the surcharge period is extended to 12 months from the date of this default.

E15c.2 The Surcharge

The amount of surcharge calculated depends on previous defaults in the current surcharge period. Customs look at the number of defaults made during the current surcharge period, 1, 2, 3, 4 or more and then the surcharge itself is a certain percentage of the unpaid VAT.

No. of defaults during current surcharge period	% of unpaid VAT
1	2
2	5
3	10
4 or more	15

For 1 default during the current surcharge period (i.e. the trader's first default during that 12-month period), 2% of the unpaid VAT will equal the amount of the surcharge. For the second default it is 5%, for the third default 10% and then for the fourth or any subsequent default 15% of the unpaid VAT is the amount of surcharge the trader has to pay.

The trader has to pay the unpaid VAT as well. The trader's default surcharge is in addition to the unpaid VAT. s.59

Customs will not assess a surcharge of less than £400 unless the 10% or the 15% rate applies in which case they will assess the surcharge, whatever amount it is and bearing in mind that there is a minimum charge of £30. Notice 700 Para 21.2

A surcharge liability will not apply if a nil or a repayment return has been submitted late. A nil return is one where the amount of VAT due is exactly nil. Nor will it apply if the tax is paid on time although the return itself is submitted late.

However, in these scenarios, there has still been a late return and so there has still been a default. So the surcharge period will still be extended. However, such an event does not increase the rate of surcharge for the next default in the surcharge liability period.

In addition, to help small businesses penalties will not be applied automatically for late payment where the taxable turnover of the business is less than £150,000.

Example 1

Alpha Ltd has submitted recent VAT returns as follows;

Quarter to	Date submitted	VAT due £	Date VAT paid	Default
31.3.04	28.4.04	5,000	28.5.04	☐
30.6.04	20.7.04	10,000	20.7.04	☐
30.9.04	25.11.04	(5,000)	N/A	☐
31.12.04	25.1.05	15,000	25.1.05	☐
31.3.05	21.4.05	12,000	21.4.05	☐
30.6.05	17.7.05	10,000	25.7.05	☐
30.9.05	2.11.05	13,000	2.11.05	☐
31.12.05	19.1.06	11,000	19.1.06	☐

Tick the box to show which returns are in default.

Illustration 1

Alpha Ltd has submitted recent VAT returns as follows;

Quarter to	Date submitted	VAT due £	Date VAT paid	Default
31.3.04	28.4.04	5,000	28.5.04	✓
30.6.04	20.7.04	10,000	20.7.04	
30.9.04	25.11.04	(5,000)	N/A	✓
31.12.04	25.1.05	15,000	25.1.05	
31.3.05	21.4.05	12,000	21.4.05	
30.6.05	17.7.05	10,000	25.7.05	
30.9.05	2.11.05	13,000	2.11.05	✓
31.12.05	19.1.06	11,000	19.1.06	

The first default return is the return to 31 March 2004. This is the first ever default so a warning is issued, in other words a surcharge liability notice (SLN) is issued which covers the 12 month period from 1 April 2004 to 31 March 2005.

The next default return is the return to 30 September 2004, this is during the surcharge period and so a surcharge will be calculated.

This is the first default in the surcharge period - 2% surcharge.

However, it is repayment return, so there is actually no VAT due to Customs and 2% of nothing is nothing. Thus, effectively, no surcharge is actually charged. However, the surcharge period is still extended to 30 September 2005, i.e. 12 months from this current default. The 2% penalty rate is not used and is 'saved' for next time!

The next default just falls into the 12-month surcharge period because it is the return to 30 September 2005.

The 2% surcharge is still available. Thus 2% of £13,000, the VAT that was due, gives a £260 default surcharge penalty. However, since this is less than £400 it will not be collected by Customs. The surcharge period is also extended to 30 September 2006.

E15c.3 Avoiding Default Surcharge

Effectively the only way to **"escape" from the surcharge period is to submit 4 quarterly returns**, or for monthly returns 12 monthly returns, **on time and pay the VAT due on time**. In this way the surcharge period then just elapses and the trader starts again with a clean sheet. If a trader defaulted again that would be the first default, a warning would be issued, in other words a surcharge liability notice would be issued for the next 12 months, but no penalty as yet. If the trader then defaulted in that surcharge period he would be into the 2% penalty and so on.

The trader must get those 4 quarterly returns in on time and the VAT paid on time if he wants to start all over again with a clean sheet.

A **default can be disregarded** for the purposes of the penalty in two situations. The first situation is where the **return and/or the tax were dispatched** to Customs at such a time and in such a manner that it was **expected that they would arrive on time**. Customs have indicated that posting a return first class at least 1 working day prior to the due date is accepted as reasonable.

The second situation is where the trader had a **reasonable excuse for his default.** Although it is far from easy to satisfy Customs that a reasonable s.59 s.71 excuse exists, case law indicates that a distinction should be drawn between the reason for the failure and the excuse. That is if the trader's lateness can be traced not to say an insufficiency of funds, but rather to some underlying cause of that insufficiency of funds then a reasonable excuse may be accepted. VAT Noti For example, the Bank has made an error and has added an extra zero on to 700/50/0 some money going out of the account and hence wiped out all funds resulting in Paras 3.2 anc the cheque to Customs bouncing. That presumably could be a reasonable excuse for not paying VAT on time.

Default surcharge **cannot be mitigated**, it is an all or nothing penalty.

E15c.4 Alternatives

The default surcharge system is not appropriate for every trader. For example, a trader that submits every fifth return late, will never actually be penalised under the default surcharge system. For such traders Customs have the option of imposing an alternative daily penalty.

There is also a separate default surcharge system for large traders who have to make payments on account.

Example 2

Tick the answer box if the statement is correct:

1.	If the tax is paid on time then a late VAT return does not constitute a default	☐
2.	If the return to 30 September 2005 is late the surcharge period will run to 30 September 2006.	☐
3.	A surcharge of less than £400 will always not be collected by Customs	☐
4.	Default surcharge can be mitigated by Customs.	☐
5.	A VAT return sent on time but which arrives late due to a postal strike is disregarded for default surcharge purposes.	☐

Answer 1

Quarter to	Date submitted	VAT due £	Date VAT paid	Default
31.3.04	28.4.04	5,000	28.5.04	✓
30.6.04	20.7.04	10,000	20.7.04	
30.9.04	25.11.04	(5,000)	N/A	✓
31.12.04	25.1.05	15,000	25.1.05	
31.3.05	21.4.05	12,000	21.4.05	
30.6.05	17.7.05	10,000	25.7.05	
30.9.05	2.11.05	13,000	2.11.05	✓
31.12.05	19.1.06	11,000	19.1.06	

When looking at the return for the quarter ended March 2004 it is obvious that the VAT is paid late, although the return itself has been submitted on time, so this is a default.

In the next return, both the VAT and the cash is on time.

Looking at the return to 30 September 2004, this time the return is late, but there is no VAT to be paid because it is a repayment return. However, because the return is late it is still in default.

The next 3 returns are all submitted on time and the cash is paid on time.

The 30 September 2005 return is a situation where both the return and the cash is late - thus another default.

Answer 2

1.	If the tax is paid on time then a late VAT return does not constitute a default	X
2.	If the return to 30 September 2005 is late the surcharge period will run to 30 September 2006.	✓
3.	A surcharge of less than £400 will always not be collected by Customs	X
4.	Default surcharge can be mitigated by Customs.	X
5.	A VAT return sent on time but which arrives late due to a postal strike is disregarded for default surcharge purposes.	✓

SUMMARY - DEFAULT SURCHARGE

A default is where either a VAT return is submitted late or a payment of VAT is made late.

For the first default, Customs issue a warning called a surcharge liability notice which outlines a period of 12 months starting with the end of the tax return of default. This 12 month period is called the surcharge period.

The default during the 12 month surcharge period has two consequences. Firstly a surcharge is calculated which could be at a 2% rate for a first default, 5% for a second default, 10% for a third default, 15% for a fourth or more default. The percentage is of the unpaid VAT.

The second consequence is that the current surcharge period is extended to 12 months from the date of the current default.

Customs will not assess a surcharge of less than £400 unless the 10% or 15% rate is applying. There is a minimum charge of £30.

A surcharge liability will not apply if a nil or repayment VAT return has been submitted late. However, because there has been a late return the surcharge period will still be extended.

E15d: REPEATED MISDECLARATION PENALTY

The repeated misdeclaration penalty applies in situations where the misdeclaration penalty will not apply but the trader is making repeated small errors. This chapter will look at:

- where the repeated misdeclaration penalty applies;
- how much is charged;
- how to avoid the penalty.

E15d.1 Introduction

There is a penalty called the repeated misdeclaration penalty which only applies to errors that are constantly being repeated but are of such a size that they are too small to suffer a penalty under the misdeclaration penalty regime. The repeated misdeclaration penalty itself is 15% of the tax lost if the error had not s.64
been discovered. Repeated misdeclaration penalty does not apply to under assessments but only applies where VAT returns understate the output tax that is due or overstate the entitlement to input tax recovery. When contrasting repeated misdeclaration penalty to the straightforward misdeclaration penalty, this penalty only applies to VAT returns whereas the other penalty applies to both VAT returns and assessments.

E15d.2 Material Inaccuracy

For the repeated misdeclaration penalty to apply there needs to be a material inaccuracy in a return, the quantity of which equals or exceeds the lower of two things - £500,000 and 10% of the gross amount of tax for the period.

The gross amount of tax (GAT) for the period is calculated in exactly the same way as for the misdeclaration penalty; it is the correct amount of output tax added to the correct amount of input tax. However, this time only 10% of GAT is used to decide if the error, (inaccuracy) warrants a penalty being charged.

Illustration 1

Jules submits her VAT return to 31 December 2005 showing:

	£
Output tax	137,500
Input tax	(57,500)
Net output tax due	80,000

The correct amount of output tax is later established as £160,000.

Thus output tax was originally understated by £22,500.

The understatement is quantified at £22,500. Is that sizeable enough to be considered a material inaccuracy for the purposes of repeated misdeclaration penalty?

The £22,500 understatement is a material inaccuracy if it equals or exceeds the lower of:

(i) £500,000

(ii) 10% of GAT.

GAT = £(137,500 + 22,500 + 57,500)

10% of £217,500 = £21,750

The lower figure is £21,750. £22,500 error exceeds this so it is a material inaccuracy.

Example 1

XYZ Ltd submits its VAT return to 31 March 2006 showing:

	£
Output tax	720,000
Input tax	480,000
VAT Payable	240,000

It is later discovered that input tax should have been £400,000.

Is there a material inaccuracy?

E15d.3Penalty Liability Notice

Once a material inaccuracy has been made, then Customs have the power to issue something known as a Penalty Liability Notice (PLN). The PLN covers a certain period of time (see below). s.64

A Penalty Liability Notice must be issued by the end of the fourth consecutive return period after the return period in which the material inaccuracy was made. The PLN will cover a period equal to eight consecutive VAT returns beginning with the VAT return in which that PLN is issued.

Illustration 2

Consider again Illustration 1 and Jules. The VAT return that Jules submitted which had the material inaccuracy on it was the return for the quarter ended 31 December 2005. Customs can issue a PLN at any time to the end of the fourth consecutive return period that follows this return Period. So basically, they can issue a PLN at any point up to the 31 December 2006.

Customs issue a PLN on 25 November 2006, which is within our time period. This PLN will cover eight consecutive return periods beginning with the one in which the PLN is issued. This PLN is issued in November 2006 which is the quarterly return running from 1 October 2006 to 31 December 2006. That is the first return that will be covered by the eight return periods. The PLN will cover the period from 1 October 2006 until the 30 September 2008. This period is an eight VAT returns period.

A trader is only actually liable to pay a repeated misdeclaration penalty if he makes a material inaccuracy during the eight VAT returns PLN period. Even then he does not pay a penalty on his first material inaccuracy in that period - he will only suffer a penalty for any second or subsequent material inaccuracy. The material inaccuracy is always calculated to see if the error exceeds or equals the lower of the two figures.

Illustration 3

Consider the previous Illustration and say that after the penalty liability notice is issued, Jules makes two more material inaccuracies in the eight returns period. The first material inaccuracy is in the VAT return period to 31 March 2007 and totals £45,000 - that is the amount of her error. The second material inaccuracy is in the VAT return period to 31 December 2007 and totals £52,000.

There is no penalty in respect of the first material inaccuracy made in that eight returns period. But for any second or subsequent material inaccuracy there is a penalty and the penalty is 15% of the error - 15% x £52,000 = a £7,800 penalty. The penalty is paid in addition to the extra tax that needs to be paid.

E15d.4 Other points

An error attracting a misdeclaration penalty will not also be subject to a repeated misdeclaration penalty. But, an error can count as a material inaccuracy for which Customs could issue a penalty liability notice or if a notice has already been issued and an eight return penalty period is running, then it could be treated as a first material inaccuracy during that penalty period. s.64

An error will not count as a material inaccuracy (MI) no matter what its size is if there is a reasonable excuse for the error. Thus if the person who has made an inaccuracy on a VAT return has a reasonable excuse for doing so, then the error is not treated as an MI. s.71

An error will also not count as an MI if there is a full voluntary disclosure to Customs of the error at a time when the trader has no reason to believe he is being investigated by Customs - so it is purely voluntary. The extra tax due because of the error will have to be paid, but the penalty will not be incurred or the regime will not be triggered on top.

If a repeated misdeclaration penalty is charged then mitigation against the penalty is available at Custom's discretion. s.70

Example 2

In the previous example involving XYZ Limited, assuming that the VAT return to the 31st of March 2006 did contain a material inaccuracy. Up to which date can Customs issue a Penalty Liability Notice?

a) 31.3.2007
b) 31.3.2008
c) 31.3.2009
d) 31.3.20010

Answer 1

Inaccuracy	=	over declaration of input VAT.
	=	£80,000

Material inaccuracy if equals or exceeds the lower of:

(i) £500,000

(ii) 10% x GAT
10% x £(720,000 + 400,000)
10% x £1,120,000 = £112,000

Lower figure is £112,000.

£80,000 does not equal/exceed this thus not material inaccuracy.

Answer 2

The answer is A.

The PLN must be issued before the end of the fourth consecutive return period after the return period in which the material inaccuracy is made.

SUMMARY - REPEATED MISDECLARATION PENALTY

A repeated misdeclaration penalty only applies where a VAT return understates the output tax due or overstates the entitlement to input tax recovery. It does not apply to under-assessments.

The penalty applies where there is a material inaccuracy in a return which equals or exceeds the lower of £500,000 and 10% of the gross amount of tax for the period. The gross amount of tax is the output tax plus the input tax as corrected for the error.

Once a material inaccuracy has been made, Customs have the power to issue a penalty liability notice.

This notice must be issued by the end of the fourth consecutive return period after the VAT return period in which the material inaccuracy was made.

The penalty liability notice will cover a period of 8 consecutive VAT returns beginning with the VAT return in which the penalty liability notice is issued.

If a trader makes a material inaccuracy during the 8 VAT return penalty liability notice period, then he will not pay a penalty on his first material inaccuracy in that period. Rather, he will suffer a penalty for his second or subsequent material inaccuracy in that period.

The penalty will be equal to 15% of the inaccuracy.

E15e: OTHER PENALTIES, INTEREST AND MITIGATION

This chapter looks at a variety of penalties and the potential mitigation of those penalties, including:

- when criminal prosecution may occur as an alternative to a penalty for civil fraud;
- what happens when VAT invoices or certificates of zero rating are issued without authority;
- the variety of penalties to discourage traders from making a variety of breaches of the regulations;
- when interest is charged on VAT that is overdue;
- what happens when errors are discovered;
- when Customs are willing to mitigate penalties that they have charged the trader.

E15e.1 Criminal Prosecution

A criminal prosecution can result for offences such as; s. 72

- fraudulent evasion of VAT;
- furnishing false documents or information;
- making false statements.

Criminal prosecution is reserved for the more serious VAT offences.

Criminal fraud is where a person knowingly takes steps to evade VAT or to enable another person to evade VAT. Criminal proceedings will be taken in such a case. The level of penalty that will result from the criminal proceedings depends on whether the conviction is secured as a summary conviction, in other words in a magistrates court, or a conviction on indictment, which is basically a conviction before a jury, so in a Crown Court. In either case the penalty consists of a fine and/or imprisonment.

If someone is held to be guilty of criminal fraud in a Magistrates court, the maximum term of imprisonment is 6 months and the maximum fine that can be imposed is the greater of £5,000 or 3 times the tax evaded. Contrast this to where someone is found guilty in a criminal court, i.e. a proper Crown Court, where the maximum **imprisonment** is 7 years and the fine is unlimited.

E15e.2 Civil Fraud

Civil fraud is basically the civil equivalent of criminal fraud, but it is easier for Customs to prove civil fraud since they only have to prove it on the "balance of probabilities" which is contrasted with a Criminal Court where proof has to be "beyond reasonable doubt" that fraud was committed. Civil fraud arises where a person takes steps or omits to take steps in order to evade VAT and his conduct involves dishonesty. s. 60 s. 71

The **penalty for civil fraud is 100% of the tax evaded.** The tax evaded has to be paid as well so effectively you are paying this amount twice. Customs have the power to mitigate this penalty by up to 100%.

Customs have tested a new approach to civil evasion investigations and have decided to "roll out" the new approach across the country. The new approach will be offered by Customs to "suitable cases". It will be made clear at the outset that the taxpayer is subject to an investigation which is intended to lead to civil evasion penalties. VAT Notice 730 & VAT Information Sheet 1/02

Customs will arrange for a meeting with the trader, at which the new approach will be explained, and the trader will be offered the chance to make disclosures (without any prior hint of what Customs already know). The trader will be offered the chance to make a report without a Customs investigation. If this offer is taken, a timetable will be agreed, and this will be monitored by Customs officers. If the trader does not appear to be complying with the timetable, Customs may return to the more traditional investigation under their own control.

E15e.3 Unauthorised Issue of VAT invoices

Customs have a whole range of civil penalties that they can charge a taxpayer who has done something wrong. These penalties allow Customs to ensure that compliance with VAT legislation is the number one concern with VAT registered traders, because not to comply can cost them quite dearly. s. 67

E15e.4 Incorrect Certificates

There are a number of situations where a person has to supply a certificate to show that zero rating applies, for example to a supply of land and buildings, or that a reduced rate of VAT applies to a supply. If someone gives an incorrect certificate they are liable to a penalty and the **penalty is equal to the tax thereby undercharged**. Once again, the penalty can be appealed against on the grounds of reasonable excuse for the misdemeanour. s. 62

E15e.5 Breaches of Regulations

Also included in the legislation is a real 'catch everything else' type clause; breaches of regulations. Effectively these are penalties for breaches of VAT regulations of any kind. There are different breaches outlined and different penalties outlined below. s. 69

Breach	Penalty
Failure to notify cessation of taxable supplies (Note 1)	Fixed Daily Rate (FDR)
Failure to make records	FDR
Failure to retain records	£500
Failure to furnish information and documents	FDR
Failure to make a VAT return (Note 2) Failure to pay VAT due on time	Greater of FDR and tax geared penalty
Any other breach of regulations	FDR

Note 1

The first breach is the failure to notify cessation of taxable supplies - i.e. a trader doesn't tell Customs that he is no longer making taxable supplies. The penalty for this is the fixed daily rate penalty.

Note 2

For a failure to make a VAT return and a failure to pay the VAT due on time - the penalty in this case is the greater of the fixed daily rate and a tax geared penalty. An earlier session looked at default surcharge which penalised a trader for making VAT returns late and failing to pay VAT on time. This penalty is an alternative for Customs to using the default surcharge penalty regime.

The penalty charged depends on the number of previous failures in the last two years.

Number of previous failures	Fixed Daily Rate	Tax Geared Penalty
No failure in previous 2 years	£5	1/6% of tax due
One failure in previous 2 years	£10	1/3% of tax due
Two failures in previous 2 years	£15	1/2% of tax due

If there has been no failure, (no breach of regulation in the previous two years) the fixed daily rate is £5 per day and the tax geared penalty is one sixth of 1% of the tax due.

With one failure in the previous two years the fixed daily rate penalty goes up to £10 per day and the tax geared penalty is one third of 1% of the tax due.

With 2 failures in the previous 2 years, the fixed daily rate is £15, the tax geared penalty is one-half of one per cent of the tax due.

The minimum penalty charged is £50. The maximum penalty charged is 100 days worth of the appropriate penalty.

The daily penalty can only be assessed, in the case of a failure to submit returns or pay tax on time, if Customs have issued a written warning of the consequences of the trader's failure to comply with his obligations.

Example 1

Paul's VAT return for the quarter to 31 December 2005 was received by Customs 55 days late. The tax due was £8,900. Paul's return for the 31st March 2005 had also been late although all of the other returns due have been filed on time.

Assume that an appropriate warning has been given by Customs and calculate the penalty Paul will have to pay under the breaches of regulations legislation.

Example 2

Match the misdemeanour to the correct penalty. Outlined below are lots of boxes containing a wrongdoing and then lots of boxes with a penalty in it. Draw a line to match the two together.

VAT evasion; Dishonest conduct	5% of VAT due
Failure to retain records	100% of the VAT undercharged
5 months late registering for VAT	100% of VAT lost
Issuing a VAT invoice when not VAT registered	15% of the VAT due or £50 if greater
Certificate of zero-rating issued when property did not qualify for zero-rating.	£500

E15e.6 Interest

A charge to interest will arise when an assessment is issued to collect an underpayment of VAT or when an assessment could have been issued, but the trader pays the tax before Customs in fact assess him. s. 74

Effectively this means that interest will be charged on any late payment of VAT, the only exception being when tax is liable to a late registration penalty because this is not subject to interest.

Customs have actually indicated that in practice they will not seek to assess interest in cases where it does not represent commercial restitution. In other words a charge to interest is not appropriate where there has been no overall loss to the Exchequer.

An example of such a situation would be where a trader makes a standard rated supply to another business, but in error treats the supply as zero rated and does not charge 17.5% VAT. If the supplier had charged VAT then the customer would have reclaimed that VAT as input tax and so there has been no overall loss to the Exchequer. In a case like this Customs will raise an assessment for the VAT that the trader should have charged at the standard rate, but will not, in addition, charge interest.

Interest rates are fixed by Customs and changed periodically.

Interest is calculated on a daily basis from the date the original VAT was due to the date the assessed VAT is paid. In practice **Customs assess from the date the original VAT was due until** a different date - **the date of the assessment.**

Illustration 1

J Limited omitted £10,000 of output tax from its VAT return to 30 September 2004. The error is discovered at a control visit and an assessment is raised on 21 May 2005. J Limited pays the VAT due on 28 May 2005.

For which time period is interest charged?

The VAT return is to 30 September 2004 from which VAT has been omitted. The VAT return to 30 September 2004 was due at the end of October, i.e. by 31 October 2004 and that is when the VAT on the return should have been paid.

The assessment was raised on 21 May 2005 and the VAT assessed was paid on 28 May 2005.

In practice Customs will charge interest from the date the VAT was due until the date the assessment is raised so the interest period is 31.10.2004 to 21.5.2005.

The legislation it says that interest could be charged from the date the VAT was due to be paid until the date it actually is paid. So in this example Customs would be entitled to an extra 7 days worth of interest to 28.5.2005, but in practice they don't.

Where an assessment is raised to collect outstanding VAT, interest is calculated from a point no earlier than 3 years from the assessment date. In other words, if an assessment is raised to collect VAT that should have been paid 5 years ago, interest on that outstanding VAT can only run for a maximum of 3 years. Thus the interest period is capped to a maximum of 3 years prior to the date the error is found.

Interest is also charged where an unregistered person issues a VAT invoice and shows an amount of VAT on this invoice. The amount of VAT shown will suffer interest from the date of the invoice until the date the amount of VAT is paid over to Customs.

Interest also applies where a person who is not registered under the flat rate farmer scheme charges a flat rate commission on his invoices as if he was a flat rate farmer.

Basically interest will catch both of the above wrongdoers on the amount they are purporting to charge their customers for VAT or for flat rate addition.

E15e.7 Discovery of Errors

If a trader discovers an error himself it really is best to disclose that error to Customs immediately.

A **voluntary disclosure** of an error should be made by letter to the local VAT office or on form **VAT 652.**

Why should a trader make a voluntary disclosure?

Because it will enable the trader to **avoid any misdeclaration penalty**. However, interest is not avoided and will be charged.

However, **net errors of £2,000 or less** in total do not have to be disclosed, but **can be corrected for by adjusting the VAT account** and including the net amount of the adjustment in the VAT due or the VAT reclaimed box on the current VAT return i.e. the next VAT return due to be submitted. This £2,000 test relates to net errors discovered in an accounting period, even though those errors themselves may relate to different accounting periods. What is important is what is discovered at the current point in time.

When net errors of £2,000 or less are discovered interest will also not be charged. The discovery of overstated output tax of £3,000 and also of overstated input tax of £4,000 would give a net error of £1,000 being discovered and this of course can be adjusted for in the VAT account.

Example 3

Mr A Simple has reviewed his 2006 VAT returns and found the following errors:

Quarter to:	
31.3.06	Overstated input tax £4,000
30.6.06	Overstated output tax £1,000
30.9.06	Understated output tax £2,000
31.12.06	Understated input tax £4,500

What is the amount of the net error?

To summarise:

- Interest will be imposed to provide commercial restitution where tax has been understated on a VAT return.
- Interest will also be charged where an unregistered person issues an invoice charging VAT.
- Interest cannot run from a date more than 3 years before the date of assessment/payment.
- Net errors of £2,000 or less can be corrected by a trader adjusting the VAT account.
- Net errors exceeding £2,000 require a formal disclosure to Customs and interest will be charged.

E15e.8 Mitigation

Mitigation is basically reduction of a penalty and it is only allowed in respect of certain offences. s. 70

These offences are:

- **Tax evasion**; conduct involving dishonesty. The original penalty for that offence was 100% of the tax evaded. s. 60
- **Misdeclaration penalty.**
- **Repeated misdeclaration penalty.** s.63
- **Late notification** of a liability to register results in a VAT penalty. s. 64
- **Unauthorised issue of VAT invoices** can also result in a penalty. s. 67

Mitigation can be made by Customs or by a VAT appeal body on appeal. s. 70
Customs or the VAT appeal body can reduce the penalty to whatever amount it thinks proper which can even include nil.

A VAT appeal body can reverse any reduction in penalty that was granted by Customs, although this does not happen very often.

Customs have stated what their policy on mitigation of penalties is in Notice 730. They envisage maximum discounts as follows:

- 40% for prompt and accurate disclosure. Notice 730
- Up to 25% for full co-operation.
- 10% for production of documents and attendance of interviews.
- This leaves a balance of 25% which Customs have said could be mitigated in exceptional circumstances.

Where Customs have charged a penalty and the trader would like the penalty to be mitigated he will need to provide Customs with good reason.

By law none of the following items can be taken into account when deciding on the mitigation of a penalty by Customs or an appeal body;

- An insufficiency of funds to pay the tax due or to pay the penalty
- The fact that there has been no loss of tax or no significant loss of tax
- The fact that the person liable for the penalty or a person acting on his behalf has acted in good faith.

Basically some of the major reasons for claiming mitigation are gone, and cannot be considered by Customs when deciding whether to mitigate a penalty or not.

To conclude if a penalty is charged it may be worth claiming mitigation if the trader feels he has a good case. If the trader has been dishonest, hasn't co-operated, hasn't produced information then maybe it is not worth asking.

Answer 1

Paul will pay a penalty that is the greater of two things; the fixed daily rate penalty or the tax geared penalty.

Starting with the fixed daily rate penalty with one failure in the previous two years Paul would be looking at a fixed daily rate of £10 per day. The return is 55 days late at £10 per day which would give Paul £550 of penalty.

Alternatively, Paul could be looking at the tax-geared penalty with one failure in the previous two years that would be one-third of 1% of the tax due. The tax due is £8,900, a third of 1% of this daily, so for 55 days £1,632.

The greater of the two figures is the penalty which Paul will have to pay which comes to £1,632.

Answer 2

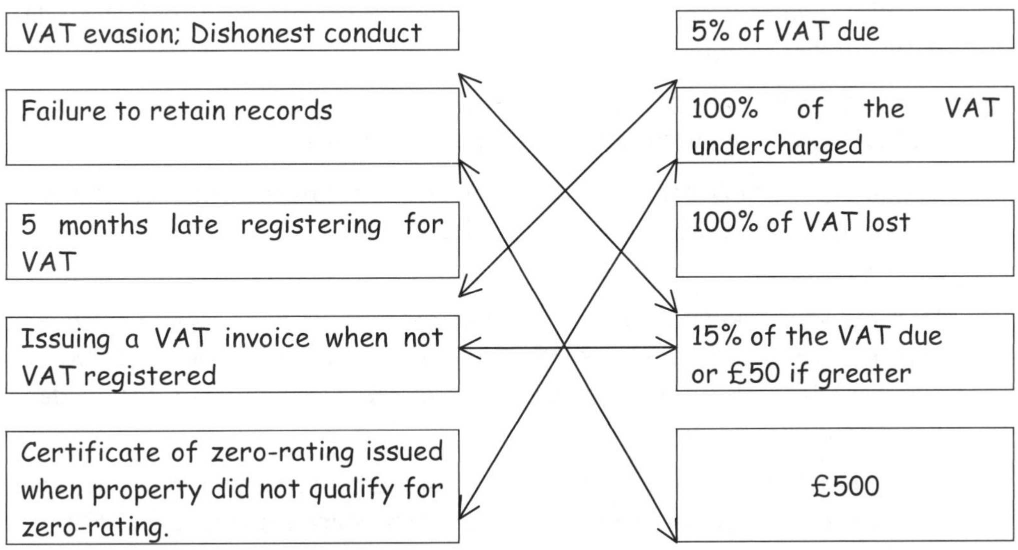

Answer 3

The way to approach this sort of question is to look at the output tax and the input tax separately.

	Output tax	Input tax
	£	£
31.3.06		(4,000)
30.6.06	(1,000)	
30.9.06	2,000	
31.12.06		4,500
	1,000	500

£1,000 output tax payable and £500 input tax repayable means net £500 output tax payable.

In the return to the end of March the trader has overstated input tax by £4,000 - £4,000 of input tax originally claimed back from Customs which we now owe to Customs. It is a negative £4,000 in the input tax column.

In the return to June the trader has overstated output tax, and paid Customs £1,000 of output tax too much. It is a negative figure, but this time in the output tax column.

In the quarter to September the trader has understated output tax by £2,000, - £2,000 owed to Customs in the output tax column.

In the return to December the trader has understated the input tax by £4,500 - thus another £4,500 claimed as input tax from Customs in the input tax column.

In summary, looking at the output tax column, Customs owe the trader £1,000 and the trader owes Customs £2,000. Overall the trader owes £1,000. Looking in the input tax column, the trader owes £4,000, Customs owes the trader £4,500 so overall Customs owe £500.

There is £1,000 of output tax payable and £500 of input tax repayable, so the net figure is £500 of output tax payable and because this is £2,000 or less the trader will adjust for it on the next VAT return to be submitted.

SUMMARY – OTHER PENALTIES, INTEREST & MITIGATION

Customs have a choice of criminal prosecution or a civil penalty when encountering fraud.

Unauthorised issue of invoices and incorrect certificates of zero rating result in penalties.

In addition Customs have a whole range of penalties for a whole range of misdemeanours.

If VAT has not been shown as due on a VAT return and is later collected by assessment, then Customs may charge interest on that unpaid VAT.

Interest is not charged in cases where it does not represent commercial restitution.

Interest is calculated on a daily basis from the date the original VAT was due to the date the assessed VAT is paid. In practice Customs only assess interest until the date an assessment is actually issued.

Interest cannot run from a date more than 3 years before the date of the assessment.

Net errors of £2,000 or less can be corrected by a trader adjusting the VAT account and no interest will be charged.

Net errors exceeding £2,000 require a formal disclosure to Customs and interest will be charged.

Mitigation can be given by Customs or by a VAT Tribunal on appeal.

E16: REFUNDS, REPAYMENT SUPPLEMENT AND INTEREST

This chapter covers three topics:
- refunds;
- repayment supplement;
- interest.

E16.1 Introduction

This chapter covers four topics; refunds, repayment supplement, interest and security. The first three items are roughly connected because they are all to do with the situation when VAT is refunded to the taxpayer. Security is a different topic and shall be dealt with on its own at the end of the session.

E16.2 Refunds

Refunds of VAT can take two forms; firstly Customs will make a refund of VAT when the output tax is less than the input tax on a VAT return. In such a case there will be a negative figure calculated on the VAT return and this figure will be refunded to the trader, usually when the VAT return is submitted. s.80

The trader may also get a refund of VAT that he has overpaid at an earlier point in time - an overpayment may have occurred if he incorrectly classified something as standard rated when it should have been zero-rated, etc. Thus the VAT he paid over and above the amount due will be refunded to him.

E16.3 Refund of VAT shown on a VAT return

Once a VAT return showing that VAT is repayable to the taxpayer is submitted to Southend the refund due will be automatically dealt with by the VAT Central Unit. They will issue instructions to issue a cheque or make a refund payment into a notified Bank account. If the time taken to sort out the repayment exceeds the set limit then repayment supplement will be added on to the repayment made. s.80

E16.4 Repayment Supplement

Repayment supplement is added to a repayment if the Commissioners fail to issue an instruction for a repayment within a 30-day period. s.79

Provided certain conditions are met, repayment supplement is the **greater of £50 or 5% of the repayment of tax due.** Notice 700/58/02

The 30-day period is not the 30-day period from submitting the return. The 30-day period begins on the later of two dates;

- the day after the last day of the prescribed accounting period to which the claim relates.
- the date of the receipt of the claim, i.e. the day that the VAT return is submitted.

Certain periods are ignored when calculating that 30-day period.

The periods left out of account when calculating the 30-day period are those where it is necessary to raise reasonable enquiries or correct errors. **The period to leave out of the 30 days is defined as beginning when the Commissioners first decide that it is necessary to make enquiries and then ends when they satisfy themselves that they have received complete answers to the questions they raised**, or when they decide not to pursue the enquiries any further. Any delay on Customs part in acting on that decision is included. In practice it is Customs policy not to "stop the clock", so to speak, until they have notified the trader of an enquiry.

Repayment supplement is denied if the repayment on the return turns out to be incorrect and thus no repayment supplement will be given to the trader for his repayment. The definition of "incorrect" is that the return is overstated by more than the greater of £250 or 5% of the correct repayment.

In addition to this, no repayment supplement is paid at all if the VAT return in question was submitted late. Thus if a trader submits his VAT return on time he will not get any repayment supplement.

Illustration 1

Joe submits his VAT return for the quarter to 31 December 2005 on 28 January 2006 showing a VAT repayment due of £1,800.

Joe is rarely in a repayment situation so Customs decide on 3 February to start an enquiry and they notify Joe of this enquiry on 10 February 2006.

After answering a few questions and amending the repayment due from £1,800 down to £1,700, the enquiry is completed on 20 February 2006. But, due to some sort of administrative error, the repayment is not made to Joe until 12 March 2006.

Will there be any repayment supplement paid to Joe in addition to the £1,700 repayment? To answer this question the first step is to decide whether the repayment was issued late; late being in excess of the 30-day period. Start by looking at the time between the receipt of the return, which was 28 January 2006, and the issue of the repayment order, which was 12 March 2006 which is 42 days.

Initially it looks as if a repayment supplement will be due since 42 days is definitely in excess of 30 days.

However, there was an enquiry during this period of time and the enquiry period has to be deducted from the 42 days. The enquiry period was from 10 February 2006 to the 20 February, which is 11 days long.

42 days minus 11 days is 31 days. This exceeds the 30-day cut-off point and hence repayment supplement will be due.

However, the original repayment claim for £1,800 had to be amended and was adjusted downwards by £100. To be entitled to repayment supplement the £100 adjustment needs to be less than the greater of two figures – the greater of £250 or 5% of the correct payment. The correct repayment was £1,700, which at 5% gives £85. The greater of £250 and £85 is £250. So, the £100 adjustment needs to be less than £250, which it is. By being less than £250, repayment supplement is due which is 5% of the repayment made of £1,700, i.e. £85. The repayment paid to Joe will be £1,700 plus £85.

One further thing to note about the original 42-day period. It is the time between the date the return was received by Customs and the issue of the repayment order. Do not include 28 January or 12 March when working out the period. A common error is to calculate a period of 44 days by counting the first day (the start date), and the last day (the end date). Those dates are actually ignored.

When looking at the enquiry period do add a start and end date. Thus include 10 February and 20 February to get to 11 days.

Example 1

Alpha Limited submits its VAT return for the quarter to 31 March 2005 on 22 April 2005. The return shows a repayment of £2,500.

On 5 May 2005 Customs start an enquiry into the return notifying Alpha Limited of this on 8 May 2005. After a control visit, which discovers no irregularity, the enquiry is closed down on 24 May 2005.

Alpha Limited receives its repayment on 8 June 2005.

Will repayment supplement also be paid?

E16.5 Refund of overpaid VAT

A refund of overpaid VAT would occur where a person has paid more VAT to Customs than was originally due. For example, a trader has treated certain supplies as standard rated when really they should have been zero-rated. On s.80(1)
the receipt of the claim, Customs will make a refund of the overpaid VAT to the trader.

The Commissioners have the power to withhold a refund of VAT if they feel that it would **unjustly enrich** the claimant. The concept of unjust enrichment is quite a difficult one, but as a general rule the repayment cannot unjustly enrich a business if it passes the repayment on to its customers. From the Commissioners point of view it is unfair for a business to gain from the sort of windfall that is a refund of VAT.

s.80(3)

There is a restriction where a trader makes the claim for a refund of VAT which he originally paid because he had a mistaken assumption about the way the VAT rules applied. In a case like this a refund will only be made to the extent of the loss or the damage which the trader can show he has suffered as a result of the mistaken assumption. Otherwise, Customs will allege that any repayment will give unjust enrichment.

s.80(3A) - (

Repayments will be allowed on the basis that they will be repaid to the customer - this will prevent the taxpayer being unjustly enriched and Customs have the power to make regulations for overseeing the reimbursement of traders' customers where a refund has been made to the trader just for that purpose. By the same token, Customs can make regulations to claw back any refund which was supposed to be passed on to the customer but the trader did not do this.

Notice 700/4

Customs are **not liable to refund tax paid to them more than 3 years before the date of the claim**, or 3 years before the date the trader commenced legal proceedings if this is earlier. This 3 year limit applies to all claims for input tax, correction of errors, adjustments to take account of a change in the consideration for a supply, pre-registration expenses, post deregistration expenses, adjustments under the Capital Goods Scheme and claims for bad debt relief. It is an all encompassing three year limit.

Following FA 2005 the start date for the three year time limit for claiming refunds in the case of errors on returns or voluntary disclosures or tax accounted for on assessments, is the end of the relevant accounting period. In the case of a duplicate payment, it is the date of the payment.

Example 2

Paul mistakenly charged standard rate VAT on all Widget A supplies made since 1 January 1980. He appealed to a VAT Appeal body on 14 April 2005 that supplies of Widget A should be zero-rated. The Appeal body ruled in Paul's favour on 12 September 2005. A claim was lodged for a VAT refund the next day.

The refund is restricted to VAT paid from which date?

A	1 January 1980	D	14 April 2002
B	14 April 2005	E	12 September 2002
C	12 September 2005	F	13 September 2002

E16.6 Interest on overpaid VAT

This will be interest that is paid in addition to the overpaid tax being refunded to the trader. If a trader has overpaid VAT then there has been a period of time when he has been unable to use his own money because effectively Customs have had his money. If this overpayment arose as a result of an error on the part of Customs, then interest can be paid to the trader. There are many s.78
reasons why VAT might have been overpaid ; maybe too much VAT was paid to Customs in the first place; maybe too little input VAT was reclaimed on a VAT return; or maybe the trader in some way was prevented from recovering VAT at the proper time.

Interest will be applied to the repayment of VAT and is calculated on a daily basis at fixed rates. There is a **three-year restriction** as seen before. Just as overpaid tax is restricted to tax paid in the prior three-year period, similarly interest is restricted to the same three years. To claim the interest a trader must make a claim in writing within three years of the end of the period to which it relates.

Interest is calculated on a daily basis but there are some days that Customs can ignore for the calculation. These days are periods of time resulting from an unreasonable delay by the claimant in making the claim, or maybe in providing information so that Customs can establish the claim both in quantity and suitability for repayment.

Example 3

This is a summary of the chapter so far - fill in the missing words, out of the three options, only one of which is correct.

Select the correct answer:

- Repayment supplement is the greater of **£250 / £150/ £50** or **15% / 10% / 5%** of the repayment due and is given on repayments of VAT where the VAT return was submitted on time and where a repayment order was not made within **10 / 30 / 60 days.**
- Overpayments of VAT will be refunded provided the claimant will not be **unjustly enriched / unfairly gained / unjustly profited**.
- The right to a refund and, if appropriate, interest is limited to VAT paid in the **1 / 3 / 6** years prior to the claim.

Answer 1

Date return submitted *(Note 1)*	22 April 2005
Date repayment made	8 June 2005
	46 days
Less:	
Enquiry notified *(Note 2)*	8 May 2005
Enquiry ceased	24 May 2005
	17 days
Total (46 – 17) *(Note 3)*	29 days

Repayment not late – no repayment supplement due.

Note 1: First work out the initial period of time, i.e. from the date the return was submitted, which was 22 April 2005, until the date the repayment was made, which was 8 June. That is 46 days remembering not to count 22 April or 8 June but rather look at the period in between these dates.

Note 2: From the 46 day period deduct the enquiry period and that starts when the enquiry was notified to the company, 8 May, until the enquiry ceased on 24 May. This time do include 8 and 24 May - 17 days.

Note 3: Total period of time of 46 days minus 17 days is 29 days. The repayment effectively was made 29 days late, which is not in excess of 30 days, so it was not made late enough for repayment supplement to be added to it. Thus there is no repayment supplement due on top of the repayment for Alpha Limited.

Answer 2

The correct answer is D.

3 years prior to earlier of:

Date legal proceedings started		14 April 2005
Date of claim		13 September 2005
14 April 2005 less 3 years	=	14 April 2002

The claim is restricted to a three-year period which is the three years prior to the earlier of two dates. First is the date legal proceedings were started which in the example was 14 April 2005. The second date is the date of the claim. The claim was not lodged until after the Appeal hearing was heard on 13 September 2005. So the earlier of those two dates is 14 April 2005. Go back three years from this date and the claim can be made on VAT charged since 14 April 2002.

Answer 3

- Repayment supplement is the greater of **£50** or **5%** of the repayment due and is given on repayments of VAT where the VAT return was submitted on time and where a repayment order was not made within **30 days**.
- Overpayments of VAT will be refunded provided the claimant will not be **unjustly enriched**.
- The right to a refund and, if appropriate, interest is limited to VAT paid in the **3** years prior to the claim.

SUMMARY – REFUNDS, REPAYMENT SUPPLEMENT & INTEREST

Refunds of VAT can occur when input tax exceeds output tax on a VAT return.

On submission of the VAT return, a refund will automatically be made by the VAT Central Unit.

Repayment supplement will be added to a repayment if Customs failed to issue a repayment instruction within a 30 day period.

Repayment supplement is the greater of £50 or 5% of the repayment of VAT due.

VAT will also be refunded if it was overpaid in an earlier period, for example supplies which were treated as standard rated when really they should have been zero rated.

On receipt of a claim Customs will make a refund of the overpaid VAT to the trader.

The Commissioners have the power to withhold a refund of VAT if they feel it would unjustly enrich the claimant.

Where VAT has been overpaid, interest will also be paid in addition to the refund of overpaid tax if the overpayment arose as a result of an error on the part of Customs.

Interest is restricted to the prior 3 year period and is calculated on a daily basis.